G000257797

THE abc OF
BRITISH RAILWAYS
LOCOMOTIVES

COMBINED VOLUME
PARTS 1—4
Nos. 1-99999

**ALSO DIESEL AND ELECTRIC LOCOMOTIVES
AND MULTIPLE UNITS**

SUMMER
1959
EDITION

BCA

LONDON   NEW YORK   SYDNEY   TORONTO

NOTES ON THE USE OF THIS BOOK

THE following notes are a guide to the system of reference marks and other details given in the lists of dimensions shown for each class.

1. Many of the classes listed are sub-divided by reason of mechanical or constructional differences (on the Eastern and North Eastern Regions the sub-divisions are denoted in some cases by " Parts," shown thus : D16/3). At the head of each class will be found a list of such sub-divisions, if any, usually arranged in order of introduction. Each part is given there a reference mark by which its relevant dimensions, if differing from those of other parts, and the locomotives included in this sub-division, or part, may be indentified. Any other differences between locomotives are also indicated, with reference marks, below the details of the class's introduction.

2. The lists of dimensions at the head of each class show locomotives fitted with two inside cylinders, Stephenson valve gear and slide valves, unless otherwise stated, e.g. (O) = two outside cylinders, P.V. = piston valves.

3. The following method is used to denote superheated locomotives, the letters being inserted, where applicable, after the boiler pressure details : Su = All engines superheated.
SS = Some engines superheated.

4. The date on which the first locomotive of a class was built or modified is denoted by " Introduced."

5. S. denotes Service (Departmental) locomotive still carrying B.R. number. This reference letter is introduced only for the reader's guidance and is not borne by the locomotive concerned.

Note :

   (a) On the Southern Region the letters " DS " preceding a number indicate a Service Locomotive. On the S.R. (only) this marking appears on the locomotive.

   (b) The Eastern and North Eastern Regions number their departmental locomotives in a separate series, as shown in Part IV.

ABBREVIATIONS USED

C W — Crewe Works
H W — Horwich Works
R W — St. Rollox Works
R T S — Rugby Testing Station
S T S — Swindon Testing Station
W W — Wolverton Works

BRITISH RAILWAYS LOCOMOTIVE SHEDS AND SHED CODES

ALL B.R. LOCOMOTIVES CARRY THE CODE OF THEIR HOME DEPOT ON A SMALL PLATE AFFIXED TO THE SMOKEBOX DOOR.

LONDON MIDLAND REGION

1A	**Willesden**	9A	**Longsight (Manchester)**
1B	Camden	9B	Stockport (Edgeley)
1C	Watford	9C	Macclesfield
1D	Devons Road (Bow)	9D	Buxton
1E	Bletchley	9E	Trafford Park
	Leighton Buzzard		Glazebrook
		9F	Heaton Mersey
			Gowhole
2A	**Rugby**	9G	Gorton
2B	Nuneaton		Ardwick
2D	Coventry		Dinting
2E	Northampton		Guide Bridge
2F	Woodford Halse		Mottram
			Reddish
3A	**Bescot**		
3B	Bushbury	11A	**Barrow**
3C	Walsall	11B	Workington
3D	Aston	11C	Oxenholme
3E	Monument Lane	11D	Tebay
5A	**Crewe North**	12A	**Carlisle (Kingmoor)**
	Whitchurch	12B	Carlisle (Upperby)
	Crewe (Gresty Lane)		Penrith
5B	Crewe South	12C	Carlisle (Canal)
5C	Stafford	12D	Kirkby Stephen
5D	Stoke		
5E	Alsager	14A	**Cricklewood**
5F	Uttoxeter	14B	Kentish Town
		14C	St. Albans
6A	**Chester (Midland)**	14D	Neasden
6B	Mold Junction		Aylesbury
6C	Birkenhead		Chesham
6D	Chester (Northgate)		Marylebone
6E	Chester (West)		Rickmansworth
6F	Bidston	14E	Bedford
6G	Llandudno Junction		
6H	Bangor	15A	**Wellingborough**
6J	Holyhead	15B	Kettering
6K	Rhyl	15C	Leicester (Midland)
		15D	Coalville
8A	**Edge Hill**	15E	Leicester (Central)
8B	Warrington (Dallam)	15F	Market Harborough
	Warrington (Arpley)		Seaton
8C	Speke Junction		
8D	Widnes	16A	**Nottingham**
8E	Northwich	16B	Kirkby-in-Ashfield
8F	Springs Branch (Wigan)	16C	Mansfield
8G	Sutton Oak	16D	Annesley
			Nottingham (Victoria)
			Kirkby Bentinck

17A	**Derby**		24E	Blackpool
	Derby (Friargate)		24F	Fleetwood
17B	Burton		24G	Skipton
	Horninglow		24H	Hellifield
	Overseal		24J	Lancaster (Green Ayre)
17D	Rowsley		24K	Preston
	Cromford		24L	Carnforth
	Middleton			
	Sheep Pasture			
			26A	**Newton Heath**
			26B	Agecroft
18A	**Toton (Stapleford &**		26C	Bolton
	Sandiacre)		26D	Bury
18B	Westhouses		26E	Lees (Oldham)
18C	Hasland		26F	Patricroft
21A	**Saltley**		27A	**Bank Hall**
21B	Bournville		27B	Aintree
			27C	Southport
24A	**Accrington**		27D	Wigan
24B	Rose Grove		27E	Walton-on-the-Hill
24C	Lostock Hall		27F	Brunswick (Liverpool)
24D	Lower Darwen			Warrington (Central)

EASTERN REGION

30A	**Stratford**		32C	Lowestoft Central
	Chelmsford		32D	Yarmouth South Town
	Enfield Town		32E	Yarmouth Vauxhall
	Southend (Victoria)		32G	Melton Constable
	Wood St. (Walthamstow)			Norwich City
30B	Hertford East			
	Buntingford			
30C	Bishops Stortford		33A	**Plaistow**
30E	Colchester		33B	Tilbury
	Braintree		33C	Shoeburyness
	Clacton			
	Maldon			
	Walton-on-Naze		34A	**Kings Cross**
30F	Parkeston		34B	Hornsey
			34C	Hatfield
			34D	Hitchin
31A	**Cambridge**		34E	New England
	Ely		34F	Grantham
	Huntingdon East			
	Saffron Walden			
31B	March		36A	**Doncaster**
	Wisbech East		36C	Frodingham
31C	Kings Lynn		36E	Retford
	Hunstanton			
31D	South Lynn			
31E	Bury St. Edmunds		40A	**Lincoln**
	Sudbury (Suffolk)		40B	Immingham
31F	Spital Bridge (Peterboro')			Grimsby
				New Holland
			40E	Colwick
32A	**Norwich (Thorpe)**		40F	Boston
	Cromer Beach			Sleaford
	Dereham			Spalding
	Wymondham			
32B	Ipswich			
	Felixstowe Town			
	Stowmarket			

4

41A	Sheffield (Darnall)	41F	Mexborough
41B	Sheffield (Grimesthorpe)		Wath
41C	Millhouses	41G	Barnsley
41D	Canklow	41H	Staveley (ex-G.C.)
41E	Staveley (Barrow Hill)	41J	Langwith
		41K	Tuxford

NORTH EASTERN REGION

50A	York	52H	Tyne Dock
50B	Leeds (Neville Hill)		Pelton Level
50C	Selby	52J	Borough Gardens
50D	Starbeck	52K	Consett
50E	Scarborough		
50F	Malton	53A	Hull (Dairycoates)
	Pickering	53B	Hull (Botanic Gardens)
50G	Whitby	53D	Bridlington
		53E	Goole
51A	Darlington		
	Middleton-in-Teesdale		
51C	West Hartlepool	55A	Leeds (Holbeck)
51E	Stockton	55B	Stourton
51F	West Auckland	55C	Farnley
51G	Haverton Hill	55D	Royston
51J	Northallerton	55E	Normanton
51L	Thornaby	55F	Manningham
			Keighley
52A	Gateshead		Ilkley
	Bowes Bridge	55G	Huddersfield
52B	Heaton		
52C	Blaydon		
	Alston	56A	Wakefield
	Hexham		Knottingley
52D	Tweedmouth	56B	Ardsley
	Alnmouth	56C	Copley Hill
52E	Percy Main	56D	Mirfield
52F	North and South Blyth	56E	Sowerby Bridge
52G	Sunderland	56F	Low Moor
	Durham	56G	Bradford

SCOTTISH REGION

60A	Inverness	62A	Thornton
	Dingwall		Anstruther
	Kyle of Lochalsh		Burntisland
60B	Aviemore		Kirkcaldy
	Boat of Garten		Ladybank
60C	Helmsdale		Methil
	Dornoch	62B	Dundee (Tay Bridge)
	Tain		Arbroath
60D	Wick		Montrose
	Thurso		St. Andrews
60E	Forres	62C	Dunfermline
			Alloa
			Kelty
61A	Kittybrewster	63A	Perth
	Ballater		Aberfeldy
	Fraserburgh		Blair Atholl
	Inverurie		Crieff
	Peterhead	63B	Stirling
61B	Aberdeen (Ferryhill)		Killin
61C	Keith	63C	Forfar
	Banff	63D	Oban
	Elgin		Pallachulish

5

64A	**St. Margarets**		65E	Kipps
	(Edinburgh)		65F	Grangemouth
	Dunbar		65G	Yoker
	Galashiels		65H	Helensburgh
	Hardengreen		65I	Balloch
	Longniddry		65J	Fort William
	North Berwick			Mallaig
	Seafield			
	South Leith		66A	**Polmadie (Glasgow)**
64B	Haymarket		66B	Motherwell
64C	Dalry Road		66C	Hamilton
64D	Carstairs		66D	Greenock (Ladyburn)
64E	Polmont			
64F	Bathgate		67A	**Corkerhill (Glasgow)**
64G	Hawick		67B	Hurlford
	Riccarton Junction			Beith
	St. Boswells			Muirkirk
			67C	Ayr
65A	**Eastfield (Glasgow)**		67D	Adrossan
	Arrochar			
65B	St. Rollox		68B	Dumfries
65C	Parkhead		68C	Stranraer
65D	Dawsholm			Newton Stewart
	Dumbarton		68D	Beattock

SOUTHERN REGION

70A	**Nine Elms**		72B	Salisbury
70B	Feltham		72C	Yeovil Town
70C	Guildford		72E	Barnstaple Junction
70D	Basingstoke			Ilfracombe
70E	Reading South			Torrington
70F	Fratton		72F	Wadebridge
70H	Ryde (I.O.W.)			
			73A	**Stewarts Lane**
71A	**Eastleigh**		73B	Bricklayers Arms
	Andover Junction		73C	Hither Green
	Lymington		73D	Gillingham (Kent)
	Southampton Terminus		73E	Faversham
	Winchester City		73F	Ashford (Kent)
71B	Bournemouth Central		73G	Ramsgate
	Branksome		73H	Dover
71G	Weymouth			Folkestone
	Bridport		73J	Tonbridge
71I	Southampton Docks			
			75A	**Brighton**
72A	**Exmouth Junction**			Newhaven
	Bude		75B	Redhill
	Callington		75C	Norwood Junction
	Exmouth		75D	Horsham
	Lyme Regis		75E	Three Bridges
	Okehampton		75F	Tunbridge Wells West
	Seaton			

WESTERN REGION

81A	**Old Oak Common**		82A	**Bristol (Bath Road)**
81B	Slough			Bath
	Marlow			Wells
81C	Southall			Weston-super-Mare
81D	Reading			Yatton
	Henley-on-Thames			
81E	Didcot		82B	St. Phillip's Marsh
81F	Oxford		82C	Swindon
	Fairford			Chippenham

82D	Westbury		85E	Gloucester (Barnwood)
	Frome			Dursley
82E	Bristol (Barrow Rd.)			Tewkesbury
82F	Bath (Green Park)		85F	Bromsgrove
	Radstock West			Redditch
	Highbridge East			
82G	Templecombe		86A	Newport
				(Ebbw Junction)
			86B	Newport (Pill)
83A	Newton Abbot		86C	Cardiff (Canton)
	Kingsbridge		86D	Llantrisant
83B	Taunton		86E	Severn Tunnel Junction
	Bridgwater		86F	Tondu
83C	Exeter		86G	Pontypool Road
	Tiverton Junction		86H	Aberbeeg
83D	Laira (Plymouth)		86J	Aberdare
	Launceston		86K	Tredegar
83E	St. Blazey			
	Bodmin		87A	Neath
	Moorswater			Glyn Neath
83F	Truro			Neath (N. & B.)
83G	Penzance		87B	Duffryn Yard
	Helston		87C	Danygraig
	St. Ives		87D	Swansea East Dock
83H	Plymouth (Friary)		87E	Landore
			87F	Llanelly
				Burry Port
84A	Wolverhampton			Pantyffynnon
	(Stafford Road)		87G	Carmarthen
84B	Oxley		87H	Neyland
84C	Banbury			Cardigan
84D	Leamington Spa			Milford Haven
84E	Tyseley			Pembroke Dock
	Stratford-on-Avon			Whitland
84F	Stourbridge Junction		87J	Goodwick
84G	Shrewsbury		87K	Swansea (Paxton Street)
	Clee Hill			Gurnos
	Craven Arms			Llandovery
	Knighton			Upper Bank
	Builth Road			
84H	Wellington (Salop)		88A	Cardiff (Radyr)
84J	Croes Newydd			Cathays
	Bala		88B	Cardiff East Dock
	Penmaenpool		88C	Barry
	Trawsfynydd		88D	Merthyr
84K	Wrexham (Rhosddu)			Dowlais Cae Harris
				Dowlais Central
				Rhymney
85A	Worcester		88E	Abercynon
	Evesham		88F	Treherbert
	Kingham			Ferndale
85B	Gloucester			
	Brimscombe		89A	Oswestry
	Cheltenham (Malvern Rd.)			Llanidloes
	Cirencester			Moat Lane
	Lydney		89B	Brecon
	Tetbury		89C	Machynlleth
85C	Hereford			Aberayron
	Leominster			Aberystwyth
	Ross			Aberystwyth (V. of R.)
85D	Kidderminster			Portmadoc
				Pwllheli

SUMMARY OF WESTERN REGION
STEAM LOCOMOTIVE CLASSES
WITH HISTORICAL NOTES AND DIMENSIONS

The code given in smaller bold type at the head of each Class,
e.g. " 6MT " denotes its British Railways power classification.

The numbers of locomotives in service have been checked to January 21st, 1959.

4-6-0 **6MT** **1000 Class**
" County "

Introduced 1945. Hawksworth design.
*Fitted with double chimney.
Weight: Loco.   76 tons 17 cwt.
Tender 49 tons 0 cwt.
Pressure: 280 lb. Su.
Cyls.: (O) 18½″ × 30″.
Driving Wheels: 6′ 3″.
T.E.: 32,580 lb. P.V.

1005/17/9/21/5
*1000–4/6–16/8/20/2–4/6–9

Total 30

4-6-0 **7P** **4073 Class**
" Castle "

*Introduced 1923. Collett design,
developed from " Star " (4037,
5083–92 converted from " Star ").
†Introduced 1946. Fitted with 3-row
superheater.
‡Introduced 1947. Fitted with 4-row
superheater.
¶Introduced 1956. Fitted with double
chimney.
Weight: Loco.   79 tons 17 cwt.
Tender 46 tons 14 cwt.
Pressure: 225 lb. Su.
Cyls.: (4) 16″ × 26″.
Driving Wheels: 6′ 8½″.
T.E.: 31,625 lb.
Inside Walschaerts valve gear and
rocking shafts. P.V.

*4037/73/5/7/9/81–6/9/92/4–6/
8/9, 5001–25/7–32/4/5/7–42/
4–8/51–6/8–60/2/6–70/6/
8/80/4/7/9–92
†5000/50/63/5/72/4/5/7/9/81/2/93
/6–9/7000–3/5–12/4–7/20/1/5–8
/31–3/5/7
‡4074/8, 5026/33/6/49/71/3/94/5,
7019/24/9/30/4/6

†¶7023
‡¶4080/7/8/90/3/7, 5043/57/61/
4/88, 7004/13/8/22 **Total 163**

4-6-0 **5MT** **4900 Class**
" Hall "

*Introduced 1924. Collett rebuild with
6′ 0″ driving wheels of " Saint "
(built 1907).
†Introduced 1928. Modified design for
new construction, with higher-
pitched boiler, modified footplating
and detail differences.
Weight: Loco. { 72 tons 10 cwt.*
{ 75 tons 0 cwt.†
Tender 46 tons 14 cwt.
Pressure: 225 lb. Su.
Cyls.: (O) 18½″ × 30″.
Driving Wheels: 6′ 0″.
T.E.: 27,275 lb.
P.V.

*4900
†4901–10/2–99, 5900–99, 6900–58

Total 258

4-6-0 **8P** **6000 Class**
" King "

Introduced 1927. Collett design.
All engines modified since 1947 with
4-row superheater and since 1955
with double chimney.
Weight: Loco.   89 tons 0 cwt.
Tender 46 tons 14 cwt.
Pressure: 250 lb. Su.
Cyls.: (4) 16¼″ × 28″.
Driving Wheels: 6′ 6″.
T.E.: 40,285 lb.
Inside Walschaerts valve gear and
rocking shafts. P.V.

6000–29

Total 30

8

4-6-0   5MT   6800 Class
" Grange "

Introduced 1936. Collett design, variation of " Hall " with smaller wheels, incorporating certain parts of withdrawn 4300 2-6-0 locos.

Weight: Loco.   74 tons 0 cwt.
       Tender 40 tons 0 cwt.
Pressure: 225 lb. Su.
Cyls.: (O) 18½″ × 30″.
Driving Wheels: 5′ 8″.
T.E.: 28,875 lb.
P.V.

6800–79   **Total 80**

4-6-0   5MT   6959 Class
" Modified Hall "

Introduced 1944. Hawksworth development of "Hall," with larger superheater, "one-piece" main frames and plate-framed bogie.

Weight: Loco. 75 tons 16 cwt.
       Tender 46 tons 14 cwt.
Pressure: 225 lb. Su.
Cyls.: (O) 18½″ × 30″.
Driving Wheels: 6′ 0″.
T.E.: 27,275 lb
P.V

6959–99, 7900–29   **Total 71**

4-6-0   5MT   7800 Class
" Manor "

Introduced 1938. Collett design for secondary lines, incorporating certain parts of withdrawn 4300 2-6-0 locos.

Weight: Loco. 68 tons 18 cwt.
       Tender 40 tons 0 cwt.
Pressure: 225 lb. Su.
Cyls.: (O) 18″ × 30″.
Driving Wheels: 5′ 8″.
T.E.: 27,340 lb.
P.V.

7800–29   **Total 30**

4-4-0   " City " Class

Introduced 1903. Churchward design.
Weight: Loco.   55 tons 6 cwt.
       Tender 36 tons 15 cwt.
Pressure: 200 lb. Su.
Cyls.: 18″ × 26″.
Driving Wheels: 6′ 8½″.
T.E.: 17,790 lb.

3440

Withdrawn 1931 and preserved in York Museum. Returned to service 1957.

            Total 1

4-4-0   2P   9000 Class

Introduced 1936. Collett rebuild, incorporating " Duke " type boiler and " Bulldog " frames for light lines.
Weight: Loco.   49 tons 0 cwt.
       Tender { 40 tons 0 cwt.
              36 tons 15 cwt.
Pressure: 180 lb. SS.
Cyls.: 18″ × 26″.
Driving Wheels: 5′ 8″.
T.E.: 18,955 lb.

9004/5/14/5/7/8

            Total 6

2-8-0   8F   2800 Class

*Introduced 1903. Churchward design, earlier locos. subsequently fitted with new boiler and superheater.

†Introduced 1938. Collett locos., with side-window cab and detail alterations.

Weight: Loco. { 75 tons 10 cwt.*
              76 tons 5 cwt.†
       Tender 40 tons 0 cwt.
Pressure: 225 lb. Su.
Cyls.: (O) 18½″ × 30″.
Driving Wheels: 4′ 7½″.
T.E.: 35,380 lb.
P.V.

*2803–11/3/5–9/21–6/31–83
†2884–99, 3800–66

            Total 157

2-8-0 7F 4700 Class

Introduced 1919. Churchward mixed traffic design (4700 built with smaller boiler and later rebuilt).

Weight: Loco. 82 tons 0 cwt.
        Tender 46 tons 14 cwt.

Pressure: 225 lb. Su.

Cyls.: (O) 19″ × 30″.

Driving Wheels: 5′ 8″.

T.E.: 30,460 lb.

P.V.

4700–8   Total 9

2-6-0 4MT 4300 Class

*Introduced 1911. Churchward design.
†Introduced 1925. Locos. with detail alteration affecting weight.
‡Introduced 1932. Locos. with side window cab and detail alterations.

Weight: Loco. { 62 tons 0 cwt.*
               { 64 tons 0 cwt.†
               { 65 tons 6 cwt.‡
        Tender 40 tons 0 cwt.

Pressure: 200 lb. Su.

Cyls.: (O) 18½″ × 30″.

Driving Wheels: 5′ 8″.

T.E.: 25,670 lb.

P.V.

*4358, 5306/11/8/9/21/2/4/6/30–
3/6/7/9/41/5/50/1/3/5–8/61/9/
70/5/6/8/80–2/4/5/8/93/6/9,
6300–14/6/7/9/20/3–7/9–53/5–
82/4–95/7–9, 7305–21
†7300–4
‡7322–8/9/32/6/8/9/40/1, 930/8/
9/15

                              Total 169

0-6-0 3MT 2251 Class

Introduced 1930. Collett design.
Weight:
    Loco.   43 tons 8 cwt.
    Tender { 36 tons 15 cwt.
           { 47 tons 6 cwt. (ex-R.O.D.
             tender from 3000 Class
             2-8-0).

Pressure: 200 lb. Su.

Cyls.: 17½″ × 24″.

Driving Wheels: 5′ 2″.

T.E.: 20,155 lb.

2200–53/5–7/9–62/4–8/70–8/
80–99, 3200–19

                              Total 115

2-8-2T 8F 7200 Class

Introduced 1934. Collett rebuild, with extended bunker and trailing wheels, of Churchward 4200 class 2-8-0T.

Weight: 92 tons 2 cwt.

Pressure: 200 lb. Su.

Cyls.: (O) 19″ × 30″.

Driving Wheels: 4′ 7½″.

T.E.: 33,170 lb.

P.V.

7200–53   Total 54

2-8-0T {7F*} 4200 Class
           {8F†}

*Introduced 1910. Churchward design.
†5205 class. Introduced 1923. With enlarged cyls. and detail alterations.

Weight: { 81 tons 12 cwt.*
        { 82 tons 2 cwt.†

Pressure: 200 lb. Su.

Cyls.: { (O) 18½″ × 30″*.
       { (O) 19″ × 30″†.

Driving Wheels: 4′ 7½″.

T.E.: { 31,450 lb.*
      { 33,170 lb.†

P.V.

*4200/1/3/6–8/11–5/7/8/21–3/5–
33/5–8/41–3/6–8/50–99,
5200–4
†5205–64   Total 150

10

2-6-2T 4MT 3100 Class

Introduced 1938. Collett rebuild, with
higher pressure and smaller wheels, of
Churchward 3150 class (introduced
1906).
Weight: 81 tons 9 cwt.
Pressure: 225 lb. Su.
Cyls.: (O) 18½″ × 30″.
Driving Wheels: 5′ 3″.
T.E.: 31,170 lb.
P.V.

3103   **Total 1**

2-6-2T 4MT 4500 Class

*Introduced 1906. Churchward design
for light branches, developed from
4400 class with larger wheels, earlier
locos. subsequently fitted with superheater.
†4575 class. Introduced 1927. With
detail alterations and increased
weight.
‡Introduced 1953. Push-and-pull fitted.

Weight: {57 tons 0 cwt.*
        {61 tons 0 cwt.†‡
Pressure: 200 lb. Su.
Cyls.: (O) 17″ × 24″.
Driving Wheels: 4′ 7½″.
T.E.: 21,250 lb.
P.V.

*4507/8/36/40/7/9/50/2/5–67/9–
71/3/4

†4575/7/85/7/8/91–4/9, 5500/3/
4/8–10/4–6/8–23/5–8/30–3/
6–44/6–54/6–8/61–5/7/9–71/3

‡4589, 5511/24/9/34/45/55/9
/60/8/72   **Total 101**

2-6-2T 4MT 5100 & 6100 Classes

*5100 class. Introduced 1928. Collett
rebuild, with detail alterations and
increased weight, of Churchward 3100
class (introduced 1903 and subsequently fitted with superheater).
†5101 class. Introduced 1929. Modified
design for new construction.

‡6100 class. Introduced 1931. Locos
for London suburban area with
increased boiler pressure.
Weight: {75 tons 10 cwt.*
        {78 tons 9 cwt.†‡
Pressure: {200 lb. Su.*†
          {225 lb. Su.‡
Cyls.: (O) 18″ × 30″.
Driving Wheels: 5′ 8″.
T.E.: {24,300 lb.*†
      {27,340 lb.‡
P.V.

*5148

†4100–37/40–79, 5101–4/6/10/
50–5/8/63/4/6/7/9/70/3–99

‡6101–69   **Total 194**

2-6-2T 4MT 8100 Class

Introduced 1938. Collett rebuild, with
higher pressure and smaller wheels, of
Churchward locos. in 5100 class.
Weight: 76 tons 11 cwt.
Pressure: 225 lb. Su.
Cyls.: (O) 18″ × 30″.
Driving Wheels: 5′ 6″.
T.E.: 28,165 lb.
P.V.

8100–4/6–9   **Total 9**

2-6-2T unclass. V. of R.

*Introduced 1902. Davies and Metcalfe
design for V. of. R. 1′ 11½″ gauge.
†Introduced 1923. G.W. development
of V. of R. design.
Weight: 25 tons 0 cwt.
Gauge: 1′ 11½″.
Pressure: 165 lb.
Cyls.: (O) {11″ × 17″.*
            {11½″ × 17″.†
Driving Wheels: 2′ 6″.
T.E.: {9,615 lb.*
      {10,510 lb.†
Walschaerts valve gear.

*9   †7/8   **Total 3**

11

NOTE

The following abbreviations are used to indicate the pre-grouping owners of certain Western Region locomotives :

B.P.G.V.	Burry Port & Gwendraeth Valley Railway.
Car.R.	Cardiff Railway.
P. & M.	Powlesland & Mason (Contractor).
S.H.T.	Swansea Harbour Trust.
V. of R.	Cambrian Railways (Vale of Rheidol).
W. & L.	Cambrian Railways (Welshpool & Llanfair).

0-6-2T 5MT 5600 Class

*Introduced 1924. Collett design for service in Welsh valleys.
†Introduced 1927. Locos. with detail alterations.
Weight: { 68 tons 12 cwt.*
              { 69 tons 7 cwt.†
Pressure: 200 lb. Su.
Cyls.: 18″ × 26″.
Driving Wheels: 4′ 7½″.
T.E.: 25,800 lb.
P.V.

*5600–99
†6600–99   **Total 200**

0-6-0PT 2F 850 Class

Introduced 1910. Dean saddletanks, subsequently rebuilt with pannier tanks.
Weight: 36 tons 3 cwt.
Pressure: 165 lb.
Cyls.: 16″ × 24″.
Driving Wheels: 4′ 1½″.
T.E.: 17,410 lb.

2012   **Total 1**

0-6-0ST 0F 1361 Class

Introduced 1910. Churchward design for dock shunting.
Weight: 35 tons 4 cwt.
Pressure: 150 lb.
Cyls.: (O) 16″ × 20″.
Driving Wheels: 3′ 8″.
T.E.: 14,835 lb.
1361–5   **Total 5**

0-6-0PT 1F 1366 Class

Introduced 1934. Collett development of 1361 class, with pannier tanks.
Weight: 35 tons 4 cwt.
Pressure: 165 lb.
Cyls.: 16″ × 20″.
Driving Wheels: 3′ 8″.
T.E.: 16,320 lb.
1366–71   **Total 6**

0-6-0PT 4F 1500 Class

Introduced 1949. Hawksworth short-wheelbase heavy shunting design.
Weight: 58 tons 4 cwt.
Pressure: 200 lb.
Cyls.: (O) 17½″ × 24″.
Driving Wheels: 4′ 7½″.
T.E.: 22,515 lb.
Walschaerts valve gear. P.V.
1500–9   **Total 10**

0-6-0PT 2F 1600 Class

Introduced 1949. Hawksworth light branch line and shunting design.
Weight: 41 tons 12 cwt.
Pressure: 165 lb.
Cyls.: 16½″ × 24″.
Driving Wheels: 4′ 1½″.
T.E.: 18,515 lb.
1600–69   **Total 70**

0-6-0PT 2F 2021 Class

Introduced 1897. Dean saddletank, subsequently rebuilt with pannier tanks.
Weight: 39 tons 15 cwt.
Pressure: 165 lb.
Cyls.: 16½″ × 24″.
Driving Wheels: 4′ 1½″.
T.E.: 18,515 lb.
2069   **Total 1**

0-6-0PT 1P 5400 Class

Introduced 1931. Collett design for light passenger work, push-and-pull fitted.

Weight: 46 tons 12 cwt.
Pressure: 165 lb.
Cyls.: 16½″ × 24″.
Driving Wheels: 5′ 2″.
T.E.: 14,780 lb.

5400/7/9/10/2/4/6–8/20–4
Total 14

0-6-0PT 3F 5700 Class

*Introduced 1929. Collett design for shunting and light goods work developed from 2021 class.
†Introduced 1930. Locos. with steam brake and no A.T.C. fittings, for shunting only.
§Introduced 1933. Locos. with detail alterations, modified cab (except 8700) and increased weight.
‡Introduced 1933. Locos. with condensing apparatus for working over L.T. Metropolitan line.
¶Introduced 1948. Steam brake locos. with increased weight.
Weight: { 47 tons 10 cwt.*†
{ 50 tons 15 cwt.‡
{ 49 tons 0 cwt.§¶
Pressure: 200 lb.
Cyls.: 17½″ × 24″.
Driving Wheels: 4′ 7½″.
T.E.: 22,515 lb.

*5702/4–9/13/7/20/1/6–8/31/4/7/8/40/4–50/3–9/61/3–6/8–71/3–6/8–80/3/4/7–91/3–6/8/9, 7700–9/12/3/5–37/9–49/51–3/5–78/80–/91/3/4/6–9, 8701/2/4–49
†6700–2/7/11/2/4/9/20/4/5/8/9/35/8/9/41–3/5/9
§3600–3739/41–92/4–9, 4600–99, 8700/50–4/6/7/9–99, 9600–82, 9711–71/3–99
‡9700–7/9/10
¶6750–70/2–9
Total 779

0-6-0PT 2P* 2F†
6400 & 7400 Classes

*6400 class. Introduced 1932. Collett design for light passenger work, variation of 5400 class with smaller wheels, push-and-pull fitted.

†7400 class. Introduced 1936. Non-push-and-pull fitted locos.
Weight: { 45 tons 12 cwt.*
{ 45 tons 9 cwt.†
Pressure: 180 lb.
Cyls.: 16½″ × 24″.
Driving Wheels: 4′ 7½″.
T.E.: 18,010 lb.

*6400–6/8–22/4–6/8–39
†7400–14/7–37/9–49

**Total : 6400 Class 37
7400 Class 47**

0-6-0PT 4F 9400 Class

*Introduced 1947. Hawksworth taper boiler design for heavy shunting.
†Introduced 1949. Locos. with non-superheated boiler.
Weight: 55 tons 7 cwt.
Pressure: 200 lb. SS.
Cyls.: 17½″ × 24″.
Driving Wheels: 4′ 7½″.
T.E.: 22,515 lb.

*9400–9
†3400–9, 8400–99, 9410–99
Total 210

0-6-0T 1F B.P.G.V.

Introduced 1910. Hudswell Clarke design for B.P.G.V., rebuilt by G.W.R.
Weight: 37 tons 15 cwt.
Pressure: 165 lb.
Cyls.: (O) 15″ × 22″.
Driving Wheels: 3′ 9″.
T.E.: 15,430 lb.

2198
Total 1

0-6-0T Unclass. W. & L.

(Line closed: locos. stored.)

Introduced 1902. Beyer Peacock design for 2′ 6″ gauge W. & L. Section, Cambrian Railways.
Weight: 19 tons 18 cwt.

Gauge: 2' 6".
Pressure: 150 lb.
Cyls.: (O) 11½" × 16".
Driving Wheels: 2' 9".
T.E.: 8,175 lb.
Walschaerts valve gear.

822/3 **Total 2**

0-4-2T 1P
1400 & 5800 Classes

*1400 class introduced 1932. Collett design for light branch work (originally designated 4800 class). Push-and-pull fitted.

†5800 class introduced 1933. Non-push-and-pull fitted locos.
Weight: 41 tons 6 cwt.
Pressure: 165 lb.
Cyls.: (O) 16" × 24".
Driving Wheels: 5' 2".
T.E.: 13,900 lb.

*1407/9/10/2/9–21/4/6–9/31–5/
8/4/2/4/5/7–55/8/62–4/6–8/
70–4
†5804/9/15/8

Total 47

0-4-0T 3F 1101 Class

Introduced 1926. Avonside Engine Co. design to G.W. requirements for dock shunting.
Weight: 38 tons 4 cwt.
Pressure: 170 lb.
Cyls.: (O) 16" × 24".
Driving Wheels: 3' 9½".
T.E.: 19,510 lb.
Walschaerts valve gear.

1101–6 **Total 6**

0-4-0ST OF Cardiff Rly.

Introduced 1893. Kitson design for Cardiff Railway.
Weight: 25 tons 10 cwt.
Pressure: 160 lb.
Cyls.: (O) 14" × 21".

Driving Wheels: 3' 2½".
T.E.: 14,540 lb.
Hawthorn Kitson valve gear.

1338 **Total 1**

0-4-0ST OF P. & M.

Introduced 1907. Peckett design for P. & M.
Weight: 33 tons 10 cwt.
Pressure: 150 lb.
Cyls.: (O) 15" × 21".
Driving Wheels: 3' 7".
T.E.: 14,010 lb.

1151/2 **Total 2**

0-4-0ST S.H.T.

Introduced 1906. Peckett design for S.H.T. (similar to 1151/2).
Weight: 33 tons 10 cwt.
Pressure: 150 lb.
Cyls.: (O) 15" × 21".
Driving Wheels: 3' 7".
T.E.: 14,010 lb.

1143/5 **Total 2**

Introduced 1909. Hawthorn Leslie design for S.H.T.
Weight: 26 tons 17 cwt.
Pressure: 150 lb.
Cyls.: (O) 14" × 22".
Driving Wheels: 3' 6".
T.E.: 13,090 lb.

1144 **Total 1**

Introduced 1911. Hudswell Clarke design for S.H.T.
Weight: 28 tons 15 cwt.
Pressure: 160 lb.
Cyls.: (O) 15" × 22".
Driving Wheels: 3' 4".
T.E.: 16,830 lb.

1142 **Total 1**

NUMERICAL LIST OF WESTERN REGION STEAM LOCOMOTIVES

Locomotives are of G.W. origin except where indicated by other initials

2-6-2T   V. of R.

7	Owain Glyndŵr
8	Llywelyn
9	Prince of Wales

0-6-0T   W. & L.

822   823

(Line closed : locos. stored.)

4-6-0   1000 Class
"County"

1000	County of Middlesex
1001	County of Bucks
1002	County of Berks
1003	County of Wilts
1004	County of Somerset
1005	County of Devon
1006	County of Cornwall
1007	County of Brecknock
1008	County of Cardigan
1009	County of Carmarthen
1010	County of Caernarvon
1011	County of Chester
1012	County of Denbigh
1013	County of Dorset
1014	County of Glamorgan
1015	County of Gloucester
1016	County of Hants
1017	County of Hereford
1018	County of Leicester
1019	County of Merioneth
1020	County of Monmouth
1021	County of Montgomery
1022	County of Northampton
1023	County of Oxford
1024	County of Pembroke
1025	County of Radnor
1026	County of Salop
1027	County of Stafford
1028	County of Warwick
1029	County of Worcester

0-4-0T   1101 Class

1101	1103	1105
1102	1104	1106

0-4-0ST   S.H.T.

1142	1143	1144	1145

0-4-0ST   P.M.

1151   1152

0-4-0ST   Car. R.

1338

0-6-0ST   1361 Class

1361	1363	1365
1362	1364	

0-6-0PT   1366 Class

1366	1368	1370
1367	1369	1371

0-4-2T   1400 Class

1407	1420	1428	1434
1409	1421	1429	1435
1410	1424	1431	1438
1412	1426	1432	1440
1419	1427	1433	1441

1442-2861

1442	1450	1458	1468
1444	1451	1462	1470
1445	1452	1463	1471
1447	1453	1464	1472
1448	1454	1466	1473
1449	1455	1467	1474

0-6-0PT   1500 Class

1500	1503	1506	1509
1501	1504	1507	
1502	1505	1508	

0-6-0PT   1600 Class

1600	1618	1636	1654
1601	1619	1637	1655
1602	1620	1638	1656
1603	1621	1639	1657
1604	1622	1640	1658
1605	1623	1641	1659
1606	1624	1642	1660
1607	1625	1643	1661
1608	1626	1644	1662
1609	1627	1645	1663
1610	1628	1646	1664
1611	1629	1647	1665
1612	1630	1648	1666
1613	1631	1649	1667
1614	1632	1650	1668
1615	1633	1651	1669
1616	1634	1652	
1617	1635	1653	

0-6-0PT   850 Class

2012

0-6-0PT   2021 Class

2069

0-6-0T   B.P.G.V.

2198

0-6-0   2251 Class

2200	2224	2248	2276
2201	2225	2249	2277
2202	2226	2250	2278
2203	2227	2251	2280
2204	2228	2252	2281
2205	2229	2253	2282
2206	2230	2255	2283
2207	2231	2256	2284
2208	2232	2257	2285
2209	2233	2259	2286
2210	2234	2260	2287
2211	2235	2261	2288
2212	2236	2262	2289
2213	2237	2264	2290
2214	2238	2265	2291
2215	2239	2266	2292
2216	2240	2267	2293
2217	2241	2268	2294
2218	2242	2270	2295
2219	2243	2271	2296
2220	2244	2272	2297
2221	2245	2273	2298
2222	2246	2274	2299
2223	2247	2275	

2-8-0   2800 Class

2803	2818	2836	2849
2804	2819	2837	2850
2805	2821	2838	2851
2806	2822	2839	2852
2807	2823	2840	2853
2808	2824	2841	2854
2809	2825	2842	2855
2810	2826	2843	2856
2811	2831	2844	2857
2813	2832	2845	2858
2815	2833	2846	2859
2816	2834	2847	2860
2817	2835	2848	2861

2862	2872	2882	2891	3612	3659	3706	3753
2863	2873	2883	2892	3613	3660	3707	3754
2864	2874	2884	2893	3614	3661	3708	3755
2865	2875	2885	2894	3615	3662	3709	3756
2866	2876	2886	2895	3616	3663	3710	3757
2867	2877	2887	2896	3617	3664	3711	3758
2868	2878	2888	2897	3618	3665	3712	3759
2869	2879	2889	2898	3619	3666	3713	3760
2870	2880	2890	2899	3620	3667	3714	3761
2871	2881			3621	3668	3715	3762
				3622	3669	3716	3763
				3623	3670	3717	3764
				3624	3671	3718	3765

2-6-2T   3100 Class

3103

0-6-0   2251 Class

3200	3205	3210	3215
3201	3206	3211	3216
3202	3207	3212	3217
3203	3208	3213	3218
3204	3209	3214	3219

0-6-0PT   9400 Class

3400	3403	3406	3408
3401	3404	3407	3409
3402	3405		

4-4-0   " City " Class

3440   City of Truro

0-6-0PT   5700 Class

3600	3603	3606	3609
3601	3604	3607	3610
3602	3605	3608	3611

3625	3672	3719	3766
3626	3673	3720	3767
3627	3674	3721	3768
3628	3675	3722	3769
3629	3676	3723	3770
3630	3677	3724	3771
3631	3678	3725	3772
3632	3679	3726	3773
3633	3680	3727	3774
3634	3681	3728	3775
3635	3682	3729	3776
3636	3683	3730	3777
3637	3684	3731	3778
3638	3685	3732	3779
3639	3686	3733	3780
3640	3687	3734	3781
3641	3688	3735	3782
3642	3689	3736	3783
3643	3690	3737	3784
3644	3691	3738	3785
3645	3692	3739	3786
3646	3693	3741	3787
3647	3694	3742	3788
3648	3695	3743	3789
3649	3696	3744	3790
3650	3697	3745	3791
3651	3698	3746	3792
3652	3699	3747	3794
3653	3700	3748	3795
3654	3701	3749	3796
3655	3702	3750	3797
3656	3703	3751	3798
3657	3704	3752	3799
3658	3705		

2-8-0   2800 Class

3800	3817	3834	3851
3801	3818	3835	3852
3802	3819	3836	3853
3803	3820	3837	3854
3804	3821	3838	3855
3805	3822	3839	3856
3806	3823	3840	3857
3807	3824	3841	3858
3808	3825	3842	3859
3809	3826	3843	3860
3810	3827	3844	3861
3811	3828	3845	3862
3812	3829	3846	3863
3813	3830	3847	3864
3814	3831	3848	3865
3815	3832	3849	3866
3816	3833	3850	

4-6-0   4073 Class
" Castle "

4037	The South Wales Borderers
4073	Caerphilly Castle
4074	Caldicot Castle
4075	Cardiff Castle
4076	Carmarthen Castle
4077	Chepstow Castle
4078	Pembroke Castle
4079	Pendennis Castle
4080	Powderham Castle
4081	Warwick Castle
4082	Windsor Castle
4083	Abbotsbury Castle
4084	Aberystwyth Castle
4085	Berkeley Castle
4086	Builth Castle
4087	Cardigan Castle
4088	Dartmouth Castle
4089	Donnington Castle
4090	Dorchester Castle
4092	Dunraven Castle
4093	Dunster Castle
4094	Dynevor Castle
4095	Harlech Castle
4096	Highclere Castle
4097	Kenilworth Castle
4098	Kidwelly Castle
4099	Kilgerran Castle

2-6-2T   5100 Class

4100	4120	4142	4161
4101	4121	4143	4162
4102	4122	4144	4163
4103	4123	4145	4164
4104	4124	4146	4165
4105	4125	4147	4166
4106	4126	4148	4167
4107	4127	4149	4168
4108	4128	4150	4169
4109	4129	4151	4170
4110	4130	4152	4171
4111	4131	4153	4172
4112	4132	4154	4173
4113	4133	4155	4174
4114	4134	4156	4175
4115	4135	4157	4176
4116	4136	4158	4177
4117	4137	4159	4178
4118	4140	4160	4179
4119	4141		

2-8-0T   4200 Class

4200	4222	4238	4257
4201	4223	4241	4258
4203	4225	4242	4259
4206	4226	4243	4260
4207	4227	4246	4261
4208	4228	4247	4262
4211	4229	4248	4263
4212	4230	4250	4264
4213	4231	4251	4265
4214	4232	4252	4266
4215	4233	4253	4267
4217	4235	4254	4268
4218	4236	4255	4269
4221	4237	4256	4270

4271	4279	4287	4295
4272	4280	4288	4296
4273	4281	4289	4297
4274	4282	4290	4298
4275	4283	4291	4299
4276	4284	4292	
4277	4285	4293	
4278	4286	4294	

4644	4658	4672	4686
4645	4659	4673	4687
4646	4660	4674	4688
4647	4661	4675	4689
4648	4662	4676	4690
4649	4663	4677	4691
4650	4664	4678	4692
4651	4665	4679	4693
4652	4666	4680	4694
4653	4667	4681	4695
4654	4668	4682	4696
4655	4669	4683	4697
4656	4670	4684	4698
4657	4671	4685	4699

2-6-0   4300 Class

4358

2-8-0   4700 Class

4700	4703	4705	4707
4701	4704	4706	4708
4702			

2-6-2T   4500 Class

4507	4557	4567	4588
4508	4558	4569	4589
4536	4559	4570	4591
4540	4560	4571	4592
4547	4561	4573	4593
4549	4562	4574	4594
4550	4563	4575	4599
4552	4564	4577	
4555	4565	4585	
4556	4566	4587	

4-6-0 " Hall " 4900 Class

4900	Saint Martin
4901	Adderley Hall
4902	Aldenham Hall
4903	Astley Hall
4904	Binnegar Hall
4905	Barton Hall
4906	Bradfield Hall
4907	Broughton Hall
4908	Broome Hall
4909	Blakesley Hall
4910	Blaisdon Hall
4912	Berrington Hall
4913	Baglan Hall
4914	Cranmore Hall
4915	Condover Hall
4916	Crumlin Hall
4917	Crosswood Hall
4918	Dartington Hall
4919	Donnington Hall
4920	Dumbleton Hall
4921	Eaton Hall
4922	Enville Hall

0-6-0PT   5700 Class

4600	4611	4622	4633
4601	4612	4623	4634
4602	4613	4624	4635
4603	4614	4625	4636
4604	4615	4626	4637
4605	4616	4627	4638
4606	4617	4628	4639
4607	4618	4629	4640
4608	4619	4630	4641
4609	4620	4631	4642
4610	4621	4632	4643

4923	Evenley Hall
4924	Eydon Hall
4925	Eynsham Hall
4926	Fairleigh Hall
4927	Farnborough Hall
4928	Gatacre Hall
4929	Goytrey Hall
4930	Hagley Hall
4931	Hanbury Hall
4932	Hatherton Hall
4933	Himley Hall
4934	Hindlip Hall
4935	Ketley Hall
4936	Kinlet Hall
4937	Lanelay Hall
4938	Liddington Hall
4939	Littleton Hall
4940	Ludford Hall
4941	Llangedwyn Hall
4942	Maindy Hall
4943	Marrington Hall
4944	Middleton Hall
4945	Milligan Hall
4946	Moseley Hall
4947	Nanhoran Hall
4948	Northwick Hall
4949	Packwood Hall
4950	Patshull Hall
4951	Pendeford Hall
4952	Peplow Hall
4953	Pitchford Hall
4954	Plaish Hall
4955	Plaspower Hall
4956	Plowden Hall
4957	Postlip Hall
4958	Priory Hall
4959	Purley Hall
4960	Pyle Hall
4961	Pyrland Hall
4962	Ragley Hall
4963	Rignall Hall
4964	Rodwell Hall
4965	Rood Ashton Hall
4966	Shakenhurst Hall
4967	Shirenewton Hall
4968	Shotton Hall
4969	Shrugborough Hall

4970	Sketty Hall
4971	Stanway Hall
4972	Saint Brides Hall
4973	Sweeney Hall
4974	Talgarth Hall
4975	Umberslade Hall
4976	Warfield Hall
4977	Watcombe Hall
4978	Westwood Hall
4979	Wootton Hall
4980	Wrottesley Hall
4981	Abberley Hall
4982	Acton Hall
4983	Albert Hall
4984	Albrighton Hall
4985	Allesley Hall
4986	Aston Hall
4987	Brockley Hall
4988	Bulwell Hall
4989	Cherwell Hall
4990	Clifton Hall
4991	Cobham Hall
4992	Crosby Hall
4993	Dalton Hall
4994	Downton Hall
4995	Easton Hall
4996	Eden Hall
4997	Elton Hall
4998	Eyton Hall
4999	Gopsal Hall

4-6-0　　　　　**4073 Class**
" Castle "

5000	Launceston Castle
5001	Llandovery Castle
5002	Ludlow Castle
5003	Lulworth Castle
5004	Llanstephan Castle
5005	Manorbier Castle
5006	Tregenna Castle
5007	Rougemont Castle
5008	Raglan Castle
5009	Shrewsbury Castle
5010	Restormel Castle
5011	Tintagel Castle
5012	Berry Pomeroy Castle

5013	Abergavenny Castle	5059	Earl St. Aldwyn
5014	Goodrich Castle	5060	Earl of Berkeley
5015	Kingswear Castle	5061	Earl of Birkenhead
5016	Montgomery Castle	5062	Earl of Shaftesbury
5017	The Gloucestershire Regiment 28th, 61st	5063	Earl Baldwin
5018	St. Mawes Castle	5064	Bishop's Castle
5019	Treago Castle	5065	Newport Castle
5020	Trematon Castle	5066	Sir Felix Pole
5021	Whittington Castle	5067	St. Fagans Castle
5022	Wigmore Castle	5068	Beverston Castle
5023	Brecon Castle	5069	Isambard Kingdom Brunel
5024	Carew Castle	5070	Sir Daniel Gooch
5025	Chirk Castle	5071	Spitfire
5026	Criccieth Castle	5072	Hurricane
5027	Farleigh Castle	5073	Blenheim
5028	Llantilio Castle	5074	Hampden
5029	Nunney Castle	5075	Wellington
5030	Shirburn Castle	5076	Gladiator
5031	Totnes Castle	5077	Fairy Battle
5032	Usk Castle	5078	Beaufort
5033	Broughton Castle	5079	Lysander
5034	Corfe Castle	5080	Defiant
5035	Coity Castle	5081	Lockheed Hudson
5036	Lyonshall Castle	5082	Swordfish
5037	Monmouth Castle	5084	Reading Abbey
5038	Morlais Castle	5085	Evesham Abbey
5039	Rhuddlan Castle	5087	Tintern Abbey
5040	Stokesay Castle	5088	Llanthony Abbey
5041	Tiverton Castle	5089	Westminister Abbey
5042	Winchester Castle	5090	Neath Abbey
5043	Earl of Mount Edgcumbe	5091	Cleeve Abbey
5044	Earl of Dunraven	5092	Tresco Abbey
5045	Earl of Dudley	5093	Upton Castle
5046	Earl Cawdor	5094	Tretower Castle
5047	Earl of Dartmouth	5095	Barbury Castle
5048	Earl of Devon	5096	Bridgwater Castle
5049	Earl of Plymouth	5097	Sarum Castle
5050	Earl of St. Germans	5098	Clifford Castle
5051	Earl Bathurst	5099	Compton Castle
5052	Earl of Radnor		
5053	Earl Cairns		
5054	Earl of Ducie		
5055	Earl of Eldon		
5056	Earl of Powis		
5057	Earl Waldegrave		
5058	Earl of Clancarty		

2-6-2T   5100 Class

5101	5103	5106	5148
5102	5104	5110	5150

21

5151	5169	5181	5191
5152	5170	5182	5192
5153	5173	5183	5193
5154	5174	5184	5194
5155	5175	5185	5195
5158	5176	5186	5196
5163	5177	5187	5197
5164	5178	5188	5198
5166	5179	5189	5199
5167	5180	5190	

5376	5381	5385	5396
5378	5382	5388	5399
5380	5384	5393	

0-6-0PT   5400 Class

5400	5412	5418	5422
5407	5414	5420	5423
5409	5416	5421	5424
5410	5417		

2-8-0T   4200 Class

5200	5217	5233	5249
5201	5218	5234	5250
5202	5219	5235	5251
5203	5220	5236	5252
5204	5221	5237	5253
5205	5222	5238	5254
5206	5223	5239	5255
5207	5224	5240	5256
5208	5225	5241	5257
5209	5226	5242	5258
5210	5227	5243	5259
5211	5228	5244	5260
5212	5229	5245	5261
5213	5230	5246	5262
5214	5231	5247	5263
5215	5232	5248	5264
5216			

2-6-2T   4500 Class

5500	5524	5541	5557
5503	5525	5542	5558
5504	5526	5543	5559
5508	5527	5544	5560
5509	5528	5545	5561
5510	5529	5546	5562
5511	5530	5547	5563
5514	5531	5548	5564
5515	5532	5549	5565
5516	5533	5550	5567
5518	5534	5551	5568
5519	5536	5552	5569
5520	5537	5553	5570
5521	5538	5554	5571
5522	5539	5555	5572
5523	5540	5556	5573

2-6-0   4300 Class

5306	5326	5339	5356
5311	5330	5341	5357
5318	5331	5345	5358
5319	5332	5350	5361
5321	5333	5351	5369
5322	5336	5353	5370
5324	5337	5355	5375

0-6-2T   5600 Class

5600	5602	5604	5606
5601	5603	5605	5607

5608	5631	5654	5677
5609	5632	5655	5678
5610	5633	5656	5679
5611	5634	5657	5680
5612	5635	5658	5681
5613	5636	5659	5682
5614	5637	5660	5683
5615	5638	5661	5684
5616	5639	5662	5685
5617	5640	5663	5686
5618	5641	5664	5687
5619	5642	5665	5688
5620	5643	5666	5689
5621	5644	5667	5690
5622	5645	5668	5691
5623	5646	5669	5692
5624	5647	5670	5693
5625	5648	5671	5694
5626	5649	5672	5695
5627	5650	5673	5696
5628	5651	5674	5697
5629	5652	5675	5698
5630	5653	5676	5699

0-4-2T 5800 Class

5804	5809	5815	5818

4-6-0 4900 Class "Hall"

5900 Hinderton Hall
5901 Hazel Hall
5902 Howick Hall
5903 Keele Hall
5904 Kelham Hall
5905 Knowsley Hall
5906 Lawton Hall
5907 Marble Hall
5908 Moreton Hall
5909 Newton Hall
5910 Park Hall
5911 Preston Hall
5912 Queen's Hall
5913 Rushton Hall
5914 Ripon Hall
5915 Trentham Hall
5916 Trinity Hall
5917 Westminster Hall
5918 Walton Hall
5919 Worsley Hall
5920 Wycliffe Hall
5921 Bingley Hall
5922 Caxton Hall
5923 Colston Hall
5924 Dinton Hall
5925 Eastcote Hall
5926 Grotrian Hall
5927 Guild Hall
5928 Haddon Hall
5929 Hanham Hall
5930 Hannington Hall
5931 Hatherley Hall
5932 Haydon Hall
5933 Kingsway Hall
5934 Kneller Hall

0-6-0PT 5700 Class

5702	5737	5759	5780
5704	5738	5761	5783
5705	5740	5763	5784
5706	5744	5764	5787
5707	5745	5765	5788
5708	5746	5766	5789
5709	5747	5768	5790
5713	5748	5769	5791
5717	5749	5770	5793
5720	5750	5771	5794
5721	5753	5773	5795
5726	5754	5774	5796
5727	5755	5775	5798
5728	5756	5776	5799
5731	5757	5778	
5734	5758	5779	

23

5935	Norton Hall
5936	Oakley Hall
5937	Stanford Hall
5938	Stanley Hall
5939	Tangley Hall
5940	Whitbourne Hall
5941	Campion Hall
5942	Doldowlod Hall
5943	Elmdon Hall
5944	Ickenham Hall
5945	Leckhampton Hall
5946	Marwell Hall
5947	Saint Benet's Hall
5948	Siddington Hall
5949	Trematon Hall
5950	Wardley Hall
5951	Clyffe Hall
5952	Cogan Hall
5953	Dunley Hall
5954	Faendre Hall
5955	Garth Hall
5956	Horsley Hall
5957	Hutton Hall
5958	Knolton Hall
5959	Mawley Hall
5960	Saint Edmund Hall
5961	Toynbee Hall
5962	Wantage Hall
5963	Wimpole Hall
5964	Wolseley Hall
5965	Woollas Hall
5966	Ashford Hall
5967	Bickmarsh Hall
5968	Cory Hall
5969	Honington Hall
5970	Hengrave Hall
5971	Merevale Hall
5972	Olton Hall
5973	Rolleston Hall
5974	Wallsworth Hall
5975	Winslow Hall
5976	Ashwicke Hall
5977	Beckford Hall
5978	Bodinnick Hall
5979	Cruckton Hall
5980	Dingley Hall
5981	Frensham Hall

5982	Harrington Hall
5983	Henley Hall
5984	Linden Hall
5985	Mostyn Hall
5986	Arbury Hall
5987	Brocket Hall
5988	Bostock Hall
5989	Cransley Hall
5990	Dorford Hall
5991	Gresham Hall
5992	Horton Hall
5993	Kirby Hall
5994	Roydon Hall
5995	Wick Hall
5996	Mytton Hall
5997	Sparkford Hall
5998	Trevor Hall
5999	Wollaton Hall

4-6-0   6000 Class

" King "

6000	King George V
6001	King Edward VII
6002	King William IV
6003	King George IV
6004	King George III
6005	King George II
6006	King George I
6007	King William III
6008	King James II
6009	King Charles II
6010	King Charles I
6011	King James I
6012	King Edward VI
6013	King Henry VIII
6014	King Henry VII
6015	King Richard III
6016	King Edward V
6017	King Edward IV
6018	King Henry VI
6019	King Henry V
6020	King Henry IV

6021	King Richard II
6022	King Edward III
6023	King Edward II
6024	King Edward I
6025	King Henry III
6026	King John
6027	King Richard I
6028	King George VI
6029	King Edward VIII

2-6-2T   6100 Class

6101	6119	6136	6153
6102	6120	6137	6154
6103	6121	6138	6155
6104	6122	6139	6156
6105	6123	6140	6157
6106	6124	6141	6158
6107	6125	6142	6159
6108	6126	6143	6160
6109	6127	6144	6161
6110	6128	6145	6162
6111	6129	6146	6163
6112	6130	6147	6164
6113	6131	6148	6165
6114	6132	6149	6166
6115	6133	6150	6167
6116	6134	6151	6168
6117	6135	6152	6169
6118			

2-6-0   4300 Class

6300	6312	6329	6341
6301	6313	6330	6342
6302	6314	6331	6343
6303	6316	6332	6344
6304	6317	6333	6345
6305	6319	6334	6346
6306	6320	6335	6347
6307	6323	6336	6348
6308	6324	6337	6349
6309	6325	6338	6350
6310	6326	6339	6351
6311	6327	6340	6352

6353	6366	6377	6389
6355	6367	6378	6390
6356	6368	6379	6391
6357	6369	6380	6392
6358	6370	6381	6393
6359	6371	6382	6394
6360	6372	6384	6395
6361	6373	6385	6396
6362	6374	6386	6397
6363	6375	6387	6398
6364	6376	6388	6399
6365			

0-6-0PT   6400 Class

6400	6411	6420	6431
6401	6412	6421	6432
6402	6413	6422	6433
6403	6414	6424	6434
6404	6415	6425	6435
6405	6416	6426	6436
6406	6417	6428	6437
6408	6418	6429	6438
6409	6419	6430	6439
6410			

0-6-2T   5600 Class

6600	6620	6640	6660
6601	6621	6641	6661
6602	6622	6642	6662
6603	6623	6643	6663
6604	6624	6644	6664
6605	6625	6645	6665
6606	6626	6646	6666
6607	6627	6647	6667
6608	6628	6648	6668
6609	6629	6649	6669
6610	6630	6650	6670
6611	6631	6651	6671
6612	6632	6652	6672
6613	6633	6653	6673
6614	6634	6654	6674
6615	6635	6655	6675
6616	6636	6656	6676
6617	6637	6657	6677
6618	6638	6658	6678
6619	6639	6659	6679

6680	6685	6690	6695
6681	6686	6691	6696
6682	6687	6692	6697
6683	6688	6693	6698
6684	6689	6694	6699

0-6-0PT   5700 Class

6700	6735	6755	6767
6701	6738	6756	6768
6702	6739	6757	6769
6707	6741	6758	6770
6711	6742	6759	6772
6712	6743	6760	6773
6714	6745	6761	6774
6719	6749	6762	6775
6720	6750	6763	6776
6724	6751	6764	6777
6725	6752	6765	6778
6728	6753	6766	6779
6729	6754		

4-6-0   6800 Class
" Grange "

6800 Arlington Grange
6801 Aylburton Grange
6802 Bampton Grange
6803 Bucklebury Grange
6804 Brockington Grange
6805 Broughton Grange
6806 Blackwell Grange
6807 Birchwood Grange
6808 Beenham Grange
6809 Burghclere Grange
6810 Blakemere Grange
6811 Cranbourne Grange
6812 Chesford Grange
6813 Eastbury Grange

6814 Enborne Grange
6815 Frilford Grange
6816 Frankton Grange
6817 Gwenddwr Grange
6818 Hardwick Grange
6819 Highnam Grange
6820 Kingstone Grange
6821 Leaton Grange
6822 Manton Grange
6823 Oakley Grange
6824 Ashley Grange
6825 Llanvair Grange
6826 Nannerth Grange
6827 Llanfrechfa Grange
6828 Trellech Grange
6829 Burmington Grange
6830 Buckenhill Grange
6831 Bearley Grange
6832 Brockton Grange
6833 Calcot Grange
6834 Dummer Grange
6835 Eastham Grange
6836 Estevarney Grange
6837 Forthampton Grange
6838 Goodmoor Grange
6839 Hewell Grange
6840 Hazeley Grange
6841 Marlas Grange
6842 Nunhold Grange
6843 Poulton Grange
6844 Penhydd Grange
6845 Paviland Grange
6846 Ruckley Grange
6847 Tidmarsh Grange
6848 Toddington Grange
6849 Walton Grange
6850 Cleeve Grange
6851 Hurst Grange
6852 Headbourne Grange
6853 Morehampton Grange
6854 Roundhill Grange
6855 Saighton Grange
6856 Stowe Grange
6857 Tudor Grange
6858 Woolston Grange
6859 Yiewsley Grange
6860 Aberporth Grange

6861	Crynant Grange
6862	Derwent Grange
6863	Dolhywel Grange
6864	Dymock Grange
6865	Hopton Grange
6866	Morfa Grange
6867	Peterston Grange
6868	Penrhos Grange
6869	Resolven Grange
6870	Bodicote Grange
6871	Bourton Grange
6872	Crawley Grange
6873	Caradoc Grange
6874	Haughton Grange
6875	Hindford Grange
6876	Kingsland Grange
6877	Llanfair Grange
6878	Longford Grange
6879	Overton Grange

4-6-0   4900 Class
" Hall "

6900	Abney Hall
6901	Arley Hall
6902	Butlers Hall
6903	Belmont Hall
6904	Charfield Hall
6905	Claughton Hall
6906	Chicheley Hall
6907	Davenham Hall
6908	Downham Hall
6909	Frewin Hall
6910	Gossington Hall
6911	Holker Hall
6912	Helmster Hall
6913	Levens Hall
6914	Langton Hall
6915	Mursley Hall
6916	Misterton Hall
6917	Oldlands Hall
6918	Sandon Hall
6919	Tylney Hall
6920	Barningham Hall
6921	Borwick Hall
6922	Burton Hall
6923	Croxteth Hall

6924	Grantley Hall
6925	Hackness Hall
6926	Holkham Hall
6927	Lilford Hall
6928	Underley Hall
6929	Whorlton Hall
6930	Aldersey Hall
6931	Aldborough Hall
6932	Burwarton Hall
6933	Birtles Hall
6934	Beachamwell Hall
6935	Browsholme Hall
6936	Breccles Hall
6937	Conyngham Hall
6938	Corndean Hall
6939	Calveley Hall
6940	Didlington Hall
6941	Fillongley Hall
6942	Eshton Hall
6943	Farnley Hall
6944	Fledborough Hall
6945	Glasfryn Hall
6946	Heatherden Hall
6947	Helmingham Hall
6948	Holbrooke Hall
6949	Haberfield Hall
6950	Kingsthorpe Hall
6951	Impney Hall
6952	Kimberley Hall
6953	Leighton Hall
6954	Lotherton Hall
6955	Lydcott Hall
6956	Mottram Hall
6957	Norcliffe Hall
6958	Oxburgh Hall

4-6-0   6959 Class
" Modified Hall "

6959	Peatling Hall
6960	Raveningham Hall
6961	Stedham Hall
6962	Soughton Hall
6963	Throwley Hall
6964	Thornbridge Hall
6965	Thirlestaine Hall
6966	Witchingham Hall

27

6967	Willesley Hall
6968	Woodcock Hall
6969	Wraysbury Hall
6970	Whaddon Hall
6971	Athelhampton Hall
6972	Beningbrough Hall
6973	Bricklehampton Hall
6974	Bryngwyn Hall
6975	Capesthorne Hall
6976	Graythwaite Hall
6977	Grundisburgh Hall
6978	Haroldstone Hall
6979	Helperly Hall
6980	Llanrumney Hall
6981	Marbury Hall
6982	Melmerby Hall
6983	Otterington Hall
6984	Owsden Hall
6985	Parwick Hall
6986	Rydal Hall
6987	Shervington Hall
6988	Swithland Hall
6989	Wightwick Hall
6990	Witherslack Hall
6991	Acton Burnell Hall
6992	Arborfield Hall
6993	Arthog Hall
6994	Baggrave Hall
6995	Benthall Hall
6996	Blackwell Hall
6997	Bryn-Ivor Hall
6998	Burton Agnes Hall
6999	Capel Dewi Hall

4-6-0   4073 Class
" Castle "

7000	Viscount Portal
7001	Sir James Milne
7002	Devizes Castle
7003	Elmley Castle
7004	Eastnor Castle
7005	Sir Edward Elgar
7006	Lydford Castle
7007	Great Western
7008	Swansea Castle

7009	Athelney Castle
7010	Avondale Castle
7011	Banbury Castle
7012	Barry Castle
7013	Bristol Castle
7014	Caerhays Castle
7015	Carn Brea Castle
7016	Chester Castle
7017	G. J. Churchward
7018	Drysllwyn Castle
7019	Fowey Castle
7020	Gloucester Castle
7021	Haverfordwest Castle
7022	Hereford Castle
7023	Penrice Castle
7024	Powis Castle
7025	Sudeley Castle
7026	Tenby Castle
7027	Thornbury Castle
7028	Cadbury Castle
7029	Clun Castle
7030	Cranbrook Castle
7031	Cromwell's Castle
7032	Denbigh Castle
7033	Hartlebury Castle
7034	Ince Castle
7035	Ogmore Castle
7036	Taunton Castle
7037	Swindon

2-8-2T   7200 Class

7200	7214	7228	7241
7201	7215	7229	7242
7202	7216	7230	7243
7203	7217	7231	7244
7204	7218	7232	7245
7205	7219	7233	7246
7206	7220	7234	7247
7207	7221	7235	7248
7208	7222	7236	7249
7209	7223	7237	7250
7210	7224	7238	7251
7211	7225	7239	7252
7212	7226	7240	7253
7213	7227		

2-6-0   4300 Class

7300	7310	7320	7332
7301	7311	7321	7333
7302	7312	7322	7334
7303	7313	7323	7335
7304	7314	7324	7336
7305	7315	7325	7338
7306	7316	7326	7339
7307	7317	7327	7340
7308	7318	7328	7341
7309	7319	7329	

0-6-0PT   7400 Class

7400	7412	7426	7439
7401	7413	7427	7440
7402	7414	7428	7441
7403	7417	7429	7442
7404	7418	7430	7443
7405	7419	7431	7444
7406	7420	7432	7445
7407	7421	7433	7446
7408	7422	7434	7447
7409	7423	7435	7448
7410	7424	7436	7449
7411	7425	7437	

0-6-0PT   5700 Class

7700	7721	7740	7760
7701	7722	7741	7761
7702	7723	7742	7762
7703	7724	7743	7763
7704	7725	7744	7764
7705	7726	7745	7765
7706	7727	7746	7766
7707	7728	7747	7767
7708	7729	7748	7768
7709	7730	7749	7769
7712	7731	7751	7770
7713	7732	7752	7771
7715	7733	7753	7772
7716	7734	7755	7773
7717	7735	7756	7774
7718	7736	7757	7775
7719	7737	7758	7776
7720	7739	7759	7777

7778	7784	7789	7796
7780	7785	7790	7797
7781	7786	7791	7793
7782	7787	7793	7799
7783	7788	7794	

4-6-0   7800 Class
" Manor "

7800	Torquay Manor
7801	Anthony Manor
7802	Bradley Manor
7803	Barcote Manor
7804	Baydon Manor
7805	Broome Manor
7806	Cockington Manor
7807	Compton Manor
7808	Cookham Manor
7809	Childrey Manor
7810	Draycott Manor
7811	Dunley Manor
7812	Erlestoke Manor
7813	Freshford Manor
7814	Fringford Manor
7815	Fritwell Manor
7816	Frilsham Manor
7817	Garsington Manor
7818	Granville Manor
7819	Hinton Manor
7820	Dinmore Manor
7821	Ditcheat Manor
7822	Foxcote Manor
7823	Hook Norton Manor
7824	Iford Manor
7825	Lechlade Manor
7826	Longworth Manor
7827	Lydham Manor
7828	Odney Manor
7829	Ramsbury Manor

4-6-0   6959 Class
" Modified Hall "

7900	Saint Peter's Hall
7901	Dodington Hall
7902	Eaton Mascot Hall
7903	Foremarke Hall
7904	Fountains Hall

7905	Fowey Hall
7906	Fron Hall
7907	Hart Hall
7908	Henshall Hall
7909	Heveningham Hall
7910	Hown Hall
7911	Lady Margaret Hall
7912	Little Linford Hall
7913	Little Wyrley Hall
7914	Lleweni Hall
7915	Mere Hall
7916	Mobberley Hall
7917	North Aston Hall
7918	Rhose Wood Hall
7919	Runter Hall
7920	Coney Hall
7921	Edstone Hall
7922	Salford Hall
7923	Speke Hall
7924	Thornycroft Hall
7925	Westol Hall
7926	Willey Hall
7927	Willington Hall
7928	Wolf Hall
7929	Wyke Hall

8456	8467	8478	8489
8457	8468	8479	8490
8458	8469	8480	8491
8459	8470	8481	8492
8460	8471	8482	8493
8461	8472	8483	8494
8462	8473	8484	8495
8463	8474	8485	8496
8464	8475	8486	8497
8465	8476	8487	8498
8466	8477	8488	8499

2-6-2T   8100 Class

8100	8103	8106	8108
8101	8104	8107	8109
8102			

0-6-0PT   9400 Class

8400	8414	8428	8442
8401	8415	8429	8443
8402	8416	8430	8444
8403	8417	8431	8445
8404	8418	8432	8446
8405	8419	8433	8447
8406	8420	8434	8448
8407	8421	8435	8449
8408	8422	8436	8450
8409	8423	8437	8451
8410	8424	8438	8452
8411	8425	8439	8453
8412	8426	8440	8454
8413	8427	8441	8455

0-6-0PT   5700 Class

8700	8726	8751	8778
8701	8727	8752	8779
8702	8728	8753	8780
8704	8729	8754	8781
8705	8730	8756	8782
8706	8731	8757	8783
8707	8732	8759	8784
8708	8733	8760	8785
8709	8734	8761	8786
8710	8735	8762	8787
8711	8736	8763	8788
8712	8737	8764	8789
8713	8738	8765	8790
8714	8739	8766	8791
8715	8740	8767	8792
8716	8741	8768	8793
8717	8742	8769	8794
8718	8743	8770	8795
8719	8744	8771	8796
8720	8745	8772	8797
8721	8746	8773	8798
8722	8747	8774	8799
8723	8748	8775	
8724	8749	8776	
8725	8750	8777	

4-4-0   9000 Class

9004	9014	9017	9018
9005	9015		

2-6-0   4300 Class

9308	9309	9315

0-6-0PT   9400 Class

9400	9425	9450	9475
9401	9426	9451	9476
9402	9427	9452	9477
9403	9428	9453	9478
9404	9429	9454	9479
9405	9430	9455	9480
9406	9431	9456	9481
9407	9432	9457	9482
9408	9433	9458	9483
9409	9434	9459	9484
9410	9435	9460	9485
9411	9436	9461	9486
9412	9437	9462	9487
9413	9438	9463	9488
9414	9439	9464	9489
9415	9440	9465	9490
9416	9441	9466	9491
9417	9442	9467	9492
9418	9443	9468	9493
9419	9444	9469	9494
9420	9445	9470	9495
9421	9446	9471	9496
9422	9447	9472	9497
9423	9448	9473	9498
9424	9449	9474	9499

0-6-0PT   5700 Class

9600	9610	9620	9630
9601	9611	9621	9631
9602	9612	9622	9632
9603	9613	9623	9633
9604	9614	9624	9634
9605	9615	9625	9635
9606	9616	9626	9636
9607	9617	9627	9637
9608	9618	9628	9638
9609	9619	9629	9639

9640	9676	9730	9766
9641	9677	9731	9767
9642	9678	9732	9768
9643	9679	9733	9769
9644	9680	9734	9770
9645	9681	9735	9771
9646	9682	9736	9773
9647	9700	9737	9774
9648	9701	9738	9775
9649	9702	9739	9776
9650	9703	9740	9777
9651	9704	9741	9778
9652	9705	9742	9779
9653	9706	9743	9780
9654	9707	9744	9781
9655	9709	9745	9782
9656	9710	9746	9783
9657	9711	9747	9784
9658	9712	9748	9785
9659	9713	9749	9786
9660	9714	9750	9787
9661	9715	9751	9788
9662	9716	9752	9789
9663	9717	9753	9790
9664	9718	9754	9791
9665	9719	9755	9792
9666	9720	9756	9793
9667	9721	9757	9794
9668	9722	9758	9795
9669	9723	9759	9796
9670	9724	9760	9797
9671	9725	9761	9798
9672	9726	9762	9799
9673	9727	9763	
9674	9728	9764	
9675	9729	9765	

SERVICE LOCOMOTIVES

Diesel Mechanical

20
PWM 650   **Total 2**

Petrol

22   24   27
    Total 3

POWER AND WEIGHT CLASSIFICATION

Since 1920 Western Region locomotives have been classified for power and weight by a letter on a coloured disc on the cab side. The letter represents the power of the locomotive and is approximately proportional to the tractive effort as under :

Power class	Tractive effort lb.	Power class	Tractive effort lb.
Special	Over 38,000	B	18,501–20,500
E	33,001–38,000	A	16,500–18,500
D	25,001–33,000	Un-grouped	
C	20,501–25,000		Below 16,500

The colour of the circle represents the routes over which the engine may work. Red engines are limited to the main lines and lines capable of carrying the heaviest locomotives ; blue engines are allowed over additional routes, yellow engines over nearly the whole system and uncoloured engines are more or less unrestricted. The double red circles on the " King " class represent special restrictions for these engines.

Class	Power Class	Route Restriction Colour	Class	Power Class	Route Restriction Colour
4-6-0			**0-6-2T**		
1000	D	Red	5600	D	Red
4073	D	Red			
4900	D	Red			
6000	Special	Double Red	**0-6-0T**		
6800	D	Red	850	—	—
6959	D	Red	1361	—	—
7800	D	Blue	1366	—	—
4-4-0			1500	C	Red
9000	B	Yellow	1600	A	—
2-8-0			2021	A	—
2800	E	Blue	5400	—	Yellow
4700	D	Red	5700	C	Yellow
2-6-0			9700–10	C	Blue
4300	D	Blue	6400	A	Yellow
9305	D	Red	7400	A	Yellow
0-6-0			9400	C	Red
2251	B	Yellow	(2198)	—	—
2-8-2T			**0-4-2T**		
7200	E	Red	1400	—	—
2-8-0T			5800	—	—
4200	E	Red			
2-6-2T			**0-4-0T**		
3100	D	Red	1101	B	Red
4500	C	Yellow	(1338)	—	—
5100	D	Blue	(1151)	—	—
6100	D	Blue	(1143)	—	Blue
8100	D	Blue	(1144)	—	Yellow
(7)	—	—	(1142)	A	Yellow

Top: 1101 Class
0-4-0T No. 1101
[K. L. Cook

Centre: 1400 Class
0-4-2T No. 1412
[G. Wheeler

Right: 1361 Class
0-6-0ST No. 1363
[L. Marshall

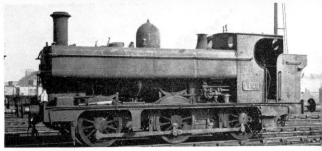

2021 Class 0-6-0PT No. 2069   [K. R. Pir

5700 Class 0-6-0PT No. 8700   [J. Davenport

5700 Class 0-6-0PT No. 9651 (with detail differences)   [K. R. Pirt

1600 Class 0-6-0PT No. 1641

[Brian E. Morrison

2251 Class 0-6-0 No. 2200

[P. H. Wells

400 Class 0-6-0PT No. 8405

[K. R. Pirt

A*

1500 Class 0-6-0PT No. 1503 [R. K. Evans

1366 Class 0-6-0PT No. 1370 [J. B. Bucknall

1000 Class 4-6-0 No. 1010 *County of Caernarvon* [G. Wheeler

4900 Class 4-6-0 No. 4905 *Barton Hall* [G. Wheeler

6959 Class 4-6-0 No. 6978 *Haroldstone Hall* [R. C. Riley

6000 Class 4-6-0 No. 6018 *King Henry VI*   [*G. Wheeler*

4073 Class 4-6-0 No. 7005 *Sir Edward Elgar*   [*G. Wheeler*

4073 Class 4-6-0 No. 7022 *Hereford Castle* (fitted with extended smokebox and double chimney)   [*J. Davenport*

6800 Class 4-6-0 No. 6821 *Leaton Grange*

[*G. Wheeler*

7800 Class 4-6-0 No. 7817 *Garsington Manor*

[*P. H. Wells*

000 Class 4-4-0 No. 9018

[*P. H. Wells*

4700 Class 2-8-0 No. 4701   [Brian E. Morrison

2800 Class 2-8-0 No. 2880   [L. Marshall

2800 Class 2-8-0 No. 3808 (with side-window cab)   Brian E. Morrison

SUMMARY OF SOUTHERN REGION STEAM LOCOMOTIVE CLASSES
IN ALPHABETICAL ORDER
WITH HISTORICAL NOTES AND DIMENSIONS

The Code given in smaller bold type at the head of each Class, e.g. " 2F " denotes its British Railways power classification. The number of locomotives in service has been checked to March 11th, 1959.

Classes

0-6-0T 0P A1 & A1X

*A1. Introduced 1872. Stroudley L.B.S.C. " Terrier," later fitted with Marsh boiler, retaining original type smokebox.

†A1X. Introduced 1911. Rebuild of A1 with Marsh boiler and extended smokebox.

‡A1 X. Loco. with increased cylinder diameter.

Weight: { 27 tons 10 cwt.*†
            { 28 tons 5 cwt.†‡
Pressure: 150 lb.
Cyls.: { 12"   × 20".*†
        { 14³⁄₁₆" × 20".‡
Driving Wheels: 4' 0".
T.E.: { 7,650 lb.*†
       { 10,695 lb.‡

*DS680
†DS681, 32635/40/6/50/5/61/2/
    70/7/8
‡32636   **Total A1   1
                          A1X 12**

0-4-0T 1F Class B4

*Introduced 1891. Adams L.S.W. design for dock shunting.
†Introduced 1908. Drummond K14 locos., with smaller boiler and detail alterations.

Weight: { 33 tons 9 cwt.*
         { 32 tons 18 cwt.†
Pressure: 140 lb. Cyls. (O): 16" × 22".
Driving Wheels: 3' 9¾".
T.E.: 14,650 lb.

*30088/9/93/6, 30102
†30083/4   **Total 7**

0-6-0 2F Class C

Introduced 1900. Wainwright S.E.C. design.
Weight: Loco. 43 tons 16 cwt.
Pressure: 160 lb.
Cyls.: 18½" × 26".
Driving Wheels: 5' 2".
T.E.: 19,520 lb.

31004/33/7/54/61/8/71/86,
    31102/12/3/50/91, 31218/9/21⟩
    3/7/9/42 – 5/52/3/5/6/67/8/70 –
    2/80/7/93/7/8, 31317, 31480/1/
    95/8, 31510/73/5/6/8/9/81/3/4/
    8–90/2, 31682–4/6/8–95, 31714
    –7/9–25   **Total 78**

0-6-0 2F Class C2X

Introduced 1908. Marsh rebuild of R. J. Billinton L.B.S.C. C2 with larger C3-type boiler, extended smokebox, etc.
Weight: Loco. 45 tons 5 cwt.
Pressure: 170 lb.
Cyls.: 17½" × 26".
Driving Wheels: 5' 0".
T.E.: 19,175 lb.

32437/8/41–51, 32521–3/5–9/32/
    4–6/8/9/41/3–54   **Total 40**

0-4-0T 0P Class C14

Introduced 1923. Urie rebuild as shunting loco. of Drummond L.S.W. motor-train 2-2-0T (originally introduced 1906).
Weight: 25 tons 15 cwt.
Pressure: 150 lb.
Cyls.: (O) 14" × 14".
Driving Wheels: 3' 0".
T.E.: 9,720 lb.
Walschaerts valve gear.

DS77   **Total 1**

4-4-0   3P   Class D1

Introduced 1921. Maunsell rebuild of Wainwright S.E.C. D, with larger superheated boiler, Belpaire firebox and long-travel piston valves.
Weight: Loco. 52 tons 4 cwt.
Pressure: 180 lb. Su.
Cyls.: 19″ × 26″.
Driving Wheels: 6′ 8″.
T.E.: 17,950 lb.

31145, 31246/7, 31470/87/9/92/4, 31505/9/45, 31727/35/9/41/3/9

Total 17

4-4-0   3P   Class E1

Introduced 1919. Maunsell rebuild of Wainwright S.E.C. E, with larger superheated boiler, Belpaire firebox and long-travel piston valves.
Weight: Loco. 53 tons 9 cwt.
Pressure: 180 lb.
Cyls.: 19″ × 26″.
Driving Wheels: 6′ 6″.
T.E.: 18,410 lb.

31019/67, 31165, 31497, 31507

Total 5

0-6-0T   2F   Class E1

Introduced 1874. Stroudley L.B.S.C. design, reboiled by Marsh.
Weight: 44 tons 3 cwt.
Pressure: 170 lb.
Cyls.: 17″ × 24″.
Driving Wheels: 4′ 6″.
T.E.: 18,560 lb.

3/4, 32151, 32689/94

Total 5

0-6-2T   1P2F   Class E1/R

Introduced 1927. Maunsell rebuild of Stroudley L.B.S.C. E1, with radial trailing axle and larger bunker for passenger service in West of England.
Weight: 50 tons 5 cwt.
Pressure: 170 lb.
Cyls.: 17″ × 24″.
Driving Wheels: 4′ 6″.
T.E.: 18,560 lb.

32135, 32697

Total 2

0-6-0T   3F   Class E2

*Introduced 1913. L. B. Billinton L.B.S.C. design.
†Introduced 1915. Later locos. with tanks extended further forward.
Weight: { 52 tons 15 cwt.*
          { 53 tons 10 cwt.†
Pressure: 170 lb.
Cyls.: 17½″ × 26″.
Driving Wheels: 4′ 6″.
T.E.: 21,305 lb.

*32100-4
†32105-9

Total 10

0-6-2T   2F   Class E3

Introduced 1894. R. J. Billinton L.B.S.C. design, development of Stroudley " West Brighton " (introduced 1891), reboiled and fitted with extended smokebox, 1918 onwards; cylinder diameter reduced from 18″ by S.R.
Weight: 56 tons 10 cwt.
Pressure: 170 lb.
Cyls.: 17½″ × 26″.
Driving Wheels: 4′ 6″.
T.E.: 21,305 lb.

32165/6, 32456

Total 3

0-6-2T   2P2F   Class E4

E4. Introduced 1897. R. J. Billinton L.B.S.C. design, development of E3 with larger wheels, reboiled with Marsh boiler and extended smokebox, cylinder diameter reduced from 18″ by S.R.
Weight: 57 tons 10 cwt.
Pressure: 170 lb.
Cyls.: 17½″ × 26″.
Driving Wheels: 5′ 0″.
T.E.: 19,175 lb.

32463/8 –75/9/80/4/7/91/4/5/7/8, 32500/3 –10/2/5/7/9/56/7/9/62– 6/77–81

Total 44

Classes E6-H15

0-6-2T 3F Class E6

*‡**E6.** Introduced 1904. R. J. Billinton L.B.S.C. design, development of E5 with smaller wheels, some with higher pressure.

Weight: 61 tons.*‡
Pressure: { 160 lb.*
{ 175 lb.‡
Cyls.: 18" × 26".
Driving Wheels: 4' 6".
T.E.: { 21,215 lb.*
{ 23,205 lb.‡

*‡32408/10/5-8

Total 6

0-6-0T 2F Class G6

*Introduced 1894. Adams L.S.W. design, later additions by Drummond, but with Adams type boiler.
†Introduced 1925. Fitted with Drummond type boiler.
Weight: 47 tons 13 cwt.
Pressure: 160 lb.
Cyls.: 17½" × 24".
Driving Wheels: 4' 10".
T.E.: 17,235 lb.

*30238/58/66/77, 30349,
DS3152
†30160, 30274

Total 10

4-8-0T 8F Class G16

Introduced 1921. Urie L.S.W. "Hump" loco.
Weight: 95 tons 2 cwt.
Pressure: 180 lb. Su.
Cyls.: (O) 22" × 28".
Driving Wheels: 5' 1".
T.E.: 33,990 lb.
Walschaerts valve gear. P.V.

30493-5

Total 3

0-4-4T 1P Class H

Introduced 1904. Wainwright S.E.C. design.
*Introduced 1949. Fitted for push-and-pull working.
Weight: 54 tons 8 cwt.
Pressure: 160 lb.
Cyls.: 18" × 26".
Driving Wheels: 5' 6".
T.E.: 17,360 lb.

31005, 31259/61/3/5/6, 31305-7/
24/6/8, 31500/3/33/40/2/50-3
*31161/2/4/77/93, 31239/69/76/
8/9/95, 31308/10/9/22/7/9,
31512/7-22/30/43/4/8/54

Total 50

4-6-0 4P5F Class H15

*Introduced 1914. Urie L.S.W. design, fitted with "Maunsell" superheater from 1927, replacing earlier types.
†Introduced 1915. Urie rebuild with two outside cylinders of Drummond E14 4-cyl. 4-6-0 introduced 1907, retaining original boiler retubed and fitted with superheater.
‡Introduced 1924. Maunsell locos. with N15-type boiler and smaller tender.
§Introduced 1924. Maunsell rebuild of Drummond F13 4-cyl. 4-6-0 introduced 1905, with detail differences from rebuild of E14.
¶Introduced 1927. Urie loco. (built 1914 saturated), rebuilt with later N15-type boiler, with smaller firebox.

Weight: Loco. { 81 tons 5 cwt.*
{ 82 tons 1 cwt.†
{ 79 tons 19 cwt.‡¶
{ 80 tons 11 cwt.§
Pressure: { 180 lb. Su.*‡¶
{ 175 lb. Su.†§
Cyls.: (O) 21" × 28".
Driving Wheels: 6' 0".
T.E. { 26,240 lb.*‡¶
{ 25,510 lb.†§
Walschaerts valve gear. P.V.

*30482/4/6/8/9 †30335
‡30473-8, 30521-4 §30331
¶30491

Total 18

43

4-6-2T   6F   Class H16

Introduced 1921. Urie L.S.W. design for heavy freight traffic.
Weight: 96 tons 8 cwt.
Pressure: 180 lb. Su.
Cyls.: (O) 21″ × 28″.
Driving Wheels: 5′ 7″.
T.E.: 28,200 lb.
Walschaerts valve gear. P.V.

30516–20   **Total 5**

2-6-0   4P5F   Class K

Introduced 1913. L. B. Billinton L.B.S.C. design.
Weight: Loco. 63 tons 15 cwt.
Pressure: 180 lb. Su.
Cyls.: (O) 21″ × 26″.
Driving Wheels: 5′ 6″.
T.E.: 26,580 lb.
P.V.

32337–53   **Total 17**

4-4-0   3P   Class L

Introduced 1914. Wainwright S.E.C. design, with detail alterations by Maunsell.
Weight: Loco. 57 tons 9 cwt.
Pressure: 160 lb. Su.
Cyls.: 20½″ × 26″.
Driving Wheels: 6′ 8″.
T.E.: 18,575 lb.
P.V.

31760/2–6/8/70/1/3/5–81
                                Total 17

4-4-0   3P   Class L1

Introduced 1926. Maunsell post-grouping development of L, with long-travel valves, side window cab and detail alterations.
Weight: Loco. 57 tons 16 cwt.
Pressure: 180 lb. Su.
Cyls.: 19½″ × 26″.
Driving Wheels: 6′ 8″.
T.E.: 18,910 lb.
P.V.

31753–9/82–9   **Total 15**

4-6-0   7P   Class LN

*Introduce 1926. Maunsell design, cylinders and tender modified by Bulleid from 1938, and fitted with multiple-je blastpipe and large-diameter chimney.
†Introduced 1929. Loco. fitted experimentally with smaller driving wheels.
‡Introduced 1929. Loco. fitted experimentally with longer boiler.

Weight: Loco. $\begin{cases} 83 \text{ tons } 10 \text{ cwt.}^{*}\dagger \\ 84 \text{ tons } 16 \text{ cwt.}\ddagger \end{cases}$
Pressure: 220 lb. Su.
Cyls.: (4) 16½″ × 26″.
Driving Wheels: $\begin{cases} 6′ 7″.^{*}\ddagger \\ 6′ 3″.\dagger \end{cases}$
T.E.: $\begin{cases} 33,510 \text{ lb.}^{*}\ddagger \\ 35,300 \text{ lb.}\dagger \end{cases}$
Walschaerts valve gear. P.V.

*30350–8/61–5
†30859   ‡30860
                                Total 16

0-4-4T   2P   Class M7

*Introduced 1897. Drummond L.S.W. M7 design.
†Introduced 1903. Drummond X14 design, with increased front overhang, steam reverser and detail alterations, now classified M7 (30254 originally M7).
‡Introduced 1925. X14 design fitted for push-and-pull working.

Weight: $\begin{cases} 60 \text{ tons } 4 \text{ cwt.}^{*} \\ 60 \text{ tons } 3 \text{ cwt.}\dagger \\ 62 \text{ tons } 0 \text{ cwt.}\ddagger \end{cases}$
Pressure: 175 lb.
Cyls.: 18½″ × 26″.
Driving Wheels: 5′ 7″.
T.E.: 19,755 lb.

*30023–6/31–6/9/40/3/4, 30112, 30241/5–9/51/3/5/6, 30318–21/ 3/4/57, 30667–71/3/4/6

†30030, 30123/4/7/30/2/3, 30254, 30374/6/5/7/8, 30479

‡30021 /7/8 /9 / 45 /7 – 53 / 5 – 60, 30104–11/25/8/9/31, 30328/79, 30480/1

                                Total 88

44

Classes MN-O2

4-6-2   8P   Class MN

*Introduced 1941. Bulleid design originally with 280 lb. pressure, multiple-jet blastpipe and Bulleid Valve gear.
†Introduced 1956. Rebuilt with Walschaerts valve gear, modified details and air-smoothed casing removed.

Weight: Loco. $\begin{cases} 94 \text{ tons } 15 \text{ cwt.*} \\ 97 \text{ tons } 18 \text{ cwt.†} \end{cases}$

Pressure: 250 lb.
Cyls.: (3) 18″ × 24″.
Driving Wheels: 6′ 2″.
T.E.: 33,495 lb.
P.V.

*35001/3/5/6/11/9/21/4/8/9
†35002/4/7–10/2–8/20/2/3/5–7/30

Total 30

2-6-0   4P5F   Classes N & N1

*N. Introduced 1917. Maunsell S.E.C. mixed traffic design.
†N1. Introduced 1922. 3-cylinder development of N.

Weight: Loco. $\begin{cases} 61 \text{ tons } 4 \text{ cwt.*} \\ 64 \text{ tons } 5 \text{ cwt.†} \end{cases}$

Pressure: 200 lb. Su.
Cyls.: $\begin{cases} (O) 19″ × 28″.* \\ (3) 16″ × 28″.† \end{cases}$
Driving Wheels: 5′ 6″.
T.E.: $\begin{cases} 26,035 \text{ lb.*} \\ 27,695 \text{ lb.†} \end{cases}$
Walschaerts valve gear.   P.V.

*31400–14, 31810–21/3–75
†31822/76–80

Total   N 80
             N1 6

4-6-0   5P   Class N15

*Introduced 1925. Maunsell locos. with long-travel valves, increased boiler pressure, smaller fireboxes, and tenders from Drummond G14 4-6-0s.

†Introduced 1925. Later locos. with detail alterations and increased weight.
‡Introduced 1925. Locos. with modified cabs to suit Eastern Section, and new bogie tenders.
§Introduced 1926. Locos. with detail alterations and most with six-wheeled tenders for Central Section.

Weight: Loco. $\begin{cases} 79 \text{ tons } 18 \text{ cwt.*} \\ 80 \text{ tons } 19 \text{ cwt.†‡} \\ 81 \text{ tons } 17 \text{ cwt.§} \end{cases}$

Pressure: 200 lb. Su.
Cyls.: (O) 20½″ × 28″.
Driving Wheels: 6′ 7″.
T.E.: 25,320 lb.
Walschaerts valve gear.   P.V.

*30453/5–7   †30448–52
‡30763–5/7–75/7–86/8–91/2
§30793–30806

Total 49

0-6-0   2F   Class O1

*Introduced 1903. Wainwright rebuild with domed boiler and new cab of Stirling S.E. Class O 0-6-0 (introduced 1878).
†Introduced 1903. Loco. with smaller driving wheels.
Weight: Loco. 41 tons 1 cwt.
Pressure: 150 lb.
Cyls.: 18″ × 26″.

Driving Wheels: $\begin{cases} 5′ 2″.* \\ 5′ 1″.† \end{cases}$
T.E.: $\begin{cases} 17,325 \text{ lb.*} \\ 17,610 \text{ lb.†} \end{cases}$

*31065, 31258, 31370, 31425/30/4
†31048

Total 7

0-4-4T   0P   Class O2

*Introduced 1889. Adams L.S.W. design.
†Introduced 1923. Fitted with Westinghouse brake for I.O.W. Bunkers enlarged from 1932.
‡Fitted with Drummond-type boiler.
§Fitted for push-and-pull working.
Weight: $\begin{cases} 46 \text{ tons } 18 \text{ cwt.*‡} \\ 48 \text{ tons } 8 \text{ cwt.†} \end{cases}$
Pressure: 160 lb.
Cyls.: 17½″ × 24″.
Driving Wheels: 4′ 10″.
T.E.: 17,235 lb

*30177/9/92/3/9, 30200/12/25/9/
32/6
†14/6–8/20–2/4–33
†§35/6
‡30223　　　‡§30182/3
Total 33

0-6-0T　Unclass　Class P

Introduced 1909. Wainwright S.E.C.
design for push-and-pull work, now
used for shunting.
Weight: 28 tons 10 cwt.
Pressure: 160 lb.
Cyls.: 12″ × 18″.
Driving Wheels: 3′ 9⅛″.
T.E.: 7,810 lb.
31027, 31323/5, 31556/8
Total 5

0-6-0　4F　Class Q

Introduced 1938. Maunsell design, later
fitted with multiple-jet blastpipe and
large-diameter chimney.
Weight: Loco. 49 tons 10 cwt.
Pressure 200 lb. Su.
Cyls.: 19″ × 26″.
Driving Wheels: 5′ 1″.
T.E.: 26,160 lb.
P.V.
30530–49
Total 20

Classes P-R1

0-6-0　5F　Class Q1

Introduced 1942. Bulleid " Austerity "
design.
Weight: Loco. 51 tons 5 cwt.
Pressure: 230 lb. Su.
Cyls.: 19″ × 26″.
Driving Wheels: 5′ 1″.
T.E.: 30,080 lb.
P.V.
33001–40
Total 40

0-6-0T　2F　Class R1

*Introduced 1888. Stirling S.E. design
later rebuilt with domed boiler.
†Introduced 1938. Fitted with Urie
type short chimney for Whitstable
branch and fitted with or retaining
original Stirling-type cab.
Weight: { 46 tons 15 cwt.*
         { 46 tons 8 cwt.†
Pressure: 160 lb.
Cyls.: 18″ × 26″.
Driving Wheels: { 5′ 2″.*
                { 5′ 1″.†
T.E.: { 18,480 lb.*
      { 18,780 lb.†
*31047, 31107/28/74, 31337/40
†31010
Total 7

SOUTHERN REGION SERVICE LOCOMOTIVES

No.	Old No.	Class	Station
DS 49	—	—	Broad Clyst
*DS 74	—	Bo-Bo	{ Durnsford Road Power Station
*DS 75	—	Bo	Waterloo & City
DS 77	0745	C14	{ Redbridge Sleeper Depot
DS 600	—	0-4-0 Diesel	{ Eastleigh Carriage Works
DS 680	{ L.B.S.C. 654 S.E.C. 751 }	A1	{ Lancing Carriage Works
DS 681	L.B.S.C. 659	A1X	{ Lancing Carriage Works
DS 1169	—	—	Folkestone Warren
DS 1173	2217	0-6-0 Diesel	Engineer's Department
DS 3152	30272	G6	Meldon Quarry

* Electric.　　　　† Repainted 1947 in Stroudley livery.

Classes S15-V

4-6-0　　6F　　Class S15

*Introduced 1920. Urie L.S.W. design, development of N15 for mixed traffic work.

†Introduced 1927. Maunsell design, with higher pressure, smaller grate, modified footplating and other detail differences. 30833-7 with 6-wheel tenders for Central Section.

‡Introduced 1936. Later locos. with detail differences and reduced weight.

Weight: Loco. $\begin{cases} 79 \text{ tons } 16 \text{ cwt.*} \\ 80 \text{ tons } 14 \text{ cwt.†} \\ 79 \text{ tons } 5 \text{ cwt.‡} \end{cases}$

Pressure: $\begin{cases} 180 \text{ lb. Su.*} \\ 200 \text{ lb. Su.†‡} \end{cases}$

Cyls.: $\begin{cases} (O) 21'' \times 28''.* \\ (O) 20\frac{1}{2}'' \times 28''.†‡ \end{cases}$

Driving Wheels: 5′ 7″.

T.E. $\begin{cases} 28,200 \text{ lb.*} \\ 29,855 \text{ lb.†‡} \end{cases}$

Walschaerts valve gear. P.V.

*30496-30515　　†30823-37
‡30838-47

Total 45

4-4-0　　3P　　Class T9

*Introduced 1899. Drummond L.S.W. design, fitted with superheater and larger cylinders by Urie from 1922.

†Introduced 1899. Locos. with detail differences (originally fitted with firebox watertubes).

‡Introduced 1900. Locos. with wider cab and splashers, without coupling rod splashers and originally fitted with firebox watertubes.

Weight: Loco. $\begin{cases} 51 \text{ tons } 18 \text{ cwt.*} \\ 51 \text{ tons } 16 \text{ cwt.†} \\ 51 \text{ tons } 7 \text{ cwt.‡} \end{cases}$

Pressure: 175 lb. Su.

Cyls.: 19″ × 26″.

Driving Wheels: 6′ 7″.

T.E.: 17,675 lb.

*30117/20, 30287-9
†30702/6/7/9/11/5/7-9/24/6/9/32
‡30300/1/10/3/38

Total 23

Classes
2-6-0　　4P3F　　U & UI

*U. Introduced 1928. Rebuild of Maunsell S.E.C. Class K ("River") 2-6-4T (introduced 1917).

†U. Introduced 1928. Locos. built as Class U, with smaller splashers and detail alterations.

‡UI. Introduced 1928. 3-cylinder development of Class U (prototype 31890, rebuilt from 2-6-4T, originally built 1925).

Weight: Loco. $\begin{cases} 63 \text{ tons.*} \\ 62 \text{ tons } 6 \text{ cwt.†} \\ 65 \text{ tons } 6 \text{ cwt.‡} \end{cases}$

Pressure: 200 lb. Su.

Cyls.: $\begin{cases} (O) 19'' \times 28''.*† \\ (3) 16'' \times 28''.‡ \end{cases}$

Driving Wheels: 6′ 0″.

T.E. $\begin{cases} 23,865 \text{ lb.*†} \\ 25,385 \text{ lb.‡} \end{cases}$

Walschaerts valve gear.

*31790-31809　　†31610-39
‡31890-31910

Total Class U 50
Class UI 21

0-6-0T　　3F　　Class USA

Introduced 1942. U.S. Army Transportation Corps design, purchased by S.R. 1946, and fitted with modified cab and bunker and other detail alterations.

Weight: 46 tons 10 cwt.
Pressure: 210 lb.
Cyls.: (O) 16½″ × 24″.
Driving Wheels: 4′ 6″.
T.E.: 21,600 lb.
Walschaerts valve gear.　P.V.
30061-74　　　　　　Total 14

4-4-0　　5P　　Class V

*Introduced 1930. Maunsell design.
†Introduced 1938. Fitted with multiple-jet blastpipe and large-diameter chimney by Bulleid.

Weight: Loco. 67 tons 2 cwt.
Pressure: 220 lb. Su.
Cyls.: (3) 16½″ × 26″.
Driving Wheels: 6′ 7″.
T.E.: 25,135 lb.
Walschaerts valve gear.　P.V.

*30902-6/8/10-2/6/22/3/5-8/
32/5/6
†30900/1/7/9/13-5/7-21/4/29-
31/3/4/7-9　　　　Total 40

2-6-4T   6F   **Class W**

Introduced 1931. Maunsell design, developed from Class N1 2-6-0.
Weight: 90 tons 14 cwt.
Pressure: 200 lb. Su.
Cyls.: (3) $16\frac{1}{2}'' \times 28''$.
Driving Wheels: 5' 6".
T.E.: 29,450 lb.
Walschaerts valve gear. P.V.

31911–25   **Total 15**

Classes
4-6-2   7P5F   **WC & BB**

*Introduced 1945. Bulleid " West Country " Class, with Bulleid valve gear.
†Introduced 1946. Bulleid " Battle of Britain " Class, with Bulleid valve gear.
‡Introduced 1948. Locos. with larger tenders.
§Introduced 1957. Rebuilt with Walschaerts valve gear, modified details and air-smoothed casing removed.
Weight: Loco. $\begin{cases} 86 \text{ tons } 0 \text{ cwt.}*\dagger\ddagger \\ 90 \text{ tons } 1 \text{ cwt.}\S \end{cases}$
Pressure: 250 lb. Su.
Cyls.: (3) $16\frac{3}{8}'' \times 24''$.
Driving Wheels: 6' 2".
T.E.: 27,715 lb.
Bulleid valve gear. P.V.
*34002/6 – 9/11/5/9/20/3/4/30/2 – 6/8/40/1/3/4
†34049/51/4–61/3–70
†‡34071–90, 34109/10
*‡34091–34108
*§34001/3–5/10/2–4/6–8/21/2/5– 9/31/7/9/42/5–8
†§34050/2/3/62

                    Total 110

0-8-0T   6F   **Class Z**

Introduced 1929. Maunsell design for heavy shunting.
Weight: 71 tons 12 cwt.
Pressure: 180 lb.
Cyls.: (3) $16'' \times 28''$.
Driving Wheels: 4' 8".
T.E.: 29,375 lb.
Walschaerts valve gear. P.V.
30950–7   **Total 8**

0-6-0   3F   **Class 700**

Introduced 1897. Drummond L.S.W. design, superheated from 1921.
Weight: Loco. 46 tons 14 cwt.
Pressure: 180 lb. Su.
Cyls.: $19'' \times 26'$.
Driving Wheels: 5' 1".
T.E.: 23,540 lb.
30306/8/9/15- 7/25–7/39/46/50/2/ 5/68, 30687/9–30701

                    Total 29

2-4-0WT   0P   **Class 0298**

Introduced 1874. Beattie L.S.W. design, rebuilt by Adams (1884–92). Urie (1921–2) and Maunsell (1931–5).
Weight: 37 tons 16 cwt.
Pressure: 160 lb.
Cyls.: (O) $16\frac{1}{2}'' \times 20''$.
Driving Wheels: 5' 7".
T.E.: 11,050 lb.

30585–7   **Total 3**

0-6-0   2F   **Class 0395**

*Introduced 1881. Adams L.S.W. design, later reboilered with ex-L.C. & D. Class M3 4-4-0 boiler.
Weight: Loco. $\begin{cases} 37 \text{ tons } 12 \text{ cwt.}*\ddagger \\ 38 \text{ tons } 14 \text{ cwt.}\dagger\ddagger \end{cases}$
Pressure: $\begin{cases} 140 \text{ lb.}*\dagger \\ 150 \text{ lb.}\ddagger \end{cases}$
Driving Wheels: 5' 1".
T.E.: $\begin{cases} 15,535 \text{ lb.}*\dagger \\ 16,645 \text{ lb.}\ddagger \end{cases}$
*‡30567

                    Total 1

4-4-2T   1P   **Class 0415**

Introduced 1882. Adams L.S.W. design, later reboilered.
Weight: 55 tons 2 cwt.
Pressure: 160 lb.
Cyls.: (O) $17\frac{1}{2}'' \times 24''$.
Driving Wheels: 5' 7".
T.E.: 14,920 lb.

30582–4   **Total 3**

BRITISH RAILWAYS LOCOMOTIVES
Nos. 30021-35030, 3-36

Named Engines are indicated by an asterisk (*)

No.	Class	No.	Class	No.	Class	No.	Class
30021	M7	30065	U.S.A.	30133	M7	30306	700
30023	M7	30066	U.S.A.	30160	G6	30308	700
30024	M7	30067	U.S.A.	30177	O2	30309	700
30025	M7	30068	U.S.A.	30179	O2	30310	T9
30026	M7	30069	U.S.A.	30182	O2	30313	T9
30027	M7	30070	U.S.A.	30183	O2	30315	700
30028	M7	30071	U.S.A.	30192	O2	30316	700
30029	M7	30072	U.S.A.	30193	O2	30317	700
30030	M7	30073	U.S.A.	30199	O2	30318	M7
30031	M7	30074	U.S.A.	30200	O2	30319	M7
30032	M7	30083	B4	30212	O2	30320	M7
30033	M7	30084	B4	30223	O2	30321	M7
30034	M7	30088	B4	30225	O2	30323	M7
30035	M7	30089	B4	30229	O2	30324	M7
30036	M7	30093	B4	30232	O2	30325	700
30039	M7	30096	B4	30236	O2	30326	700
30040	M7	30102	B4	30238	G6	30327	700
30043	M7	30104	M7	30241	M7	30328	M7
30044	M7	30105	M7	30245	M7	30331	H15
30045	M7	30106	M7	30246	M7	30335	H15
30047	M7	30107	M7	30247	M7	30338	T9
30048	M7	30108	M7	30248	M7	30339	700
30049	M7	30109	M7	30249	M7	30346	700
30050	M7	30110	M7	30251	M7	30349	G6
30051	M7	30111	M7	30253	M7	30350	700
30052	M7	30112	M7	30254	M7	30352	700
30053	M7	30117	T9	30255	M7	30355	700
30055	M7	30120	T9	30256	M7	30357	M7
30056	M7	30123	M7	30258	G6	30368	700
30057	M7	30124	M7	30266	G6	30374	M7
30058	M7	30125	M7	30274	G6	30375	M7
30059	M7	30127	M7	30277	G6	30377	M7
30060	M7	30128	M7	30287	T9	30378	M7
30061	U.S.A.	30129	M7	30288	T9	30379	M7
30062	U.S.A.	30130	M7	30289	T9	30448*	N15
30063	U.S.A.	30131	M7	30300	T9	30449*	N15
30064	U.S.A.	30132	M7	30301	T9	30450*	N15

No.	Class	No.	Class	No.	Class	No.	Class
30451*	N15	30517	H16	30690	700	30785*	N15
30452*	N15	30518	H16	30691	700	30786*	N15
30453*	N15	30519	H16	30692	700	30788*	N15
30455*	N15	30520	H16	30693	700	30789*	N15
30456*	N15	30521	H15	30694	700	30790*	N15
30457*	N15	30522	H15	30695	700	30791*	N15
30473	H15	30523	H15	30696	700	30793*	N15
30474	H15	30524	H15	30697	700	30794*	N15
30475	H15	30530	Q	30698	700	30795*	N15
30476	H15	30531	Q	30699	700	30796*	N15
30477	H15	30532	Q	30700	700	30797*	N15
30478	H15	30533	Q	30701	700	30798*	N15
30479	M7	30534	Q	30702	T9	30799*	N15
30480	M7	30535	Q	30706	T9	30800*	N15
30481	M7	30536	Q	30707	T9	30801*	N15
30482	H15	30537	Q	30709	T9	30802*	N15
30484	H15	30538	Q	30711	T9	30803*	N15
30486	H15	30539	Q	30715	T9	30804*	N15
30488	H15	30540	Q	30717	T9	30805*	N15
30489	H15	30541	Q	30718	T9	30806*	N15
30491	H15	30542	Q	30719	T9	30823	S15
30493	G16	30543	Q	30724	T9	30824	S15
30494	G16	30544	Q	30726	T9	30825	S15
30495	G16	30545	Q	30729	T9	30826	S15
30496	S15	30546	Q	30732	T9	30827	S15
30497	S15	30547	Q	30763*	N15	30828	S15
30498	S15	30548	Q	30764*	N15	30829	S15
30499	S15	30549	Q	30765*	N15	30830	S15
30500	S15	30567	0395	30767*	N15	30831	S15
30501	S15	30582	0415	30768*	N15	30832	S15
30502	S15	30583	0415	30769*	N15	30833	S15
30503	S15	30584	0415	30770*	N15	30834	S15
30504	S15	30585	0298	30771*	N15	30835	S15
30505	S15	30586	0298	30772*	N15	30836	S15
30506	S15	30587	0298	30773*	N15	30837	S15
30507	S15	30667	M7	30774*	N15	30838	S15
30508	S15	30668	M7	30775*	N15	30839	S15
30509	S15	30669	M7	30777*	N15	30840	S15
30510	S15	30670	M7	30778*	N15	30841	S15
30511	S15	30671	M7	30779*	N15	30842	S15
30512	S15	30673	M7	30780*	N15	30843	S15
30513	S15	30674	M7	30781*	N15	30844	S15
30514	S15	30676	M7	30782*	N15	30845	S15
30515	S15	30687	700	30783*	N15	30846	S15
30516	H16	30689	700	30784*	N15	30847	S15

No.	Class	No.	Class	No.	Class	No.	Class
30850*	LN	30929*	V	31165	EI	31307	H
30851*	LN	30930*	V	31174	RI	31308	H
30852*	LN	30931*	V	31177	H	31310	H
30853*	LN	30932*	V	31191	C	31317	C
30854*	LN	30933*	V	31193	H	31319	H
30855*	LN	30934*	V	31218	C	31322	H
30856*	LN	30935*	V	31219	C	31323	P
30857*	LN	30936*	V	31221	C	31324	H
30858*	LN	30937*	V	31223	C	31325	P
30859*	LN	30938*	V	31227	C	31326	H
30860*	LN	30939*	V	31229	C	31327	H
30861*	LN	30950	Z	31239	H	31328	H
30862*	LN	30951	Z	31242	C	31329	H
30863*	LN	30952	Z	31243	C	31337	RI
30864*	LN	30953	Z	31244	C	31340	RI
30865*	LN	30954	Z	31245	C	31370	OI
30900*	V	30955	Z	31246	DI	31400	N
30901*	V	30956	Z	31247	DI	31401	N
30902*	V	30957	Z	31252	C	31402	N
30903*	V	31004	C	31253	C	31403	N
30904*	V	31005	H	31255	C	31404	N
30905*	V	31010	RI	31256	C	31405	N
30906*	V	31019	EI	31258	OI	31406	N
30907*	V	31027	P	31259	H	31407	N
30908*	V	31033	C	31261	H	31408	N
30909*	V	31037	C	31263	H	31409	N
30910*	V	31047	RI	31265	H	31410	N
30911*	V	31048	OI	31266	H	31411	N
30912*	V	31054	C	31267	C	31412	N
30913*	V	31061	C	31268	C	31413	N
30914*	V	31065	OI	31269	H	31414	N
30915*	V	31067	EI	31270	C	31425	OI
30916*	V	31068	C	31271	C	31430	OI
30917*	V	31071	C	31272	C	31434	OI
30918*	V	31086	C	31276	H	31470	DI
30919*	V	31102	C	31278	H	31480	C
30920*	V	31107	RI	31279	H	31481	C
30921*	V	31112	C	31280	C	31487	DI
30922*	V	31113	C	31287	C	31489	DI
30923*	V	31128	RI	31293	C	31492	DI
30924*	V	31145	DI	31295	H	31494	DI
30925*	V	31150	C	31297	C	31495	C
30926*	V	31161	H	31298	C	31497	EI
30927*	V	31162	H	31305	H	31498	C
30928*	V	31164	H	31306	H	31500	H

No.	Class	No.	Class	No.	Class	No.	Class
31503	H	31616	U	31724	C	31795	U
31505	DI	31617	U	31725	C	31796	U
31507	EI	31618	U	31727	DI	31797	U
31509	DI	31619	U	31735	DI	31798	U
31510	C	31620	U	31739	DI	31799	U
31512	H	31621	U	31741	DI	31800	U
31517	H	31622	U	31743	DI	31801	U
31518	H	31623	U	31749	DI	31802	U
31519	H	31624	U	31753	LI	31803	U
31520	H	31625	U	31754	LI	31804	U
31521	H	31626	U	31755	LI	31805	U
31522	H	31627	U	31756	LI	31806	U
31530	H	31628	U	31757	LI	31807	U
31533	H	31629	U	31758	LI	31808	U
31540	H	31630	U	31759	LI	31809	U
31542	H	31631	U	31760	L	31810	N
31543	H	31632	U	31762	L	31811	N
31544	H	31633	U	31763	L	31812	N
31545	DI	31634	U	31764	L	31813	N
31548	H	31635	U	31765	L	31814	N
31550	H	31636	U	31766	L	31815	N
31551	H	31637	U	31768	L	31816	N
31552	H	31638	U	31770	L	31817	N
31553	H	31639	U	31771	L	31818	N
31554	H	31682	C	31773	L	31819	N
31556	P	31683	C	31775	L	31820	N
31558	P	31684	C	31776	L	31821	N
31573	C	31686	C	31777	L	31822	NI
31575	C	31688	C	31778	L	31823	N
31576	C	31689	C	31779	L	31824	N
31578	C	31690	C	31780	L	31825	N
31579	C	31691	C	31781	L	31826	N
31581	C	31692	C	31782	LI	31827	N
31583	C	31693	C	31783	LI	31828	N
31584	C	31694	C	31784	LI	31829	N
31588	C	31695	C	31785	LI	31830	N
31589	C	31714	C	31786	LI	31831	N
31590	C	31715	C	31787	LI	31832	N
31592	C	31716	C	31788	LI	31833	N
31610	U	31717	C	31789	LI	31834	N
31611	U	31719	C	31790	U	31835	N
31612	U	31720	C	31791	U	31836	N
31613	U	31721	C	31792	U	31837	N
31614	U	31722	C	31793	U	31838	N
31615	U	31723	C	31794	U	31839	N

No.	Class	No.	Class	No.	Class	No.	Class
31840	N	31894	UI	32166	E3	32474	E4
31841	N	31895	UI	32337	K	32475	E4
31842	N	31896	UI	32338	K	32479	E4
31843	N	31897	UI	32339	K	32480	E4
31844	N	31898	UI	32340	K	32484	E4
31845	N	31899	UI	32341	K	32487	E4
31846	N	31900	UI	32342	K	32491	E4
31847	N	31901	UI	32343	K	32494	E4
31848	N	31902	UI	32344	K	32495	E4
31849	N	31903	UI	32345	K	32497	E4
31850	N	31904	UI	32346	K	32498	E4
31851	N	31905	UI	32347	K	32500	E4
31852	N	31906	UI	32348	K	32503	E4
31853	N	31907	UI	32349	K	32504	E4
31854	N	31908	UI	32350	K	32505	E4
31855	N	31909	UI	32351	K	32506	E4
31856	N	31910	UI	32352	K	32507	E4
31857	N	31911	W	32353	K	32508	E4
31858	N	31912	W	32408	E6	32509	E4
31859	N	31913	W	32410	E6	32510	E4
31860	N	31914	W	32415	E6	32512	E4
31861	N	31915	W	32416	E6	32515	E4
31862	N	31916	W	32417	E6	32517	E4
31863	N	31917	W	32418	E6	32519	E4
31864	N	31918	W	32437	C2X	32521	C2X
31865	N	31919	W	32438	C2X	32522	C2X
31866	N	31920	W	32441	C2X	32523	C2X
31867	N	31921	W	32442	C2X	32525	C2X
31868	N	31922	W	32443	C2X	32526	C2X
31869	N	31923	W	32444	C2X	32527	C2X
31870	N	31924	W	32445	C2X	32528	C2X
31871	N	31925	W	32446	C2X	32529	C2X
31872	N	32100	E2	32447	C2X	32532	C2X
31873	N	32101	E2	32448	C2X	32534	C2X
31874	N	32102	E2	32449	C2X	32535	C2X
31875	N	32103	E2	32450	C2X	32536	C2X
31876	NI	32104	E2	32451	C2X	32538	C2X
31877	NI	32105	E2	32456	E3	32539	C2X
31878	NI	32106	E2	32463	E4	32541	C2X
31879	NI	32107	E2	32468	E4	32543	C2X
31880	NI	32108	E2	32469	E4	32544	C2X
31890	UI	32109	E2	32470	E4	32545	C2X
31891	UI	32135	EI/R	32471	E4	32546	C2X
31892	UI	32151	EI	32472	E4	32547	C2X
31893	UI	32165	E3	32473	E4	32548	C2X

No.	Class	No.	Class	No.	Class	No.	Class
32549	C2X	33014	Q1	34019*	WC	34064*	BB
32550	C2X	33015	Q1	34020*	WC	34065*	BB
32551	C2X	33016	Q1	34021*	WC	34066*	BB
32552	C2X	33017	Q1	34022*	WC	34067*	BB
32553	C2X	33018	Q1	34023*	WC	34068*	BB
32554	C2X	33019	Q1	34024*	WC	34069*	BB
32556	E4	33020	Q1	34025*	WC	34070*	BB
32557	E4	33021	Q1	34026*	WC	34071*	BB
32559	E4	33022	Q1	34027*	WC	34072*	BB
32562	E4	33023	Q1	34028*	WC	34073*	BB
32563	E4	33024	Q1	34029*	WC	34074*	BB
32564	E4	33025	Q1	34030*	WC	34075*	BB
32565	E4	33026	Q1	34031*	WC	34076*	BB
32566	E4	33027	Q1	34032*	WC	34077*	BB
32577	E4	33028	Q1	34033*	WC	34078*	BB
32578	E4	33029	Q1	34034*	WC	34079*	BB
32579	E4	33030	Q1	34035*	WC	34080*	BB
32580	E4	33031	Q1	34036*	WC	34081*	BB
32581	E4	33032	Q1	34037*	WC	34082*	BB
32636	A1X	33033	Q1	34038*	WC	34083*	BB
32640	A1X	33034	Q1	34039*	WC	34084*	BB
32646	A1X	33035	Q1	34040*	WC	34085*	BB
32650	A1X	33036	Q1	34041*	WC	34086*	BB
32655	A1X	33037	Q1	34042*	WC	34087*	BB
32661	A1X	33038	Q1	34043*	WC	34088*	BB
32662	A1X	33039	Q1	34044*	WC	34089*	BB
32670	A1X	33040	Q1	34045*	WC	34090*	BB
32677	A1X	34001*	WC	34046*	WC	34091*	WC
32678	A1X	34002*	WC	34047*	WC	34092*	WC
32689	E1	34003*	WC	34048*	WC	34093*	WC
32694	E1	34004*	WC	34049*	BB	34094*	WC
32697	E1/R	34005*	WC	34050*	BB	34095*	WC
33001	Q1	34006*	WC	34051*	BB	34096*	WC
33002	Q1	34007*	WC	34052*	BB	34097*	WC
33003	Q1	34008*	WC	34053*	BB	34098*	WC
33004	Q1	34009*	WC	34054*	BB	34099*	WC
33005	Q1	34010*	WC	34055*	BB	34100*	WC
33006	Q1	34011*	WC	34056*	BB	34101*	WC
33007	Q1	34012*	WC	34057*	BB	34102*	WC
33008	Q1	34013*	WC	34058*	BB	34103*	WC
33009	Q1	34014*	WC	34059*	BB	34104*	WC
33010	Q1	34015*	WC	34060*	BB	34105*	WC
33011	Q1	34016*	WC	34061*	BB	34106*	WC
33012	Q1	34017*	WC	34062*	BB	34107*	WC
33013	Q1	34018*	WC	34063*	BB	34108*	WC

No.	Class	No.	Class	No.	Class	No.	Class
34109*	BB	35007*	MN	35015*	MN	35023*	MN
34110*	BB	35008*	MN	35016*	MN	35024*	MN
35001*	MN	35009*	MN	35017*	MN	35025*	MN
35002*	MN	35010*	MN	35018*	MN	35026*	MN
35003*	MN	35011*	MN	35019*	MN	35027*	MN
35004*	MN	35012*	MN	35020*	MN	35028*	MN
35005*	MN	35013*	MN	35021*	MN	35029*	MN
35006*	MN	35014*	MN	35022*	MN	35030*	MN

Isle of Wight Locomotives

No.	Class	No.	Class	No.	Class	No.	Class
3*	E1	20*	O2	26*	O2	31*	O2
4*	E1	21*	O2	27*	O2	32*	O2
14*	O2	22*	O2	28*	O2	33*	O2
16*	O2	24*	O2	29*	O2	35*	O2
17*	O2	25*	O2	30*	O2	36*	O2
18*	O2						

BRITISH RAILWAYS LOCOMOTIVES

Nos. 30021-35030 and 3-36

NAMED LOCOMOTIVES

CLASS N15 " KING ARTHUR " 4-6-0

30448	Sir Tristram	30769	Sir Balan
30449	Sir Torre	30770	Sir Prianius
30450	Sir Kay	30771	Sir Sagramore
30451	Sir Lamorak	30772	Sir Percivale
30452	Sir Meliagrance	30773	Sir Lavaine
30453	King Arthur	30774	Sir Gaheris
30455	Sir Launcelot	30775	Sir Agravaine
30456	Sir Galahad	30777	Sir Lamiel
30457	Sir Bedivere	30778	Sir Pelleas
30763	Sir Bors de Ganis	30779	Sir Colgrevance
30764	Sir Gawain	30780	Sir Persant
30765	Sir Gareth	30781	Sir Aglovale
30767	Sir Valence	30782	Sir Brian
30768	Sir Balin	30783	Sir Gillemere

30784	Sir Nerovens	30797	Sir Blamor de Ganis
30785	Sir Mador de la Porte	30798	Sir Hectimere
30786	Sir Lionel	30799	Sir Ironside
30788	Sir Urre of the Mount	30800	Sir Meleaus de Lile
30789	Sir Guy	30801	Sir Meliot de Logres
30790	Sir Villiars	30802	Sir Durnore
30791	Sir Uwaine	30803	Sir Harry le Fise Lake
30793	Sir Ontzlake	30804	Sir Cador of Cornwall
30794	Sir Ector de Maris	30805	Sir Constantine
30795	Sir Dinadan	30806	Sir Galleron
30796	Sir Dodinas le Savage		

CLASS LN "LORD NELSON" 4-6-0

30850	Lord Nelson	30858	Lord Duncan
30851	Sir Francis Drake	30859	Lord Hood
30852	Sir Walter Raleigh	30860	Lord Hawke
30853	Sir Richard Grenville	30861	Lord Anson
30854	Howard of Effingham	30862	Lord Collingwood
30855	Robert Blake	30863	Lord Rodney
30856	Lord St. Vincent	30864	Sir Martin Frobisher
30857	Lord Howe	30865	Sir John Hawkins

CLASS V "SCHOOLS" 4-4-0

30900	Eton	30914	Eastbourne
30901	Winchester	30915	Brighton
30902	Wellington	30916	Whitgift
30903	Charterhouse	30917	Ardingly
30904	Lancing	30918	Hurstpierpoint
30905	Tonbridge	30919	Harrow
30906	Sherborne	30920	Rugby
30907	Dulwich	30921	Shrewsbury
30908	Westminster	30922	Marlborough
30909	St. Paul's	30923	Bradfield
30910	Merchant Taylors	30924	Haileybury
30911	Dover	30925	Cheltenham
30912	Downside	30926	Repton
30913	Christ's Hospital	30927	Clifton

30928	Stowe	30934	St. Lawrence
30929	Malvern	30935	Sevenoaks
30930	Radley	30936	Cranleigh
30931	King's Wimbledon	30937	Epsom
30932	Blundells	30938	St. Olave's
30933	King's Canterbury	30939	Leatherhead

CLASSES WC & BB 4–6–2

"WEST COUNTRY" and "BATTLE OF BRITAIN"

34001	Exeter	34036	Westward Ho
34002	Salisbury	34037	Clovelly
34003	Plymouth	34038	Lynton
34004	Yeovil	34039	Boscastle
34005	Barnstaple	34040	Crewkerne
34006	Bude	34041	Wilton
34007	Wadebridge	34042	Dorchester
34008	Padstow	34043	Combe Martin
34009	Lyme Regis	34044	Woolacombe
34010	Sidmouth	34045	Ottery St. Mary
34011	Tavistock	34046	Braunton
34012	Launceston	34047	Callington
34013	Okehampton	34048	Crediton
34014	Budleigh Salterton	34049	Anti-Aircraft Command
34015	Exmouth	34050	Royal Observer Corps
34016	Bodmin	34051	Winston Churchill
34017	Ilfracombe	34052	Lord Dowding
34018	Axminster	34053	Sir Keith Park
34019	Bideford	34054	Lord Beaverbrook
34020	Seaton	34055	Fighter Pilot
34021	Dartmoor	34056	Croydon
34022	Exmoor	34057	Biggin Hill
34023	Blackmore Vale	34058	Sir Frederick Pile
34024	Tamar Valley	34059	Sir Archibald Sinclair
34025	Whimple	34060	25 Squadron
34026	Yes Tor	34061	73 Squadron
34027	Taw Valley	34062	17 Squadron
34028	Eddystone	34063	229 Squadron
34029	Lundy	34064	Fighter Command
34030	Watersmeet	34065	Hurricane
34031	Torrington	34066	Spitfire
34032	Camelford	34067	Tangmere
34033	Chard	34068	Kenley
34034	Honiton	34069	Hawkinge
34035	Shaftesbury	34070	Manston

NAMED LOCOMOTIVES—*contd.*

34071	601 Squadron	34091	Weymouth
34072	257 Squadron	34092	City of Wells
34073	249 Squadron	34093	Saunton
34074	46 Squadron	34094	Mortehoe
34075	264 Squadron	34095	Brentor
34076	41 Squadron	34096	Trevone
34077	603 Squadron	34097	Holsworthy
34078	222 Squadron	34098	Templecombe
34079	141 Squadron	34099	Lynmouth
34080	74 Squadron	34100	Appledore
34081	92 Squadron	34101	Hartland
34082	615 Squadron	34102	Lapford
34083	605 Squadron	34103	Calstock
34084	253 Squadron	34104	Bere Alston
34085	501 Squadron	34105	Swanage
34086	219 Squadron	34106	Lydford
34087	145 Squadron	34107	Blandford Forum
34088	213 Squadron	34108	Wincanton
34089	602 Squadron	34109	Sir Trafford
34090	Sir Eustace Missenden,		Leigh-Mallory
	Southern Railway	34110	66 Squadron

CLASS MN " MERCHANT NAVY " 4–6–2

35001	Channel Packet	35015	Rotterdam Lloyd
35002	Union Castle	35016	Elders Fyffes
35003	Royal Mail	35017	Belgian Marine
35004	Cunard White Star	35018	British India Line
35005	Canadian Pacific	35019	French Line CGT
35006	Peninsular & Oriental	35020	Bibby Line
	S.N. Co.	35021	New Zealand Line
35007	Aberdeen	35022	Holland-America Line
	Commonwealth	35023	Holland-Afrika Line
35008	Orient Line	35024	East Asiatic Company
35009	Shaw Savill	35025	Brocklebank Line
35010	Blue Star	35026	Lamport & Holt Line
35011	General Steam	35027	Port Line
	Navigation	35028	Clan Line
35012	United States Lines	35029	Ellerman Lines
35013	Blue Funnel	35030	Elder Dempster Lines
35014	Nederland Line		

CLASS E1 0–6–0T

3 Ryde   4 Wroxall

CLASS O2 0–4–4T

14	Fishbourne	27	Merstone
16	Ventnor	28	Ashey
17	Seaview	29	Alverstone
18	Ningwood	30	Shorwell
20	Shanklin	31	Chale
21	Sandown	32	Bonchurch
22	Brading	33	Bembridge
24	Calbourne	35	Freshwater
25	Godshill	36	Carisbrooke
26	Whitwell		

SOUTHERN RAILWAY LOCOMOTIVE SUPERINTENDENTS AND CHIEF MECHANICAL ENGINEERS OF CONSTITUENT COMPANIES

LONDON & SOUTH WESTERN RAILWAY

J. Woods ...	... ...	1835–1841
J. V. Gooch	... ...	1841–1850
J. Beattie ...	... ...	1850–1871
W. G. Beattie	... ...	1871–1878
W. Adams ...	... ...	1878–1895
D. Drummond	... ...	1895–1912
R. W. Urie...	... ...	1912–1922

LONDON, BRIGHTON AND SOUTH COAST RAILWAY

—. Statham	... ...	? –1845
J. Gray ...	... ...	1845–1847
S. Kirtley ...	... ...	1847
J. C. Craven	... ...	1847–1869
W. Stroudley	... ...	1870–1889
R. J. Billinton	... ...	1890–1904
D. Earle Marsh	... ...	1905–1911
L. B. Billinton	... ...	1911–1922

SOUTH EASTERN RAILWAY

B. Cubitt ...	... ...	1842–1845
J. Cudworth	... ...	1845–1876
A. M. Watkin	... ...	1876
R. Mansell ...	... ...	1877–1878
J. Stirling ...	... ...	1873–1898

LONDON, CHATHAM AND DOVER RAILWAY

W. Cubitt ...	... ...	1853–1860
W. Martley ...	... ...	1860–1874
W. Kirtley ...	... ...	1874–1898

SOUTH EASTERN AND CHATHAM RAILWAY

H. S. Wainwright ...	...	1899–1913
R. E. L. Maunsell ...	...	1913–1922

SOUTHERN RAILWAY

R. E. L. Maunsell ...	...	1923–1937
O. V. Bulleid	... ...	1937–1949

BRITISH RAILWAYS LOCOMOTIVES
Nos. 40000-59999

The code given in bold type to the right of each Class heading,
e.g. " 2P " denotes its British Railways power classification.
The numbers of locomotives in service have been checked to January 24th, **1959**.

2-6-2T   3

Introduced 1930. Fowler L.M.S. design
with parallel boiler.
*Introduced 1930. Condensing locos.
for working to Moorgate, London.

Weight: { 70 tons 10 cwt.
{ 71 tons 16 cwt.*
Pressure: 200 lb. Su.
Cyls.: (O) 17½″ × 26″.
Driving Wheels: 5′ 3″.
T.E.: 21,485 lb.
Walschaerts valve gear. P.V.

40001	40019	40037*	40054
40002	40020	40038*	40055
40003	40021	40039*	40056
40004	40022*	40040*	40057
40005	40023*	40041	40058
40006	40024*	40042	40059
40007	40025*	40043	40060
40008	40026*	40044	40061
40009	40027*	40045	40062
40010	40028*	40046	40063
40011	40029*	40047	40064
40012	40030*	40048	40065
40013	40031*	40049	40066
40014	40032*	40050	40067
40015	40033*	40051	40068
40016	40034*	40052	40069
40017	40035*	40053	40070
40018	40036*		

Total 70

2-6-2T   3

Introduced 1935. Stanier L.M.S. taper
boiler development of Fowler design
(above).
*Introduced 1941. Rebuilt with larger
boiler.

Weight: { 71 tons 5 cwt.
{ 72 tons 10 cwt.*
Pressure: 200 lb. Su.
Cyls.: (O) 17½″ × 26″.
Driving Wheels: 5′ 3″.

T.E.: 21,485 lb.
Walschaerts valve gear. P.V.

40071	40106	40141	40176
40072	40107	40142	40177
40073	40108	40143	40178
40074	40109	40144	40179
40075	40110	40145	40180
40076	40111	40146	40181
40077	40112	40147	40182
40078	40113	40148*	40183
40079	40114	40149	40184
40080	40115	40150	40185
40081	40116	40151	40186
40082	40117	40152	40187
40083	40118	40153	40188
40084	40119	40154	40189
40085	40120	40155	40190
40086	40121	40156	40191
40087	40122	40157	40192
40088	40123	40158	40193
40089	40124	40159	40194
40090	40125	40160	40195
40091	40126	40161	40196
40092	40127	40162	40197
40093	40128	40163*	40198
40094	40129	40164	40199
40095	40130	40165	40200
40096	40131	40166	40201
40097	40132	40167*	40202
40098	40133	40168	40203*
40099	40134	40169*	40204
40100	40135	40170	40205
40101	40136	40171	40206
40102	40137	40172	40207
40103	40138	40173	40208
40104	40139	40174	40209
40105	40140	40175	

Total 139

4-4-0   2P

Introduced 1912. Fowler rebuild of
Johnson locos. with superheater and
piston valves.

Weight: Loco. 53 tons 7 cwt.
Pressure: 160 lb. Su.
Cyls.: $20\frac{1}{2}'' \times 26''$.
Driving Wheels: 7' $0\frac{1}{2}''$.
T.E.: 17,585 lb.
P.V.

40332	40452	40501	40538
40396	40453	40502	40540
40402	40454	40504	40542
40411	40461	40511	40543
40412	40487	40513	40548
40416	40489	40534	40550
40421	40491	40536	40552
40439	40493	40537	40557
40443			

Total 33

4-4-0   2P

Introduced 1928. Post-grouping devel-
opment of Midland design, with
modified dimensions and reduced
boiler mountings.
*Introduced 1928. Locos. built for S. &
D.J.R. (taken into L.M.S. stock, 1930).
†Fitted experimentally in 1933 with
Dabeg feed-water heater.

Weight: Loco. 54 tons 1 cwt.
Pressure: 180 lb. Su.
Cyls.: $19'' \times 26''$.
Driving Wheels: 6' 9''.
T.E.: 17,730 lb.
P.V.

40563	40575	40587	40600
40564	40576	40588	40601
40565	40577	40589	40602
40566	40578	40590	40603
40567	40579	40592	40604
40568	40580	40593	40605
40569	40581	40594	40606
40570	40582	40595	40607
40571	40583	40596	40608
40572	40584	40597	40609
40573	40585	40593	40610
40574	40586	40599	40611

40612	40634*	40657	40680
40613	40635*	40658	40681
40614	40636	40659	40682
40615	40637	40660	40683
40616	40638	40661	40684
40617	40640	40663	40685
40618	40641	40664	40686
40619	40642	40665	40687
40620	40643	40666	40688
40621	40644	40667	40689
40622	40645	40668	40690
40623	40646	40669	40691
40624	40647	40670	40692
40625	40648	40671	40693
40626	40649	40672	40694
40627	40650	40673	40695
40628	40651	40674	40696
40629	40652	40675	40697
40630	40653†	40677	40698
40631	40654	40678	40699
40632	40655	40679	40700
40633*†	40656		

Total 134

4-4-0 (3-Cyl. Compd.)   4P

Introduced 1924. Post-grouping
development of Johnson Midland
compound with modified dimensions
and (with some exceptions) reduced
boiler mountings.

Weight: Loco. 61 tons 14 cwt.
Pressure: 200 lb. Su.
Cyls.: $\begin{cases} \text{L.P. (2) } 21'' \times 26''. \\ \text{H.P. (1) } 19'' \times 26''. \end{cases}$
Driving Wheels: 6' 9''.
T.E. (of L.P. cyls. at
80% boiler pressure): 22,650 lb.
P.V. (H.P. cyl. only).

40907	41063	41123	41162
40925	41100	41143	41165
40936	41101	41157	41168
41049	41120	41158	41173
41062	41121		

Total 18

2-6-2T 2

Introduced 1946. Ivatt L.M.S. taper boiler design.

Weight: 63 tons 5 cwt.

Pressure: 200 lb. Su.

Cyls.: $\begin{cases} \text{(O) } 16'' \times 24''. \\ \text{(O) } 16\frac{1}{2}'' \times 24''.* \end{cases}$

Driving Wheels: 5' 0".

T.E.: $\begin{cases} 17,410 \text{ lb.} \\ 18,510 \text{ lb.}* \end{cases}$

Walschaerts valve gear. P.V.

41200	41233	41266	41298*
41201	41234	41267	41299*
41202	41235	41268	41300*
41203	41236	41269	41301*
41204	41237	41270	41302*
41205	41238	41271	41303*
41206	41239	41272	41304*
41207	41240	41273	41305*
41208	41241	41274	41306*
41209	41242	41275	41307*
41210	41243	41276	41308*
41211	41244	41277	41309*
41212	41245	41278	41310*
41213	41246	41279	41311*
41214	41247	41280	41312*
41215	41248	41281	41313*
41216	41249	41282	41314*
41217	41250	41283	41315*
41218	41251	41284	41316*
41219	41252	41285	41317*
41220	41253	41286	41318*
41221	41254	41287	41319*
41222	41255	41288	41320*
41223	41256	41289	41321*
41224	41257	41290*	41322*
41225	41258	41291*	41323*
41226	41259	41292*	41324*
41227	41260	41293*	41325*
41228	41261	41294*	41326*
41229	41262	41295*	41327*
41230	41263	41296*	41328*
41231	41264	41297*	41329*
41232	41265		

Total 130

0-4-0T 0F

Introduced 1907. Deeley Midland design.

Weight: 32 tons 16 cwt.

Pressure: 160 lb.

Cyls.: (O) 15" × 22".

Driving Wheels: 3' 9¾".

T.E.: 14,635 lb.

Walschaerts valve gear.

41528	41531	41533	41536
41529	41532	41535	41537

Total 8

0-6-0T 1F

Introduced 1878. Johnson Midland design.

*Rebuilt with Belpaire firebox.

Weight: 39 tons 11 cwt.

Pressure: $\begin{cases} 150 \text{ lb.} \\ 140 \text{ lb.}* \end{cases}$

Cyls.: 17" × 24".

Driving Wheels: 4' 7".

T.E.: $\begin{cases} 16,080 \text{ lb.} \\ 15,005 \text{ lb.}* \end{cases}$

41661*	41739*	41797*	41855*
41702*	41754*	41804*	41857*
41708*	41763*	41835	41875*
41712*	41769*	41844*	41878*
41726*	41773*	41847*	41879*
41734*	41795*		

Total 22

0-4-4T 2P

Introduced 1932. Stanier L.M.S. design. Push-and-pull fitted.

Weight: 58 tons 1 cwt.

Pressure: 160 lb.

Cyls.: 18" × 26".

Driving Wheels: 5' 7".

T.E.: 17,100 lb.

41900	41903	41906	41908
41901	41904	41907	41909
41902	41905		

Total 10

4-4-2T 3P

Introduced 1923. Midland and L.M.S. development of Whitelegg L.T. & S. "79" Class.
Weight: 71 tons 10 cwt.
Pressure: 170 lb.
Cyls.: (O) 19″ × 26″.
Driving Wheels: 6′ 6″.
T.E.: 17,390 lb.

41928	41946	41949	41975
41939	41947	41950	41977
41941	41948	41969	41978
41945			

Total 13

0-6-2T 3F

Introduced 1903. Whitelegg L.T. & S. "69" Class (Nos. 41990–3 built 1912 taken directly into M.R. stock).
Weight: 64 tons 13 cwt.
Pressure: 170 lb.
Cyls.: 18″ × 26″.
Driving Wheels: 5′ 3″.
T.E.: 19,320 lb.

41981	41984	41987	41992
41982	41985	41990	41993
41983	41986	41991	

Total 11

2-6-4T 4

*Introduced 1927. Fowler L.M.S. parallel boiler design.
†Introduced 1933. As earlier engines, but with side-window cab and doors.
‡Introduced 1934. Stanier taper-boiler 3-cylinder design for L.T. & S.
§Introduced 1935. Stanier taper-boiler 2-cylinder design.
¶Introduced 1945. Fairburn development of Stanier design with shorter wheelbase and detail alterations.

Weight:
{ 86 tons 5 cwt.*†
92 tons 5 cwt.‡
87 tons 17 cwt.§
85 tons 5 cwt.¶
Pressure (all types): 200 lb. Su.
Cyls.:
{ (O) 19″ × 26″.*†
(3) 16″ × 26″.‡
(O) 19⅝″ × 26″.§¶
Driving Wheels (all types): 5′ 9″.
T.E.:
{ 23,125 lb.*†
24,600 lb.‡
24,670 lb.§¶
Walschaerts valve gear. P.V.

¶FAIRBURN LOCOS.

42050	42095	42140	42185
42051	42096	42141	42186
42052	42097	42142	42187
42053	42098	42143	42188
42054	42099	42144	42189
42055	42100	42145	42190
42056	42101	42146	42191
42057	42102	42147	42192
42058	42103	42148	42193
42059	42104	42149	42194
42060	42105	42150	42195
42061	42106	42151	42196
42062	42107	42152	42197
42063	42108	42153	42198
42064	42109	42154	42199
42065	42110	42155	42200
42066	42111	42156	42201
42067	42112	42157	42202
42068	42113	42158	42203
42069	42114	42159	42204
42070	42115	42160	42205
42071	42116	42161	42206
42072	42117	42162	42207
42073	42118	42163	42208
42074	42119	42164	42209
42075	42120	42165	42210
42076	42121	42166	42211
42077	42122	42167	42212
42078	42123	42168	42213
42079	42124	42169	42214
42080	42125	42170	42215
42081	42126	42171	42216
42082	42127	42172	42217
42083	42128	42173	42218
42084	42129	42174	42219
42085	42130	42175	42220
42086	42131	42176	42221
42087	42132	42177	42222
42088	42133	42178	42223
42089	42134	42179	42224
42090	42135	42180	42225
42091	42136	42181	42226
42092	42137	42182	42227
42093	42138	42183	42228
42094	42139	42184	42229

42230	42248	42266	42284
42231	42249	42267	42285
42232	42250	42268	42286
42233	42251	42269	42287
42234	42252	42270	42288
42235	42253	42271	42289
42236	42254	42272	42290
42237	42255	42273	42291
42238	42256	42274	42292
42239	42257	42275	42293
42240	42258	42276	42294
42241	42259	42277	42295
42242	42260	42278	42296
42243	42261	42279	42297
42244	42262	42280	42298
42245	42263	42281	42299
42246	42264	42282	
42247	42265	42283	

*FOWLER LOCOS.

42300	42324	42348	42372
42301	42325	42349	42373
42302	42326	42350	42374
42303	42327	42351	42375
42304	42328	42352	42376
42305	42329	42353	42377
42306	42330	42354	42378
42307	42331	42355	42379
42308	42332	42356	42380
42309	42333	42357	42381
42310	42334	42358	42382
42311	42335	42359	42383
42312	42336	42360	42384
42313	42337	42361	42385
42314	42338	42362	42386
42315	42339	42363	42387
42316	42340	42364	42388
42317	42341	42365	42389
42318	42342	42366	42390
42319	42343	42367	42391
42320	42344	42368	42392
42321	42345	42369	42393
42322	42346	42370	42394
42323	42347	42371	

†FOWLER LOCOS. WITH SIDE-WINDOW CAB

42395	42403	42411	42418
42396	42404	42412	42419
42397	42405	42413	42420
42398	42406	42414	42421
42399	42407	42415	42422
42400	42408	42416	42423
42401	42409	42417	42424
42402	42410		

§STANIER 2-CYL. LOCOS.

42425	42443	42461	42479
42426	42444	42462	42480
42427	42445	42463	42481
42428	42446	42464	42482
42429	42447	42465	42483
42430	42448	42466	42484
42431	42449	42467	42485
42432	42450	42468	42486
42433	42451	42469	42487
42434	42452	42470	42488
42435	42453	42471	42489
42436	42454	42472	42490
42437	42455	42473	42491
42438	42456	42474	42492
42439	42457	42475	42493
42440	42458	42476	42494
42441	42459	42477	
42442	42460	42478	

‡STANIER 3-CYL. LOCOS.

42500	42510	42519	42528
42501	42511	42520	42529
42502	42512	42521	42530
42503	42513	42522	42531
42504	42514	42523	42532
42505	42515	42524	42533
42506	42516	42525	42534
42507	42517	42526	42535
42508	42518	42527	42536
42509			

§STANIER 2-CYL. LOCOS.

42537	42571	42605	42639
42538	42572	42606	42640
42539	42573	42607	42641
42540	42574	42608	42642
42541	42575	42609	42643
42542	42576	42610	42644
42543	42577	42611	42645
42544	42578	42612	42646
42545	42579	42613	42647
42546	42580	42614	42648
42547	42581	42615	42649
42548	42582	42616	42650
42549	42583	42617	42651
42550	42584	42618	42652
42551	42585	42619	42653
42552	42586	42620	42654
42553	42587	42621	42655
42554	42588	42622	42656
42555	42589	42623	42657
42556	42590	42624	42658
42557	42591	42625	42659
42558	42592	42626	42660
42559	42593	42627	42661
42560	42594	42628	42662
42561	42595	42629	42663
42562	42596	42630	42664
42563	42597	42631	42665
42564	42598	42632	42666
42565	42599	42633	42667
42566	42600	42634	42668
42567	42601	42635	42669
42568	42602	42636	42670
42569	42603	42637	42671
42570	42604	42638	42672

¶FAIRBURN LOCOS.

42673	42680	42687	42694
42674	42681	42688	42695
42675	42682	42689	42696
42676	42683	42690	42697
42677	42684	42691	42698
42678	42685	42692	42699
42679	42686	42693	

2-6-0   6P5F

Introduced 1926. Hughes L.M.S. design built under Fowler's direction. Walschaerts valve gear. P.V.

*Introduced 1953. Locos. rebuilt experimentally with Lentz R.C. poppet valves in 1931; rebuilt with Reidinger rotary poppet valve gear in 1953.

Weight: Loco. 66 tons 0 cwt.
Pressure: 180 lb. Su.
Cyls. :(O) $21'' \times 26''$.
Driving Wheels: 5' 6".
T.E.: 26,580 lb.

42700	42735	42770	42805
42701	42736	42771	42806
42702	42737	42772	42807
42703	42738	42773	42808
42704	42739	42774	42809
42705	42740	42775	42810
42706	42741	42776	42811
42707	42742	42777	42812
42708	42743	42778	42813
42709	42744	42779	42814
42710	42745	42780	42815
42711	42746	42781	42816
42712	42747	42782	42817
42713	42748	42783	42818*
42714	42749	42784	42819
42715	42750	42785	42820
42716	42751	42786	42821
42717	42752	42787	42822*
42718	42753	42788	42823
42719	42754	42789	42824*
42720	42755	42790	42825*
42721	42756	42791	42826
42722	42757	42792	42827
42723	42758	42793	42828
42724	42759	42794	42829*
42725	42760	42795	42830
42726	42761	42796	42831
42727	42762	42797	42832
42728	42763	42798	42833
42729	42764	42799	42834
42730	42765	42800	42835
42731	42766	42801	42836
42732	42767	42802	42837
42733	42768	42803	42838
42734	42769	42804	42839

Total 645

42840	42867	42894	42920
42841	42868	42895	42921
42842	42869	42896	42922
42843	42870	42897	42923
42844	42871	42898	42924
42845	42872	42899	42925
42846	42873	42900	42926
42847	42874	42901	42927
42848	42875	42902	42928
42849	42876	42903	42929
42850	42877	42904	42930
42851	42878	42905	42931
42852	42879	42906	42932
42853	42880	42907	42933
42854	42881	42908	42934
42855	42882	42909	42935
42856	42883	42910	42936
42857	42884	42911	42937
42858	42885	42912	42938
42859	42886	42913	42939
42860	42887	42914	42940
42861	42888	42915	42941
42862	42889	42916	42942
42863	42890	42917	42943
42864	42891	42918	42944
42865	42892	42919	
42866	42893		**Total 245**

2-6-0   6P5F

Introduced 1933. Stanier L.M.S. taper boiler design, some with safety valves mounted on the top feed.
Weight: Loco. 69 tons 2 cwt.
Pressure: 225 lb. Su.
Cyls.: (O) $18'' \times 28''$.
Driving Wheels: $5'\,6''$.
T.E.: 26,290 lb.
Walschaerts valve gear. P.V.

42945	42955	42965	42975
42946	42956	42966	42976
42947	42957	42967	42977
42948	42958	42968	42978
42949	42959	42969	42979
42950	42960	42970	42980
42951	42961	42971	42981
42952	42962	42972	42982
42953	42963	42973	42983
42954	42964	42974	42984
			Total 40

2-6-0   4

Introduced 1947. Ivatt L.M.S. taper boiler design with double chimney. Later engines introduced with single chimney, with which earlier engines are being rebuilt.
Weight: Loco. 59 tons 2 cwt.
Pressure: 225 lb. Su.
Cyls.: (O) $17\frac{1}{2}'' \times 26''$.
Driving Wheels: $5'\,3''$.
T.E.: 24,170 lb.
Walschaerts valve gear. P.V.

43000	43036	43072	43108
43001	43037	43073	43109
43002	43038	43074	43110
43003	43039	43075	43111
43004	43040	43076	43112
43005	43041	43077	43113
43006	43042	43078	43114
43007	43043	43079	43115
43008	43044	43080	43116
43009	43045	43081	43117
43010	43046	43082	43118
43011	43047	43083	43119
43012	43048	43084	43120
43013	43049	43085	43121
43014	43050	43086	43122
43015	43051	43087	43123
43016	43052	43088	43124
43017	43053	43089	43125
43018	43054	43090	43126
43019	43055	43091	43127
43020	43056	43092	43128
43021	43057	43093	43129
43022	43058	43094	43130
43023	43059	43095	43131
43024	43060	43096	43132
43025	43061	43097	43133
43026	43062	43098	43134
43027	43063	43099	43135
43028	43064	43100	43136
43029	43065	43101	43137
43030	43066	43102	43138
43031	43067	43103	43139
43032	43068	43104	43140
43033	43069	43105	43141
43034	43070	43106	43142
43035	43071	43107	43143

43144	43149	43154	43158
43145	43150	43155	43159
43146	43151	43156	43160
43147	43152	43157	43161
43148	43153		

Total 162

0-6-0   3F

Introduced 1885. Johnson Midland locos., rebuilt from 1916 by Fowler with Belpaire firebox.
*Introduced 1885. Johnson Midland locos., rebuilt from 1920 by Fowler with Belpaire firebox.
†Introduced 1896. Locos. built for S. & D.J. (taken into L.M.S. stock 1930).
Weight: Loco. 43 tons 17 cwt.
Pressure: 175 lb.
Cyls.: $18'' \times 26''$.
Driving Wheels: $\begin{cases} 5'\ 3''. \\ 5'\ 3''.† \\ 4'\ 11''.* \end{cases}$
T.E.: $\begin{cases} 19,890\ \text{lb}. \\ 19,890\ \text{lb}.† \\ 21,240\ \text{lb}.* \end{cases}$

43174*	43225	43267	43327
43178*	43233	43268	43329
43183*	43234	43271	43330
43185*	43235	43277	43333
43187*	43237	43278	43335
43188*	43240	43282	43337
43189*	43241	43284	43339
43192	43242	43287	43340
43194†	43243	43292	43342
43200	43245	43294	43344
43203	43247	43295	43355
43205	43248†	43305	43357
43207	43249	43306	43359
43210	43250	43307	43361
43211†	43251	43308	43368
43212	43253	43309	43369
43213	43254	43314	43370
43214	43256	43315	43371
43216†	43257	43318	43373
43218†	43258	43321	43374
43219	43261	43324	43378
43222	43263	43325	43379
43223	43266	43326	43381

43386	43490	43599	43679
43387	43496	43605	43680
43388	43499	43608	43681
43389	43502	43615	43682
43394	43506	43618	43687
43395	43507	43619	43693
43398	43509	43620	43705
43399	43510	43622	43709
43400	43514	43623	43711
43405	43515	43624	43714
43406	43520	43627	43715
43410	43521	43629	43721
43411	43523	43630	43727
43427	43529	43634	43728
43428	43531	43637	43729
43429	43538	43638	43731
43431	43548	43639	43734
43433	43558	43644	43735
43435	43562	43645	43737
43436	43565	43650	43749
43440	43570	43651	43750*
43444	43572	43652	43751
43446	43574	43657	43753
43449	43578	43658	43754
43453	43579	43660	43756
43456	43580	43664	43759
43457	43583	43665	43760
43459	43584	43668	43762
43464	43585	43669	43763
43468	43586	43673	43766
43474	43587	43674	43771
43482	43593	43675	43773
43484	43594	43678	

Total 223

0-6-0   3F

Introduced 1906. Deeley Midland design. Rebuilt by Fowler with
* Belpaire firebox.
Weight: Loco. 46 tons 3 cwt.
Pressure: 175 lb.
Cyls.: $18\frac{1}{2}'' \times 26''$.
Driving Wheels: $5'\ 3''$.
T.E.: 21,010 lb.

67

43778	43799	43812	43826
43784	43800	43814	43828
43785	43808	43822	43829
43789	43809	43825	43832
43793			

Total 17

0-6-0　　　　　　　　　　4F

Introduced 1911. Fowler superheated Midland design.
Weight: Loco. 48 tons 15 cwt.
Pressure: 175 lb. Su.
Cyls.: 20″ × 26″.
Driving Wheels: 5′ 3″.
T.E.: 24,555 lb.
P.V.

43836	43876	43917	43952
43839	43877	43918	43953
43840	43878	43919	43954
43841	43880	43920	43955
43842	43881	43921	43957
43843	43882	43922	43958
43844	43883	43923	43960
43845	43884	43924	43961
43846	43885	43925	43962
43848	43886	43926	43963
43849	43887	43928	43964
43850	43888	43929	43965
43853	43890	43930	43966
43854	43893	43931	43967
43855	43896	43932	43968
43856	43897	43933	43969
43858	43899	43934	43970
43859	43900	43935	43971
43860	43902	43937	43972
43861	43903	43938	43973
43863	43904	43939	43975
43864	43905	43940	43976
43865	43906	43942	43977
43866	43907	43944	43979
43868	43908	43945	43981
43869	43910	43947	43982
43870	43911	43948	43983
43871	43913	43949	43985
43872	43914	43950	43986
43873	43915	43951	43987

43988	43999	44009	44018
43989	44000	44010	44019
43990	44001	44011	44020
43991	44002	44012	44021
43994	44003	44013	44022
43995	44004	44014	44023
43996	44005	44015	44025
43997	44007	44016	44026
43998	44008		

Total 154

0-6-0　　　　　　　　　　4F

Introduced 1924. Post-grouping development of Midland design with reduced boiler mountings.
*Introduced 1922. Locos. built for S. & D.J.R. to M.R. design (taken into L.M.S. stock 1930).
Weight: Loco. 48 tons 15 cwt.
Pressure: 175 lb. Su.
Cyls.: 20″ × 26″.
Driving Wheels: 5′ 3″.
T.E.: 24,555 lb.
P.V.

44027	44048	44069	44090
44028	44049	44070	44091
44029	44050	44071	44092
44030	44051	44072	44093
44031	44052	44073	44094
44032	44053	44074	44095
44033	44054	44075	44096
44034	44055	44076	44097
44035	44056	44077	44098
44036	44057	44078	44099
44037	44058	44079	44100
44038	44059	44080	44101
44039	44060	44081	44102
44040	44061	44082	44103
44041	44062	44083	44104
44042	44063	44084	44105
44043	44064	44085	44106
44044	44065	44086	44107
44045	44066	44087	44108
44046	44067	44088	44109
44047	44068	44089	44110

44111	44158	44205	44252	44299	44346	44393	44440
44112	44159	44206	44253	44300	44347	44394	44441
44113	44160	44207	44254	44301	44348	44395	44442
44114	44161	44208	44255	44302	44349	44396	44443
44115	44162	44209	44256	44303	44350	44397	44444
44116	44163	44210	44257	44304	44351	44398	44445
44117	44164	44211	44258	44305	44352	44399	44446
44118	44165	44212	44259	44306	44353	44400	44447
44119	44166	44213	44260	44307	44354	44401	44448
44120	44167	44214	44261	44308	44355	44402	44449
44121	44168	44215	44262	44309	44356	44403	44450
44122	44169	44216	44263	44310	44357	44404	44451
44123	44170	44217	44264	44311	44358	44405	44452
44124	44171	44218	44265	44312	44359	44406	44453
44125	44172	44219	44266	44313	44360	44407	44454
44126	44173	44220	44267	44314	44361	44408	44455
44127	44174	44221	44268	44315	44362	44409	44456
44128	44175	44222	44269	44316	44363	44410	44457
44129	44176	44223	44270	44317	44364	44411	44458
44130	44177	44224	44271	44318	44365	44412	44459
44131	44178	44225	44272	44319	44366	44413	44460
44132	44179	44226	44273	44320	44367	44414	44461
44133	44180	44227	44274	44321	44368	44415	44462
44134	44181	44228	44275	44322	44369	44416	44463
44135	44182	44229	44276	44323	44370	44417	44464
44136	44183	44230	44277	44324	44371	44418	44465
44137	44184	44231	44278	44325	44372	44419	44466
44138	44185	44232	44279	44326	44373	44420	44467
44139	44186	44233	44280	44327	44374	44421	44468
44140	44187	44234	44281	44328	44375	44422	44469
44141	44188	44235	44282	44329	44376	44423	44470
44142	44189	44236	44283	44330	44377	44424	44471
44143	44190	44237	44284	44331	44378	44425	44472
44144	44191	44238	44285	44332	44379	44426	44473
44145	44192	44239	44286	44333	44380	44427	44474
44146	44193	44240	44287	44334	44381	44428	44475
44147	44194	44241	44288	44335	44382	44429	44476
44148	44195	44242	44289	44336	44383	44430	44477
44149	44196	44243	44290	44337	44384	44431	44478
44150	44197	44244	44291	44338	44385	44432	44479
44151	44198	44245	44292	44339	44386	44433	44480
44152	44199	44246	44293	44340	44387	44434	44481
44153	44200	44247	44294	44341	44388	44435	44482
44154	44201	44248	44295	44342	44389	44436	44483
44155	44202	44249	44296	44343	44390	44437	44484
44156	44203	44250	44297	44344	44391	44438	44485
44157	44204	44251	44298	44345	44392	44439	44486

44487	44517	44547	44577
44488	44518	44548	44578
44489	44519	44549	44579
44490	44520	44550	44580
44491	44521	44551	44581
44492	44522	44552	44582
44493	44523	44553	44583
44494	44524	44554	44584
44495	44525	44555	44585
44496	44526	44556	44586
44497	44527	44557*	44587
44498	44528	44558*	44588
44499	44529	44559*	44589
44500	44530	44560*	44590
44501	44531	44561*	44591
44502	44532	44562	44592
44503	44533	44563	44593
44504	44534	44564	44594
44505	44535	44565	44595
44506	44536	44566	44596
44507	44537	44567	44597
44508	44538	44568	44598
44509	44539	44569	44599
44510	44540	44570	44600
44511	44541	44571	44601
44512	44542	44572	44602
44513	44543	44573	44603
44514	44544	44574	44604
44515	44545	44575	44605
44516	44546	44576	44606

Total 580

4-6-0   5

Introduced 1934. Stanier L.M.S. taper boiler design.

Experimental locomotives:—

1. Introduced 1947. Stephenson link motion (outside), Timken roller bearings.
2. Introduced 1948. Caprotti valve gear.
3. Introduced 1948. Caprotti valve gear, Timken roller bearings.
4. Introduced 1948. Caprotti valve gear, Timken roller bearings, double chimney.
5. Introduced 1947. Timken roller bearings.
6. Introduced 1947. Timken roller bearings, double chimney.
7. Introduced 1949. Fitted with steel firebox.
8. Introduced 1950. Skefko roller bearings.
9. Introduced 1950. Timken roller bearings on driving coupled axle only.
10. Introduced 1950. Skefko roller bearings on driving coupled axle only.
11. Introduced 1951. Caprotti valve gear, Skefko roller bearings.

Weight: Loco.
72 tons 2 cwt.
75 tons 6 cwt. (1, 5, 6, 8, 9, 10).
74 tons 0 cwt. (2, 3, 4, 11).
72 tons 2 cwt. (7).

Pressure: 225 lb. Su.
Cyls.: (O) 18½" × 28".
Driving Wheels: 6' 0".
T.E.: 25,455 lb.

Walschaerts valve gear and P.V. except where otherwise shown.

44658	44684[8]	44710	44736
44659	44685[8]	44711	44737
44660	44686[11]	44712	44738[2]
44661	44687[11]	44713	44739[2]
44662	44688[9]	44714	44740[2]
44663	44689[9]	44715	44741[2]
44664	44690[9]	44716	44742[2]
44665	44691[9]	44717	44743[2]
44666	44692[9]	44718[9]	44744[2]
44667	44693[9]	44719[9]	44745[2]
44668[10]	44694[9]	44720[7]	44746[2]
44669[10]	44695[9]	44721[7]	44747[2]
44670[10]	44696[9]	44722[7]	44748[3]
44671[10]	44697[9]	44723[7]	44749[3]
44672[10]	44698	44724[7]	44750[3]
44673[10]	44699	44725[7]	44751[3]
44674[10]	44700	44726[7]	44752[3]
44675[10]	44701	44727[7]	44753[3]
44676[10]	44702	44728	44754[3]
44677[10]	44703	44729	44755[4]
44678[8]	44704	44730	44756[4]
44679[8]	44705	44731	44757[4]
44680[8]	44706	44732	44758[5]
44681[8]	44707	44733	44759[5]
44682[8]	44708	44734	44760[5]
44683[8]	44709	44735	44761[5]

44762[5]	44809	44856	44903	44950	44997	45044	45091
44763[5]	44810	44857	44904	44951	44998	45045	45092
44764[5]	44811	44858	44905	44952	44999	45046	45093
44765[6]	44812	44859	44906	44953	45000	45047	45094
44766[6]	44813	44860	44907	44954	45001	45048	45095
44767[1]	44814	44861	44908	44955	45002	45049	45096
44768	44815	44862	44909	44956	45003	45050	45097
44769	44816	44863	44910	44957	45004	45051	45098
44770	44817	44864	44911	44958	45005	45052	45099
44771	44818	44865	44912	44959	45006	45053	45100
44772	44819	44866	44913	44960	45007	45054	45101
44773	44820	44867	44914	44961	45008	45055	45102
44774	44821	44868	44915	44962	45009	45056	45103
44775	44822	44869	44916	44963	45010	45057	45104
44776	44823	44870	44917	44964	45011	45058	45105
44777	44824	44871	44918	44965	45012	45059	45106
44778	44825	44872	44919	44966	45013	45060	45107
44779	44826	44873	44920	44967	45014	45061	45108
44780	44827	44874	44921	44968	45015	45062	45109
44781	44828	44875	44922	44969	45016	45063	45110
44782	44829	44876	44923	44970	45017	45064	45111
44783	44830	44877	44924	44971	45018	45065	45112
44784	44831	44878	44925	44972	45019	45066	45113
44785	44832	44879	44926	44973	45020	45067	45114
44786	44833	44880	44927	44974	45021	45068	45115
44787	44834	44881	44928	44975	45022	45069	45116
44788	44835	44882	44929	44976	45023	45070	45117
44789	44836	44883	44930	44977	45024	45071	45118
44790	44837	44884	44931	44978	45025	45072	45119
44791	44838	44885	44932	44979	45026	45073	45120
44792	44839	44886	44933	44980	45027	45074	45121
44793	44840	44887	44934	44981	45028	45075	45122
44794	44841	44888	44935	44982	45029	45076	45123
44795	44842	44889	44936	44983	45030	45077	45124
44796	44843	44890	44937	44984	45031	45078	45125
44797	44844	44891	44938	44985	45032	45079	45126
44798	44845	44892	44939	44986	45033	45080	45127
44799	44846	44893	44940	44987	45034	45081	45128
44800	44847	44894	44941	44988	45035	45082	45129
44801	44848	44895	44942	44989	45036	45083	45130
44802	44849	44896	44943	44990	45037	45084	45131
44803	44850	44897	44944	44991	45038	45085	45132
44804	44851	44898	44945	44992	45039	45086	45133
44805	44852	44899	44946	44993	45040	45087	45134
44806	44853	44900	44947	44994	45041	45088	45135
44807	44854	44901	44948	44995	45042	45089	45136
44808	44855	44902	44949	44996	45043	45090	45137

45138	45179	45220	45261	45302	45349	45396	45443
45139	45180	45221	45262	45303	45350	45397	45444
45140	45181	45222	45263	45304	45351	45398	45445
45141	45182	45223	45264	45305	45352	45399	45446
45142	45183	45224	45265	45306	45353	45400	45447
45143	45184	45225	45266	45307	45354	45401	45448
45144	45185	45226	45267	45308	45355	45402	45449
45145	45186	45227	45268	45309	45356	45403	45450
45146	45187	45228	45269	45310	45357	45404	45451
45147	45188	45229	45270	45311	45358	45405	45452
45148	45189	45230	45271	45312	45359	45406	45453
45149	45190	45231	45272	45313	45360	45407	45454
45150	45191	45232	45273	45314	45361	45408	45455
45151	45192	45233	45274	45315	45362	45409	45456
45152	45193	45234	45275	45316	45363	45410	45457
45153	45194	45235	45276	45317	45364	45411	45458
45154*	45195	45236	45277	45318	45365	45412	45459
45155	45196	45237	45278	45319	45366	45413	45460
45156*	45197	45238	45279	45320	45367	45414	45461
45157*	45198	45239	45280	45321	45368	45415	45462
45158*	45199	45240	45281	45322	45369	45416	45463
45159	45200	45241	45282	45323	45370	45417	45464
45160	45201	45242	45283	45324	45371	45418	45465
45161	45202	45243	45284	45325	45372	45419	45466
45162	45203	45244	45285	45326	45373	45420	45467
45163	45204	45245	45286	45327	45374	45421	45468
45164	45205	45246	45287	45328	45375	45422	45469
45165	45206	45247	45288	45329	45376	45423	45470
45166	45207	45248	45289	45330	45377	45424	45471
45167	45208	45249	45290	45331	45378	45425	45472
45168	45209	45250	45291	45332	45379	45426	45473
45169	45210	45251	45292	45333	45380	45427	45474
45170	45211	45252	45293	45334	45381	45428	45475
45171	45212	45253	45294	45335	45382	45429	45476
45172	45213	45254	45295	45336	45383	45430	45477
45173	45214	45255	45296	45337	45384	45431	45478
45174	45215	45256	45297	45338	45385	45432	45479
45175	45216	45257	45298	45339	45386	45433	45480
45176	45217	45258	45299	45340	45387	45434	45481
45177	45218	45259	45300	45341	45388	45435	45482
45178	45219	45260	4530!	45342	45389	45436	45483
				45343	45390	45437	45484
				45344	45391	45438	45485
				45345	45392	45439	45486
				45346	45393	45440	45487
				45347	45394	45441	45488
				45348	45395	45442	45489

* NAMES :

45154	Lanarkshire Yeomanry
45156	Ayrshire Yeomanry
45157	The Glasgow Highlander
45158	Glasgow Yeomanry

4300 Class 2-6-0 No. 5369   [G. Wheeler

4300 Class 2-6-0 No. 6319 (with detail differences)   [L. Marshall

4300 Class 2-6-0 No. 7341 (with side-window cab)   [L. Marshall

B

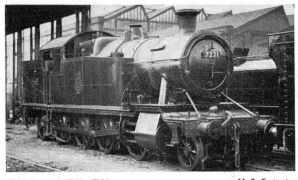

7200 Class 2-8-2T No. 7221   [A. R. Carpenter

4200 Class 2-8-0T No. 4281   [B. K. B. Gree

4200 Class 2-8-0T No. 4247 (with outside steampipes)   [A. W. Martin

Top: 4500 Class
2-6-2T No. 4507
[*G. Wheeler*

Centre: 4575 Class
2-6-2T No. 4575
[*K. R. Pirt*

Right: "City" Class
4-4-0 No. 3440 *City
of Truro*
P. Ransome-Wallis

B*

5101 Class 2-6-2T No. 5153 [L. King

3100 Class 2-6-2T No. 3103 [K. R. Pirt

8100 Class 2-6-2T No. 8108 [B. K. B. Green

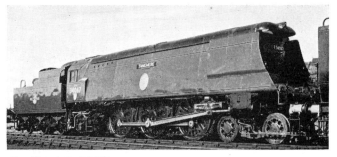

Class BB 4-6-2 No. 34067 *Tangmere*

[L. Elsey

Rebuilt Class WC 4-6-2 No. 34014 *Budleigh Salterton*

[G. Wheeler

Rebuilt Class MN 4-6-2 No. 35004 *Cunard White Star*

[G. Wheeler

Class LN 4-6-0 No. 30854 *Howard of Effingham*

[J. B. Bucknall

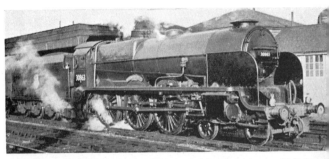

Class LN 4-6-0 No. 30863 *Lord Rodney* (with shortened smokebox)

[G. D. Parkes

Class V 4-4-0 No. 30907 *Dulwich*

[L. Else

Class N15 (Maunsell) 4-6-0 No. 30453 *King Arthur*   [*R. C. Riley*

Class N15 (Maunsell) 4-6-0 No. 30803 *Sir Harry le Fise Lake* (with six-wheel tender)
[*A. A. Cameron*

Class S15 4-6-0 (Urie) No. 30498   [*R. J. Buckley*

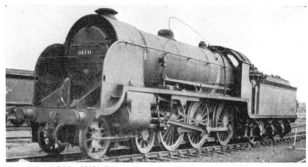

Class H15 4-6-0 No. 30331 (Maunsell rebuild of Drummond F13) [L. King

Class H15 4-6-0 (Maunsell) No. 30477 [L. Marshall

Class U1 2-6-0 No. 31909 [B. K. B. Green

Class K 2-6-0 No. 32343   [*L. King*

Class T9 4-4-0 No. 30289   [*R. C. Riley*

Class T9 4-4-0 No. 30313 (with wider cab and splashers and six-wheel tender)
                                                           [*L. Elsey*

Class L 4-4-0 No. 31778   [L. Marshall

Class D1 4-4-0 No. 31487   [L. King

Class L1 4-4-0 No. 31754   [J. H. Asto

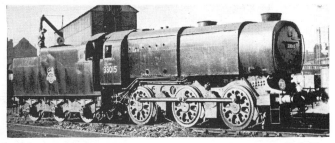

Class Q1 0-6-0 No. 33015   [*R. C. Riley*

Class Q 0-6-0 No. 30541   [*R. C. Riley*

Class 0395 0-6-0 No. 30575   [*C. P. Boocock*

Class M7 0-4-4T No. 30668   *[J. Robertson*

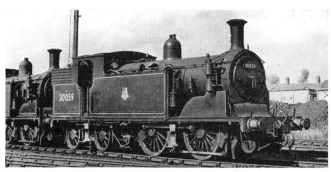

Class M7 0-4-4T No. 30059 (push-and-pull fitted)   *[L. Marshall*

Class O2 0-4-4T No. 30225   *G. Wheeler*

Class W 2-6-4T No. 31917 [L. King

Class Z 0-8-0T No. 30953 [J. A. Coiley

Class H16 4-6-2T No. 30520 [L. Elsey

Class A1X 0-6-0T No. 32640   [*C. P. Boocock*

Class E1 0-6-0T No. 32151   [*L. Elsey*

Class E2 0-6-0T No. 32108   [*G. Wheeler*

Class P 0-6-0T No. 31323

[J. H. Aston

Class R1 0-6-0T No. 31047

[L. Marshall

Class USA 0-6-0T No. 30062

[B. K. B. Green

Class 0415 4-4-2T No. 30583   [L. Marshall

Class 0298 2-4-0WT No. 30586   [L. King

Class B4 0-4-0T No. 30083   [J. Hodge

45490	45493	45496	45498
45491	45494	45497	45499
45492	45495		

Total 842

"Patriot" Class
4-6-0   6P5F & 7P

*6P5F. Introduced 1930. Fowler 3-cyl. rebuild of L.N.W. "Claughton" Class (introduced 1912), retaining original wheels and other details.

Remainder. Introduced 1933. New locos. to Fowler design (45502–41 were officially considered as rebuilds).

†7P. Introduced 1946. Ivatt rebuild of Fowler locos. with larger taper boiler, new cylinders and double chimney.

Weight: Loco. $\begin{cases} 80 \text{ tons } 15 \text{ cwt.} \\ 80 \text{ tons } 15 \text{ cwt.*} \\ 82 \text{ tons } 0 \text{ cwt.†} \end{cases}$

Pressure: $\begin{cases} 200 \text{ lb. Su.} \\ 200 \text{ lb. Su.*} \\ 250 \text{ lb. Su.†} \end{cases}$

Cyls : $\begin{cases} (3) \ 18'' \times 26''. \\ (3) \ 18'' \times 26''.* \\ (3) \ 17'' \times 26''.† \end{cases}$

Driving Wheels: 6' 9".

T.E.: $\begin{cases} 26,520 \text{ lb.} \\ 26,520 \text{ lb.*} \\ 29,570 \text{ lb.†} \end{cases}$

Walschaerts valve gear. P.V.

45500*	Patriot
45501*	St. Dunstan's
45502	Royal Naval Division
45503	The Royal Leicestershire Regiment
45504	Royal Signals
45505	The Royal Army Ordnance Corps
45506	The Royal Pioneer Corps
45507	Royal Tank Corps
45508	
45509	The Derbyshire Yeomanry

45510	
45511	Isle of Man
45512†	Bunsen
45513	
45514†	Holyhead
45515	Caernarvon
45516	The Bedfordshire and Hertfordshire Regiment
45517	
45518	Bradshaw
45519	Lady Godiva
45520	Llandudno
45521†	Rhyl
45522†	Prestatyn
45523†	Bangor
45524	Blackpool
45525†	Colwyn Bay
45526†	Morecambe and Heysham
45527†	Southport
45528†	
45529†	Stephenson
45530†	Sir Frank Ree
45531†	Sir Frederick Harrison
45532†	Illustrious
45533	Lord Rathmore
45534†	E. Tootal Broadhurst
45535†	Sir Herbert Walker K.C.B.
45536†	Private W. Wood, V.C.
45537	Private E. Sykes, V.C.
45538	Giggleswick
45539	E. C. Trench
45540†	Sir Robert Turnbull
45541	Duke of Sutherland
45542	
45543	Home Guard
45544	
45545†	Planet
45546	Fleetwood
45547	
45548	Lytham St. Annes
45549	
45550	
45551	

Total 52

" Jubilee " Class

4-6-0   6P5F & 7P

6P5F. Introduced 1934. Stanier L.M.S. taper boiler development of the " Patriot " class.

*7P. Introduced 1942. Rebuilt with larger boiler and double chimney.

Weight: Loco. $\begin{cases} 79 \text{ tons } 11 \text{ cwt.} \\ 82 \text{ tons } 0 \text{ cwt.*} \end{cases}$

Pressure: $\begin{cases} 225 \text{ lb. Su.} \\ 250 \text{ lb. Su.*} \end{cases}$

Cyls.: (3) 17" × 26".

Driving Wheels: 6' 9".

T.E.: $\begin{cases} 26,610 \text{ lb.} \\ 29,570 \text{ lb.*} \end{cases}$

Walschaerts valve gear. P.V.

45552	Silver Jubilee
45553	Canada
45554	Ontario
45555	Quebec
45556	Nova Scotia
45557	New Brunswick
45558	Manitoba
45559	British Columbia
45560	Prince Edward Island
45561	Saskatchewan
45562	Alberta
45563	Australia
45564	New South Wales
45565	Victoria
45566	Queensland
45567	South Australia
45568	Western Australia
45569	Tasmania
45570	New Zealand
45571	South Africa
45572	Eire
45573	Newfoundland
45574	India
45575	Madras
45576	Bombay
45577	Bengal
45578	United Provinces
45579	Punjab
45580	Burma
45581	Bihar and Orissa
45582	Central Provinces
45583	Assam
45584	North West Frontier
45585	Hyderabad
45586	Mysore
45587	Baroda
45588	Kashmir
45589	Gwalior
45590	Travancore
45591	Udaipur
45592	Indore
45593	Kolhapur
45594	Bhopal
45595	Southern Rhodesia
45596	Bahamas
45597	Barbados
45598	Basutoland
45599	Bechuanaland
45600	Bermuda
45601	British Guiana
45602	British Honduras
45603	Solomon Islands
45604	Ceylon
45605	Cyprus
45606	Falkland Islands
45607	Fiji
45608	Gibraltar
45609	Gilbert and Ellice Islands
45610	Ghana
45611	Hong Kong
45612	Jamaica
45613	Kenya
45614	Leeward Islands
45615	Malay States
45616	Malta G.C.
45617	Mauritius
45618	New Hebrides
45619	Nigeria
45620	North Borneo
45621	Northern Rhodesia
45622	Nyasaland
45623	Palestine
45624	St. Helena
45625	Sarawak
45626	Seychelles
45627	Sierra Leone

45628	Somaliland
45629	Straits Settlements
45630	Swaziland
45631	Tanganyika
45632	Tonga
45633	Aden
45634	Trinidad
45635	Tobago
45636	Uganda
45638	Zanzibar
45639	Raleigh
45640	Frobisher
45641	Sandwich
45642	Boscawen
45643	Rodney
45644	Howe
45645	Collingwood
45646	Napier
45647	Sturdee
45648	Wemyss
45649	Hawkins
45650	Blake
45651	Shovell
45652	Hawke
45653	Barham
45654	Hood
45655	Keith
45656	Cochrane
45657	Tyrwhitt
45658	Keyes
45659	Drake
45660	Rooke
45661	Vernon
45662	Kempenfelt
45663	Jervis
45664	Nelson
45665	Lord Rutherford of Nelson
45666	Cornwallis
45667	Jellicoe
45668	Madden
45669	Fisher
45670	Howard of Effingham
45671	Prince Rupert
45672	Anson
45673	Keppel
45674	Duncan

45675	Hardy
45676	Codrington
45677	Beatty
45678	De Robeck
45679	Armada
45680	Camperdown
45681	Aboukir
45682	Trafalgar
45683	Hogue
45684	Jutland
45685	Barfleur
45686	St. Vincent
45687	Neptune
45688	Polyphemus
45689	Ajax
45690	Leander
45691	Orion
45692	Cyclops
45693	Agamemnon
45694	Bellerophon
45695	Minotaur
45696	Arethusa
45697	Achilles
45698	Mars
45699	Galatea
45700	Amethyst
45701	Conqueror
45702	Colossus
45703	Thunderer
45704	Leviathan
45705	Seahorse
45706	Express
45707	Valiant
45708	Resolution
45709	Implacable
45710	Irresistible
45711	Courageous
45712	Victory
45713	Renown
45714	Revenge
45715	Invincible
45716	Swiftsure
45717	Dauntless
45718	Dreadnought
45719	Glorious
45720	Indomitable
45721	Impregnable

45722	Defence
45723	Fearless
45724	Warspite
45725	Repulse
45726	Vindictive
45727	Inflexible
45728	Defiance
45729	Furious
45730	Ocean
45731	Perseverance
45732	Sanspareil
45733	Novelty
45734	Meteor
45735*	Comet
45736*	Phoenix
45737	Atlas
45738	Samson
45739	Ulster
45740	Munster
45741	Leinster
45742	Connaught

Total 190

" Royal Scot " Class
4-6-0   7P

Introduced 1943. Stanier rebuild of Fowler L.M.S locos. (introduced 1927) with taper boiler, new cylinders and double chimney.

*Introduced 1935. Stanier taper boiler rebuild with simple cylinders of experimental high pressure compound loco. No. 6399 *Fury*. (Introduced 1929.)

Weight: Loco. {83 tons. / 84 tons 1 cwt.*

Pressure: 250 lb. Su.

Cyls.: (3) 18″ × 26″.

Driving Wheels: 6′ 9″.

T.E.: 33,150 lb.

Walschaerts valve gear. P.V.

46100	Royal Scot
46101	Royal Scots Grey
46102	Black Watch
46103	Royal Scots Fusilier
46104	Scottish Borderer
46105	Cameron Highlander
46106	Gordon Highlander
46107	Argyll and Sutherland Highlander
46108	Seaforth Highlander
46109	Royal Engineer
46110	Grenadier Guardsman
46111	Royal Fusilier
46112	Sherwood Forester
46113	Cameronian
46114	Coldstream Guardsman
46115	Scots Guardsman
46116	Irish Guardsman
46117	Welsh Guardsman
46118	Royal Welch Fusilier
46119	Lancashire Fusilier
46120	Royal Inniskilling Fusilier
46121	Highland Light Infantry, City of Glasgow Regiment
46122	Royal Ulster Rifleman
46123	Royal Irish Fusilier
46124	London Scottish
46125	3rd Carabinier
46126	Royal Army Service Corps
46127	Old Contemptibles
46128	The Lovat Scouts
46129	The Scottish Horse
46130	The West Yorkshire Regiment
46131	The Royal Warwickshire Regiment
46132	The King's Regiment Liverpool
46133	The Green Howards
46134	The Cheshire Regiment
46135	The East Lancashire Regiment
46136	The Border Regiment
46137	The Prince of Wales's Volunteers (South Lancashire)
46138	The London Irish Rifleman
46139	The Welch Regiment

46140	The King's Royal Rifle Corps
46141	The North Staffordshire Regiment
46142	The York & Lancaster Regiment
46143	The South Staffordshire Regiment
46144	Honourable Artillery Company
46145	The Duke of Wellington's Regt. (West Riding)
46146	The Rifle Brigade
46147	The Northamptonshire Regiment
46148	The Manchester Regiment
46149	The Middlesex Regiment
46150	The Life Guardsman
46151	The Royal Horse Guardsman
46152	The King's Dragoon Guardsman
46153	The Royal Dragoon
46154	The Hussar
46155	The Lancer
46156	The South Wales Borderer
46157	The Royal Artilleryman
46158	The Loyal Regiment
46159	The Royal Air Force
46160	Queen Victoria's Rifleman
46161	King's Own
46162	Queen's Westminster Rifleman
46163	Civil Service Rifleman
46164	The Artists' Rifleman
46165	The Ranger (12th London Regt.)
46166	London Rifle Brigade
46167	The Hertfordshire Regiment
46168	The Girl Guide
46169	The Boy Scout
46170*	British Legion

Total 71

"Princess" Class

4-6-2   8P

*Introduced 1933. Stanier L.M.S. taper boiler design.

Remainder. Introduced 1935. Development of original design with alterations to valve gear, boiler and other details.

Weight: Loco. 104 tons 10 cwt.

Pressure: 250 lb. Su.

Cyls.: (4) 16¼" × 28".

Driving Wheels: 6' 6".

T.E.: 40,285 lb.

Walschaerts valve gear (inside valves operated by rocking shafts on No. 46205; remainder have four sets of valve gear). P.V.

46200*	The Princess Royal
46201*	Princess Elizabeth
46203	Princess Margaret Rose
46204	Princess Louise
46205	Princess Victoria
46206	Princess Marie Louise
46207	Princess Arthur of Connaught
46208	Princess Helena Victoria
46209	Princess Beatrice
46210	Lady Patricia
46211	Queen Maud
46212	Duchess of Kent

Total 12

"Coronation" Class

4-6-2   8P

Introduced 1937. Stanier L.M.S. enlargement of "Princess Royal" class. All except Nos. 46230-4/49-55 originally streamlined. (Streamlining removed from 1946.)

*Introduced 1947. Ivatt development with roller bearings and detail alterations.

Weight: Loco. { 105 tons 5 cwt.
{ 106 tons 8 cwt.*

93

Pressure: 250 lb. Su.
Cyls.: (4) 16¼" × 28".
Driving Wheels: 6' 9".
T.E.: 40,000 lb.
Walschaerts valve gear and rocking shafts. P.V.

46220	Coronation
46221	Queen Elizabeth
46222	Queen Mary
46223	Princess Alice
46224	Princess Alexandra
46225	Duchess of Gloucester
46226	Duchess of Norfolk
46227	Duchess of Devonshire
46228	Duchess of Rutland
46229	Duchess of Hamilton
46230	Duchess of Buccleuch
46231	Duchess of Atholl
46232	Duchess of Montrose
46233	Duchess of Sutherland
46234	Duchess of Abercorn
46235	City of Birmingham
46236	City of Bradford
46237	City of Bristol
46238	City of Carlisle
46239	City of Chester
46240	City of Coventry
46241	City of Edinburgh
46242	City of Glasgow
46243	City of Lancaster
46244	King George VI
46245	City of London
46246	City of Manchester
46247	City of Liverpool
46248	City of Leeds
46249	City of Sheffield
46250	City of Lichfield
46251	City of Nottingham
46252	City of Leicester
46253	City of St. Albans
46254	City of Stoke-on-Trent
46255	City of Hereford
46256*	Sir William A. Stanier, F.R.S.
46257*	City of Salford

Total 38

2-6-0　　　　　2

Introduced 1946. Ivatt L.M.S. taper boiler design.
Weight: Loco. 47 tons 2 cwt.
Pressure: 200 lb. Su.
Cyls.: $\begin{cases}(O) 16" \times 24". \\ (O) 16\frac{1}{2}" \times 24".* \end{cases}$
Driving Wheels: 5' 0".
T.E.: $\begin{cases}17,410 \text{ lb.} \\ 18,510 \text{ lb.*} \end{cases}$
Walschaerts valve gear. P.V.

46400	46434	46468*	46498*
46401	46435	46469*	46499*
46402	46436	46470*	46500*
46403	46437	46471*	46501*
46404	46438	46472*	46502*
46405	46439	46473*	46503*
46406	46440	46474*	46504*
46407	46441	46475*	46505*
46408	46442	46476*	46506*
46409	46443	46477*	46507*
46410	46444	46478*	46508*
46411	46445	46479*	46509*
46412	46446	46480*	46510*
46413	46447	46481*	46511*
46414	46448	46482*	46512*
46415	46449	46483*	46513*
46416	46450	46484*	46514*
46417	46451	46485*	46515*
46418	46452	46486*	46516*
46419	46453	46487*	46517*
46420	46454	46488*	46518*
46421	46455	46489*	46519*
46422	46456	46490*	46520*
46423	46457	46491*	46521*
46424	46458	46492*	46522*
46425	46459	46493*	46523*
46426	46460	46494*	46524*
46427	46461	46495*	46525*
46428	46462	46496*	46526*
46429	46463	46497*	46527*
46430	46464		
46431	46465*		
46432	46466*		
46433	46467*		

Total 128

94

0-4-0ST   0F

Introduced 1932. Kitson design prepared to Stanier's requirements for L.M.S.

*Introduced 1953. Extended side tanks and coal space.

Weight: { 33 tons 0 cwt.
{ 34 tons 0 cwt.*

Pressure: 160 lb.
Cyls.: (O) 15½" × 30".
Driving Wheels: 3' 10".
T.E.: 14,205 lb.

47000	47003	47006*	47008*
47001	47004	47007*	47009*
47002	47005*		

Total 10

0-6-0T   2F

Introduced 1928. Fowler L.M.S. short-wheelbase dock tanks.
Weight: 43 tons 12 cwt.
Pressure: 160 lb.
Cyls.: (O) 17" × 22".
Driving Wheels: 3' 11".
T.E.: 18,400 lb.
Walschaerts valve gear.

47160	47163	47166	47168
47161	47164	47167	47169
47162	47165		

Total 10

0-4-0T   Sentinel

Geared Sentinel locos.

Introduced 1929. Single-speed locos. for S. & D.J. (taken into L.M.S. stock 1930).
Weight: 27 tons 15 cwt.
Pressure: 275 lb. Su.
Cyls.: (4) 6¾" × 9".
Driving Wheels: 3' 1½".
T.E.: 15,500 lb.
Poppet valves.

47190   47191

Total 2

0-6-0T   3F

Introduced 1899. Johnson large Midland design, rebuilt with Belpaire firebox from 1919; fitted with condensing apparatus for London area.

*Introduced 1899. Non-condensing locos.
Weight: 48 tons 15 cwt.
Pressure: 160 lb.
Cyls.: 18" × 26".
Driving Wheels: 4' 7".
T.E.: 20,835 lb.

47200	47212	47226	47241
47201*	47213	47228	47246*
47202	47214	47229	47247
47203	47216	47230*	47248*
47204	47217	47231*	47250*
47205	47218	47235*	47254*
47207	47221	47236*	47255*
47209	47223	47238*	47257*
47210	47224	47239*	47259*
47211	47225		

Total 38

0-6-0T   3F

Introduced 1924. Post-grouping development of Midland design with detail alterations.

*Introduced 1929. Locos. built for S. & D.J. (taken into L.M.S. stock 1930).
†Push-and-pull fitted.
Weight: 49 tons 10 cwt.
Pressure: 160 lb.
Cyls.: 18" × 26".
Driving Wheels: 4' 7".
T.E.: 20,835 lb.

47260	47273	47286	47299
47261	47274	47287	47300
47262	47275	47288	47301
47263	47276	47289	47302
47264	47277	47290	47303
47265	47278	47291	47304
47266	47279	47292	47305
47267	47280	47293	47306
47268	47281	47294	47307
47269	47282	47295	47308
47270	47283	47296	47309
47271	47284	47297	47310*
47272	47285	47298	47311*

47312*	47359	47406	47453	47501	47546	47592S	47638
47313*	47360	47407	47454	47502	47547	47593	47639
47314*	47361	47408	47455	47503	47548	47594	47640
47315*	47362	47409	47457	47504	47549	47595	47641
47316*	47363	47410	47458	47505	47550	47596	47642
47317	47364	47411	47459	47506	47551	47597	47643
47318	47365	47412	47460	47507	47552	47598	47644
47319	47366	47413	47461	47508	47554	47599	47645
47320	47367	47414	47462	47509	47555	47600	47646
47321	47368	47415	47463	47510	47556	47601	47647
47322	47369	47416	47464	47511	47557	47602	47648
47323	47370	47417	47465	47512	47558	47603	47649
47324	47371	47418	47466	47513	47559	47604	47650
47325	47372	47419	47467	47514	47560	47605	47651
47326	47373	47420	47468	47515	47561	47606	47652
47327	47374	47421	47469	47516	47562	47607	47653
47328	47375	47422	47470	47517	47563	47608	47654
47329	47376	47423	47471	47518	47564	47609	47655†
47330	47377	47424	47472	47519	47565	47610	47656
47331	47378	47425	47473	47520	47566	47611	47657
47332	47379	47426	47474	47521	47567	47612	47658
47333	47380	47427	47475	47522	47568	47614	47659
47334	47381	47428	47476	47523	47569	47615	47660
47335	47382	47429	47477††	47524	47570	47616	47661
47336	47383	47430	47478†	47525	47571	47618	47662
47337	47384	47431	47479†	47526	47572	47619	47664
47338	47385	47432	47480†	47527	47573	47620	47665
47339	47386	47433	47481†	47528	47574	47621	47666
47340	47387	47434	47482	47529	47575	47622	47667
47341	47388	47435	47483	47530	47576	47623	47668
47342	47389	47436	47484	47531	47577	47624	47669
47343	47390	47437	47485	47532	47578	47625	47670
47344	47391	47438	47486	47533	47579	47626	47671
47345	47392	47439	47487	47534	47580	47627	47672
47346	47393	47440	47488	47535	47581	47628	47673
47347	47394	47441	47489	47536	47582	47629	47674
47348	47395	47442	47490	47537	47583	47630	47675
47349	47396	47443	47491	47538	47584	47631	47676
47350	47397	47444	47492	47539	47585	47632	47677
47351	47398	47445	47493	47540	47586	47633	47678
47352	47399	47446	47494	47541	47587	47634	47679
47353	47400	47447	47495	47542	47588	47635	47680
47354	47401	47448	47496	47543	47589	47636	47681†
47355	47402	47449	47497	47544	47590	47637	
47356	47403	47450	47498	47545	47591		
47357	47404	47451	47499				
47358	47405	47452	47500				Total 417

96

2-8-0   8F

Introduced 1935. Stanier L.M.S. taper
  boiler design.
Weight: Loco. 72 tons 2 cwt.
Pressure: 225 lb. Su.
Cyls.: (O) $18\frac{1}{2}'' \times 28''$.
Driving Wheels: 4' $8\frac{1}{2}''$.
T.E.: 32,440 lb.
Walschaerts valve gear. P.V.

48000	48063	48107	48144	48181	48248	48295	48345
48001	48064	48108	48145	48182	48249	48296	48346
48002	48065	48109	48146	48183	48250	48297	48347
48003	48067	48110	48147	48184	48251	48301	48348
48004	48069	48111	48148	48185	48252	48302	48349
48005	48070	48112	48149	48186	48253	48303	48350
48006	48073	48113	48150	48187	48254	48304	48351
48007	48074	48114	48151	48188	48255	48305	48352
48008	48075	48115	48152	48189	48256	48306	48353
48009	48076	48116	48153	48190	48257	48307	48354
48010	48077	48117	48154	48191	48258	48308	48355
48011	48078	48118	48155	48192	48259	48309	48356
48012	48079	48119	48156	48193	48260	48310	48357
48016	48080	48120	48157	48194	48261	48311	48358
48017	48081	48121	48158	48195	48262	48312	48359
48018	48082	48122	48159	48196	48263	48313	48360
48020	48083	48123	48160	48197	48264	48314	48361
48024	48084	48124	48161	48198	48265	48315	48362
48026	48085	48125	48162	48199	48266	48316	48363
48027	48088	48126	48163	48200	48267	48317	48364
48029	48089	48127	48164	48201	48268	48318	48365
48033	48090	48128	48165	48202	48269	48319	48366
48035	48092	48129	48166	48203	48270	48320	48367
48036	48093	48130	48167	48204	48271	48321	48368
48037	48094	48131	48168	48205	48272	48322	48369
48039	48095	48132	48169	48206	48273	48323	48370
48045	48096	48133	48170	48207	48274	48324	48371
48046	48097	48134	48171	48208	48275	48325	48372
48050	48098	48135	48172	48209	48276	48326	48373
48053	48099	48136	48173	48210	48277	48327	48374
48054	48100	48137	48174	48211	48278	48328	48375
48055	48101	48138	48175	48212	48279	48329	48376
48056	48102	48139	48176	48213	48280	48330	48377
48057	48103	48140	48177	48214	48281	48331	48378
48060	48104	48141	48178	48215	48282	48332	48379
48061	48105	48142	48179	48216	48283	48333	48380
48062	48106	48143	48180	48217	48284	48334	48381
				48218	48285	48335	48382
				48219	48286	48336	48383
				48220	48287	48337	48384
				48221	48288	48338	48385
				48222	48289	48339	48386
				48223	48290	48340	48387
				48224	48291	48341	48388
				48225	48292	48342	48389
				48246	48293	48343	48390
				48247	48294	48344	48391

48392	48439	48500	48547	48634	48670	48706	48742
48393	48440	48501	48548	48635	48671	48707	48743
48394	48441	48502	48549	48636	48672	48708	48744
48395	48442	48503	48550	48637	48673	48709	48745
48396	48443	48504	48551	48638	48674	48710	48746
48397	48444	48505	48552	48639	48675	48711	48747
48398	48445	48506	48553	48640	48676	48712	48748
48399	48446	48507	48554	48641	48677	48713	48749
48400	48447	48508	48555	48642	48678	48714	48750
48401	48448	48509	48556	48643	48679	48715	48751
48402	48449	48510	48557	48644	48680	48716	48752
48403	48450	48511	48558	48645	48681	48717	48753
48404	48451	48512	48559	48646	48682	48718	48754
48405	48452	48513	48600	48647	48683	48719	48755
48406	48453	48514	48601	48648	48684	48720	48756
48407	48454	48515	48602	48649	48685	48721	48757
48408	48455	48516	48603	48650	48686	48722	48758
48409	48456	48517	48604	48651	48687	48723	48759
48410	48457	48518	48605	48652	48688	48724	48760
48411	48458	48519	48606	48653	48689	48725	48761
48412	48459	48520	48607	48654	48690	48726	48762
48413	48460	48521	48608	48655	48691	48727	48763
48414	48461	48522	48609	48656	48692	48728	48764
48415	48462	48523	48610	48657	48693	48729	48765
48416	48463	48524	48611	48658	48694	48730	48766
48417	48464	48525	48612	48659	48695	48731	48767
48418	48465	48526	48613	48660	48696	48732	48768
48419	48466	48527	48614	48661	48697	48733	48769
48420	48467	48528	48615	48662	48698	48734	48770
48421	48468	48529	48616	48663	48699	48735	48771
48422	48469	48530	48617	48664	48700	48736	48772
48423	48470	48531	48618	48665	48701	48737	48773
48424	48471	48532	48619	48666	48702	48738	48774
48425	48472	48533	48620	48667	48703	48739	48775
48426	48473	48534	48621	48668	48704	48740	
48427	48474	48535	48622	48669	48705	48741	
48428	48475	48536	48623				
48429	48476	48537	48624				
48430	48477	48538	48625				
48431	48478	48539	48626				
48432	48479	48540	48627				
48433	48490	48541	48628				
48434	48491	48542	48629				
48435	48492	48543	48630				
48436	48493	48544	48631				
48437	48494	48545	48632				
48438	48495	48546	48633				

Total 666

0-8-0   7F

Introduced 1936. L.N.W. G2a Class.
Bowen-Cooke G1 superheated design
of 1912, rebuilt with G2 boiler and
Belpaire firebox.
Weight: Loco. 62 tons 0 cwt.
Pressure: 175 lb. Su.
Cyls.: $20\frac{1}{2}'' \times 24''$.
Driving Wheels: $4' 5\frac{1}{2}''$.
T.E.: 28,045 lb.
Joy valve gear. P.V.

48895	49079	49164	49301
48898	49081	49173	49304
48905	49082	49177	49306
48915	49087	49180	49303
48922	49093	49181	49310
48926	49094	49191	49311
48927	49099	49196	49313
48930	49104	49198	49314
48932	49105	49199	49315
48942	49106	49200	49321
48943	49109	49203	49323
48945	49112	49209	49327
48950	49114	49210	49328
48951	49115	49216	49330
48953	49116	49224	49335
48964	49117	49226	49340
49002	49119	49228	49342
49007	49120	49229	49343
49003	49122	49234	49344
49009	49125	49240	49348
49010	49126	49243	49350
49018	49129	49245	49352
49020	49130	49246	49355
49021	49132	49249	49357
49023	49134	49252	49361
49025	49137	49262	49366
49027	49139	49266	49368
49034	49141	49267	49373
49037	49142	49268	49375
49044	49143	49270	49377
49045	49144	49275	49378
49048	49147	49277	49381
49049	49149	49278	49382
49061	49150	49281	49386
49063	49153	49287	49387
49064	49154	49288	49391
49070	49155	49289	49392
49077	49158	49293	49394
49078	49160		

Total 154

0-8-0   7F

Introduced 1921. Development of L.N.W. G2 Class. Bowen-Cooke G1 superheated design of 1912 with higher pressure boiler. Many later rebuilt with Belpaire firebox.
Weight: Loco. 62 tons 0 cwt.
Pressure: 175 lb. Su.
Cyls.: 20½" × 24".
Driving Wheels: 4' 5½".
T.E.: 28,045 lb.
Joy valve gear. P.V.

49395	49410	49425	49440
49396	49411	49426	49441
49397	49412	49427	49442
49398	49413	49428	49443
49399	49414	49429	49444
49400	49415	49430	49445
49401	49416	49431	49446
49402	49417	49432	49447
49403	49418	49433	49448
49404	49419	49434	49449
49405	49420	49435	49450
49406	49421	49436	49451
49407	49422	49437	49452
49408	49423	49438	49453
49409	49424	49439	49454

Total 60

0-8-0   7F

Introduced 1929. Fowler L.M.S. design, developed from L.N.W. G2.
Weight: Loco. 60 tons 15 cwt.
Pressure: 200 lb. Su.
Cyls.: 19½" × 26".
Driving Wheels: 4' 8½".
T.E.: 29,745 lb.
Walschaerts valve gear. P.V.

49505	49544	49618	49662
49508	49578	49624	49667
49509	49582	49627	49668
49511	49586	49637	49674
49515	49592	49640	

Total 19

2-4-2T   2P

Introduced 1889. Aspinall L. & Y. Class 5 with 2 tons coal capacity.
*Introduced 1890. Locos. built or rebuilt with smaller cylinders.

99

†Introduced 1898. Locos. with longer
tanks and 4 tons coal capacity. Rebuilt
1910 with Belpaire firebox and extended smokebox.

Weight: {
55 tons 19 cwt.
55 tons 19 cwt.*
59 tons 3 cwt.†
}
Pressure: 180 lb.
Cyls.: {
$17\frac{1}{2}'' \times 26''$.*
$18'' \times 26''$. (Remainder)
}
Driving Wheels: 5' 8".
T.E.: {
18,360 lb.*
18,955 lb. (Remainder)
}
Joy valve gear.

50647	50721	50781	50850†
50712	50746	50795*	

Total 7

0-4-0ST 0F

Introduced 1891. Aspinall L. & Y.
Class 21.
Weight: 21 tons 5 cwt.
Pressure: 160 lb.
Cyls.: (O) $13'' \times 18''$.
Driving Wheels: 3' $0\frac{3}{4}''$.
T.E.: 11,335 lb.

51204	51218	51229	51241
51206	51221	51231	51244
51207	51222	51232	51246
51217	51227	51237	51253

Total 16

0-6-0ST 2F

Introduced 1891. Aspinall rebuild of
L. & Y. Barton Wright Class 23 0-6-0.
Originally introduced 1877.
Weight: 43 tons 17 cwt.
Pressure: 140 lb.
Cyls.: $17\frac{1}{2}'' \times 26''$.
Driving Wheels: 4' 6".
T.E.: 17,545 lb.

See also Service locomotives.

51319	51343	51371	51404
51336	51358	51397	51408

51412S	51441	51457	51496
51413	51444S	51458	51497
51419	51445	51484	51498
51429S	51446S	51486	51524

Total 29

0-6-0T 1F

Introduced 1897. Aspinall L. & Y.
Class 24 dock tanks.
Weight: 50 tons 0 cwt.
Pressure: 140 lb.
Cyls.: (O) $17'' \times 24''$.
Driving Wheels: 4' 0".
T.E.: 15,285 lb.
Allan straight link valve gear.

51537   51544

Total 2

0-6-0 2F

Introduced 1887. Barton Wright
L. & Y. Class 25.
Weight: Loco. 39 tons 1 cwt.
Pressure: 140 lb.
Cyls.: $17\frac{1}{2}'' \times 26''$.
Driving Wheels: 4' 6".
T.E.: 17,545 lb.

52044

Total 1

0-6-0 3F

Introduced 1889. Aspinall L. & Y. Class
27. Nos. 52515–27 built superheated
with roundtop firebox and extended
smokebox, later rebuilt with saturated boiler and short smokebox.
*Introduced 1911. Rebuilt with Belpaire
firebox and extended smokebox.
Weight: Loco. 42 tons 3 cwt.
Pressure: 180 lb.
Cyls.: $18'' \times 26''$.
Driving Wheels: 5' 1".
T.E.: {
21,130 lb.
21,130 lb.*
}
Joy valve gear.

52089	52095	52119	52129
52093S	52108	52121	52133

52135*	52237	52319	52438*
52139	52240	52322	52441S
52140*	52244	52341	52443
52141	52248	52345S	52445*
52154*	52252	52348	52452
52161*	52260	52351	52455
52162*S	52268	52355	52456
52171	52269	52378	52458
52179	52270	52389	52459S
52182	52271	52393	52461
52183	52275	52400*	52464S
52201*	52278	52410	52466
52207S	52289	52411	52515
52218S	52290	52413*	52523
52225	52305	52415	52526
52230	52311	52429	52527
52232	52312*S	52431*	

Total 75

2-8-0   7F

Introduced 1914. Fowler design for S. & D.J.
(All taken into L.M.S. stock, 1930.)
Weight: Loco. 64 tons 15 cwt.
Pressure: 190 lb. Su.
Cyls.: (O) 21″ × 28″.
Driving Wheels: 4′ 8¼″.
T.E.: 35,295 lb.
Walschaerts valve gear. P.V.

53800	53803	53806	53809
53801	53804	53807	53810
53802	53805	53808	

Total 11

4-4-0   3P

Introduced 1916. Pickersgill Caledonian " 113 " and " 928 " classes.
Weight: Loco. 61 tons 5 cwt.
Pressure: 180 lb. Su.
Cyls.: 20″ × 26″.
Driving Wheels: 6′ 6″.
T.E.: 20,400 lb.
P.V.

54461	54465	54469	54473
54462	54466	54470	54474
54463	54467	54471	54475
54464	54468	54472	54476

Total 16

4-4-0   3P

Introduced 1920. Pickersgill Caledonian " 72 " class.
Weight: Loco. 61 tons 5 cwt.
Pressure: 180 lb. Su.
Cyls.: 20½″ × 26″.
Driving Wheels: 6′ 6″.
T.E.: 21,435 lb.
P.V.

54477	54486	54494	54502
54478	54487	54495	54503
54479	54488	54496	54504
54480	54489	54497	54505
54482	54490	54498	54506
54483	54491	54499	54507
54484	54492	54500	54508
54485	54493	54501	

Total 31

0-4-4T   2P

*Introduced 1895. McIntosh Caledonian " 19 " class, with railed coal bunker.
†Introduced 1897. McIntosh " 92 " class, developed from " 29 " class with larger tanks and highsided coal bunker (both classes originally fitted for condensing on Glasgow Central Low Level lines).
Weight: { 53 tons 16 cwt.*
       { 53 tons 19 cwt.
Pressure: 180 lb.
Cyls.: 18″ × 26″.
Driving Wheels: 5′ 9″.
T.E.: 18,680 lb.

55124*   55126†

Total 2

0-4-4T   2P

Introduced 1900. McIntosh Caledonian " 439 " or " Standard Passenger " class.
*Introduced 1915. Pickersgill locos. with detail alterations.
Weight: { 53 tons 19 cwt.
       { 57 tons 12 cwt.*
Pressure: 180 lb.
Cyls.: 18″ × 26″.
Driving Wheels: 5′ 9″.
T.E.: 18,680 lb.

55165	55202	55216	55227*
55167	55203	55217	55228*
55169	55204	55218	55229*
55173	55206	55219	55230*
55185	55207	55220	55231*
55189	55208	55221	55232*
55195	55209	55222	55233*
55198	55210	55223	55234*
55199	55211	55224	55235*
55200	55214	55225	55236*
55201	55215	55226	

Total 43

0-4-4T   2P

Introduced 1922. Pickersgill Caledonian
"431" class (developed from "439"
class) with cast-iron front buffer
beam for banking.
Weight: 57 tons 17 cwt.
Pressure: 180 lb.
Cyls.: $18\frac{1}{4}'' \times 26''$.
Driving Wheels: 5' 9".
T.E.: 19,200 lb.

55237	55238	55239	55240

Total 4

0-4-4T   2P

Introduced 1925. Post-Grouping devel-
opment of Caledonian "439" class.
Weight: 59 tons 12 cwt.
Pressure: 180 lb.
Cyls.: $18\frac{1}{4}'' \times 26''$.
Driving Wheels: 5' 9".
T.E.: 19,200 lb.

55260	55263	55266	55268
55261	55264	55267	55269
55262	55265		

Total 10

0-4-0ST   0F

Introduced 1885. Drummond and
McIntosh Caledonian "Pugs."
Weight: 27 tons 7 cwt.
Pressure: 160 lb.
Cyls.: (O) $14'' \times 20''$.
Driving Wheels: 3' 8".
T.E.: 12,115 lb.

56025S	56029	56032S	56038
56027S	56031	56035	56039

Total 8

0-6-0T   2F

Introduced 1911. McIntosh Caledonian
dock shunters, "498" class.
Weight: 47 tons 15 cwt.
Pressure: 160 lb.
Cyls.: (O) $17'' \times 22''$.
Driving Wheels: 4' 0".
T.E.: 18,015 lb.

56151	56158	56166	56170
56152	56159	56167	56171
56153	56160	56168	56172
56154	56163	56169	56173
56156	56165		

Total 18

0-6-0T   3F

Introduced 1895. McIntosh Caledonian
"29" and "782" classes (56232-9
originally condensing).
Weight: 47 tons 15 cwt.
Pressure: 160 lb.
Cyls.: $18'' \times 26''$.
Driving Wheels: 4' 6".
T.E.: 21,215 lb.

56232	56287	56321	56349
56235	56289	56322	56352
56239	56290	56324	56356
56240	56291	56325	56359
56241	56292	56326	56360
56242	56295	56327	56361
56245	56296	56331	56362
56246	56298	56332	56363
56252	56300	56333	56364
56256	56302	56335	56365
56259	56304	56336	56367
56260	56305	56337	56368
56264	56308	56338	56370
56266	56309	56340	56371
56269	56310	56341	56372
56278	56312	56343	56373
56279	56313	56344	56374
56285	56316	56347	56376
56286	56318	56348	

Total 75

0-6-0   2F

Introduced 1883. Drummond Caledonian "Standard Goods"; later additions by Lambie and McIntosh.
*Some rebuilt with L.M.S. boiler.

Weight: Loco. $\begin{cases} 41 \text{ tons } 6 \text{ cwt.} \\ 42 \text{ tons } 4 \text{ cwt.*} \end{cases}$

Pressure: 180 lb.
Cyls.: 18" × 26".
Driving Wheels: 5' 0".
T.E.: 21,480 lb.

57232	57271	57338	57389
57233	57273	57339	57392
57236	57274	57340	57398
57237	57275	57341	57404
57238	57276	57345	57407
57239	57278	57347	57411
57240	57279	57348	57414
57241	57284	57349	57416
57242	57285	57350	57417
57243	57287	57353	57418
57244	57288	57354	57419
57245	57291	57355	57424
57246	57292	57356	57426
57247	57295	57357	57429
57249	57296	57359	57431
57250	57299	57360	57432
57251	57300	57361	57434
57252	57302	57362	57435
57253	57303	57363	57436
57254	57307	57364	57441
57256	57309	57365	57444
57257	57311	57366	57445
57258	57314	57367	57446
57259	57317	57369	57447
57261	57319	57370	57448
57262	57321	57373	57451
57263	57324	57375	57461
57264	57325	57377	57462
57265	57326	57378	57463
57266	57328	57383	57465
57267	57329	57384	57470
57268	57331	57385	57472
57269	57335	57386	57473
57270	57336		

Total 134

0-6-0   3F

Introduced 1899. McIntosh Caledonian "812" (Nos. 57550–57623) and "652" (remainder) classes.
Weight: Loco. 45 tons 14 cwt.
Pressure: 180 lb.
Cyls.: 18½" × 26".
Driving Wheels: 5' 0".
T.E.: 22,690 lb.

57550	57575	57600	57622
57552	57576	57601	57623
57553	57577	57602	57625
57554	57579	57603	57626
57555	57580	57604	57627
57557	57581	57605	57628
57558	57583	57607	57630
57559	57585	57608	57631
57560	57586	57609	57632
57562	57587	57611	57633
57563	57590	57612	57634
57564	57591	57613	57635
57565	57592	57614	57637
57566	57593	57615	57638
57568	57594	57617	57640
57569	57595	57618	57642
57570	57596	57619	57643
57571	57597	57620	57644
57572	57599	57621	57645

Total 76

0-6-0   3F

Introduced 1918. Pickersgill Caledonian "294" class (superheated) and "670" classes.
Weight: Loco. 50 tons 13 cwt.
Pressure: 180 lb. Su.
Cyls.: 18½" × 26".
Driving Wheels: 5' 0".
T.E.: 22,690 lb.
P.V.

57650	57661	57670	57682
57651	57663	57671	57684
57652	57665	57672	57686
57653	57666	57673	57688
57654	57667	57674	57689
57655	57668	57679	57690
57658	57669	57681	57691
57659			

Total 29

0-4-4T   IP

*Introduced 1889. Johnson Midland design of 1881 with larger cylinders and higher boiler pressure. Rebuilt with Belpaire firebox.
†Introduced 1895. Final Johnson 0-4-4T design, with higher-pitched boiler and larger tanks, later rebuilt with Belpaire firebox.
Push-and-pull fitted.
Weight: 53 tons 4 cwt.
Pressure: 150 lb.
Cyls.: $\begin{cases} 18'' \times 24''.^* \\ 17'' \times 24''.† \end{cases}$
Driving Wheels: 5' 4".
T E.: $\begin{cases} 18,225 \text{ lb.}^* \\ 16,255 \text{ lb.}† \end{cases}$

58065* 58085† 58086†

Total 3

0-6-0   2F

*Introduced 1875. Johnson Midland 4' 11" design with round top firebox.
†Introduced 1917. Johnson 4' 11" design rebuilt with Belpaire firebox.
§Introduced 1917. Johnson Midland 5' 3" design rebuilt with Belpaire firebox.
Weight: Loco. Various—
37 tons 12 cwt. to 40 tons 3 cwt.
Pressure: 160 lb.
Cyls.: 18" × 26".
Driving Wheels: $\begin{cases} 4' 11''.^* \\ 4' 11''.† \\ 5' 3''.§ \end{cases}$
T.E.: $\begin{cases} 19,420 \text{ lb.}^* \\ 19,420 \text{ lb.}† \\ 18,185 \text{ lb.}§ \end{cases}$

58115†	58137†	58168†	58186†
58116†	58138†	58169†	58190§
58118†	58143†	58170†	58191§
58119†	58144†	58171†	58197§
58120†	58146†	58173†	58198§
58122†	58148†	58174†	58199§
58123†	58153†	58175†	58204§
58124†	58158†	58177†	58209§
58128†	58160†	58178†	58213§
58130†	58163†	58181†	58214§
58131†	58165†	58182†	58215§
58132†	58166†	58183†	58217§
58135†	58167†	58185†	58218§

58219§	58260§	58283§	58295§
58220§	58261§	58287§	58298§
58221§	58271§	58291§	58305§
58228§	58279§	58293§	58308§
58246*	58281§		

Total 70

0-6-0T   2F

Introduced 1879. Park North London design.
Weight: 45 tons 10 cwt.
Pressure: 160 lb.
Cyls.: (O) 17" × 24".
Driving Wheels: 4' 4".
T.E.: 18,140 lb.

58850

Total 1

4-2-2

Introduced 1886. Neilson & Co. design for the Caledonian Railway incorporating Drummond details.
Weight: Engine and Tender: 75 tons.
Pressure: 150 lb.
Cyls.: 18" × 26".
Driving Wheels: 7' 0".
T.E.: 12,785 lb.

123   **Total 1**

Withdrawn as L.M.S. No. 14010 in 1935. Returned to service for special use 1958.

SERVICE LOCOS.

Details of Diesel Service Locomotives are shown in ABC of British Railways Diesels and the Diesel section of the Combined Volume of ABC of British Railways Locomotives.

0-4-0   Diesel

E.D.I	E.D.4	E.D.6
E.D.2	E.D.5	E.D.7
E.D.3		

0-4-0 (3′0″ gauge)   Diesel

E.D.10

0-4-0 (2′ 6″ gauge)   Diesel

ZM 32

0-6-0ST   2F

Introduced 1870. Webb version of Ramsbottom " Special Tank."

Weight: 34 tons 10 cwt.

Pressure: 140 lb.

Cyls.: 17″ × 24″.

Driving Wheels: 4′ 5½″.

T.E.: 17,005 lb.

C.D.3 Wolverton Carriage Works
C.D.6   ,,   ,,   ,,
C.D.7   ,,   ,,   ,,
C.D.8 Earlestown, Wolverton C.W.

0-6-0ST   2F

For details see Nos. 51319-51524.

| 11304 | 11324 | 11368 | 11394 |
| 11305 | | | |

CHIEF MECHANICAL ENGINEERS

BRITISH RAILWAYS (L.M. Region)

H. G. Ivatt ... 1948–1951

L.M.S.

George Hughes	1923–1925	Sir William Stanier	...	1932–1944
Sir Henry Fowler ...	1925–1931	Charles E. Fairburn	...	1944–1945
E. H. J. Lemon	1931–1932	H. G. Ivatt	...	1945–1947
(Sir Ernest Lemon)				

LOCOMOTIVE SUPERINTENDENTS AND C.M.E.'S—L.M.S. CONSTITUENT COMPANIES

CALEDONIAN RAILWAY

Robert Sinclair (First loco. engineer)*	1847–1856
Benjamin Connor	1856–1876
George Brittain ...	1876–1882
Dugald Drummond ...	1882–1890
Hugh Smellie ...	1890
J. Lambie	1890–1895
J. F. McIntosh ...	1895–1914
William Pickersgill ...	1914–1923

L. & Y.R.

Sir John Hawkshaw (Consultant),*		
Hurst and Jenkins successively to 1868		
W. Hurst	...	1868–1876
W. Barton Wright ...		1876–1886
John A. F. Aspinall ...		1886–1899
H. A. Hoy	...	1899–1904
George Hughes ...		1904–1921

The L. & Y. amalgamated with L.N.W.R. as from January 1st, 1922.

FURNESS RAILWAY

R. Mason	1890–1897
W. F. Pettigrew ...	1897–1918
D. J. Rutherford ...	1918–1923

GLASGOW AND SOUTH WESTERN RAILWAY

Patrick Stirling ...	1853–1866
James Stirling ...	1866–1878
Hugh Smellie ...	1878–1890
James Manson ...	1890–1912
Peter Drummond ...	1912–1918
R. H. Whitelegg ...	1918–1923

L.N.W.R.

Francis Trevithick and J. E. McConnell, first loco. engineers, 1846, with Alexander Allan largely responsible for design at Crewe.*

John Ramsbottom ...	...	1857–1871
Francis William Webb ...		1871–1903
George Whale ...		1903–1909
Charles John Bowen-Cooke ...		1909–1920
Capt. Hewitt Pearson Montague Beames ...		1920–1921
George Hughes ...		1922

HIGHLAND RAILWAY

William Stroudley (First loco. engineer) ...	1866–1869
David Jones	1869–1896
Peter Drummond ...	1896–1911
F. G. Smith	1912–1915
C. Cumming	1915–1923

L.T. & S.R.

Thomas Whitelegg	1880–1910
Robert Harben Whitelegg	1910–1912

(L.T. & S.R. absorbed by M.R., control of locos. transferred to Derby as from August, 1912.)

---

* Exclusive of previous service with constituent company.

LOCOMOTIVE SUPERINTENDENTS AND C.M.E.'S (continued)

MARYPORT & CARLISLE

Hugh Smellie	... ...	1870–1878
J. Campbell	...	1878–
William Coulthard	... *	–1904
J. B. Adamson	... ...	1904–1923

MIDLAND RAILWAY

Matthew Kirtley (First loco. engineer)	...	1844–1873
Samuel Waite Johnson		1873–1903
Richard Mountford Deeley		1903–1909
Henry Fowler	... ...	1909–1923

SOMERSET AND DORSET JOINT RAILWAY

Until leased by Mid. and L. & S. W. (as from 1st November, 1875) locomotives were bought from outside builders, principally George England of Hatcham Iron Works, S.E. After the above date, Derby and its various Loco. Supts. and C.M.E.'s have acted for S. & D.J. aided by a resident Loco. Supt. stationed at Highbridge Works.

NORTH STAFFORDSHIRE RAILWAY

L. Clare	... ...	1876–1882
L. Longbottom	... ...	1882–1902
J. H. Adams	... ...	1902–1915
J. A. Hookham	... ...	1915–1923

W. Angus was Loco. Supt. at Stoke prior to 1876. No earlier records can be traced.

WIRRAL

Eric G. Barker	... ...	1892–1902
T. B. Hunter	... ...	1903–1923

Barker of the Wirral Railway is noteworthy for originating the 4-4-4 tank type in this country (1896).

NORTH LONDON RAILWAY

(Worked by L. & N.W. by agreement dated December, 1908.)

William Adams	... ...	1853–1873
J. C. Park	... ...	1873–1893
Henry J. Pryce	... ...	1893–1908

* Date of actual entry into office not known.

HISTORIC LOCOMOTIVES PRESERVED IN STORE

Type	Originating Company	Pre-Grouping No.	L.M.S. No.	Name	Place of Preservation
4-2-2	M.R.	118	(673)	—	Derby
2-4-0	M.R.	158A	—	—	Derby
*4-4-0	M.R.	(1000)	(1000)	—	Crewe
4-4-2T	L.T. & S.	80	(2148)	Thundersley	Derby
2-2-2	L.N.W.	(49)	—	Columbine	York Museum
2-2-2	L.N.W.	3020	—	Cornwall	Crewe
2-4-0	L.N.W.	790	(5031)	Hardwicke	Crewe
0-4-0ST	L.N.W.	1439	—	—	Crewe
†0-4-0T	L.N.W.	—	—	Pet	Crewe
2-4-2T	L. & Y.	1008	(10621)	—	Horwich
0-4-0	F.R.	3	—	Coppernob	Horwich
0-4-2	Liverpool & Manchester	—	—	Lion	Crewe
4-6-0	H.R.	103	(17916)	—	St. Rollox
‡4-4-0	H.R.	(2)	(14398)	Ben Alder	Boat of Garten

The unbracketed numbers are the ones at present carried by the locos.
* Present number 41000.
† 18 in. gauge works shunter.
‡ Present number 54398.

NUMERICAL LIST OF ENGINES

The code given in smaller bold type at the head of each class, e.g. "4MT" denotes its British Railways power classification.
The numbers of locomotives in service have been checked to February 28th, 1959.

4-6-2   8P6F   Class A4

Introduced 1935. Gresley streamlined design with corridor tender (except those marked †). All fitted with double blastpipe and chimney.
*Inside cylinder reduced to 17".
Weight: Loco.   102 tons 19 cwt.
Tender $\begin{cases} 64 \text{ tons 19 cwt.} \\ 60 \text{ tons 7 cwt.†} \end{cases}$
Pressure: 250 lb. P.V.
Cyls.: $\begin{cases} (3) \ 18\frac{1}{2}'' \times 26''. \\ (2) \ 18\frac{1}{2}'' \times 26'' \ (1) \ 17'' \times 26''.* \end{cases}$
Driving Wheels: 6' 8".
T.E.: $\begin{cases} 35,455 \text{ lb.} \\ 33,616 \text{ lb.*} \end{cases}$
Walschaerts valve gear and derived motion. P.V.

60001† Sir Ronald Matthews
60002† Sir Murrough Wilson
60003 Andrew K. McCosh
60004 William Whitelaw
60005† Sir Charles Newton
60006† Sir Ralph Wedgwood
60007 Sir Nigel Gresley
60008† Dwight D. Eisenhower
60009 Union of South Africa
60010 Dominion of Canada
60011 Empire of India
60012* Commonwealth of Australia
60013 Dominion of New Zealand
60014 Silver Link
60015 Quicksilver
60016† Silver King
60017 Silver Fox
60018† Sparrow Hawk
60019† Bittern
60020*†Guillemot
60021 Wild Swan
60022 Mallard
60023† Golden Eagle
60024 Kingfisher
60025 Falcon

60026† Miles Beevor
60027 Merlin
60028 Walter K. Whigham
60029 Woodcock
60030 Golden Fleece
60031* Golden Plover
60032 Gannet
60033 Seagull
60034 Lord Faringdon

Total 34

4-6-2   7P6F   Class A3

Introduced 1927. Development of Gresley G.N. 180 lb. Pacific (introduced 1922, L.N.E.R. A1, later A10) with 220 lb. pressure (prototype and others rebuilt from A10). Some have G.N.-type tender with coal rails†, remainder L.N.E.R. pattern.
*Double blast pipe and chimney.
Weight: Loco.   96 tons 5 cwt.
Tender $\begin{cases} 56 \text{ tons 6 cwt.†} \\ 57 \text{ tons 18 cwt.} \end{cases}$
Pressure: 220 lb. Su.
Cyls.: (3) 19" × 26".
Driving Wheels: 6' 8".
T.E.: 32,910 lb.
Walschaerts valve gear and derived motion. P.V.

60035* Windsor Lad
60036* Colombo
60037* Hyperion
60038 Firdaussi
60039 Sandwich
60040 Cameronian
60041 Salmon Trout
60042* Singapore
60043* Brown Jack
60044 Melton
60045 Lemberg
60046* Diamond Jubilee
60047 Donovan
60048 Doncaster
60049* Galtee More
60050 Persimmon

60051	Blink Bonny
60052	Prince Palatine
60053*	Sansovino
60054*	Prince of Wales
60055*	Woolwinder
60056	Centenary
60057*	Ormonde
60058*	Blair Athol
60059*	Tracery
60060	The Tetrarch
60061*	Pretty Polly
60062*	Minoru
60063*	Isinglass
60064	Tagalie
60065*	Knight of Thistle
60066*	Merry Hampton
60067	Ladas
60068	Sir Visto
60069	Sceptre
60070	Gladiateur
60071*	Tranquil
60072	Sunstar
60073*	St. Gatien
60074	Harvester
60075	St. Frusquin
60076	Galopin
60077	The White Knight
60078	Night Hawk
60079	Bayardo
60080	Dick Turpin
60081*	Shotover
60082	Neil Gow
60083	Sir Hugo
60084*	Trigo
60085*	Manna
60086	Gainsborough
60087*	Blenheim
60088	Book Law
60089	Felstead
60090*	Grand Parade
60091	Captain Cuttle
60092*	Fairway
60093	Coronach
60094	Colorado
60095*	Flamingo
60096*	Papyrus
60097*	Humorist

60098	Spion Kop
60099*	Call Boy
60100*	Spearmint
60101	Cicero
60102	Sir Frederick Banbury
60103*	Flying Scotsman
60104	Solario
60105*	Victor Wild
60106*	Flying Fox
60107*	Royal Lancer
60108	Gay Crusader
60109*	Hermit
60110	Robert the Devil
60111	Enterprise
60112*	St. Simon

Total 78

4-6-2   8P6F   Class A1

A1/1* Introduced 1945. Thompson rebuild of A10.
A1 Peppercorn development of A1/1 for new construction.
A1† Fitted with roller bearings.
Weight: Loco. { 101 tons.*
{ 104 tons 2 cwt.
Tender 60 tons 7 cwt.
Pressure: 250 lb. Su.
Cyls.: (3) 19″ × 26″.
Driving Wheels: 6′ 8″.
T.E.: 37,400 lb.
Walschaerts valve gear. P.V.

60113*	Great Northern
60114	W. P. Allen
60115	Meg Merrilies
60116	Hal o' the Wynd
60117	Bois Roussel
60118	Archibald Sturrock
60119	Patrick Stirling
60120	Kittiwake
60121	Silurian
60122	Curlew
60123	H. A. Ivatt
60124	Kenilworth
60125	Scottish Union
60126	Sir Vincent Raven
60127	Wilson Worsdell
60128	Bongrace
60129	Guy Mannering
60130	Kestrel

60131	Osprey
60132	Marmion
60133	Pommern
60134	Foxhunter
60135	Madge Wildfire
60136	Alcazar
60137	Redgauntlet
60138	Boswell
60139	Sea Eagle
60140	Balmoral
60141	Abbotsford
60142	Edward Fletcher
60143	Sir Walter Scott
60144	King's Courier
60145	Saint Mungo
60146	Peregrine
60147	North Eastern
60148	Aboyeur
60149	Amadis
60150	Willbrook
60151	Midlothian
60152	Holyrood
60153†	Flamboyant
60154†	Bon Accord
60155†	Borderer
60156†	Great Central
60157†	Great Eastern
60158	Aberdonian
60159	Bonnie Dundee
60160	Auld Reekie
60161	North British
60162	Saint Johnstoun

Total 50

4-6-2 (A2/1: 7P6F) 8P7F Class A2

A2/2* Introduced 1943. Thompson rebuild of Gresley Class P2 2-8-2 (introduced 1934).
Weight: Loco. 101 tons 10 cwt.
Pressure: 225 lb. Su.
Cyls.: (3) 20″ × 26″.
Driving Wheels: 6′ 2″.
T.E.: 40,320 lb.

A2/1† Introduced 1944. Development of Class A2/2, incorporating Class V2 2-6-2 boiler.
Weight: Loco. 98 tons.
Pressure: 225 lb. Su.
Cyls.: (3) 19″ × 26″.
Driving Wheels: 6′ 2″.   T.E.: 36,385 lb.

A2/3‡ Introduced 1946. Development of Class A2/2 for new construction.
Weight: Loco. 101 tons 10 cwt.
Pressure: 250 lb. Su.
Cyls.: (3) 19″ × 26″.
Driving Wheels: 6′ 2″.
T.E.: 40,430 lb.

A2§ Introduced 1947. Peppercorn development of Class A2/2 with shorter wheelbase. (No. 60539 built with double blast pipe.)

A2** Rebuilt with double blast pipe and multiple valve regulator.
Weight: Loco. 101 tons.
Pressure: 250 lb. Su.
Cyls.: (3) 19″ × 26″.
Driving Wheels: 6′ 2″.
T.E.: 40,430 lb.
Tender weight (all parts): 60 tons 7 cwt.
Walschaerts valve gear.   P.V.

60500‡	Edward Thompson
60501*	Cock o' the North
60502*	Earl Marischal
60503*	Lord President
60504*	Mons Meg
60505*	Thane of Fife
60506*	Wolf of Badenoch
60507†	Highland Chieftain
60508†	Duke of Rothesay
60509†	Waverley
60510†	Robert the Bruce
60511‡	Airborne
60512‡	Steady Aim
60513‡	Dante
60514‡	Chamossaire
60515‡	Sun Stream
60516‡	Hycilla
60517‡	Ocean Swell
60518‡	Tehran
60519‡	Honeyway
60520‡	Owen Tudor
60521‡	Watling Street
60522‡	Straight Deal
60523‡	Sun Castle
60524‡	Herringbone
60525§	A. H. Peppercorn
60526**	Sugar Palm
60527§	Sun Chariot
60528§	Tudor Minstrel
60529**	Pearl Diver
60530§	Sayajirao

110

60531 § Bahram	60812
60532 ** Blue Peter	60813
60533 ** Happy Knight	60814
60534 § Irish Elegance	60315
60535 § Hornet's Beauty	60816
60536 § Trimbush	60817
60537 § Bachelor's Button	60818
60538 ** Velocity	60819
60539 § Bronzino	60820

Total

Class A2	15	Class A2/2	6
Class A2/1	4	Class A2/3	15

4-6-4   8P7F   Class W1

Introduced 1937. Rebuilt from Gresley experimental high-pressure 4-cyl. compound with water-tube boiler, introduced 1929.
Weight: Loco. 107 tons 17 cwt.
       Tender 60 tons 7 cwt.
Pressure: 250 lb. Su.
Cyls.: (3) 19″ × 26″.
Driving Wheels: 6′ 8″.
T.E.: 37,400 lb.
Walschaerts valve gear and derived motion. P.V.

60700   **Total 1**

2-6-2   7P6F   Class V2

Introduced 1936. Gresley design.
Weight: Loco. 93 tons 2 cwt.
       Tender 52 tons.
Pressure: 220 lb. Su.
Cyls.: (3) 18½″ × 26″.
Driving Wheels: 6′ 2″.
T.E.: 33,730 lb.
Walschaerts valve gear and derived motion. P.V.

60800	Green Arrow
60801	
60802	
60803	
60804	
60805	
60806	
60807	
60808	
60809	The Snapper, The East Yorkshire Regiment, The Duke of York's Own
60810	
60811	

60821	
60822	
60823	
60824	
60825	
60826	
60827	
60828	
60829	
60830	
60831	
60832	
60833	
60834	
60835	The Green Howard, Alexandra, Princess of Wales's Own Yorkshire Regiment
60836	
60837	
60838	
60839	
60840	
60841	
60842	
60843	
60844	
60845	
60846	
60847	St. Peter's School York, A.D. 627
60848	
60849	
60850	
60851	
60852	
60853	
60854	

60855			
60856			
60857			
60858			
60859			
60860	Durham School		
60861			
60862			
60863			
60864			
60865			
60866			
60867			
60868			
60869			
60870			
60871			
60872	King's Own Yorkshire Light Infantry		
60873	Coldstreamer		
60874			

60875	60897	60919	60941
60876	60898	60920	60942
60877	60899	60921	60943
60878	60900	60922	60944
60879	60901	60923	60945
60880	60902	60924	60946
60881	60903	60925	60947
60882	60904	60926	60948
60883	60905	60927	60949
60884	60906	60928	60950
60885	60907	60929	60951
60886	60908	60930	60952
60887	60909	60931	60953
60888	60910	60932	60954
60889	60911	60933	60955
60890	60912	60934	60956
60891	60913	60935	60957
60892	60914	60936	60958
60893	60915	60937	60959
60894	60916	60938	60960
60895	60917	60939	60961
60896	60918	60940	60962
60963			

60964	The Durham Light Infantry		
60965	60967	60969	
60966	60968	60970	

60971	60975	60979	60983
60972	60976	60980	
60973	60977	60981	
60974	60978	60982	

Total 184

4-6-0   5MT   Class B1

Introduced 1942. Thompson design.
Weight: Loco. 71 tons 3 cwt.
　　　　　Tender 52 tons.
Pressure: 225 lb. Su.
Cyls.: (O) 20″ × 26″.
Driving Wheels: 6′ 2″.
T.E.: 26,880 lb.
Walschaerts valve gear. P.V.

61000	Springbok
61001	Eland
61002	Impala
61003	Gazelle
61004	Oryx
61005	Bongo
61006	Blackbuck
61007	Klipspringer
61008	Kudu
61009	Hartebeeste
61010	Wildebeeste
61011	Waterbuck
61012	Puku
61013	Topi
61014	Oribi
61015	Duiker
61016	Inyala
61017	Bushbuck
61018	Gnu
61019	Nilghal
61020	Gemsbok
61021	Reitbok
61022	Sassaby
61023	Hirola
61024	Addax
61025	Pallah
61026	Ourebi
61027	Madoqua
61028	Umseke
61029	Chamois
61030	Nyala
61031	Reedbuck

61032	Stembok			61190	
61033	Dibatag			61191	
61034	Chiru			61192	
61035	Pronghorn			61193	
61036	Ralph Assheton			61194	
61037	Jairou			61195	
61038	Blacktail			61196	
61039	Steinbok			61197	
61040	Roedeer			61198	
61041	61079	61116	61153	61199	
61042	61080	61117	61154	61200	
61043	61081	61118	61155	61201	
61044	61082	61119	61156	61202	
61045	61083	61120	61157	61203	
61046	61084	61121	61158	61204	
61047	61085	61122	61159	61205	
61048	61086	61123	61160	61206	
61049	61087	61124	61161	61207	
61050	61088	61125	61162	61208	
61051	61089	61126	61163	61209	
61052	61090	61127	61164	61210	
61053	61091	61128	61165	61211	
61054	61092	61129	61166	61212	
61055	61093	61130	61167	61213	
61056	61094	61131	61168	61214	
61058	61095	61132	61169	61215	William Henton Carver
61059	61096	61133	61170	61216	
61060	61097	61134	61171	61217	
61061	61098	61135	61172	61218	
61062	61099	61136	61173	61219	
61063	61100	61137	61174	61220	
61064	61101	61138	61175	61221	Sir Alexander Erskine-Hill
61065	61102	61139	61176		
61066	61103	61140	61177	61222	
61067	61104	61141	61178	61223	
61068	61105	61142	61179	61224	
61069	61106	61143	61180	61225	
61070	61107	61144	61181	61226	
61071	61108	61145	61182	61227	
61072	61109	61146	61183	61228	
61073	61110	61147	61184	61229	
61074	61111	61148	61185	61230	
61075	61112	61149	61186	61231	
61076	61113	61150	61187	61232	
61077	61114	61151	61188	61233	
61078	61115	61152		61234	
61189	Sir William Gray			61235	

61236	
61237	Geoffrey H. Kitson
61238	Leslie Runciman
61239	
61240	Harry Hinchcliffe
61241	Viscount Ridley
61242	Alexander Reith Gray
61243	Sir Harold Mitchell
61244	Strang Steel
61245	Murray of Elibank
61246	Lord Balfour of Burleigh
61247	Lord Burghley
61248	Geoffrey Gibbs
61249	FitzHerbert Wright
61250	A. Harold Bibby
61251	Oliver Bury

61252	61283	61314	61345
61253	61284	61315	61346
61254	61285	61316	61347
61255	61286	61317	61348
61256	61287	61318	61349
61257	61288	61319	61350
61258	61289	61320	61351
61259	61290	61321	61352
61260	61291	61322	61353
61261	61292	61323	61354
61262	61293	61324	61355
61263	61294	61325	61356
61264	61295	61326	61357
61265	61296	61327	61358
61266	61297	61328	61359
61267	61298	61329	61360
61268	61299	61330	61361
61269	61300	61331	61362
61270	61301	61332	61363
61271	61302	61333	61364
61272	61303	61334	61365
61273	61304	61335	61366
61274	61305	61336	61367
61275	61306	61337	61368
61276	61307	61338	61369
61277	61308	61339	61370
61278	61309	61340	61371
61279	61310	61341	61372
61280	61311	61342	61373
61281	61312	61343	61374
61282	61313	61344	61375

61376	61377		61378
61379	Mayflower		
61380	61388	61396	61404
61381	61389	61397	61405
61382	61390	61398	61406
61383	61391	61399	61407
61384	61392	61400	61408
61385	61393	61401	61409
61386	61394	61402	
61387	61395	61403	

Total 409

4-6-0   5MT   Class B16

B16/1 Introduced 1920. Raven N.E. design with Stephenson valve gear.

B16/2* Introduced 1937. Gresley rebuild of B16/1 with Walschaerts valve gear and derived motion for inside cylinder.

B16/3† Introduced 1944. Thompson rebuild of B16/1 with individual sets of Walschaerts valve gear for each cylinder.

Weight: Loco. $\begin{cases} 77 \text{ tons } 14 \text{ cwt.} \\ 79 \text{ tons } 4 \text{ cwt.*} \\ 78 \text{ tons } 19 \text{ cwt.†} \end{cases}$
Tender 46 tons 12 cwt.
Pressure: 180 lb. Su.
Cyls.: (3) 18½″ × 26″.
Driving Wheels: 5′ 8″.
T.E.: 30,030 lb.   P.V.

61410	61427	61444†	61461†
61411	61428	61445	61462
61412	61429	61446	61453†
61413	61430	61447	61464†
61414	61431	61448†	61465
61415	61432	61449†	61466
61416	61433	61450	61467†
61417†	61434†	61451	61468†
61418†	61435*	61452	61469
61419	61436	61453†	61470
61420†	61437*	61454†	61471
61421*	61438*	61455*	61472†
61422	61439†	61456	61473
61423	61440	61457*	61475*
61424	61441	61458	61476†
61425	61442	61459	61477
61426	61443	61460	61478

Total: Class B16/1 44
Class B16/3 17 Class B16/2 7

4-6-0   4P3F   Class B12

B12/3 Introduced 1932. Gresley rebuild of Holden G.E. design of 1911 with large boiler, round-topped firebox and long-travel valves.
(B12/2 was a development of B12/1 with Lentz valves, since rebuilt to B12/3.)

Weight: Loco.   69 tons 10 cwt.
　　　　Tender 39 tons 6 cwt.
Pressure: 180 lb. Su.
Cyls.: 20″ × 28″.
Driving Wheels: 6′ 6″.
T.E.: 21,970 lb.
P.V.

61514	61546	61563	61575
61530	61558	61571	61577
61533	61564	61572	61580
61535			

Total 13

4-6-0   4MT (B2 and   B17/6: 5P4F)   Classes B2 & B17

B17/1[1] Introduced 1928. Gresley design for G.E. section with G.E.-type tender.
B17/6[2] Introduced 1947. B17/1 fitted with 100A (B1-type) boiler.
B17/4[3] Introduced 1936. Locos. with L.N.E.R. 4,200-gallon tender.
B17/6[4] Introduced 1943. B17/4 fitted with 100A (B1-type) boiler.
B17/6[5] Rebuild of streamlined B17/5 introduced in 1937. Rebuilt with 100A boiler and de-streamlined in 1951.

Weight: Loco.   77 tons 5 cwt.
　　　　Tender $\begin{cases} 39 \text{ tons } 6 \text{ cwt.}^{13} \\ 52 \text{ tons.}^{345} \end{cases}$
Pressure: $\begin{cases} 180 \text{ lb.}^{13} \\ 225 \text{ lb.}^{245} \end{cases}$ Su.
Cyls.: (3) 17½″ × 26″.
Driving Wheels: 6′ 8″.
T.E.: $\begin{cases} 22,485 \text{ lb.}^{13} \\ 28,555 \text{ lb.}^{245} \end{cases}$
Walschaerts valve gear and derived motion. P.V.

B2[6] Introduced 1945. Thompson 2-cyl. rebuild of B17, with 100A boiler and N.E. tender.
B2[7] Introduced 1945, with L.N.E.R. tender.

Weight: Loco.   73 tons 10 cwt.
　　　　Tender $\begin{cases} 46 \text{ tons } 12 \text{ cwt.}^4 \\ 52 \text{ tons.}^7 \end{cases}$
Pressure: 225 lb. Su.
Cyls.: (O) 20″ × 26″.
Driving Wheels: 6′ 8″.
T.E.: 24,865 lb.
Walschaerts valve gear.   P.V.

61607[6]	Blickling
61608[2]	Gunton
61610[2]	Honingham Hall
61611[2]	Raynham Hall
61612[2]	Houghton Hall
61613[2]	Woodbastwick Hall
61614[6]	Castle Hedingham
61616[6]	Fallodon
61618[2]	Wynyard Park
61620[2]	Clumber
61623[2]	Lambton Castle
61625[1]	Raby Castle
61626[2]	Brancepeth Castle
61627[2]	Aske Hall
61629[1]	Naworth Castle
61631[2]	Serlby Hall
61633[2]	Kimbolton Castle
61636[6]	Harlaxton Manor
61637[2]	Thorpe Hall
61639[6]	Norwich City
61641[2]	Gayton Hall
61644[6]	Earlham Hall
61647[2]	Helmingham Hall
61651[4]	Derby County
61652[2]	Darlington
61653[4]	Huddersfield Town
61654[4]	Sunderland
61655[4]	Middlesbrough
61656[4]	Leeds United
61657[4]	Doncaster Rovers
61658[4]	The Essex Regiment
61659[5]	East Anglian
61660[3]	Hull City
61661[4]	Sheffield Wednesday
61662[4]	Manchester United
61663[4]	Everton

61664⁴ Liverpool
61665⁴ Leicester City
61666⁴ Nottingham Forest
61668⁴ Bradford City
61670⁵ City of London
61672⁴ West Ham United

Total

Class B2   5   Class B17/4   2
Class B17/1 2   Class B17/6 33

2-6-0 4MT Class K2

K2/2 Introduced 1914. Gresley G.N. design.
K2/1* Introduced 1931. Rebuilt from small-boilered K1 (introduced 1912).
†K2/2 with side-window cab.
‡K2/1 with side-window cab.

Weight: Loco.   64 tons 8 cwt.
         Tender 43 tons 2 cwt.
Pressure: 180 lb. Su.
Cyls.: (O) 20″ × 26″.
Driving Wheels: 5′ 8″.
T.E.: 23,400 lb.
Walschaerts valve gear. P.V.

61721‡	61741†	61751	61758†
61723*	61742	61752	61759
61728*	61743	61753	61760
61730	61745	61754	61761
61731	61747	61755†	61762
61738	61748	61756	61763
61740	61750		

61764† Loch Arkaig
61766
61767
61769†
61770†
61771
61772† Loch Lochy
61773
61776†
61777
61778

61779†
61780
61782† Loch Eil
61783† Loch Shiel
61784†
61785†
61786†
61787† Loch Quoich
61788† Loch Rannoch
61789† Loch Laidon
61790† Loch Lomond
61791† Loch Laggan
61792†
61794† Loch Oich

Total

Class K2/1   3   Class K2/2 48

Classes
2-6-0 5P6F K3 & K5

K3/2 Introduced 1924. Development of Gresley G.N. design, built to L.N.E.R. loading gauge.
K3/3* Introduced 1929. Differ in details only, such as springs, from K3/2.
‡K3/2 fitted with G.N. tender.
(K3/1 were G.N. locos. (introduced 1920), with G.N. cabs, and K3/4, K3/5 and K3/6 were variations of K3/2 differing in weight and details. These locos. have now been modified to K3/2.)
Weight: Loco.   72 tons 12 cwt.
         Tender { 52 tons.
                 43 tons 2 cwt.‡
Pressure: 180 lb. Su.
Cyls.: (3) 18½″ × 26″.
Driving Wheels: 5′ 8″.
T.E.: 30,030 lb.
Walschaerts valve gear and derived motion. P.V.
K5† Introduced 1945. Thompson 2-cyl. rebuild of K3.
Weight: Loco.   71 tons 5 cwt.
         Tender 52 tons.
Pressure: 225 lb. Su.
Cyls.: (O) 20″ × 26″.
Driving Wheels: 5′ 8″.
T.E.: 29,250 lb.
Walschaerts valve gear. P.V.

61800	61802	61804	61806
61801	61803	61805	61807

61808	61855‡	61902	61949
61809	61856‡	61903	61950
61810	61857‡	61904	61951
61811	61858‡	61905	61952
61812‡	61859‡	61906	61953
61813	61860	61907	61954
61814	61861	61908	61955
61815	61862	61909	61956
61816	61863†	61910	61957
61817	61864	61911	61958
61818	61865	61912	61959
61819	61866	61913	61960
61820	61867	61914	61961
61821	61868	61915	61962
61822	61869	61916	61963
61823	61870*	61917	61964
61824	61871*	61918	61965
61825	61872*	61919	61966
61826	61873*	61920	61967
61827	61874*	61921	61968
61828	61875*	61922	61969
61829	61876*	61923	61970
61830	61877*	61924	61971
61831	61878*	61925	61972
61832	61879*	61926	61973
61833	61880*	61927	61974
61834	61881*	61928	61975
61835	61882*	61929	61976
61836	61883*	61930	61977
61837	61884*	61931	61978
61838	61885*	61932	61979
61839	61886*	61933	61980
61840	61887*	61934	61981
61841‡	61888*	61935	61982
61842	61889*	61936	61983
61843	61890	61937	61984
61844	61891	61938	61985
61845	61892	61939	61986
61846	61893	61940	61987
61847	61894	61941	61988
61848	61895	61942	61989
61849	61896	61943	61990
61850	61897	61944	61991
61851	61898	61945	61992
61852	61899	61946	
61853	61900	61947	
61854‡	61901	61948	

Total
Class K3/2 172 **Class K5 1**
Class K3/3 20

Classes
2-6-0 5P6F K1 & K4

K4* Introduced 1937. Gresley locos.
for West Highland line.
Weight: Loco. 68 tons 8 cwt.
         Tender 44 tons 4 cwt.
Pressure: 200 lb. Su.
Cyls.: (3) $18\frac{1}{2}'' \times 26''$.
Driving Wheels: 5' 2".
T.E.: 36,600 lb.
Walschaerts valve gear and derived
motion. P.V.

K1/1† Introduced 1945. Thompson
2-cyl. loco. Rebuilt from K4.
P.V.

K1 Introduced 1949. Peppercorn
development of Thompson K1/1 (No.
61997) for new construction, with
increased length.
Weight: Loco. 66 tons 17 cwt.
         Tender 44 tons 4 cwt.
Pressure: 225 lb. Su.
Cyls.: (O) $20'' \times 26''$.
Driving Wheels: 5' 2".
T.E.: 32,080 lb.
Walschaerts valve gear. P.V.

61993* Loch Long
61994* The Great Marquess
61995* Cameron of Lochiel
61996* Lord of the Isles
61997† MacCailin Mor
61998* Macleod of Macleod

62001	62017	62033	62049
62002	62018	62034	62050
62003	62019	62035	62051
62004	62020	62036	62052
62005	62021	62037	62053
62006	62022	62038	62054
62007	62023	62039	62055
62008	62024	62040	62056
62009	62025	62041	62057
62010	62026	62042	62058
62011	62027	62043	62059
62012	62028	62044	62060
62013	62029	62045	62061
62014	62030	62046	62062
62015	62031	62047	62063
62016	62032	62048	62064

62065	62067	62069
62066	62068	62070

Total

Class K1 70   **Class K4 5**

Class K1/1 1

4-4-0   3P   Class D30

D30/2 Introduced 1914. Development
of D30/1, introduced 1912 (Reid N.B.
"Scott" class) with detail differences.
Weight: Loco.   57 tons 16 cwt.
        Tender 46 tons 13 cwt.
Pressure: 165 lb. Su.
Cyls.: 20″ × 26″.
Driving Wheels: 6′ 6″.
T.E.: 18,700 lb.
P.V.

62418	The Pirate
62421	Laird o' Monkbarns
62426	Cuddie Headrigg
62427	Dumbiedykes
62436	Lord Glenvarloch
62439	Father Ambrose

Total 6

4-4-0   3P   Class D34

Introduced 1913. Reid N.B. " Glen "
class.
Weight: Loco.   57 tons 4 cwt.
        Tender 46 tons 13 cwt.
Pressure: 165 lb. Su.
Cyls.: 20″ × 26″.
Driving Wheels: 6′ 0″.

T.E.: 20,260 lb.
P.V.

62467	Glenfinnan
62469	Glen Douglas
62470	Glen Roy
62471	Glen Falloch
62472	Glen Nevis
62474	Glen Croe
62475	Glen Beasdale
62477	Glen Dochart
62478	Glen Quoich
62479	Glen Sheil
62480	Glen Fruin
62482	Glen Mamie
62483	Glen Garry
62484	Glen Lyon
62485	Glen Murran
62487	Glen Arklet
62488	Glen Aladale
62489	Glen Dessary
62490	Glen Fintaig
62492	Glen Garvin
62493	Glen Gloy
62494	Glen Gour
62495	Glen Luss
62496	Glen Loy
62497	Glen Mallie
62498	Glen Moidart

Total 26

HISTORIC LOCOMOTIVES PRESERVED IN STORE

Type	Originating Company	Pre-Grouping No.	L.N.E.R. No.	Name	Place of Preservation
4-2-2	G.N.R.	1	—	—	York Museum
4-4-2	G.N.R.	990	(3990)	Henry Oakley	York Museum
4-4-2	G.N.R.	251	(3251)	—	York Museum
2-2-4T	N.E.R.	66	66	Aerolite	York Museum
2-4-0	N.E.R.	910	910	—	York Museum
2-4-0	N.E.R.	1463	1463	—	York Museum
4-4-0	N.E.R.	1621	1621	—	York Museum
4-4-0	G.N.S.	49	(6849)	Gordon Highlander	Inverurie Works

The unbracketed numbers are the ones at present carried by the locos.

4-4-0 3P1F Class D16

D16/3¹ Introduced 1933. Gresley rebuild of D15 with larger boiler, round-topped firebox and modified footplating. D15 was Belpaire firebox development of original J. Holden (G.E.) " Claud Hamilton " class.

D16/3² Introduced 1938. Rebuild of D16/2 with round-topped firebox, but retaining original footplating and slide valves.

Weight: Loco. 55 tons 18 cwt.
       Tender 39 tons 5 cwt.
Pressure: 180 lb. Su.
Cyls.: 19″ × 26″.
Driving Wheels: 7′ 0″.
T.E.: 17,095 lb.

62511¹	62540¹	62597¹	62613²
62517¹	62544²	62604¹	62618²
62524¹	62570²	62606²	
62529¹	62589²	62612²	

Total 14

4-4-0 3P2F Class D11

D11/1* Introduced 1920. Robinson G.C. " Large Director "development of D10 (introduced 1913).

D11/2 Introduced 1924. Post-grouping locos. built to Scottish loading gauge. From 1938 the class has been rebuilt with long-travel valves.

Weight: Loco. 61 tons 3 cwt.
       Tender 48 tons 6 cwt.
Pressure: 180 lb. Su.
Cyls.: 20″ × 26″.
Driving Wheels: 6′ 9″.
T.E.: 19,645 lb.
P.V.

62660* Butler-Henderson
62661* Gerard Powys Dewhurst
62662* Prince of Wales
62663* Prince Albert
62664* Princess Mary
62665* Mons
62666* Zeebrugge
62667* Somme
62668* Jutland
62669* Ypres
62670* Marne
62671 Bailie MacWheeble
62672 Baron of Bradwardine

62673 Evan Dhu
62674 Flora MacIvor
62675 Colonel Gardiner
62676 Jonathan Oldbuck
62677 Edie Ochiltree
62678 Luckie Mucklebackit
62680 Lucy Ashton
62681 Captain Craigengelt
62682 Haystoun of Bucklaw
62684 Wizard of the Moor
62685 Malcolm Graeme
62686 The Fiery Cross
62687 Lord James of Douglas
62688 Ellen Douglas
62689 Maid of Lorn
62690 The Lady of the Lake
62691 Laird of Balmawhapple
62692 Allan-:ane
62693 Roderick Dhu
62694 James Fitzjames

Total
Class D11/1 11 Class D11/2 22

4-4-0 4P Class D49

D49/1* Introduced 1927. Gresley design with piston valves. Walschaerts valve gear and derived motion.

D49/2† Introduced 1928. Development of D49/1 with Lentz Rotary Cam poppet valves.

D49/2‡ Introduced 1949. Fitted with Reidinger R.R. Rotary valve gear.
(D49/3 comprised locos. 62720-5 as built with Lentz Oscillating Cam poppet valves. From 1938 these locos. were converted to D49/1. 62751-75 have larger valves than the earlier D49/2, and were at first classified D49/4).
¹Fitted with G.C. tender.
²Fitted with N.E. tender.
³The remainder have L.N.E.R. tenders.

Weight: Loco. $\begin{cases} 66 \text{ tons.}*† \\ 64 \text{ tons 10 cwt.}‡ \\ 48 \text{ tons } 6 \text{ cwt.}¹ \end{cases}$
     Tender $\begin{cases} 44 \text{ tons } 2 \text{ cwt.}² \\ 52 \text{ tons.}³ \end{cases}$

Pressure: 180 lb. Su.
Cyls.: (3) 17″ × 26″.
Driving Wheels: 6′ 8″.
T.E.: 21,555 lb.

62701*[1] Derbyshire
62705*[1] Lanarkshire
62707*[1] Lancashire
62708*[1] Argyllshire
62709*[1] Berwickshire
62710*[1] Lincolnshire
62711*[1] Dumbartonshire
62712*[1] Morayshire
62714*[1] Perthshire
62715*[1] Roxburghshire
62716*[1] Kincardineshire
62717*[1] Banffshire
62718*[1] Kinross-shire
62719*[1] Peebles-shire
62720*[1] Cambridgeshire
62722*[1] Huntingdonshire
62723*[2] Nottinghamshire
62727†[2] The Quorn
62728*[1] Cheshire
62729*[1] Rutlandshire
62731*[1] Selkirkshire
62733*[1] Northumberland
62734*[2] Cumberland
62738†[3] The Zetland
62739†[3] The Badsworth
62740†[3] The Bedale
62743†[3] The Cleveland
62744†[3] The Holderness
62745†[3] The Hurworth
62747†[3] The Percy
62751†[3] The Albrighton
62753†[3] The Belvoir
62759†[3] The Craven
62760†[3] The Cotswold
62762†[3] The Fernie
62763†[3] The Fitzwilliam
62765†[3] The Goathland
62770†[3] The Puckeridge

Total
Class D49/1 22 Class D49/2 16

2-4-0   IMT   Class E4

Introduced 1891. J. Holden G.E. design.
Weight: Loco. 40 tons 6 cwt.
Tender 30 tons 13 cwt.

Pressure: 160 lb.   Cyls.: 17½″ × 24″.
Driving Wheels: 5′ 8″.
T.E.: 14,700 lb.

62785   **Total 1**

0-8-0   6F   Class Q6

Introduced 1913. Raven N.E. design.
*Some locos. are fitted with tender from withdrawn B15 locos.
Weight: Loco.   65 tons 18 cwt.
Tender { 44 tons 2 cwt.
       { 44 tons.*
Pressure: 180 lb. Su.
Cyls.: (O) 20″ × 26″.
Driving Wheels: 4′ 7½″.
T.E.: 28,800 lb.
P.V.

63340	63370	63400	63430
63341	63371	63401	63431
63342	63372	63402	63432
63343	63373	63403	63433
63344	63374	63404	63434
63345	63375	63405	63435
63346	63376	63406	63436
63347	63377	63407	63437
63348	63378	63408	63438
63349	63379	63409	63439
63350	63380	63410	63440
63351	63381	63411	63441
63352	63382	63412	63442
63353	63383	63413	63443
63354	63384	63414	63444
63355	63385	63415	63445
63356	63386	63416	63446
63357	63387	63417	63447
63358	63388	63418	63448
63359	63389	63419	63449
63360	63390	63420	63450
63361	63391	63421	63451
63362	63392	63422	63452
63363	63393	63423	63453
63364	63394	63424	63454
63365	63395	63425	63455
63366	63396	63426	63456
63367	63397	63427	63457
63368	63398	63428	63458
63369	63399	63429	63459

Total 120

Class 3 (Fowler) 2-6-2T No. 40018 [P. J. Sharpe

Class 3 (Stanier) 2-6-2T No. 40168 [J. Cupit

Class 3 (Stanier) 2-6-2T No. 40167 (with large boiler) [R. J. Buckley

C

Class 2P (ex-Midland) 4-4-0 No. 40413   [R. K. Evans

Class 2P (ex-L.M.S.) 4-4-0 No. 40700   [R. J. Buckley

Class 4P 4-4-0 No. 41062   [K. R. Pirt

Class 1F 0-6-0T No. 41835 (with round-top firebox)   [K. R. Pirt

Class 1F 0-6-0T No. 41795   [R. C. Riley

Class 3F (ex-Midland) 0-6-0T No. 47221 (fitted with condensing apparatus)
                                                                 [P. J. Sharpe

Class 4 (Stanier 2-cylinder) 2-6-4T No. 42643

[B. E. Morrison

Class 4 (Fowler) 2-6-4T No. 42411 (with side-window cab)

[R. J. Buckley

Class 4 (Stanier 3-cylinder) 2-6-4T No. 42524

[P. J. Sharp

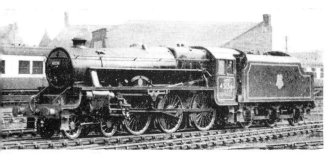

Class 5 4-6-0 No. 45156 *Ayrshire Yeomanry* [*J. Davenport*

Class 5 4-6-0 No. 44741 (with Caprotti valve gear) [*R. C. Riley*

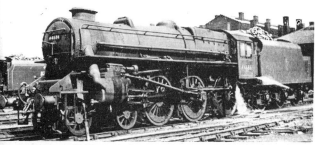

Class 5 4-6-0 No. 44636 (Caprotti valve gear and double chimney) [*B. K. B. Green*

Class 2 (Ivatt) 2-6-2T No. 41291   [R. C. Riley

Class 2 (Ivatt) 2-6-0 No. 46457   [A. A. Cameron

Class 4 (Ivatt) 2-6-0 No. 43096   [C. G. Pearson

ass 8P 4-6-2 No. 46245 *City of London*   [*J. Robertson*

ass 8P 4-6-2 No. 46256 *Sir William A. Stanier, F.R.S.* (with detail differences)
                                                               [*J. B. Bucknall*

ass 8P 4-6-2 No. 46206 *Princess Marie Louise*   [*B. E. Morrison*

Class 2F 0-6-0 No. 58246 (4′ 11″ driving wheels; with round-top firebox)

[J. B. Buckna

Class 2F 0-6-0 No. 58115 (4′ 11″ driving wheels; Deeley cab)

[J. Davenpo

Class 3F 0-6-0 No. 43828

[D. Marriott

Class 3P 4-4-0 No. 54468　　　　　　　　　　　　　[B. E. Morrison

Class 2P 0-4-4T No. 55233　　　　　　　　　　　　[L. Marshall

Class 3F 0-6-0T No. 56321　　　　　　　　　　　　[R. E. Vincent

Class 2P 2-4-2T No. 50647   T. K. Widd

Class 2F 0-6-0ST No. 51358   [D. Slater

Class 1F 0-6-0T No. 51544   [K. R. Pirt

Class 2F 0-6-0T No. 56165 [B. E. Morrison

Class 0F 0-4-0ST No. 51241 [P. J. Robinson

Class 0F 0-4-0ST No. 56038 [K. L. Cook

Class 8P 4-6-2 No. 71000 *Duke of Gloucester*　　　　　[*J. Robertson*

Class 7P6F 4-6-2 No. 70043 *Lord Kitchener*　　　　　[*J. Robertson*

Class 6P5F 4-6-2 No. 72009 *Clan Stewart*　　　　　[*P. J. Sharpe*

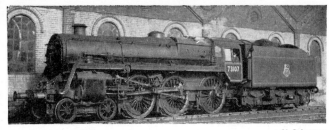

Class 5 4-6-0 No. 73107   [*J. Robertson*

Class 5 4-6-0 No. 73129 (with Caprotti valve gear)   [*R. A. Panting*

Class 4 4-6-0 No. 75029 (with double chimney)   [*L. King*

Class 3 2-6-0 No. 77008

[*L. King*

Class 4 2-6-0 No. 76027

[*G. Wheeler*

Class 9F 2-10-0 No. 92022 (with Crosti boiler)

[*H. N. James*

Class A1 4-6-2 No. 60158 *Aberdonian* [*J. Davenport*

Class A2/2 4-6-2 No. 60502 *Earl Marischal* [*C. Lawson Kerr*

Class A2/3 4-6-2 No. 60523 *Sun Castle* [*J. Davenport*

Class V2 2-6-2 No. 60848　　　　　　　　　　　　　　　　[J. Robertson

Class B1 4-6-0 No. 61034 *Chiru*　　　　　　　　　　　　　　[L. King

Class B16/3 4-6-0 No. 61417　　　　　　　　　　　　　　　　[D. Penney

0-8-0   8F   **Class Q7**

Introduced 1919. Raven N.E. design.
Weight: Loco. 71 tons 12 cwt.
          Tender 44 tons 2 cwt.
Pressure: 180 lb. Su.
Cyls.: (3) $18\frac{1}{2}'' \times 26''$.
Driving Wheels: $4' 7\frac{1}{4}''$.
T.E.: 36,965 lb.
P.V.

63460	63464	63468	63472
63461	63465	63469	63473
63462	63466	63470	63474
63463	63467	63471	

Total 15

Classes
2-8-0   8F (O1)   **O1 & O4**
        7F (O4)

O4/1[1] Introduced 1911. Robinson
G.C. design with small boiler,
Belpaire firebox, steam and vacuum
brakes and water scoop.

O4/3[2] Introduced 1917. R.O.D. locos.
with steam brake only and no scoop.

O4/2[3] Introduced 1925. O4/3 with
cabs and boiler mountings reduced.

O4/5[4] Introduced 1932. Rebuilt with
shortened O2-type boiler and separate smokebox saddle.

O4/6[5] Introduced 1924. Rebuilt from
O5 retaining higher cab (63914–20
with side windows).

O4/7[6] Introduced 1939. Rebuilt with
shortened O2-type boiler, retaining
G.C. smokebox.

O4/8[7] Introduced 1944. Rebuilt with
100A (B1) boiler, retaining original
cylinders.
(O4/4 were rebuilds with O2 boilers,
since rebuilt again; O5 was a G.C.
development of O4 with larger
boiler and Belpaire firebox.)

Weight: Loco.
- 73 tons 4 cwt.[1]
- 73 tons 4 cwt.[3]
- 73 tons 4 cwt.[3]
- 74 tons 13 cwt.[4]
- 73 tons 4 cwt.[5]
- 73 tons 17 cwt.[6]
- 72 tons 10 cwt.[7]

Tender
- 48 tons 6 cwt. (with scoop)
- 47 tons 6 cwt. (without scoop)

Pressure: 180 lb. Su.
Cyls.: (O) $21'' \times 26''$.
Driving Wheels: $4' 8''$.
T.E.: 31,325 lb.
P.V.

O1[8] Introduced 1944. Thompson rebuild with 100A boiler, Walschaerts
valve gear and new cylinders.
Weight: Loco. 73 tons 6 cwt.
          Tender as O4.
Pressure: 225 lb. Su.
Cyls.: (O) $20'' \times 26''$.
Driving Wheels: $4' 8''$.
T.E.: 35,520 lb.
Walschaerts valve gear.   P.V.

63570[6]	63606[7]	63643[6]	63679[2]
63571[8]	63607[7]	63644[7]	63680[3]
63572[1]	63608[1]	63645[6]	63681[2]
63573[7]	63609[1]	63646[8]	63682[3]
63574[1]	63610[8]	63647[7]	63683[7]
63575[7]	63611[1]	63648[3]	63684[1]
63576[1]	63612[7]	63649[2]	63685[2]
63577[1]	63613[7]	63650[8]	63686[2]
63578[8]	63614[1]	63651[7]	63687[8]
63579[8]	63615[6]	63652[8]	63688[7]
63582[6]	63616[6]	63653[7]	63689[8]
63583[1]	63617[1]	63654[1]	63690[3]
63584[1]	63618[1]	63655[7]	63691[7]
63585[1]	63619[8]	63656[2]	63692[1]
63586[1]	63621[1]	63657[2]	63693[1]
63587[1]	63622[1]	63658[1]	63694[1]
63588[6]	63623[1]	63659[2]	63695[2]
63589[8]	63624[7]	63660[1]	63696[2]
63590[8]	63625[1]	63661[6]	63697[7]
63591[8]	63626[1]	63662[6]	63698[1]
63592[8]	63628[7]	63663[8]	63699[6]
63593[1]	63630[8]	63664[1]	63700[1]
63594[8]	63631[7]	63665[2]	63701[1]
63595[6]	63632[1]	63666[2]	63702[2]
63596[8]	63633[7]	63669[6]	63703[7]
63597[1]	63634[6]	63670[8]	63704[7]
63598[1]	63635[1]	63671[1]	63705[7]
63599[1]	63636[7]	63672[7]	63706[7]
63600[6]	63637[8]	63673[8]	63707[1]
63601[1]	63638[2]	63674[7]	63708[6]
63602[1]	63639[7]	63675[7]	63709[7]
63603[6]	63640[1]	63676[2]	
63604[7]	63641[7]	63677[1]	
63605[1]	63642[2]	63678[8]	

63710¹	63757¹	63806⁸	63868⁸
63711⁸	63758⁶	63807⁸	63869⁸
63712⁸	63759²	63808⁸	63870²
63713²	63760⁸	63812²	63872⁸
63714²	63761⁶	63813²	63873⁷
63715⁷	63762¹	63816⁷	63874⁸
63716²	63763⁷	63817⁸	63876⁶
63717⁷	63764²	63818⁷	63877⁷
63718⁷	63765⁷	63819⁷	63878⁷
63719¹	63766²	63821²	63879⁸
63720⁷	63767⁷	63822²	63880⁶
63721⁷	63768⁸	63823⁷	63881⁷
63722¹	63769⁷	63824⁶	63882⁷
63723¹	63770⁶	63827⁷	63883⁷
63724²	63771²	63828⁷	63884⁷
63725⁸	63772⁶	63829⁷	63885⁷
63726⁷	63773⁸	63832⁷	63886⁸
63727¹	63774²	63833²	63887⁸
63728⁷	63775⁶	63836⁷	63888²
63729²	63776⁷	63837⁷	63889²
63730⁷	63777⁸	63838⁸	63890⁸
63731⁷	63778⁸	63839⁶	63891⁶
63732⁷	63779²	63840⁷	63893⁷
63733²	63780⁸	63841⁷	63894⁶
63734⁷	63781⁷	63842²	63895⁷
63735²	63782⁷	63843⁶	63897⁷
63736¹	63783⁷	63845²	63898⁷
63737²	63784⁸	63846²	63899⁷
63738⁷	63785⁷	63847³	63900²
63739⁷	63786⁸	63848⁶	63901⁸
63740⁸	63787²	63850⁷	63902⁵
63741⁷	63788⁷	63851⁴	63904⁵
63742⁷	63789⁸	63852⁷	63905⁵
63743¹	63790²	63853⁷	63906⁵
63744²	63791⁷	63854⁸	63907⁵
63745⁴	63792⁸	63855²	63908⁵
63746⁸	63793⁷	63856⁸	63911⁵
63747⁶	63794⁷	63857⁷	63912⁵
63748⁷	63795⁸	63858⁷	63913⁵
63749⁶	63796⁸	63859²	63914⁷
63750⁷	63798²	63860⁶	63915⁷
63751²	63799¹	63861⁸	63917⁵
63752⁸	63800⁸	63862⁷	63920⁵
63753²	63801⁷	63863⁸	
63754⁷	63802⁷	63864⁷	
63755⁸	63803⁸	63865⁸	
63756²	63804²	63867⁸	
	63805⁷		

Total

Class O1	58	Class O4/5	2
Class O4/1	52	Class O4/6	11
Class O4/2	5	Class O4/7	33
Class O4/3	60	Class O4/8	96

2-8-0   8F   Class O2

O2/1* Introduced 1921. Development of experimental Gresley G.N. 3-cyl. loco. (L.N.E.R. 3921). Subsequently rebuilt with side-window cab, and reduced boiler mountings.

O2/2† Introduced 1924. Development of O2/1 with detail differences.

O2/3 Introduced 1932. Development of O2/2 with side-window cab and reduced boiler mountings.

O2/4‡ Introduced 1943. Rebuilt with 100A (B1 type) boiler and smokebox extended backwards (63924 retaining G.N. tender).

Weight: Loco.
- 75 tons 16 cwt.*†
- 78 tons 13 cwt.
- 74 tons 2 cwt.‡

Tender
- 43 tons 2 cwt. (63922–46)
- 52 tons (63947–87).

Pressure: 180 lb. Su.
Cyls.: (3) 18½" × 26".
Driving Wheels: 4' 8".
T.E.: 36,740 lb.
Walschaerts valve gear and derived motion. P.V.

63922*	63939†	63956	63973
63923*	63940†	63957	63974
63924‡	63941†	63958	63975
63925‡	63942†	63959	63976
63926*	63943†	63960	63977
63927*	63944†	63961	63978
63928‡	63945‡	63962‡	63979
63929*	63946†	63963	63980
63930*	63947	63964	63981
63931*	63948	63965	63982‡
63932‡	63949‡	63966‡	63983‡
63933‡	63950‡	63967	63984
63934†	63951	63968	63985
63935‡	63952	63969	63986
63936†	63953	63970	63987
63937†	63954	63971	
63938‡	63955	63972	

Total

Class O2/1 **8**   Class O2/3 **35**
Class O2/2 **10**   Class O2/4 **13**

0-6-0   2P3F   **Class J6**

Introduced 1911. Gresley G.N. design.
Weight: Loco.   50 tons 10 cwt.
        Tender 43 tons 2 cwt.
Pressure: 170 lb. Su.
Cyls.: 19″ × 26″.
Driving Wheels: 5′ 2″.
T.E.: 21,875 lb.
P.V.

64170	64196	64231	64256
64171	64197	64232	64257
64172	64198	64233	64258
64173	64203	64234	64259
64174	64206	64235	64260
64175	64207	64236	64261
64176	64208	64237	64265
64177	64209	64238	64266
64178	64210	64239	64268
64179	64213	64240	64269
64180	64214	64241	64270
64181	64215	64245	64272
64182	64219	64246	64273
64184	64222	64247	64277
64185	64223	64248	64278
64188	64224	64250	64279
64190	64226	64251	
64191	64228	64253	
64192	64229	64254	

Total **73**

0-6-0   2P3F   **Class J11**

Introduced 1901. Robinson G.C. design.
Parts 1 and 4 have 3,250-gallon
tenders; Parts 2 and 5, 4,000-gallon.
Parts 1 and 2 have high boiler
mountings; Parts 4 and 5 low. All
of Parts 4 and 5 are superheated, and
some of Parts 1 and 2. There are
frequent changes between parts.

J11/3* Introduced 1942. Rebuilt with
long-travel piston valves and boiler
higher pitched.

Weight: Loco. $\begin{cases} 51 \text{ tons } 19 \text{ cwt. (Sat.)} \\ 52 \text{ tons } 2 \text{ cwt. (Su.)} \\ 53 \text{ tons } 6 \text{ cwt.*} \end{cases}$
Tender $\begin{cases} 44 \text{ tons } 3 \text{ cwt. (3,250 gall.)} \\ 48 \text{ tons } 6 \text{ cwt. (4,000 gall.)} \end{cases}$
Pressure: 180 lb. SS.
Cyls.: 18½″ × 26″.
Driving Wheels: 5′ 2″.
T.E.: 21,960 lb.

64280	64329	64377	64420*
64283*	64331	64379*	64421
64284*	64332*	64381	64423
64287	64333*	64382	64425
64288	64336	64383	64427*
64292	64337	64384	64428
64294	64341	64385	64429
64297	64346*	64386*	64430
64298	64348	64387	64433
64304*	64351	64388	64434
64305	64352*	64389	64435
64308	64354*	64393*	64437
64310	64355	64394*	64438
64311	64357	64395*	64439*
64313	64359*	64396	64440
64314*	64361	64397	64441*
64315	64362*	64402*	64442*
64316*	64363	64403	64443
64317*	64364*	64404	64444
64318*	64365	64405	64445
64319	64368	64406*	64446
64321	64371	64407	64447
64324*	64373*	64417*	64450*
64325	64375*	64418*	64451
64328	64376	64419	64452

Total

Class J11/3 **33**
Class J11 (other parts) **67**

0-6-0   3F   **Class J35**

J35/5* Introduced 1906. Reid N.B.
design with piston valves.

J35/4 Introduced 1908. Slide valves.
(Parts 1, 2 and 3 were variations of
Parts 4 and 5 before superheating.)

Weight: Loco. $\begin{cases} 51 \text{ tons.*} \\ 50 \text{ tons } 15 \text{ cwt.} \end{cases}$

Tender $\begin{cases} 38 \text{ tons } 1 \text{ cwt.*} \\ 37 \text{ tons } 15 \text{ cwt.} \end{cases}$

Pressure: 180 lb. Su.
Cyls.: 18¼″ × 26″.
Driving Wheels: 5′ 0″.
T.E.: 22,080 lb.

64460*	64480	64500	64519
64461*	64482	64501	64520
64462*	64483	64502	64521
64463*	64484	64504	64523
64466*	64485	64505	64524
64468*	64487	64506	64525
64470*	64488	64507	64527
64471*	64489	64509	64529
64472*	64490	64510	64530
64473*	64491	64511	64531
64474*	64493	64512	64532
64475*	64494	64513	64533
64476*	64496	64514	64534
64477*	64497	64515	64535
64478	64498	64516	
64479	64499	64518	

Total
Class J35/4 48   Class J35/5 14

0-6-0   5F   Class J37

Introduced 1914. Reid N.B. design.
Superheated development of J35.
Weight: Loco. 54 tons 14 cwt.
Tender 40 tons 19 cwt.
Pressure: 180 lb. Su.
Cyls.: 19½″ × 26″.
Driving Wheels: 5′ 0″.
T.E.: 25,210 lb.
P.V.

64536	64547	64558	64569
64537	64548	64559	64570
64538	64549	64560	64571
64539	64550	64561	64572
64540	64551	64562	64573
64541	64552	64563	64574
64542	64553	64564	64575
64543	64554	64565	64576
64544	64555	64566	64577
64545	64556	64567	64578
64546	64557	64568	64579

64580	64595	64610	64625
64581	64596	64611	64626
64582	64597	64612	64627
64583	64598	64613	64628
64584	64599	64614	64629
64585	64600	64615	64630
64586	64601	64616	64631
64587	64602	64617	64632
64588	64603	64618	64633
64589	64604	64619	64634
64590	64605	64620	64635
64591	64606	64621	64636
64592	64607	64622	64637
64593	64608	64623	64638
64594	64609	64624	64639

Total 104

0-6-0   3P5F   Class J19

Introduced 1916. Hill G.E. design
rebuilt with round-topped firebox
from 1934.
*Rebuilt with 19″ cyls. and 180 lb.
pressure.
Weight: Loco. 50 tons 7 cwt.
Tender 38 tons 5 cwt.
Pressure: $\begin{cases} 170 \text{ lb. Su.} \\ 180 \text{ lb. Su.*} \end{cases}$
Cyls.: $\begin{cases} 20″ × 26″. \\ 19″ × 26″.* \end{cases}$
Driving Wheels: 4′ 11″.
T.E.: $\begin{cases} 27,430 \text{ lb.} \\ 26,215 \text{ lb.*} \end{cases}$

64640	64650	64659	64668
64641	64652	64660	64669
64642	64653	64661	64670
64643	64654	64663	64671*
64644	64655	64664*	64673
64646	64656	64665	64674
64647	64657	64666	
64648	64658	64667	

Total 30

0-6-0   5F   Class J20

J20/1 Introduced 1943. Hill G.E.
design with Belpaire firebox (introduced 1920) rebuilt with B12/1-type
boiler with round-topped firebox.

140

Weight: Loco. 54 tons 15 cwt.
       Tender 38 tons 5 cwt.
Pressure: 180 lb. Su.
Cyls.: 20″ × 28″.
Driving Wheels: 4′ 11″.
T.E.: 29,045 lb.
P.V.

64675	64681	64687	64694
64676	64682	64689	64695
64677	64683	64690	64696
64678	64684	64691	64697
64679	64685	64692	64698
64680	64686	64693	64699

Total 24

0-6-0 4P5F Class J39

Introduced 1926. Gresley design.

J39/1   Standard 3,500-gallon tender.
J39/2* Standard 4,200-gallon tender.
J39/3† Various N.E. tenders (3,940-gallon on 64843-5, 4,125-gallon on 64855-9).
Weight: Loco. 57 tons 17 cwt.
       Tender { 44 tons 4 cwt.
               52 tons 13 cwt.*
               and others.
Pressure: 180 lb. Su.
Cyls.: 20″ × 26″.
Driving Wheels: 5′ 2″.
T.E.: 25,665 lb.
P.V.

64700†	64719	64738	64757
64701	64720	64739	64758
64702	64721	64740	64759
64703	64722	64741	64760
64704	64723	64742	64761
64705	64724	64743	64762
64706	64725	64744	64763
64707	64726	64745	64764
64708	64727	64746	64765
64709	64728	64747	64766
64710	64729	64748	64767
64711	64730	64749	64768
64712	64731	64750	64769
64713	64732	64751	64770
64714	64733	64752	64771
64715	64734	64753	64772
64716	64735	64754	64773
64717	64736	64755	64774
64718	64737	64756	64775

64776	64823	64870	64917*
64777	64824	64871	64918*
64778	64825	64872*	64919*
64779	64826	64873*	64920*
64780	64827	64874*	64921*
64781	64828	64875*	64922*
64782	64829	64876*	64923*
64783	64830	64877*	64924*
64784*	64831	64878*	64925*
64785*	64832	64879*	64926†
64786*	64833	64880*	64927*
64787*	64834	64881*	64928*
64788*	64835	64882*	64929*
64789*	64836	64883*	64930*
64790*	64837	64884*	64931*
64791*	64838*	64885*	64932*
64792*	64839*	64886*	64933
64793*	64840*	64887*	64934
64794*	64841*	64888*	64935
64795*	64842*	64889*	64936
64796	64843†	64890*	64937
64797	64844†	64891*	64938
64798	64845†	64892*	64939
64799	64846	64893*	64940
64800	64847	64894*	64941
64801	64848	64895*	64942
64802	64849	64896*	64943
64803	64850	64897*	64944
64804	64851	64898*	64945*
64805	64852	64899*	64946*
64806	64853	64900*	64947*
64807	64854	64901*	64948*
64808	64855†	64902*	64949*
64809	64856†	64903*	64950*
64810	64857†	64904*	64951*
64811	64858†	64905*	64952*
64812	64859†	64906*	64953*
64813	64860	64907*	64954*
64814	64861	64908*	64955*
64815	64862	64909*	64956*
64816	64863	64910*	64957*
64817	64864	64911*	64958*
64818	64865	64912*	64959*
64819	64866	64913*	64960*
64820*	64867	64914*	64961*
64821*	64868	64915*	64962*
64822*	64869	64916*	64963*

64964*	64971†	64978†	64985†
64965*	64972†	64979†	64986†
64966*	64973†	64980†	64987†
64967*	64974†	64981†	64988†
64968*	64975†	64982†	
64969*	64976†	64983†	
64970*	64977†	64984†	

Total

Class J39/1 155 Class J39/3 28
Class J39/2 106

0-6-0 2F **Class J21**

Introduced 1886. T. W. Worsdell N.E. design. Majority built as 2-cyl. compounds and later rebuilt as simple locos., subsequently rebuilt with superheater and piston valves, superheater later removed.

Weight: Loco. 42 tons 9 cwt.
Tender 36 tons 19 cwt.
Pressure: 160 lb. SS.
Cyls.: 19″ × 24″.
Driving Wheels: 5′ 1¼″.
T.E.: 19,240 lb.

65033	65070	65099	65110

Total 4

0-6-0 2F **Class J10**

J10/4* Introduced 1896. Pollitt development of J10/2 with larger bearings and larger tender.
J10/6 Introduced 1901. Robinson locos. with larger bearings and small tender.
Weight: Loco. 41 tons 6 cwt.
Tender { 37 tons 6 cwt.
        { 43 tons.*
Pressure: 160 lb.
Cyls.: 18″ × 26″.
Driving Wheels: 5′ 1″.
T.E.: 18,780 lb.

65131	65134*	65140*	65158*
65133*	65138*	65157*	65166*

65169*	65184	65192	65198
65177	65187	65194	

Total

Class J10/4 8   Class J10/6 7

0-6-0 2F **Class J36**

Introduced 1388. Holmes N.B. design.
Weight: Loco. 41 tons 19 cwt.
Tender 33 tons 9 cwt.
Pressure: 165 lb.
Cyls.: 18½″ × 26″.
Driving Wheels: 5′ 0″.
T.E.: 19,690 lb.

65210	
65211	
65214	
65216	Byng
65217	French
65218	
65221	
65222	Somme
65224	Mons
65227	
65223	
65229	
65230	
65232	
65233	Plumer
65234	
65235	Gough
65237	
65239	
65241	
65243	Maude
65246	
65247	
65249	
65251	
65252	
65253	Joffre
65257	
65258	
65259	
65260	

65261			
65265			
65266			
65267			
65268	Allenby		
65273	65282	65295	65305
65275	65285	65296	65306
65276	65287	65297	65307
65277	65288	65300	65309
65280	65290	65303	65310
65281	65293	65304	
65311	Haig		
65312	65320	65331	65342
65313	65321	65333	65343
65315	65323	65334	65344
65316	65325	65335	65345
65317	65327	65338	65346
65318	65329	65339	
65319	65330	65341	

Total 86

0-6-0   1P2F   Class J15

Introduced 1883. Worsdell G.E. design,
    modified by J. Holden.
*Fitted with side-window cab for
    Colne Valley line.
Weight: Loco. 37 tons 2 cwt.
    Tender 30 tons 13 cwt.
Pressure: 160 lb.
Cyls.: $17\frac{1}{2}'' \times 24''$.
Driving Wheels: 4' 11".
T.E.: 16,940 lb.

65361	65447	65458	65470
65388	65448	65459	65471
65389	65449	65460	65472
65420	65450	65461	65473
65424*	65451	65462	65474
65434	65452	65463	65475
65440	65453	65464	65476
65443	65454	65465	65477
65445	65455	65466	65478
65446	65457	65469	65479

Total 40

0-6-0   2P4F   Class J17

Introduced 1901. J. Holden G.E.
    design. Many rebuilt from round-top
    firebox J16, introduced 1900.
*Fitted with small tender.
Weight: Loco. 45 tons 8 cwt.
    Tender { 38 tons 5 cwt.
    { 30 tons 12 cwt.*
Pressure: 180 lb. Su.
Cyls.: 19" × 26".
Driving Wheels: 4' 11".
T.E.: 24,340 lb.

65502*	65528*	65549	65567
65503*	65530	65551	65570
65505	65531	65553	65576
65506*	65532	65554	65577
65507*	65533	65555	65578
65511*	65536	65556	65580
65512*	65538	65557	65581
65513*	65539	65558	65582
65514*	65540	65559	65583
65519*	65541	65560	65584
65520	65542	65561	65586
65521	65544	65563	65588
65525	65545	65564	65589
65526	65546	65565	
65527	65548	65566	

Total 58

0-6-0   3F   Class J25

Introduced 1898. W. Worsdell N.E.
    design.
*Original design, saturated, with slide
    valves.
†Rebuilt with superheater and piston
    valves.
‡Rebuilt with piston valves, super-
    heater removed.
Weight: Loco. { 39 tons 11 cwt.*
    { 41 tons 14 cwt.†
    { 40 tons 17 cwt.‡
    Tender 36 tons 19 cwt.
Pressure: 160 lb. SS.
Cyls.: $18\frac{1}{2}'' \times 26''$.
Driving Wheels: 4' 7¼".
T.E.: 21,905 lb.

65645†	65662†	65666*	65675*
65656*	65663*	65670*	65685*

65687*	65698*	65712*	65726*
65691*	65700*	65713*	65727*
65693*	65702‡	65714*	65728*
65695*	65706†	65720*	

Total 23

0-6-0   5F   Class J26

Introduced 1904. W. Worsdell N.E. design.

Weight: Loco. 46 tons 16 cwt.
         Tender 36 tons 19 cwt.

Pressure: 180 lb.

Cyls.: 18½″ × 26″.

Driving Wheels: 4′ 7½″.

T.E.: 24,640 lb.

65731	65747	65760	65772
65732	65749	65761	65773
65735	65751	65762	65774
65736	65753	65763	65776
65737	65755	65764	65777
65741	65756	65768	65778
65743	65757	65769	65779
65745			

Total 29

65780	65809	65838	65867†
65781	65810	65839	65868†
65782	65811	65840	65869†
65783	65812	65841	65870†
65784	65813	65842	65871*
65785	65814	65843	65872†
65786	65815	65844	65873†
65787	65816	65845	65874*
65788	65817	65846	65875†
65789	65818	65847	65876†
65790	65819	65848	65877†
65791	65820	65849	65878*
65792	65821	65850	65879†
65793	65822	65851	65880*
65794	65823	65852	65881*
65795	65824	65853	65882†
65796	65825	65854	65883*
65797	65826	65855	65884†
65798	65827	65856	65885†
65799	65828	65857	65886†
65800	65829	65858	65887*
65801	65830	65859	65888†
65802	65831	65860†	65889*
65803	65832	65861†	65890*
65804	65833	65862†	65891†
65805	65834	65863*	65892*
65806	65835	65864†	65893*
65807	65836	65865†	65894*
65808	65837	65866*	

Total 115

0-6-0   5F   Class J27

Introduced 1906. W. Worsdell N.E. design developed from J26.
*Introduced 1921. Raven locos. Superheated, with piston valves.
†Introduced 1943. Piston valves, but superheater removed.

Weight: Loco. { 47 tons Sat.
               { 49 tons 10 cwt. Su.
        Tender 36 tons 19 cwt.

Pressure: 180 lb. SS.

Cyls.: 18½″ × 26″.

Driving Wheels: 4′ 7½″.

T.E.: 24,640 lb.

0-6-0   6F   Class J38

Introduced 1926. Gresley design. Predecessor of J39, with 4′ 8″ wheels, boiler 6″ longer than J39 and smokebox 6″ shorter.

*Rebuilt with J39 boiler.

Weight: Loco. 58 tons 19 cwt.
         Tender 44 tons 4 cwt.

Pressure: 180 lb. sq.

Cyls.: 20″ × 26″.

Driving Wheels: 4′ 8″.

T.E.: 28,415 lb.

P.V.

65900	65903*	65906*	65909
65901	65904	65907	65910
65902	65905	65908*	65911

144

65912	65918*	65924	65930
65913	65919	65925	65931
65914	65920	65926*	65932
65915	65921	65927*	65933
65916	65922	65928	65934
65917*	65923	65929	

Total 35

4-4-2T 2P1F Class C13

Introduced 1903. Robinson G.C. design, later rebuilt with superheater, push-and-pull fitted.
Weight: 66 tons 13 cwt.
Pressure: 160 lb. Su.
Cyls.: 18" × 26".
Driving Wheels: 5' 7".
T.E.: 17,100 lb.

67417   Total 1

4-4-2T 2P1F Class C14

Introduced 1907. Robinson G.C. design, later superheated, development of C13, with detail differences.
Weight: 71 tons.
Pressure: 160 lb. Su.
Cyls.: 18" × 26".
Driving Wheels: 5' 7".
T.E.: 17,100 lb.

67445	67448	67450

Total 3

4-4-2T 2P Class C15

Introduced 1911. Reid N.B. design. Push-and-pull fitted.
Weight: 68 tons 15 cwt.
Pressure: 175 lb.
Cyls.: 18" × 26".
Driving Wheels: 5' 9".
T.E.: 18,160 lb.

67460	67474

Total 2

4-4-2T 2P Class C16

Introduced 1915. Reid N.B. design, superheated development of C15.
Weight: 72 tons 10 cwt.
Pressure: 165 lb. Su.
Cyls.: 19" × 26".
Driving Wheels: 5' 9".
T.E.: 19,080 lb.
P.V.

67482	67487	67491	67497
67484	67488	67492	67500
67485	67489	67494	67501
67486	67490	67496	67502

Total 16

Classes
2-6-2T V1 (3MT) V1 & V3
V3 (4MT)

V1 Introduced 1930. Gresley design.
V3* Introduced 1939. Development of V1 with higher pressure (locos. numbered from 67682 rebuilt from V1).
Weight: $\begin{cases} 84 \text{ tons.} \\ 86 \text{ tons 16 cwt.*} \end{cases}$
Pressure: $\begin{cases} 180 \text{ lb. Su.} \\ 200 \text{ lb. Su.*} \end{cases}$
Cyls.: (3) 16" × 26".
Driving Wheels: 5' 8".
T.E.: $\begin{cases} 22,465 \text{ lb.} \\ 24\ 960 \text{ lb.*} \end{cases}$
Walschaerts valve gear and derived motion. P.V.

67600*	67623	67646*	67669*
67601	67624*	67647	67670*
67602	67625*	67648	67671
67603	67626*	67649	67672*
67604*	67627*	67650*	67673
67605*	67628*	67651*	67674*
67606*	67629	67652*	67675*
67607*	67630	67653*	67676
67608	67631	67654*	67677*
67609*	67632*	67655	67678*
67610	67633	67656*	67679*
67611*	67634*	67657*	67680
67612*	67635	67658	67681*
67613	67636*	67659	67682*
67614*	67637	67660*	67683*
67615*	67638*	67661	67684*
67616	67639	67662*	67685*
67617*	67640	67663*	67686*
67618*	67641	67664	67687*
67619*	67642	67665	67688*
67620*	67643*	67666	67689*
67621	67644*	67667*	67690*
67622	67645	67668*	67691*

Total
Class V1 35   Class V3 57

145

2-6-4T   4MT   Class L1

Introduced 1945. Thompson design.

*Introduced 1954. Boiler pressure reduced to 200 lb.

†Introduced 1954. Cylinder diameter reduced.

Weight: 89 tons 9 cwt.

Pressure: $\begin{cases} 225 \text{ lb.} \\ 200 \text{ lb.*} \end{cases}$

Cyls.: $\begin{cases} (O)\ 20'' \times 26''. \\ (O)\ 18\frac{3}{4}'' \times 26''.† \end{cases}$

Driving Wheels: 5' 2".

T.E.: $\begin{cases} 32,080 \text{ lb.} \\ 28,515 \text{ lb.*} \\ 28,180 \text{ lb.†} \end{cases}$

Walschaerts valve gear. P.V.

67701	67726	67751	67776†
67702	67727	67752	67777
67703	67728	67753	67778
67704	67729	67754	67779†
67705	67730	67755	67780
67706	67731	67756	67781
67707	67732	67757	67782
67708	67733	67758	67783
67709	67734	67759	67784
67710	67735	67760	67785
67711	67736	67761*	67786
67712	67737	67762	67787
67713	67738	67763	67788
67714	67739	67764	67789
67715	67740	67765	67790
67716	67741	67766	67791
67717	67742	67767	67792
67718	67743	67768	67793
67719	67744	67769	67794
67720	67745	67770†	67795
67721	67746	67771†	67796
67722	67747*	67772†	67797
67723	67748	67773	67798*
67724	67749	67774	67799
67725	67750	67775	67800

Total 100

0-6-0ST   4F   Class J94

Introduced 1943. Riddles M.o.S. design.
  (Bought from M.o.S., 1946.)
Weight: 48 tons 5 cwt.
Pressure: 170 lb.
Cyls.: 18" × 26".
Driving Wheels: 4' 3".
T.E.: 23,870 lb.

68006	68025	68044	68063
68007	68026	68045	68064
68008	68027	68046	68065
68009	68028	68047	68066
68010	68029	68048	68067
68011	68030	68049	68068
68012	68031	68050	68069
68013	68032	68051	68070
68014	68033	68052	68071
68015	68034	68053	68072
68016	68035	68054	68073
68017	68036	68055	68074
68018	68037	68056	68075
68019	68038	68057	68076
68020	68039	68058	68077
68021	68040	68059	68078
68022	68041	68060	68079
68023	68042	68061	68080
68024	68043	68062	

Total 75

0-4-0ST   0F   Class Y9

Introduced 1882. Holmes N.B. design.
*Locos. running permanently attached
  to wooden tender.
Weight: Loco. 27 tons 16 cwt.
        Tender 6 tons.
Pressure: 130 lb.
Cyls.: (O) 14" × 20".
Driving Wheels: 3' 8".
T.E.: 9,845 lb.

68095	68104	68114*	68123
68100*	68108*	68117*	68124
68101	68110	68119*	

Total 11

0-4-0T Unclass. Class Y1

Sentinel **Wagon** Works design. Single-speed **Geared** Sentinel locomotives. The parts of this class differ in details, including size of boiler and fuel capacity.

Y1/1* Introduced 1925.
Y1/2† Introduced 1927.
§Sprocket gear ratio 9:25 (remainder 11:25).

Weight: $\begin{cases} 20 \text{ tons } 17 \text{ cwt.*} \\ 19 \text{ tons } 16 \text{ cwt.†} \end{cases}$
Pressure: 275 lb. Su.
Cyls.: $6\frac{3}{4}'' \times 9''$.
Driving Wheels: 2' 6".
T.E.: $\begin{cases} 7,260 \text{ lb.*†} \\ 8,870 \text{ lb.§} \end{cases}$
Poppet valves.
(See also E.R. Departmental Locos.)

68150†§

Total

Class Y1/1 3   Class Y1/2 2

0-4-2T 0F Class Z4

Introduced 1915. Manning-Wardle design for G.N. of S.
Weight: 25 tons 17 cwt.
Pressure: 160 lb.
Cyls.: (O) $13'' \times 20''$.
Driving Wheels: 3' 6".
T.E.: 10,945 lb.

68190 68191   **Total 2**

0-4-2T 0F Class Z5

Introduced 1915. Manning-Wardle design for G.N. of S.
Weight: 30 tons 18 cwt.
Pressure: 160 lb.
Cyls.: (O) $14'' \times 20''$.
Driving Wheels: 4' 0".
T.E.: 11,105 lb.

68192   **Total 1**

0-6-0T Unclass. Class J71

Introduced 1886. *T.* W. Worsdell N.E. design.
*Altered cylinder dimensions.
Weight: 37 tons 12 cwt.
Pressure: 140 lb.
Driving Wheels: 4' 7¼".

Cyls.: $\begin{cases} 16'' \times 22''.* \\ 16\frac{3}{4}'' \times 22''.* \end{cases}$
T.E.: $\begin{cases} 12,130 \text{ lb.} \\ 13,300 \text{ lb.*} \end{cases}$

68230*	68254	68265	68283
68233	68260	68269	68309*
68235	68262	68272	68314
68245	68263	68275	68316*
68250*	68264	68278	

Total 19

0-6-0T 0F Class J88

Introduced 1904. Reid N.B. design with short wheelbase.
Weight: 38 tons 14 cwt.
Pressure: 130 lb.
Cyls.: (O) $15'' \times 22''$.
Driving Wheels: 3' 9".
T.E.: 12,155 lb.

68320	68332	68342	68349
68325	68334	68343	68350
68326	68335	68344	68352
68329	68336	68345	68353
68331	68338	68346	68354

Total 20

0-6-0T 3F Class J73

Introduced 1891. W. Worsdell N.E. design.
Weight: 46 tons 15 cwt.
Pressure: 160 lb.
Cyls.: $19'' \times 24''$.
Driving Wheels: 4' 7¼".
T.E.: 21,320 lb.

68359	68361	68363	68364
68360			

Total 5

DEPARTMENTAL LOCOMOTIVES

(Former running no. in brackets)

0-6-0ST 3F Class J52/2

2 (68858)   9 (68840)

0-4-0T Unclass. Class Y3

Introduced 1927.
Sentinel Wagon Works design.
Two-speed Geared Sentinel locos.
Sprocket gear ratio 15 : 19.
Weight: 20 tons 16 cwt.
Pressure: 275 lb. Su.
Cyls.: $6\frac{3}{4}'' \times 9''$.
Driving Wheels: 2' 6".
T.E.: $\begin{cases} \text{Low Gear: } 15,960 \text{ lb.} \\ \text{High Gear: } 5,960 \text{ lb.} \end{cases}$
Poppet valves.

3 (68181)	38 (68168)
5 (68165)	40 (68173)
7 (68166)	41 (68177)
8 (68183)	42 (68178)
21 (68162)	57 (68160)
	Total 10

0-6-0T 2F Class J66

Introduced 1886. J. Holden G.E. design.
Weight: 40 tons 6 cwt.
Pressure: 160 lb.
Cyls.: $16\frac{1}{2}'' \times 22''$.
Driving Wheels: 4' 0".
T.E.: 16,970 lb.

31 (68382)	36 (68378)
32 (68370)	
	Total 3

0-4-0T Unclass. Class Y1/1

4 (68132)   39 (68131)
53 (68152)

0-4-0T Dock Tank Class Y4

Introduced 1913. Hill G.E. design.
Weight: 38 tons 1 cwt.
Pressure: 180 lb.
Cyls.: (O) $17'' \times 20''$.
Driving Wheels: 3' 10".
T.E.: 19,225 lb.
Walschaerts valve gear.

33 (68129)   **Total 1**

0-4-0 Diesel Mechanical

52 (11104)

0-4-0T Unclass. Class Y1/2

54 (68153)

0-4-0 Diesel Mechanical

56

0-6-0 Diesel Mechanical

91   92

Bo-Bo EB1 Electric

100 (26510)

NOTE. (For details of Departmental diesel locomotives, see ABC British Railways Diesels or Diesel Section of combined volume.)

0-6-0T 2F Class J77

Introduced 1899. W. Worsdell N.E. rebuild of Fletcher 0-4-4T originally built 1874–84.
Some engines of this class have square-cornered and some round-cornered cab roofs.

Weight: 43 tons.
Pressure: 160 lb.
Cyls.: 17" × 22".
Driving Wheels: 4' 1¼".
T.E.: 17,560 lb.

68392	68408	68410	68431
68406	68409	68425	

Total 7

0-6-0T 2F Class J83

Introduced 1900. Holmes N.B. design.

Weight: 45 tons 5 cwt.
Pressure: 150 lb.
Cyls.: 17" × 26".
Driving Wheels: 4' 6".
T.E.: 17,745 lb.

68442	68453	68459	68472
68443	68454	68467	68477
68444	68456	68468	68479
68445	68457	68470	68480
68447	68458	68471	68481
68448			

Total 21

Classes
0-6-0T 2F J67 & J69

J69/1† Introduced 1902. Development of Holden J67 with 180 lb. pressure, larger tanks and larger firebox (some rebuilt from J67).

J69/2§ Introduced 1950. J67/1 rebuilt with 180 lb. boiler and larger firebox.

Weight: 40 tons 9 cwt.
Pressure: 180 lb.

Cyls.: 16½" × 22".
Driving Wheels: 4' 0".
T.E.: 19,090 lb.

68497†	68530†	68565†	68599†
68498§	68535†	68566†	68600†
68499†	68538†	68569†	68601†
68500†	68542†	68570†	68602†
68501†	68543†	68571†	68609†
68502†	68545†	68573†	68612†
68507†	68549†	68575†	68613†
68508†	68550†	68577†	68619†
68510§	68552†	68578†	68621†
68513§	68554†	68579†	68623†
68520§	68556†	68581†	68626†
68522§	68557†	68587†	68629†
68524†	68558†	68591†	68633†
68526†	68560†	68596†	68635†
68528†	68563†		

Total
Class J69/2 5   Class J69/1 53

0-6-0T 2F Class J68

Introduced 1912. Hill G.E. development of J69 with side-window cab.

Weight: 42 tons 9 cwt.
Pressure: 180 lb.
Cyls.: 16½" × 22".
Driving Wheels: 4' 0".
T.E.: 19,090 lb.

68639	68645	68652	68661
68640	68646	68654	68663
68641	68647	68655	68665
68642	68648	68656	
68643	68649	68658	
68644	68650	68660	

Total 21

0-6-0T 2F Class J72

Introduced 1898. W. Worsdell N.E. design.
*Altered cylinder dimensions.
Weight: 38 tons 12 cwt.
Pressure: 140 lb.
Cyls.: $\begin{cases} 17'' \times 24''. \\ 18'' \times 24''.* \end{cases}$
Driving Wheels: 4' 1¼".
T.E.: $\begin{cases} 16,760 \text{ lb.} \\ 18,790 \text{ lb.}* \end{cases}$

68670	68690	68713	68734
68671	68691	68714	68736
68672	68692	68715	68737
68673	68693	68716	68738
68674	68694	68717	68739
68675	68695	68719	68740
68676	68696	68720	68741
68677	68697	68721	68742
68678	68698	68722	68743
68679	68701	68723	68744
68680	68702	68724	68745
68681	68703	68725	68747
68682	68704	68726	68749
68683	68705	68727	68750
68684	68706	68728	68751
68685*	68707	68729	68752
68686	68708	68730	68753
68687	68709	68731	68754
68688	68710	68732	
68689	68711	68733	

(Class continued with No. 69001)

0-6-0ST 3F Class J52

J52/2 Introduced 1897. Ivatt G.N. saddletank with domed boiler.
Weight: 51 tons 14 cwt.
Pressure: 170 lb.
Cyls.: 18" × 26".
Driving Wheels: 4' 8".
T.E.: 21,735 lb.

(See also E.R. Departmental Locos.)

68824	68846	68875
68834	68869	

Total 7

0-6-0T 4F Class J50

J50/2* Introduced 1922. Gresley G.N. design (68900–19 rebuilt from smaller J51, built 1915–22).

J50/3† Introduced 1926. Post-grouping development with detail differences.

J50/1‡ Introduced 1929. Rebuilt from smaller J51, built 1913–14.

J50/4§ Introduced 1937. Development of J50/3 with larger bunker.

Weight: $\begin{cases} 57 \text{ tons.}* \\ 56 \text{ tons 6 cwt.}‡ \\ 58 \text{ tons 3 cwt.}†§ \end{cases}$

Pressure: 175 lb.
Cyls.: 18½" × 26".
Driving Wheels: 4' 8".
T.E.: 23,635 lb.

68890‡	68915*	68941†	68967†
68891‡	68916*	68943†	68968†
68892‡	68917*	68944†	68969†
68893‡	68918*	68945†	68970†
68894‡	68919*	68946†	68971†
68895‡	68920*	68947†	68972†
68896‡	68921*	68948†	68973†
68897‡	68922*	68949†	68974†
68898‡	68923*	68950†	68975†
68899‡	68924*	68951†	68976†
68900‡	68925*	68952†	68977†
68901*	68926*	68953†	68979§
68902*	68927*	68954†	68980§
68903*	68928*	68955†	68981§
68904*	68929*	68956†	68982§
68905*	68930*	68957†	68983§
68906*	68931*	68958†	68984§
68907*	68932*	68959†	68985§
68908*	68933*	68960†	68986§
68909*	68934*	68961†	68987§
68910*	68935*	68962†	68988§
68911*	68936*	68963†	68989§
68912*	68937*	68964†	68990§
68913*	68938*	68965†	68991§
68914*	68939*	68966†	

Total

Class J50/1 10   Class J50/3 36
Class J50/2 40   Class J50/4 13

0-6-0T 2F Class J72

(Continued from 68754)

69001	69008	69015	69022
69002	69009	69016	69023
69003	69010	69017	69024
69004	69011	69018	69025
69005	69012	69019	69026
69006	69013	69020	69027
69007	69014	69021	69028

Total 106

0-6-2T 3F Class N10

Introduced 1902. W. Worsdell N.E. design.
Weight: 57 tons 14 cwt.
Pressure: 160 lb.
Cyls.: $18\frac{1}{2}'' \times 26''$.
Driving Wheels: 4' 7¼".
T.E.: 21,905 lb.

69092	69101	69105	69109
69097			

Total 5

0-6-2T 3MT Class N15

N15/2* Introduced 1910. Reid N.B. design developed from N14. Cowlairs Incline banking locos.
N15/1 Introduced 1910. Development of N15/2 with smaller bunker for normal duties.
Weight: $\begin{cases} 62 \text{ tons } 1 \text{ cwt.*} \\ 60 \text{ tons } 18 \text{ cwt.} \end{cases}$
Pressure: 175 lb.
Cyls.: $18'' \times 26''$.
Driving Wheels: 4' 6".
T.E.: 23,205 lb.

69126*	69131*	69134	69137
69127*	69132	69135	69138
69128*	69133	69136	69141

69143	69165	69187	69209
69144	69168	69188	69211
69145	69170	69190	69212
69146	69171	69191	69213
69149	69173	69192	69214
69150	69176	69194	69215
69151	69177	69196	69216
69154	69178	69197	69217
69155	69179	69198	69218
69156	69180	69199	69219
69159	69181	69202	69221
69161	69182	69204	69222
69162	69183	69205	69223
69163	69184	69206	69224
69164	69185	69207	
69165	69186	69208	

Total

Class N15/1 70 Class N15/2 4

0-6-2T 2MT Class N5

N5/2. Introduced 1891. Parker M.S. & L. design developed from N4.
*Push-and-pull fitted.
Weight: 62 tons 7 cwt.
Pressure: 160 lb.
Cyls.: $18'' \times 26''$.
Driving Wheels: 5' 1".
T.E.: 18,780 lb.

69257*	69276	69307	69342
69258	69286	69308	69343
69262	69290	69309	69344
69263	69292	69314	69354
69265	69293	69319	69360
69266	69294	69320	69361
69267	69296	69322	69370
69268	69298	69327	
69274	69299	69341	

Total 34

0-6-2T 2MT Class N1

†‡§Introduced 1907. Standard Ivatt G.N. design.

§Rebuilt with superheater and reduced pressure.

‡Fitted with condensing apparatus.

Weight: 65 tons 17 cwt.

Pressure: $\begin{cases} 175 \text{ lb.†‡} \\ 170 \text{ lb. Su.§} \end{cases}$

Cyls.: 18″ × 26″.

Driving Wheels: 5′ 8″.

T.E.: $\begin{cases} 18,430 \text{ lb.†‡} \\ 17,900 \text{ lb.§} \end{cases}$

69434‡	69450‡	69462‡	69477‡
69443†	69452§	69474†	

Total 7

0-6-2T 3P2F Class N2

N2/2* Introduced 1925. Post-grouping development of Gresley G.N. N2/1, introduced 1920, which class is now included in N2/2. Built with condensing apparatus and small chimney.

N2/2† Condensing apparatus removed.

N2/3‡ Introduced 1925. Locos. built non-condensing, originally fitted with large chimney. Some now with small chimney.

N2/4§ Introduced 1928. Development of N2/2, slightly heavier. Built with condensing apparatus and small chimney.

(The small chimneys are to suit the Metropolitan loading gauge, for working to Moorgate. Condensing apparatus has been removed from or added to certain locos. transferred from or to the London area.)

Weight: $\begin{cases} 70 \text{ tons } 5 \text{ cwt.*†} \\ 70 \text{ tons } 8 \text{ cwt.‡} \\ 71 \text{ tons } 9 \text{ cwt.§} \end{cases}$

Pressure: 170 lb. Su.

Cyls.: 19″ × 26″.

Driving Wheels: 5′ 8″.

T.E.: 19,945 lb.

P.V.

69490*	69523*	69546*	69576§
69492*	69524*	69547*	69577§
69498*	69525*	69548*	69578§
69504*	69526*	69549*	69579§
69505†	69528*	69552†	69580§
69506*	69529*	69553†	69581§
69507†	69530*	69555†	69582§
69508†	69531*	69556§	69583§
69509†	69532*	69560†	69584§
69510†	69533*	69561†	69585§
69511†	69535*	69563‡	69586§
69512*	69536*	69564‡	69587§
69513*	69537*	69567†	69588§
69515†	69538*	69568§	69589§
69516†	69539*	69569§	69591§
69517*	69540*	69570§	69592§
69518*	69541*	69571§	69593§
69520*	69542*	69572§	69594‡
69521*	69543*	69574§	69596‡
69522*	69545*	69575§	

Total

Class N2/2 49   Class N2/4 25

Class N2/3 5

0-6-2T 3MT Class N7

N7/3[1] Introduced 1927. Doncaster-built version of N7/2 (see below) but with round-topped firebox.

N7/3[2] Introduced 1943. N7/2 post-grouping development of Hill G.E. design (N7), rebuilt with round-topped firebox, retaining short-travel valves.

N7/4[3] Introduced 1940. Pre-grouping G.E. design (N7), rebuilt with round-topped firebox, retaining short-travel valves.

N7/5[4] Introduced 1943. Post-grouping development of G.E. design N7/1, rebuilt with round-topped firebox, retaining short-travel valves.

Weight: $\begin{cases} 64 \text{ tons.}^{1,2,4} \\ 61 \text{ tons } 16 \text{ cwt.}^{3} \\ 64 \text{ tons } 17 \text{ cwt.}^{5} \end{cases}$

Pressure: 180 lb. Su.

Cyls.: 18″ × 24″.

Driving Wheels: 4′ 10″.

T.E.: 20,515 lb.

Walschaerts valve gear.   P.V.

69602[3]	69645[4]	69674[2]	69705[1]
69603[3]	69646[4]	69675[2]	69706[1]
69604[3]	69647[4]	69677[2]	69707[1]
69611[3]	69648[4]	69678[2]	69708[1]
69612[3]	69649[4]	69679[2]	69709[1]
69613[3]	69650[4]	69680[2]	69710[1]
69614[3]	69651[4]	69681[2]	69711[1]
69615[3]	69652[4]	69682[2]	69712[1]
69617[3]	69653[4]	69683[2]	69713[1]
69618[3]	69654[4]	69684[2]	69714[1]
69620[3]	69655[4]	69685[2]	69715[1]
69621[3]	69656[4]	69686[2]	69718[1]
69622[4]	69657[4]	69687[2]	69719[1]
69625[4]	69658[4]	69688[2]	69720[1]
69626[4]	69660[4]	69690[2]	69721[1]
69627[4]	69661[4]	69691[2]	69722[1]
69629[4]	69662[4]	69692[2]	69723[1]
69630[4]	69663[4]	69693[2]	69724[1]
69631[4]	69664[4]	69694[2]	69725[1]
69632[4]	69665[4]	69696[2]	69726[1]
69633[4]	69666[4]	69697[2]	69727[1]
69635[4]	69668[4]	69698[2]	69728[1]
69636[4]	69669[4]	69699[2]	69729[1]
69637[4]	69670[4]	69700[2]	69730[1]
69638[4]	69671[4]	69701[2]	69731[1]
69640[4]	69672[4]	69702[1]	69732[1]
69642[4]	69673[2]	69704[1]	69733[1]

Total
Class N7/3 55   Class N7/4 12

Class N7/5 40

4-6-2T   3MT   Class A5

A5/1 Introduced 1911.   Robinson G.C. design.

Weight: 85 tons 18 cwt.
Pressure: 180 lb. Su.
Cyls.: 20″ × 26″.
Driving Wheels: 5′ 7″.
T.E.: 23,750 lb.
P.V.

69800	69808	69814	69823
69801	69809	69817	69825
69803	69812	69820	69827
69805	69813	69821	69829
69806			

Total 17

4-6-2T   3MT   Class A8

Introduced 1931. Gresley rebuild of Raven N.E. Class " D " 4-4-4T (introduced 1913).

Weight: 86 tons 18 cwt.
Pressure: 175 lb. Su.
Cyls.: (3) 16½″ × 26″.
Driving Wheels: 5′ 9″.
T.E.: 22,940 lb.
P.V.

69850	69858	69873	69885
69852	69859	69874	69886
69853	69860	69875	69887
69854	69861	69877	69889
69855	69867	69878	69894
69856	69869	69880	
69857	69870	69883	

Total 26

4-8-0T   5F   Class T1

Introduced 1909. W. Worsdell N.E. design.

Weight: 85 tons 8 cwt.
Pressure: 175 lb.
Cyls.: (3) 18″ × 26″.
Driving Wheels: 4′ 7½″.
T.E.: 34,080 lb.
P.V.

69910	69915	69917	69921
69912			

Total 5

69928-69936

0-8-0T 5F Class QI

Thompson rebuild of Robinson G.C.
Q4 0-8-0, introduced 1902.
QI/I* Introduced 1942. 1,500 gallon
tanks.
QI/2 Introduced 1943. 2,000 gallon
tanks.

Weight: { 69 tons 18 cwt.*
{ 73 tons 13 cwt.

Pressure: 180 lb.
Cyls.: (O) 19″ × 26″.
Driving Wheels: 4′ 8″.
T.E.: 25,645 lb.

| 69928* | 69934 | 69936 |
| 69929 | 69935 | |

Total 5

ROUTE AVAILABILITY OF LOCOMOTIVES

CLASSES OF LOCOMOTIVES

R.A. No.	Ex-L.N.E.R. including Electric Locomotives	Ex-L.M.S.	B.R. including Diesel Locomotives
1	J15, J71	2MT (2-6-2T)	DJ12, DJ13, DJ14, DJ15, DY1, DY2, DY5, DY11
2	E4, J72, J77	2MT (2-6-0)	—
3	J10, J25, J68, J69, N10	2F (0-6-0), 1F (0-6-0T), 3MT (2-6-2T P.B.), 3MT (2-6-2T T.B.)	2MT (2-6-0), 2MT (2-6-2T)
4	B12/3, J17, J26, N5, EM2 (Co-Co)	3F (0-6-0 L. & Y.), 3F (0-6-0 Mid.), 4MT (2-6-0), 1P (0-4-4T), 2P (0-4-4T), 4MT (2-6-4T 2-cyl. T.B.)	3MT (2-6-0), 4MT (2-6-0), 3MT (2-6-2T), L.M.R. DE (827 h.p.), DE1 (800 h.p. N.B.)
5	B1, B2, B17, D16/3, J6, J11, J19, J20, J27, K2, A5, A8, C13, C14, J52, J73, J94, N7, EB1 (Bo-Bo)	2P (4-4-0), 4F (0-6-0), 7F (0-8-0 Std.), 3F (0-6-0T), 4MT (2-6-4T P.B.), 3F (0-6-2T)	DE2 (1,000 h.p. N.B.), DE2 (1,100 h.p. E.E.), 4MT (2-6-4T), DEJ1, DEJ2, DEJ3, DEJ4, DEJ5, DEJ6
6	D11, J39, K1, O1, O2, O4, WD8, Q6, J50, N2, V1	8F (2-8-0 Std.), 7F (0-8-0 L.N.W.), 3P (4-4-2T)	DE1 (1,000 h.p. E.E.), DE2 (1,160 h.p. B.R.), DE2 (1,250 h.p. Brush)
7	Q7, L1, V3	5MT (4-6-0), 4P (4-4-0), 6P/5F (2-6-0 P.B.), 6P/5F (2-6-0 T.B.), 4MT (2-6-4T 3-cyl.)	4MT (4-6-0), 5MT (4-6-0), DE2 (1,160 h.p. B.C.W.), DE4 (2,000 h.p. E.E.), DE4 (2,000 h.p. N.B.)
8	B16/1, B16/2, B16/3, D49, K3, K5, QI, T1	6P (4-6-0 " Jubilee "), 6P (4-6-0 " Patriot ")	6MT (4-6-2), 7MT (4-6-2)
9	A1, A2, A3, A4, V2, W1, EM1 (Bo-Bo)	7P (4-6-0 Converted " Jubilee "), 7P (4-6-0 Converted " Patriot "), 7P (4-6-0 " Scot ")	9F (2-10-0)

BRITISH RAILWAYS
EASTERN & NORTH EASTERN REGIONS

CHIEF MECHANICAL ENGINEER
A. H. Peppercorn ... 1948–1949
(post abolished)

LOCOMOTIVE SUPERINTENDENTS AND CHIEF MECHANICAL ENGINEERS OF THE L.N.E.R.

r Nigel Gresley ... ... 1923–1941 | E. Thompson 1941–1946
A. H. Peppercorn 1946–1947

GREAT NORTHERN RAILWAY

Sturrock	...	...	1850–1866
Stirling	...	...	1866–1895
A. Ivatt	...	...	1896–1911
N. Gresley	...	...	1911–1922

NORTH EASTERN RAILWAY

Fletcher	...	...	1854–1883
McDonnell*	...	...	1883–1884
W. Worsdell	...	...	1885–1890
V. Worsdell	...	...	1890–1910
r Vincent Raven	...	...	1910–1922

GREAT EASTERN RAILWAY

Sinclair	...	...	1862–1866
W. Johnson	...	...	1866–1873
V. Adams	...	...	1873–1878
Bromley	...	...	1878–1881
W. Worsdell	...	...	1881–1885
Holden	...	...	1885–1903
D. Holden	...	...	1903–1912
J. Hill	...	...	1912–1922

LANCASHIRE, DERBYSHIRE AND EAST COAST RAILWAY

A. Thom	...	...	1902–1907

MANCHESTER, SHEFFIELD AND LINCOLNSHIRE RAILWAY

ichard Peacock	...	...	–1854
V. G. Craig	...	...	1854–1859

Charles Sacré	...	...	1859–1886
T. Parker	...	...	1886–1893
H. Pollitt	...	...	1893–1897

GREAT CENTRAL RAILWAY

H. Pollitt	...	...	1897–1900
J. G. Robinson	...	...	1900–1922

HULL AND BARNSLEY RAILWAY

M. Stirling	...	...	1885–1922

MIDLAND AND GREAT NORTHERN JOINT RAILWAY

W. Marriott	...	...	1884–1924

NORTH BRITISH RAILWAY

T. Wheatley†	...	...	1867–1874
D. Drummond	...	...	1875–1882
M. Holmes	...	...	1882–1903
W. P. Reid	...	...	1903–1919
W. Chalmers	...	...	1919–1922

GREAT NORTH OF SCOTLAND RAILWAY

D. K. Clark	...	...	1853–1855
J. F. Ruthven	...	...	1855–1857
W. Cowan	...	...	1857–1883
J. Manson	...	...	1883–1890
J. Johnson	...	...	1890–1894
W. Pickersgill	...	...	1894–1914
T. E. Heywood	...	...	1914–1922

* Between McDonnell and T. W. Worsdell there was an interval during which ne office was covered by a Locomotive Committee.

† Previous to whom the records are indeterminate.

BRITISH RAILWAYS STANDARD LOCOMOTIVES

Chief Mechanical Engineer
J. F. HARRISON

4-6-2   **7P6F**

Introduced 1951. Designed at Derby.
Weight: Loco. 94 tons 0 cwt.
Pressure: 250 lb. Su.
Cyls.: (O) 20″ × 28″.
Driving Wheels: 6′ 2″. T.E.: 32,150 lb.
Walschaerts valve gear. P.V.

70000	Britannia
70001	Lord Hurcomb
70002	Geoffrey Chaucer
70003	John Bunyan
70004	William Shakespeare
70005	John Milton
70006	Robert Burns
70007	Coeur-de-Lion
70008	Black Prince
70009	Alfred the Great
70010	Owen Glendower
70011	Hotspur
70012	John of Gaunt
70013	Oliver Cromwell
70014	Iron Duke
70015	Apollo
70016	Ariel
70017	Arrow
70018	Flying Dutchman
70019	Lightning
70020	Mercury
70021	Morning Star
70022	Tornado
70023	Venus
70024	Vulcan
70025	Western Star
70026	Polar Star
70027	Rising Star
70028	Royal Star
70029	Shooting Star
70030	William Wordsworth
70031	Byron
70032	Tennyson
70033	Charles Dickens
70034	Thomas Hardy

70035	Rudyard Kipling
70036	Boadicea
70037	Hereward the Wake
70038	Robin Hood
70039	Sir Christopher Wren
70040	Clive of India
70041	Sir John Moore
70042	Lord Roberts
70043	Lord Kitchener
70044	Earl Haig
70045	Lord Rowallan
70046	
70047	
70048	The Territorial Army 1908-1958
70049	
70050	Firth of Clyde
70051	Firth of Forth
70052	Firth of Tay
70053	Moray Firth
70054	Dornoch Firth

Total 55

4-6-2   **8P**

Introduced 1954. Designed at Derby.
Weight: Loco. 101 tons 5 cwt.
Pressure: 250 lb. Su.
Cyls.: (3) 18″ × 28″.
Driving Wheels: 6′ 2″. T.E.: 39,080 lb.
Caprotti valve gear.

71000	Duke of Gloucester

Total 1

4-6-2   **6P5F**

Introduced 1952. Designed at Derby.
Weight: Loco. 86 tons 19 cwt.
Pressure: 225 lb. Su.
Cyls.: (O) 19½″ × 28″.
Driving Wheels: 6′ 2″. T.E.: 27,520 lb.
Walschaerts valve gear. P.V.

72000	Clan Buchanan
72001	Clan Cameron
72002	Clan Campbell

72003	Clan Fraser
72004	Clan Macdonald
72005	Clan Macgregor
72006	Clan Mackenzie
72007	Clan Mackintosh
72008	Clan Macleod
72009	Clan Stewart **Total 10**

4-6-0   5

Introduced 1951. Designed at Doncaster.
*Introduced 1956. Fitted with Caprotti valve gear.
Weight: Loco. 76 tons 4 cwt.
Pressure: 225 lb. Su.
Cyls.: (O) 19″ × 28″.
Driving Wheels: 6′ 2″. T.E.: 26,120 lb.
Walschaerts valve gear. P.V.

73000	73028	73056	73084
73001	73029	73057	73085
73002	73030	73058	73086
73003	73031	73059	73087
73004	73032	73060	73088
73005	73033	73061	73089
73006	73034	73062	73090
73007	73035	73063	73091
73008	73036	73064	73092
73009	73037	73065	73093
73010	73038	73066	73094
73011	73039	73067	73095
73012	73040	73068	73096
73013	73041	73069	73097
73014	73042	73070	73098
73015	73043	73071	73099
73016	73044	73072	73100
73017	73045	73073	73101
73018	73046	73074	73102
73019	73047	73075	73103
73020	73048	73076	73104
73021	73049	73077	73105
73022	73050	73078	73106
73023	73051	73079	73107
73024	73052	73080	73108
73025	73053	73081	73109
73026	73054	73082	73110
73027	73055	73083	73111

73112	73127*	73142*	73157
73113	73128*	73143*	73158
73114	73129*	73144*	73159
73115	73130*	73145*	73160
73116	73131*	73146*	73161
73117	73132*	73147*	73162
73118	73133*	73148*	73163
73119	73134*	73149*	73164
73120	73135*	73150*	73165
73121	73136*	73151*	73166
73122	73137*	73152*	73167
73123	73138*	73153*	73168
73124	73139*	73154*	73169
73125*	73140*	73155	73170
73126*	73141*	73156	73171

Total 172

4-6-0   4

Introduced 1951. Designed at Brighton.
*Introduced 1957. Fitted with double chimney.
Weight: Loco. 69 tons 0 cwt.
Pressure: 225 lb. Su.
Cyls.: (O) 18″ × 28″.
Driving Wheels: 5′ 8″. T.E.: 25,100 lb.
Walschaerts valve gear. P.V.

75000	75020	75040	75060
75001	75021	75041	75061
75002	75022	75042	75062
75003	75023	75043	75063
75004	75024	75044	75064
75005	75025	75045	75065
75006	75026	75046	75066
75007	75027	75047	75067
75008	75028	75048	75068
75009	75029*	75049	75069
75010	75030	75050	75070
75011	75031	75051	75071
75012	75032	75052	75072
75013	75033	75053	75073
75014	75034	75054	75074
75015	75035	75055	75075
75016	75036	75056	75076
75017	75037	75057	75077
75018	75038	75058	75078
75019	75039	75059	75079

Total 80

2-6-0　　　　　　　　　　4

Introduced 1953. Designed at Doncaster.
Weight: Loco. 59 tons 2 cwt.
Pressure: 225 lb. Su.
Cyls.: (O) $17\frac{1}{2}'' \times 26''$.
Driving Wheels: 5' 3". T.E.: 24,170 lb.
Walschaerts valve gear. P.V.

76000	76029	76058	76087
76001	76030	76059	76088
76002	76031	76060	76089
76003	76032	76061	76090
76004	76033	76062	76091
76005	76034	76063	76092
76006	76035	76064	76093
76007	76036	76065	76094
76008	76037	76066	76095
76009	76038	76067	76096
76010	76039	76068	76097
76011	76040	76069	76098
76012	76041	76070	76099
76013	76042	76071	76100
76014	76043	76072	76101
76015	76044	76073	76102
76016	76045	76074	76103
76017	76046	76075	76104
76018	76047	76076	76105
76019	76048	76077	76106
76020	76049	76078	76107
76021	76050	76079	76108
76022	76051	76080	76109
76023	76052	76081	76110
76024	76053	76082	76111
76025	76054	76083	76112
76026	76055	76084	76113
76027	76056	76085	76114
76028	76057	76086	

Total 115

2-6-0　　　　　　　　　　3

Introduced 1954. Designed at Swindon.
Weight: Loco. 57 tons 9 cwt.
Pressure: 200 lb. Su.
Cyls.: (O) $17\frac{1}{2}'' \times 26''$.
Driving Wheels: 5' 3". T.E.: 21,490 lb.
Walschaerts valve gear. P.V.

77000	77005	77010	77015
77001	77006	77011	77016
77002	77007	77012	77018
77003	77008	77013	77019
77004	77009	77014	

Total 20

2-6-0　　　　　　　　　　2

Introduced 1953. Designed at Derby.
Weight: Loco. 49 tons 5 cwt.
Pressure: 200 lb. Su.
Cyls.: (O) $16\frac{1}{2}'' \times 24''$.
Driving Wheels: 5' 0". T.E.: 18,515 lb.
Walschaerts valve gear. P.V.

78000	78017	78033	78049
78001	78018	78034	78050
78002	78019	78035	78051
78003	78020	78036	78052
78004	78021	78037	78053
78005	78022	78038	78054
78006	78023	78039	78055
78007	78024	78040	78056
78008	78025	78041	78057
78009	78026	78042	78058
78010	78027	78043	78059
78011	78028	78044	78060
78012	78029	78045	78061
78013	78030	78046	78062
78014	78031	78047	78063
78015	78032	78048	78064
78016			

Total 65

2-6-4T　　　　　　　　　4

Introduced 1951. Designed at Brighton.
Weight: 88 tons 10 cwt.
Pressure: 225 lb. Su.
Cyls.: (O) $18'' \times 28''$.
Driving Wheels: 5' 8". T.E.: 25,100 lb.
Walschaerts valve gear. P.V.

80000	80005	80010	80015
80001	80006	80011	80016
80002	80007	80012	80017
80003	80008	80013	80018
80004	80009	80014	80019

80020	80054	80088	80122
80021	80055	80089	80123
80022	80056	80090	80124
80023	80057	80091	80125
80024	80058	80092	80126
80025	80059	80093	80127
80026	80060	80094	80128
80027	80061	80095	80129
80028	80062	80096	80130
80029	80063	80097	80131
80030	80064	80098	80132
80031	80065	80099	80133
80032	80066	80100	80134
80033	80067	80101	80135
80034	80068	80102	80136
80035	80069	80103	80137
80036	80070	80104	80138
80037	80071	80105	80139
80038	80072	80106	80140
80039	80073	80107	80141
80040	80074	80108	80142
80041	80075	80109	80143
80042	80076	80110	80144
80043	80077	80111	80145
80044	80078	80112	80146
80045	80079	80113	80147
80046	80080	80114	80148
80047	80081	80115	80149
80048	80082	80116	80150
80049	80083	80117	80151
80050	80084	80118	80152
80051	80085	80119	80153
80052	80086	80120	80154
80053	80087	80121	

Total 155

2-6-2T 3

Introduced 1952. Designed at Swindon.
Weight: 73 tons 10 cwt.
Pressure: 200 lb. Su.
Cyls.: (O) $17\frac{1}{2}'' \times 26''$.
Driving Wheels: 5' 3''. T.E.: 21,490 lb.
Walschaerts valve gear. P.V.

82000	82002	82004	82006
82001	82003	82005	82007

82008	82018	82027	82036
82009	82019	82028	82037
82010	82020	82029	82038
82011	82021	82030	82039
82012	82022	82031	82040
82013	82023	82032	82041
82014	82024	82033	82042
82015	82025	82034	82043
82016	82026	82035	82044
82017			

Total 45

2-6-2T 2

Introduced 1953. Designed at Derby.
Weight: 63 tons 5 cwt.
Pressure: 200 lb. Su.
Cyls.: (O) $16\frac{1}{2}'' \times 24''$.
Driving Wheels: 5' 0''. T.E.: 18,515 lb.
Walschaerts valve gear. P.V.

84000	84008	84016	84023
84001	84009	84017	84024
84002	84010	84018	84025
84003	84011	84019	84026
84004	84012	84020	84027
84005	84013	84021	84028
84006	84014	84022	84029
84007	84015		

Total 30

2-8-0 8F WD

Ministry of Supply "Austerity" 2-8-0
locomotives purchased by British
Railways, 1948.
Introduced 1943. Riddles M.o.S. design.
Weight: Loco. 70 tons 5 cwt.
Tender 55 tons 10 cwt.
Pressure: 225 lb. Su.
Cyls.: (O) 19'' × 28''.
Driving Wheels: 4' 8½''. T.E.: 34,215 lb.
Walschaerts valve gear. P.V.

90000	90009	90018	90027
90001	90010	90019	90028
90002	90011	90020	90029
90003	90012	90021	90030
90004	90013	90022	90031
90005	90014	90023	90032
90006	90015	90024	90033
90007	90016	90025	90034
90008	90017	90026	90035

90036	90083	90130	90177	90224	90271	90318	90365
90037	90084	90131	90178	90225	90272	90319	90366
90038	90085	90132	90179	90226	90273	90320	90367
90039	90086	90133	90180	90227	90274	90321	90368
90040	90087	90134	90181	90228	90275	90322	90369
90041	90088	90135	90182	90229	90276	90323	90370
90042	90089	90136	90183	90230	90277	90324	90371
90043	90090	90137	90184	90231	90278	90325	90372
90044	90091	90138	90185	90232	90279	90326	90373
90045	90092	90139	90186	90233	90280	90327	90374
90046	90093	90140	90187	90234	90281	90328	90375
90047	90094	90141	90188	90235	90282	90329	90376
90048	90095	90142	90189	90236	90283	90330	90377
90049	90096	90143	90190	90237	90284	90331	90378
90050	90097	90144	90191	90238	90285	90332	90379
90051	90098	90145	90192	90239	90286	90333	90380
90052	90099	90146	90193	90240	90287	90334	90381
90053	90100	90147	90194	90241	90288	90335	90382
90054	90101	90148	90195	90242	90289	90336	90383
90055	90102	90149	90196	90243	90290	90337	90384
90056	90103	90150	90197	90244	90291	90338	90385
90057	90104	90151	90198	90245	90292	90339	90386
90058	90105	90152	90199	90246	90293	90340	90387
90059	90106	90153	90200	90247	90294	90341	90388
90060	90107	90154	90201	90248	90295	90342	90389
90061	90108	90155	90202	90249	90296	90343	90390
90062	90109	90156	90203	90250	90297	90344	90391
90063	90110	90157	90204	90251	90298	90345	90392
90064	90111	90158	90205	90252	90299	90346	90393
90065	90112	90159	90206	90253	90300	90347	90394
90066	90113	90160	90207	90254	90301	90348	90395
90067	90114	90161	90208	90255	90302	90349	90396
90068	90115	90162	90209	90256	90303	90350	90397
90069	90116	90163	90210	90257	90304	90351	90398
90070	90117	90164	90211	90258	90305	90352	90399
90071	90118	90165	90212	90259	90306	90353	90400
90072	90119	90166	90213	90260	90307	90354	90401
90073	90120	90167	90214	90261	90308	90355	90402
90074	90121	90168	90215	90262	90309	90356	90403
90075	90122	90169	90216	90263	90310	90357	90404
90076	90123	90170	90217	90264	90311	90358	90405
90077	90124	90171	90218	90265	90312	90359	90406
90078	90125	90172	90219	90266	90313	90360	90407
90079	90126	90173	90220	90267	90314	90361	90408
90080	90127	90174	90221	90268	90315	90362	90409
90081	90128	90175	90222	90269	90316	90363	90410
90082	90129	90176	90223	90270	90317	90364	90411

90412	90459	90506	90553	90600	90634	90668	90701
90413	90460	90507	90554	90601	90635	90669	90702
90414	90461	90508	90555	90602	90636	90670	90703
90415	90462	90509	90556	90603	90637	90671	90704
90416	90463	90510	90557	90604	90638	90672	90705
90417	90464	90511	90558	90605	90639	90673	90706
90418	90465	90512	90559	90606	90640	90674	90707
90419	90466	90513	90560	90607	90641	90675	90708
90420	90467	90514	90561	90608	90642	90676	90709
90421	90468	90515	90562	90609	90643	90677	90710
90422	90469	90516	90563	90610	90644	90678	90711
90423	90470	90517	90564	90611	90645	90679	90712
90424	90471	90518	90565	90612	90646	90680	90713
90425	90472	90519	90566	90613	90647	90681	90714
90426	90473	90520	90567	90614	90648	90682	90715
90427	90474	90521	90568	90615	90649	90683	90716
90428	90475	90522	90569	90616	90650	90684	90717
90429	90476	90523	90570	90617	90651	90685	90718
90430	90477	90524	90571	90618	90652	90686	90719
90431	90478	90525	90572	90619	90653	90687	90720
90432	90479	90526	90573	90620	90654	90688	90721
90433	90480	90527	90574	90621	90655	90689	90722
90434	90481	90528	90575	90622	90656	90690	90723
90435	90482	90529	90576	90623	90657	90691	90724
90436	90483	90530	90577	90624	90658	90692	90725
90437	90484	90531	90578	90625	90659	90693	90726
90438	90485	90532	90579	90626	90660	90694	90727
90439	90486	90533	90580	90627	90661	90695	90728
90440	90487	90534	90581	90628	90662	90696	90729
90441	90488	90535	90582	90629	90663	90697	90730
90442	90489	90536	90583	90630	90664	90698	90731
90443	90490	90537	90584	90631	90665	90699	90732
90444	90491	90538	90585	90632	90666	90700	Vulcan
90445	90492	90539	90586	90633	90667		
90446	90493	90540	90587				
90447	90494	90541	90588				
90448	90495	90542	90589				
90449	90496	90543	90590				
90450	90497	90544	90591				
90451	90498	90545	90592				
90452	90499	90546	90593				
90453	90500	90547	90594				
90454	90501	90548	90595				
90455	90502	90549	90596				
90456	90503	90550	90597				
90457	90504	90551	90598				
90458	90505	90552	90599				

Total 733

2-10-0   WD

Ministry of Supply " Austerity " 2-10-0 locomotives purchased by British Railways, 1948.
Introduced 1943. Riddles M.o.S. design.
Weight: Loco. 78 tons 6 cwt.
         Tender 55 tons 10 cwt.
Pressure: 225 lb. Su.
Cyls.: (O) 19″ × 28″.
Driving Wheels: 4′ 8½″. T.E.: 34,215 lb.
Walschaerts valve gear. P.V.

90750	90757	90763	90769
90751	90758	90764	90770
90752	90759	90765	90771
90753	90760	90766	90772
90754	90761	90767	90773
90755	90762	90768	90774
90756			

Total 25

2-10-0   9F

Introduced 1954. Designed at Brighton.
*Introduced 1955. Fitted with Crosti boiler.
†Introduced 1957. Fitted with double chimney.
‡Introduced 1958. Fitted with Mechanical Stoker.

Weight: Loco. $\begin{cases} 86 \text{ tons } 14 \text{ cwt.} \\ 90 \text{ tons } 4 \text{ cwt.*} \end{cases}$
Pressure: 250 lb. Su.
Cyls.: (O) 20″ × 28″.
Driving Wheels: 5′ 0″. T.E.: 39,670 lb.
Walschaerts valve gear. P.V.

92000	92025*	92050	92075
92001	92026*	92051	92076
92002	92027*	92052	92077
92003	92028*	92053	92078
92004	92029*	92054	92079
92005	92030	92055	92080
92006	92031	92056	92081
92007	92032	92057	92082
92008	92033	92058	92083
92009	92034	92059	92084
92010	92035	92060	92085
92011	92036	92061	92086
92012	92037	92062	92087
92013	92038	92063	92088
92014	92039	92064	92089
92015	92040	92065	92090
92016	92041	92066	92091
92017	92042	92067	92092
92018	92043	92068	92093
92019	92044	92069	92094
92020*	92045	92070	92095
92021*	92046	92071	92096
92022*	92047	92072	92097
92023*	92048	92073	92098
92024*	92049	92074	92099

92100	92138	92176	92214
92101	92139	92177	92215
92102	92140	92178†	92216
92103	92141	92179	92217
92104	92142	92180	92218
92105	92143	92181	92219
92106	92144	92182	92220
92107	92145	92183	92221
92108	92146	92184†	92222
92109	92147	92185†	92223
92110	92148	92186	92224
92111	92149	92187†	92225
92112	92150	92188	92226
92113	92151	92189	92227
92114	92152	92190	92228
92115	92153	92191	92229
92116	92154	92192	92230
92117	92155	92193	92231
92118	92156	92194	92232
92119	92157	92195	92233
92120	92158	92196	92234
92121	92159	92197	92235
92122	92160	92198	92236
92123	92161	92199	92237
92124	92162	92200	92238
92125	92163	92201	92239
92126	92164	92202	92240
92127	92165‡	92203	92241
92128	92166‡	92204	92242
92129	92167‡	92205	92243
92130	92168	92206	92244
92131	92169	92207	92245
92132	92170	92208	92246
92133	92171	92209	92247
92134	92172	92210	92248
92135	92173	92211	92249
92136	92174	92212	92250
92137	92175	92213	

Engines of this class are still being delivered.

162

BRITISH RAILWAYS STANDARD TENDERS

N.B.—*These pairings are not permanent and are liable to alteration with changed operating conditions.*

Type	Capacity		Weight in full W.O.		Locos. to which Allocated
	Water galls.	Coal tons	tons	cwt.	
BRI ...	4,250	7	49	3	70000–24/30–44 72000–9 73000–49
BRIA ...	5,000	7	52	10	70025–29
BRIB ...	4,725	7	50	5	92020–29/60–6/97–9 73080–89 73100–9/20–34/45–71 75065–79 76053–69
BRIC ...	4,725	9	53	5	92015–19/45–59/77–86 92100–39/50–67 73065–79/90–9 73135–44
BRID ...	4,725	9	54	10	70045–54
BRIE ...	4,725	10	55	10	71000
BRIF ...	5,625	7	55	5	92010–14/30–44/67–76 92087–96 92140–49/68–92202 73110–19
BRIG ...	5,000	7	52	10	92000–9 73050–52
BRIH ...	4,250	7	49	3	73053–64
BR2 ...	3,500	6	42	3	75000–49 76000–44
BR2A ...	3,500	6	42	3	75050–64/80–9 76045–52/70–76114 77000–24
BR3 ...	3,000	4	36	17	78000–64

BRITISH RAILWAYS DIESEL

LOCOMOTIVE CLASSES

1Co-Co1   "4"

Introduced: 1959.
Locomotive manufacturer: B.R. Derby/Sulzer.
Total b.h.p : 2,300/2,500.
Engine(s):
Transmission: **Electric**
Weight:
Driving Wheels:
Maximum Tractive effort:

D110	D120	D130	D140
D111	D121	D131	D141
D112	D122	D132	D142
D113	D123	D133	D143
D114	D124	D134	D144
D115	D125	D135	D145
D116	D126	D136	D146
D117	D127	D137	D147
D118	D128	D138	
D119	D129	D139	

D1	Scafell Pike		
D2	D29	D56	D83
D3	D30	D57	D84
D4	D31	D58	D85
D5	D32	D59	D86
D6	D33	D60	D87
D7	D34	D61	D88
D8	D35	D62	D89
D9	D36	D63	D90
D10	D37	D64	D91
D11	D38	D65	D92
D12	D39	D66	D93
D13	D40	D67	D94
D14	D41	D68	D95
D15	D42	D69	D96
D16	D43	D70	D97
D17	D44	D71	D98
D18	D45	D72	D99
D19	D46	D73	D100
D20	D47	D74	D101
D21	D48	D75	D102
D22	D49	D76	D103
D23	D50	D77	D104
D24	D51	D78	D105
D25	D52	D79	D106
D26	D53	D80	D107
D27	D54	D81	D108
D28	D55	D82	D109

1Co-Co1   "4"

Introduced: 1958.
Locomotive manufacturer: English Electric.
Total b.h.p: 2,000.
Engine: English Electric 16SVT Mk. II of 2,000 b.h.p. at 850 r.p.m.
Transmission: **Electric.** Six English Electric nose-suspended traction motors.
Weight: 133 tons
Driving Wheels: 3′ 9″.
Maximum tractive effort: 52,000 lb.

D200	D213	D226	D239
D201	D214	D227	D240
D202	D215	D228	D241
D203	D216	D229	D242
D204	D217	D230	D243
D205	D218	D231	D244
D206	D219	D232	D245
D207	D220	D233	D246
D208	D221	D234	D247
D209	D222	D235	D248
D210	D223	D236	D249
D211	D224	D237	
D212	D225	D238	

AIA-AIA   "4"
"WARSHIP" CLASS

Introduced: 1958.
Locomotive manufacturer: North British
   Locomotive Co.
Total b.h.p.: 2,000.
Engines: Two N.B.L./M.A.N. type L12V
   18/21S 12-cyl. of 1,000 b.h.p.
Transmission: **Hydraulic.** Two Hardy
   Spicer cardan shafts to Voith-North
   British type L306r hydraulic trans-
   missions each containing three torque
   converters.
Weight: 117 tons 8 cwt.
Driving Wheels: 3′ 7″.
Maximum tractive effort: 50,000 lb.

D600 Active
D601 Ark Royal
D602 Bulldog
D603 Conquest
D604 Cossack

B-B   "4"
"WARSHIP" CLASS

Introduced: 1958.
Locomotive manufacturer: Swindon
   Works, B.R.
Total b.h.p.: 2,200 (nominal).
Engines: Two Bristol-Siddeley-Maybach
   MD 650 V-type of 1,152 b.h.p. at
   1,530 r.p.m.
   *(1,056 b.h.p. at 1,400 r.p.m.)
Transmission: **Hydraulic.** Two Mekydro
   type K104 hydraulic transmissions
   containing permanently filled single
   torque converter and four-speed
   automatic gearbox.
Weight: 78 tons.
Driving Wheels: 3′ 3½″.
Maximum tractive effort: 52,400 lb.

D800* Sir Brian Robertson
D801* Vanguard
D802* Formidable
D803 Albion

D804	D812	D320	D828
D805	D813	D821	D829
D806	D814	D822	D830
D807	D815	D823	D831
D808	D816	D824	D832
D809	D817	D825	
D810	D818	D826	
D811	D819	D827	

B-B   "4"
"WARSHIP" CLASS

To be introduced
Locomotive manufacturer: North British
   Locomotive Co.
Total b.h.p.: 2,000
Engines:
Transmission: **Hydraulic.**
Weight:
Driving Wheels:
Maximum tractive effort:

D833	D842	D851	D860
D834	D843	D852	D861
D835	D844	D853	D862
D836	D845	D854	D863
D837	D846	D855	D864
D838	D847	D856	D865
D839	D848	D857	
D840	D849	D858	
D841	D850	D859	

0-6-0   Shunter

Introduced: 1957.
Locomotive manufacturer: B.R.
Total b.h.p.: 204.
Engine: Gardner type 8L3 of 204 b.h.p.
   at 1,200 r.p.m.
Transmission: **Mechanical.** Vulcan-
   Sinclair type 23 fluid coupling.
   Wilson-Drewry C.A.5 type five-speed
   epicyclic gearbox. Type RF 11 spiral
   bevel reverse and final drive unit.
Weight: 30 tons 16 cwt.
Driving Wheels: 3′ 7″.
Maximum tractive effort: 15,650 lb.
Classified DJ15 by the E. & N.E.R.

(Original numbers in brackets)

D2000 (11187)	D2012 (11199)
D2001 (11188)	D2013 (11200)
D2002 (11189)	D2014 (11201)
D2003 (11190)	D2015 (11202)
D2004 (11191)	D2016 (11203)
D2005 (11192)	D2017 (11204)
D2006 (11193)	D2018 (11205)
D2007 (11194)	D2019 (11206)
D2008 (11195)	D2020 (11207)
D2009 (11196)	D2021 (11208)
D2010 (11197)	D2022 (11209)
D2011 (11198)	

D2023	D2053	D2083	D2113	D2200 (11100)	D2208 (11109)
D2024	D2054	D2084	D2114	D2201 (11101)	D2209 (11110)
D2025	D2055	D2085	D2115	D2202 (11102)	D2210 (11111)
D2026	D2056	D2086	D2116	D2203 (11103)	D2211 (11112)
D2027	D2057	D2087	D2117	D2204 (11105)	D2212 (11113)
D2028	D2058	D2088	D2118	D2205 (11106)	D2213 (11114)
D2029	D2059	D2089	D2119	D2206 (11107)	D2214 (11115)
D2030	D2060	D2090	D2120	D2207 (11108)	
D2031	D2061	D2091	D2121		
D2032	D2062	D2092	D2122		
D2033	D2063	D2093	D2123		
D2034	D2064	D2094	D2124		
D2035	D2065	D2095	D2125		
D2036	D2066	D2096	D2126		
D2037	D2067	D2097	D2127		
D2038	D2068	D2098	D2128		
D2039	D2069	D2099	D2129		
D2040	D2070	D2100	D2130		
D2041	D2071	D2101	D2131		
D2042	D2072	D2102	D2132		
D2043	D2073	D2103	D2133		
D2044	D2074	D2104	D2134		
D2045	D2075	D2105	D2135		
D2046	D2076	D2106	D2136		
D2047	D2077	D2107	D2137		
D2048	D2078	D2108	D2138		
D2049	D2079	D2109	D2139		
D2050	D2080	D2110	D2140		
D2051	D2081	D2111	D2141		
D2052	D2082	D2112	D2142		

0-6-0   Shunter

Introduced: 1952.
Locomotive manufacturer: Drewry.
Total b.h.p.: 204.
Engine: Gardner type 8L3 of 204 b.h.p.
   at 1,200 r.p.m.
Transmission: **Mechanical.** Vulcan-
   Sinclair type 23 fluid coupling.
   Wilson-Drewry C.A. 5 type five-speed
   epicyclic gearbox. Type RF 11 spiral
   bevel reverse and final drive unit.
Weight: 29 tons 15 cwt.
Driving Wheels: 3′ 3″.
Maximum tractive effort: 16,850 lb.
Classified **DJ12/1** by the E. & N.E.R.

(Original numbers in brackets)

0-6-0   Shunter

Introduced: 1955.
Locomotive manufacturer: Drewry.
Total b.h.p.: 204.
Engine: Gardner type 8L3 of 204 b.h.p.
   at 1,200 r.p.m.
Transmission: **Mechanical.** Vulcan-
   Sinclair type 23 fluid coupling.
   Wilson-Drewry C.A. 5 type five-speed
   epicyclic gearbox. Type RF 11 spiral
   bevel reverse and final drive unit.
Weight: 29 tons 15 cwt.
Driving Wheels: 3′ 6″.
Maximum tractive effort: 15,650 lb.
Classified **DJ12/2** by the E. & N.E.R.

(Original numbers in brackets)

D2215 (11121)	D2229 (11135)
D2216 (11122)	D2230 (11149)
D2217 (11123)	D2231 (11150)
D2218 (11124)	D2232 (11151)
D2219 (11125)	D2233 (11152)
D2220 (11126)	D2234 (11153)
D2221 (11127)	D2235 (11154)
D2222 (11128)	D2236 (11155)
D2223 (11129)	D2237 (11156)
D2224 (11130)	D2238 (11157)
D2225 (11131)	D2239 (11158)
D2226 (11132)	D2240 (11159)
D2227 (11133)	D2241 (11160)
D2228 (11134)	

0-6-0   Shunter

**D2242-D2273, FOR PARTICULARS
SEE D2200-D2214.**

(Original numbers in brackets)

D2242 (11212)	D2251 (11221)
D2243 (11213)	D2252 (11222)
D2244 (11214)	D2253 (11223)
D2245 (11215)	D2254 (11224)
D2246 (11216)	D2255 (11225)
D2247 (11217)	D2256 (11226)
D2248 (11218)	D2257 (11227)
D2249 (11219)	D2258 (11228)
D2250 (11220)	D2259 (11229)

D2260	D2267	D2274	D2281
D2261	D2268	D2275	D2282
D2262	D2269	D2276	D2283
D2263	D2270	D2277	D2284
D2264	D2271	D2278	D2285
D2265	D2272	D2279	D2286
D2266	D2273	D2280	

0-6-0   Shunter

Introduced: 1956.

Locomotive manufacturer: Barclay.

Total b.h.p.: 204.

Engine: Gardner type 8L3 of 204 b.h.p. at 1,200 r.p.m.

Transmission: **Mechanical.** Vulcan-Sinclair type 23 fluid coupling. Wilson C.A.4 type four-speed epicyclic gearbox. Wiseman type 15 RLGB reverse and final drive unit.

Weight: 32 tons 0 cwt.

Driving Wheels: 3′ 6″.

Maximum tractive effort: 15,340 lb.

Classified **DJI4** by the E. & N.E.R.

(Original numbers in brackets)

D2400 (11177)	D2405 (11182)
D2401 (11178)	D2406 (11183)
D2402 (11179)	D2407 (11184)
D2403 (11180)	D2408 (11185)
D2404 (11181)	D2409 (11186)

0-4-0   Shunter

Introduced: 1958.
Locomotive manufacturer: Barclay.
Total b.h.p.: 204.
Engine: Gardner type 8L3 of 204 b.h.p. at 1,200 r.p.m.
Transmission: **Mechanical.** Vulcan-Sinclair type 23 fluid coupling. Wilson-Drewry C.A. 5 type five-speed epicyclic gearbox. Wiseman type 15. R.L.G.B. reverse and final drive unit.
Weight: 35 tons.
Driving Wheels: 3′ 7″.
Maximum tractive effort: 20,000 lb.

D2410	D2419	D2428	D2437
D2411	D2420	D2429	D2438
D2412	D2421	D2430	D2439
D2413	D2422	D2431	D2440
D2414	D2423	D2432	D2441
D2415	D2424	D2433	D2442
D2416	D2425	D2434	D2443
D2417	D2426	D2435	D2444
D2418	D2427	D2436	

0-6-0   Shunter

Introduced: 1956.
Locomotive manufacturer: Hudswell-Clarke.
Total b.h.p.: 204.
Engine: Gardner type 8L3 of 204 b.h.p. at 1,200 r.p.m.
Transmission: **Mechanical.** S.C.R.5 type, size 23 scoop control fluid coupling. Three-speed " SSS Power-flow " double synchro-type gearbox and final drive.
Weight: 36 tons 7 cwt.
Driving Wheels: 3′ 6″.
Maximum tractive effort: 16,100 lb.

(Original numbers in brackets)

D2500 (11116)	D2505 (11144)
D2501 (11117)	D2506 (11145)
D2502 (11118)	D2507 (11146)
D2503 (11119)	D2508 (11147)
D2504 (11120)	D2509 (11148)

0-6-0   Shunter

Introduced: 1955.
Locomotive manufacturer: Hunslet.
Total b.h.p.: 204.
Engine: Gardner type 8L3 of 204 b.h.p. at 1,200 r.p.m.
Transmission: **Mechanical.** Hunslet patent friction clutch. Hunslet four-speed gearbox incorporating reverse and final drive gears.
Weight: 30 tons 0 cwt.
Driving Wheels: 3' 4".
Maximum tractive effort: 14,500 lb.
Classified **DJ13** by the E. & N.E.R.

(Original numbers in brackets)

D2550 (11136)	D2562 (11165)
D2551 (11137)	D2563 (11166)
D2552 (11138)	D2564 (11167)
D2553 (11139)	D2565 (11168)
D2554 (11140)	D2566 (11169)
D2555 (11141)	D2567 (11170)
D2556 (11142)	D2568 (11171)
D2557 (11143)	D2569 (11172)
D2558 (11161)	D2570 (11173)
D2559 (11162)	D2571 (11174)
D2560 (11163)	D2572 (11175)
D2561 (11164)	D2573 (11176)

D2574	D2586	D2598	D2610
D2575	D2587	D2599	D2611
D2576	D2588	D2600	D2612
D2577	D2589	D2601	D2613
D2578	D2590	D2602	D2614
D2579	D2591	D2603	D2615
D2580	D2592	D2604	D2616
D2581	D2593	D2605	D2617
D2582	D2594	D2606	D2618
D2583	D2595	D2607	
D2584	D2596	D2608	
D2585	D2597	D2609	

0-4-0   Shunter

Introduced: 1953.
Locomotive manufacturer: North British.
Total b.h.p.: 200.
Engine: Paxman type 6RPH of 200 b.h.p. at 1,000 r.p.m.
Transmission: **Hydraulic.** Voith-North British hydraulic torque converter type L33YU. North British bevel gears and reversing dog clutch coupled through reduction gearing to jackshaft.

Weight: 32 tons.
Driving Wheels: 3' 6".
Maximum tractive effort: 21,500 lb.
Classified **DY11** by the E. & N.E.R.

(Original numbers in brackets)

D2700 (11700)	D2704 (11704)
D2701 (11701)	D2705 (11705)
D2702 (11702)	D2706 (11706)
D2703 (11703)	D2707 (11707)

0-4-0   Shunter

Introduced: 1957.
Locomotive manufacturer: North British.
Total b.h.p.: 225.
Engine: North British type M.A.N. W6V 17.5/22A of 225 b.h.p. at 1,100 r.p.m. (12 hr. rating).
Transmission: **Hydraulic.** Voith-North British hydraulic torque converter type LCCYU. North British bevel gears and reversing dog clutch coupled through reduction gearing to jackshaft.
Weight: 30 tons.
Driving Wheels: 3' 6".
Maximum tractive effort: 20,080 lb.
Classified **DY11** by the E. & N.E.R.

(Original numbers in brackets)

D2708 (11708)	D2714 (11714)
D2709 (11709)	D2715 (11715)
D2710 (11710)	D2716 (11716)
D2711 (11711)	D2717 (11717)
D2712 (11712)	D2718 (11718)
D2713 (11713)	D2719 (11719)

D2720	D2735	D2750	D2765
D2721	D2736	D2751	D2766
D2722	D2737	D2752	D2767
D2723	D2738	D2753	D2768
D2724	D2739	D2754	D2769
D2725	D2740	D2755	D2770
D2726	D2741	D2756	D2771
D2727	D2742	D2757	D2772
D2728	D2743	D2758	D2773
D2729	D2744	D2759	D2774
D2730	D2745	D2760	D2775
D2731	D2746	D2761	D2776
D2732	D2747	D2762	D2777
D2733	D2748	D2763	D2778
D2734	D2749	D2764	D2779

Class D49/1 4-4-0 No. 62733 *Northumberland*   [*L. Marshall*

Class K2/2 2-6-0 No. 61759   [*R. C. Riley*

Class K3/2 2-6-0 No. 61811   [*P. J. Sharpe*

D

Class D30/2 4-4-0 No. 62421 *Laird o' Monkbarns*   [J. Robertson

Class D34 4-4-0 No. 62497 *Glen Mallie*   [K. L. Cook

Class D16/3 4-4-0 No. 62589   L. King

Class D11/2 4-4-0 No. 62693 *Roderick Dhu*   [J. Robertson

Class Q6 0-8-0 No. 63437   [L. King

Class Q7 0-8-0 No. 63473   [T. E. K. Chambers

D*

Class O2/3 2-8-0 No. 63974

[B. K. B. Green

Class J38 0-6-0 No. 65932

[David A. Anderson

Class J39/2 0-6-0 No. 64893

[T. Booth

Class J6 0-6-0 No. 64190   [R. C. Riley

Class J36 0-6-0 No. 65285   [Brian E. Morrison

Class J37 0-6-0 No. 64560   [K. L. Cook

Class J19 0-6-0 No. 64652

[R. E. Vincent

Class J20/1 0-6-0 No. 64691

[J. Davenport

Class T1 4-8-0T No. 69910

[R. A. Panting

Class L1 2-6-4T No. 67791   [A. R. Carpenter

Class V1 2-6-2T No. 67664   [K. L. Cook

Class C16 4-4-2T No. 67492   [K. R. Pirt

Class N5/2 0-6-2T No. 69258

[R. C. Riley

Class C14 4-4-2T No. 67448

[T. K. Wide

Class N15/1 0-6-2T No. 69180

[J. Robertson

Class N7/5 0-6-2T No. 69658 [R. C. Riley

Class N2/2 0-6-2T No. 69493 (since withdrawn) [Brian E. Morrison

Class N2/4 0-6-2T No. 69591 [A. W. Martin

Class A8 4-6-2T No. 69850   [L. King

Class Z5 0-4-2T No. 68192   [Brian E. Morrison

Class Z4 0-4-2T No. 68191   [K. L. Cook

Class J52/2 0-6-0ST No. 68846 [R. C. Riley

Class J72 0-6-0T No. 69012 [K. L. Cook

Class J77 0-6-0T No. 68410 [A. W. Martin

Class 9F 2-10-0 No. 92066 (fitted with air pumps for working Tyne Dock—Consett iron ore trains) [B. K. B. Green

Class WD 2-8-0 No. 90052 [T. K. Widd

Class WD 2-10-0 No. 90760 [R. E. Vincent

Drewry 204 b.h.p. 0-6-0 diesel-mechanical shunter (E.R. class DJ12/2) No. D2223
[C. P. Boocock

North British 330 b.h.p. 0-4-0 diesel-hydraulic shunter No. D2905   [B. K. B. Green

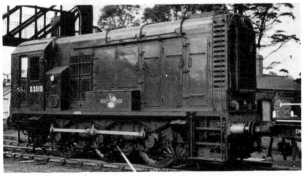

400 b.h.p. 0-6-0 diesel-electric shunter (E.R. class DEJ4) No. D3510   [B. A. Butt

Left: Type 2 Derb
B.T.H. 1,160 b.h
Bo-Bo No. D5001
        [J. B. Buckn

Centre: Type 2 Bru
Traction 1,250 b.h
A1A-A1A No. D55
        [B. A. Haresna

Bottom: Type
English Electric 1,0
b.h.p.   Bo-Bo   N
D8012
        [P. H. Groc

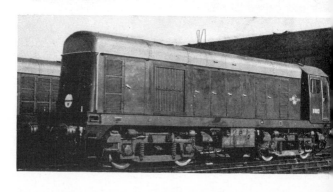

Type 4 North British 2,000 b.h.p. A1A-A1A D601 *Ark Royal* [*J. H. Aston*

Type 4 English Electric 2,000 b.h.p. 1Co-Co1 D202 [*P. Tait*

English Electric 3,300 b.h.p. "Deltic" Co-Co locomotive [*Eric Treacy*

Class 5P/5F Co-Co locomotives 10000/1

[R. Leslie

Class 6P/6F 1Co-Co1 No. 10203

[S. D. Wainwright

Class 3P/3F North British 827 b.h.p. Bo-Bo No. 10800

[P. H. Groom

0-4-0 Shunter

Introduced: 1958.
Locomotive manufacturer: North British Locomotive Co.
Total b.h.p.: 330.
Engine: North British/M.A.N. type W6V 17.5/22 AS, super-charged.
Transmission: **Hydraulic.** Voith-North British hydraulic torque converter type L24V. North British spiral bevel gears, reversing and reduction gears to jackshaft.
Weight: 36 tons.
Driving Wheels: 3' 9".
Maximum tractive effort: 24,100 lb.

D2900	D2903	D2906	D2909
D2901	D2904	D2907	D2910
D2902	D2905	D2908	

0-4-0 Shunter

Introduced: 1955.
Locomotive manufacturer: Hunslet.
Total b.h.p.: 153.
Engine: Gardner type 6L3 of 153 b.h.p. at 1,200 r.p.m.
Transmission: **Mechanical.** Hunslet patent friction clutch. Hunslet four-speed gearbox incorporating reverse and final drive gears.
Weight: 22 tons 9 cwt.
Driving Wheels: 3' 4".
Maximum tractive effort: 10,800 lb.
Classified **DY1** by E. & N.E.R.
(Original numbers in brackets)

| D2950 (11500) | D2952 (11502) |
| D2951 (11501) | |

0-4-0 Shunter

Introduced: 1956.
Locomotive manufacturer: Barclay.
Total b.h.p.: 153.
Engine: Gardner type 6L3 of 153 b.h.p. at 1,200 r.p.m.
Transmission: **Mechanical.** Vulcan-Sinclair rigid type hydraulic coupling. Wilson S.E.4 type four-speed epicyclic gearbox. Wiseman type 15 RLGB reverse and final drive unit.
Weight: 25 tons.
Driving Wheels: 3' 2".
Maximum tractive effort: 12,750 lb.
Classified **DY2** by E. & N.E.R.
(Original numbers in brackets)

| D2953 (11503) | D2955 (11505) |
| D2954 (11504) | D2956 (11506) |

0-4-0 Shunter

Introduced: 1956.
Locomotive manufacturer: Ruston & Hornsby.
Total b.h.p.: 165.
Engine: Ruston type 6VPHL of 165 b.h.p. at 1,250 r.p.m. (1 hr. rating).
Transmission: **Mechanical.** Oil pressure-operated S.L.M. type friction clutches incorporated in Ruston constant mesh type gearbox. Reverse gear and final drive unit incorporating bevel gears and dog clutches and reduction gear to final drive.
Weight: 28 tons.
Driving Wheels: 3' 4".
Maximum tractive effort: 14,350 lb.
Classified **DY5** by the E. & N.E.R.
(Original numbers in brackets)

| D2957 (11507) | D2958 (11508) |

0-6-0 Shunter

Engines D3000-D3336 were originally numbered 13000-13336 and are being renumbered as they are overhauled.

Introduced: 1953.
Locomotive manufacturer: British Railways.
Total b.h.p.: 400.
Engine: English Electric 6 cyl. type 6KT of 400 b.h.p. at 630 r.p.m.
Transmission: **Electric.** Two English Electric nose-suspended traction motors. Double reduction gear drive.
Weight: 49 tons 0 cwt.
Driving Wheels: 4' 6".
Maximum tractive effort: 35,000 lb.
Classified **DEJ4** by the E. & N.E.R.
Note: Nos. D3000-91 and 3102-3116 fitted with vacuum brake operation.

D3000	D3014	D3028	D3042
D3001	D3015	D3029	D3043
D3002	D3016	D3030	D3044
D3003	D3017	D3031	D3045
D3004	D3018	D3032	D3046
D3005	D3019	D3033	D3047
D3006	D3020	D3034	D3048
D3007	D3021	D3035	D3049
D3008	D3022	D3036	D3050
D3009	D3023	D3037	D3051
D3010	D3024	D3038	D3052
D3011	D3025	D3039	D3053
D3012	D3026	D3040	D3054
D3013	D3027	D3041	D3055

D3056	D3072	D3088	D3104
D3057	D3073	D3089	D3105
D3058	D3074	D3090	D3106
D3059	D3075	D3091	D3107
D3060	D3076	D3092	D3108
D3061	D3077	D3093	D3109
D3062	D3078	D3094	D3110
D3063	D3079	D3095	D3111
D3064	D3080	D3096	D3112
D3065	D3081	D3097	D3113
D3066	D3082	D3098	D3114
D3067	D3083	D3099	D3115
D3068	D3084	D3100	D3116
D3069	D3085	D3101	
D3070	D3086	D3102	
D3071	D3087	D3103	

0-6-0 Shunter

Introduced: 1955.
Locomotive manufacturer: British Railways.
Total b.h.p.: 350.
Engine: Crossley 6-cyl. type ESNT 6 of 350 b.h.p. at 825 r.p.m. (continuous rating).
Transmission: **Electric.** Two Crompton Parkinson nose-suspended traction motors. Double reduction gear drive.
Weight: 47 tons 10 cwt.
Driving Wheels: 4' 6".
Maximum tractive effort: 35,000 lb.

D3117	D3120	D3123	D3126
D3118	D3121	D3124	
D3119	D3122	D3125	

0-6-0 Shunter

Introduced: 1953.
Locomotive manufacturer: British Railways.
Total b.h.p.: 400.
Engine: English Electric 6-cyl. type 6KT of 400 b.h.p. at 680 r.p.m.
Transmission: **Electric.** Two English Electric nose-suspended traction motors. Double reduction gear drive.
Weight: 48 tons 0 cwt.
Driving Wheels: 4' 6".
Maximum tractive effort: 35,000 lb.
Fitted for vacuum brake operation.
Classified **DEJ4** by the E. & N.E.R.

D3127	D3130	D3133	D3136
D3128	D3131	D3134	
D3129	D3132	D3135	

0-6-0 Shunter

Introduced: 1955.
Locomotive manufacturer: British Railways.
Total b.h.p.: 370.
Engine: Blackstone 6-cyl. type ER6T of 370 b.h.p. at 750 r.p.m.
Transmission: **Electric.** Two G.E.C. nose-suspended traction motors. Double reduction gear drive.
Weight: 47 tons 10 cwt.
Driving Wheels: 4' 6".
Maximum tractive effort: 35,000 lb.
Fitted for vacuum brake operation.

D3137	D3141	D3145	D3149
D3138	D3142	D3146	D3150
D3139	D3143	D3147	D3151
D3140	D3144	D3148	

0-6-0 Shunter

Introduced: 1955.
Locomotive manufacturer: British Railways.
Total b.h.p.: 370.
Engine: Blackstone 6-cyl. type ER6T of 370 b.h.p. at 750 r.p.m.
Transmission: **Electric.** Two B.T.H. nose-suspended traction motors. Double reduction gear drive.
Weight: 47 tons 0 cwt.
Driving Wheels: 4' 6".
Maximum tractive effort: 35,000 lb.
Classified **DEJ6** by the E. & N.E.R.

D3152	D3156	D3160	D3164
D3153	D3157	D3161	D3165
D3154	D3158	D3162	D3166
D3155	D3159	D3163	

D3167-D3438. FOR PARTICULARS SEE Nos. D3127-D3136.

D3167	D3180	D3193	D3206
D3168	D3181	D3194	D3207
D3169	D3182	D3195	D3208
D3170	D3183	D3196	D3209
D3171	D3184	D3197	D3210
D3172	D3185	D3198	D3211
D3173	D3186	D3199	D3212
D3174	D3187	D3200	D3213
D3175	D3188	D3201	D3214
D3176	D3189	D3202	D3215
D3177	D3190	D3203	D3216
D3178	D3191	D3204	D3217
D3179	D3192	D3205	D3218

D3219	D3265	D3311	D3357
D3220	D3266	D3312	D3358
D3221	D3267	D3313	D3359
D3222	D3268	D3314	D3360
D3223	D3269	D3315	D3361
D3224	D3270	D3316	D3362
D3225	D3271	D3317	D3363
D3226	D3272	D3318	D3364
D3227	D3273	D3319	D3365
D3228	D3274	D3320	D3366
D3229	D3275	D3321	D3367
D3230	D3276	D3322	D3368
D3231	D3277	D3323	D3369
D3232	D3278	D3324	D3370
D3233	D3279	D3325	D3371
D3234	D3280	D3326	D3372
D3235	D3281	D3327	D3373
D3236	D3282	D3328	D3374
D3237	D3283	D3329	D3375
D3238	D3284	D3330	D3376
D3239	D3285	D3331	D3377
D3240	D3286	D3332	D3378
D3241	D3287	D3333	D3379
D3242	D3288	D3334	D3380
D3243	D3289	D3335	D3381
D3244	D3290	D3336	D3382
D3245	D3291	D3337	D3383
D3246	D3292	D3338	D3384
D3247	D3293	D3339	D3385
D3248	D3294	D3340	D3386
D3249	D3295	D3341	D3387
D3250	D3296	D3342	D3388
D3251	D3297	D3343	D3389
D3252	D3298	D3344	D3390
D3253	D3299	D3345	D3391
D3254	D3300	D3346	D3392
D3255	D3301	D3347	D3393
D3256	D3302	D3348	D3394
D3257	D3303	D3349	D3395
D3258	D3304	D3350	D3396
D3259	D3305	D3351	D3397
D3260	D3306	D3352	D3398
D3261	D3307	D3353	D3399
D3262	D3308	D3354	D3400
D3263	D3309	D3355	D3401
D3264	D3310	D3356	D3402

D3403	D3412	D3421	D3430
D3404	D3413	D3422	D3431
D3405	D3414	D3423	D3432
D3406	D3415	D3424	D3433
D3407	D3416	D3425	D3434
D3408	D3417	D3426	D3435
D3409	D3418	D3427	D3436
D3410	D3419	D3428	D3437
D3411	D3420	D3429	D3438

D3439-D3453. FOR PARTICULARS SEE D3137-3151.

D3439	D3443	D3447	D3451
D3440	D3444	D3448	D3452
D3441	D3445	D3449	D3453
D3442	D3446	D3450	

D3454-D3472. FOR PARTICULARS SEE D3127-D3136.

D3454	D3459	D3464	D3469
D3455	D3460	D3465	D3470
D3456	D3461	D3466	D3471
D3457	D3462	D3467	D3472
D3458	D3463		

D3473-D3502. FOR PARTICULARS SEE D3137-3151.

D3473	D3481	D3489	D3497
D3474	D3482	D3490	D3498
D3475	D3483	D3491	D3499
D3476	D3484	D3492	D3500
D3477	D3485	D3493	D3501
D3478	D3486	D3494	D3502
D3479	D3487	D3495	
D3480	D3488	D3496	

D3503-D3611. FOR PARTICULARS SEE D3127-D3136.

D3503	D3515	D3527	D3539
D3504	D3516	D3528	D3540
D3505	D3517	D3529	D3541
D3506	D3518	D3530	D3542
D3507	D3519	D3531	D3543
D3508	D3520	D3532	D3544
D3509	D3521	D3533	D3545
D3510	D3522	D3534	D3546
D3511	D3523	D3535	D3547
D3512	D3524	D3536	D3548
D3513	D3525	D3537	D3549
D3514	D3526	D3538	D3550

D3551	D3567	D3583	D3599
D3552	D3568	D3584	D3600
D3553	D3569	D3585	D3601
D3554	D3570	D3586	D3602
D3555	D3571	D3587	D3603
D3556	D3572	D3588	D3604
D3557	D3573	D3589	D3605
D3558	D3574	D3590	D3606
D3559	D3575	D3591	D3607
D3560	D3576	D3592	D3608
D3561	D3577	D3593	D3609
D3562	D3578	D3594	D3610
D3563	D3579	D3595	D3611
D3564	D3580	D3596	
D3565	D3581	D3597	
D3566	D3582	D3598	

D3612-D3651. FOR PARTICULARS SEE D3137-D3151.

D3612	D3622	D3632	D3642
D3613	D3623	D3633	D3643
D3614	D3624	D3634	D3644
D3615	D3625	D3635	D3645
D3616	D3626	D3636	D3646
D3617	D3627	D3637	D3647
D3618	D3628	D3638	D3648
D3619	D3629	D3639	D3649
D3620	D3630	D3640	D3650
D3621	D3631	D3641	D3651

D3652-D3831. FOR PARTICULARS SEE D3127-D3136.

D3652	D3665	D3678	D3691
D3653	D3666	D3679	D3692
D3654	D3667	D3680	D3693
D3655	D3668	D3681	D3694
D3656	D3669	D3682	D3695
D3657	D3670	D3683	D3696
D3658	D3671	D3684	D3697
D3659	D3672	D3685	D3698
D3660	D3673	D3686	D3699
D3661	D3674	D3687	D3700
D3662	D3675	D3688	D3701
D3663	D3676	D3689	D3702
D3664	D3677	D3690	D3703

D3704	D3736	D3768	D3800
D3705	D3737	D3769	D3801
D3706	D3738	D3770	D3802
D3707	D3739	D3771	D3803
D3708	D3740	D3772	D3804
D3709	D3741	D3773	D3805
D3710	D3742	D3774	D3806
D3711	D3743	D3775	D3807
D3712	D3744	D3776	D3808
D3713	D3745	D3777	D3809
D3714	D3746	D3778	D3810
D3715	D3747	D3779	D3811
D3716	D3748	D3780	D3812
D3717	D3749	D3781	D3813
D3718	D3750	D3782	D3814
D3719	D3751	D3783	D3815
D3720	D3752	D3784	D3816
D3721	D3753	D3785	D3817
D3722	D3754	D3786	D3818
D3723	D3755	D3787	D3819
D3724	D3756	D3788	D3820
D3725	D3757	D3789	D3821
D3726	D3758	D3790	D3822
D3727	D3759	D3791	D3823
D3728	D3760	D3792	D3824
D3729	D3761	D3793	D3825
D3730	D3762	D3794	D3826
D3731	D3763	D3795	D3827
D3732	D3764	D3796	D3828
D3733	D3765	D3797	D3829
D3734	D3766	D3798	D3830
D3735	D3767	D3799	D3831

Bo-Bo   "2"

Introduced: 1958.
Locomotive manufacturer: B.R./B.T.H.
Total b.h.p.: 1,160.
Engine: Sulzer 6-cyl. type 6LDA28 of 1,160 b.h.p. at 750 r.p.m.
Transmission: **Electric.** Four B.T.H. axle-hung, nose-suspended traction motors of 213 h.p. (continuous rating).
Weight: 75 tons.
Driving Wheels: 3' 9".
Maximum tractive effort: 40,000 lb.

D5000	D5029	D5058	D5087
D5001	D5030	D5059	D5088
D5002	D5031	D5060	D5089
D5003	D5032	D5061	D5090
D5004	D5033	D5062	D5091
D5005	D5034	D5063	D5092
D5006	D5035	D5064	D5093
D5007	D5036	D5065	D5094
D5008	D5037	D5066	D5095
D5009	D5038	D5067	D5096
D5010	D5039	D5068	D5097
D5011	D5040	D5069	D5098
D5012	D5041	D5070	D5099
D5013	D5042	D5071	D5100
D5014	D5043	D5072	D5101
D5015	D5044	D5073	D5102
D5016	D5045	D5074	D5103
D5017	D5046	D5075	D5104
D5018	D5047	D5076	D5105
D5019	D5048	D5077	D5106
D5020	D5049	D5078	D5107
D5021	D5050	D5079	D5108
D5022	D5051	D5080	D5109
D5023	D5052	D5081	D5110
D5024	D5053	D5082	D5111
D5025	D5054	D5083	D5112
D5026	D5055	D5084	D5113
D5027	D5056	D5085	
D5028	D5057	D5086	

Bo-Bo   "2"

Introduced: 1958.
Locomotive manufacturer: Birmingham R.C. & W. Co.
Total b.h.p.: 1,160.
Engine: Vickers Armstrong/Sulzer 6-cyl. type of 1,160 b.h.p. at 750 r.p.m.
Transmission: **Electric.** Four Crompton Parkinson axle-hung, nose-suspended traction motors.
Weight: 77 tons 10 cwt.
Driving Wheels: 3' 7".
Maximum tractive effort: 42,000 lb.

D5300	D5312	D5324	D5336
D5301	D5313	D5325	D5337
D5302	D5314	D5326	D5338
D5303	D5315	D5327	D5339
D5304	D5316	D5328	D5340
D5305	D5317	D5329	D5341
D5306	D5318	D5330	D5342
D5307	D5319	D5331	D5343
D5308	D5320	D5332	D5344
D5309	D5321	D5333	D5345
D5310	D5322	D5334	D5346
D5311	D5323	D5335	

AIA-AIA   "2"

Introduced: 1957.
Locomotive manufacturer: Brush Traction Ltd.
Total b.h.p.: { 1,250. { 1,350.*
Engine: Mirrlees, Bickerton & Day 12-cyl. JVS12T of 1,250 (1,350*) b.h.p. at 850 r.p.m.
Transmission: **Electric.** Four Brush 250 h.p. traction motors, single reduction gear drive.
Weight: 104 tons.
Driving Wheels: 3' 7".
Maximum tractive effort: 42,000 lb.

D5500	D5514	D5528*	D5542*
D5501	D5515	D5529*	D5543*
D5502	D5516	D5530*	D5544*
D5503	D5517	D5531*	D5545*
D5504	D5518	D5532*	D5546*
D5505	D5519	D5533*	D5547*
D5506	D5520*	D5534*	D5548*
D5507	D5521*	D5535*	D5549*
D5508	D5522*	D5536*	D5550*
D5509	D5523*	D5537*	D5551*
D5510	D5524*	D5538*	D5552*
D5511	D5525*	D5539*	D5553*
D5512	D5526*	D5540*	D5554*
D5513	D5527*	D5541*	D5555*

D5556*	D5562*	D5568*	D5574*
D5557*	D5563*	D5569*	D5575*
D5558*	D5564*	D5570*	D5576*
D5559*	D5565*	D5571*	D5577*
D5560*	D5566*	D5572*	D5578*
D5561*	D5567*	D5573*	D5579*

Co-Bo   "2"

Introduced: 1958.
Locomotive manufacturer: Metropolitan Vickers.
Total b.h.p.: 1,200.
Engine: Crossley 8-cyl. HST Vee 8 of 1,200 b.h.p. at 625 r.p.m. (continuous).
Transmission: **Electric.** Five Metropolitan-Vickers 180 h.p. axle-hung nose-suspended traction motors.
Weight: 97 tons.
Driving Wheels: 3' 3½".
Maximum tractive effort: 50,000 lb.

D5700	D5705	D5710	D5715
D5701	D5706	D5711	D5716
D5702	D5707	D5712	D5717
D5703	D5708	D5713	D5718
D5704	D5709	D5714	D5719

Bo-Bo   "2"

To be introduced:
Locomotive manufacturer: English Electric.
Total b.h.p.: 1,100.
Engine: English Electric 9-cyl. " Deltic " type of 1,100 b.h.p.
Transmission: **Electric.** Four English Electric nose-suspended traction motors.
Weight: 72 tons.
Driving Wheels:
Maximum tractive effort:

D5900	D5903	D5906	D5909
D5901	D5904	D5907	
D5902	D5905	D5908	

Bo-Bo   "2"

To be introduced:
Locomotive manufacturer: North British Locomotive Co.
Total b.h.p.: { 1,000.
                1,160.*
Engine: { M.A.N. 1,000 b.h.p.
          M.A.N. 1,160 b.h.p.*
Transmission: **Electric.** Four G.E.C. nose-suspended traction motors.
Weight: 72 tons.
Driving Wheels: 3' 7".
Maximum tractive effort: 45,000 lb.

D6100	D6115*	D6130*	D6145*
D6101	D6116*	D6131*	D6146*
D6102	D6117*	D6132*	D6147*
D6103	D6118*	D6133*	D6148*
D6104	D6119*	D6134*	D6149*
D6105	D6120*	D6135*	D6150*
D6106	D6121*	D6136*	D6151*
D6107	D6122*	D6137*	D6152*
D6108	D6123*	D6138*	D6153*
D6109	D6124*	D6139*	D6154*
D6110*	D6125*	D6140*	D6155*
D6111*	D6126*	D6141*	D6156*
D6112*	D6127*	D6142*	D6157*
D6113*	D6128*	D6143*	
D6114*	D6129*	D6144*	

B-B   "2"

Introduced: 1959.
Locomotive manufacturer: North British Locomotive Co.
Total b.h.p.: 1,000.
Engine(s):
Transmission: **Hydraulic.**
Weight:
Driving Wheels:
Maximum tractive effort:

D6300	D6306	D6312	D6318
D6301	D6307	D6313	D6319
D6302	D6308	D6314	D6320
D6303	D6309	D6315	D6321
D6304	D6310	D6316	D6322
D6305	D6311	D6317	D6323

D6324	D6333	D6342	D6351
D6325	D6334	D6343	D6352
D6326	D6335	D6344	D6353
D6327	D6336	D6345	D6354
D6328	D6337	D6346	D6355
D6329	D6338	D6347	D6356
D6330	D6339	D6348	D6357
D6331	D6340	D6349	
D6332	D6341	D6350	

Bo-Bo   " 1 "

Introduced: 1957.
Locomotive manufacturer: English Electric Co./Vulcan Foundry Ltd.
Total b.h.p.: 1,000.
Engine: English Electric 8 SVT Mk. II of 1,000 b.h.p. at 850 r.p.m. (continuous).
Transmission: **Electric.** Four axle-hung, nose-suspended d.c. traction motors.
Weight: 72 tons.
Driving Wheels: 3' 7".
Maximum tractive effort: 42,000 lb.

D8000	D8013	D8026	D8039
D8001	D8014	D8027	D8040
D8002	D8015	D8028	D8041
D8003	D8016	D8029	D8042
D8004	D8017	D8030	D8043
D8005	D8018	D8031	D8044
D8006	D8019	D8032	D8045
D8007	D8020	D8033	D8046
D8008	D8021	D8034	D8047
D8009	D8022	D8035	D8048
D8010	D8023	D8036	D8049
D8011	D8024	D8037	
D8012	D8025	D8038	

Bo-Bo   " 3 "

To be introduced:
Locomotive manufacturer: Birmingham R.C. & W. Co.
Total b.h.p.: 1,550.
Engine(s):
Transmission: **Electric.**
Weight:
Driving Wheels:
Maximum tractive effort:

D6500	D6517	D6534	D6551
D6501	D6518	D6535	D6552
D6502	D6519	D6536	D6553
D6503	D6520	D6537	D6554
D6504	D6521	D6538	D6555
D6505	D6522	D6539	D6556
D6506	D6523	D6540	D6557
D6507	D6524	D6541	D6558
D6508	D6525	D6542	D6559
D6509	D6526	D6543	D6560
D6510	D6527	D6544	D6561
D6511	D6528	D6545	D6562
D6512	D6529	D6546	D6563
D6513	D6530	D6547	D6564
D6514	D6531	D6548	
D6515	D6532	D6549	
D6516	D6533	D6550	

Bo-Bo   " 1 "

Introduced: 1957.
Locomotive manufacturer: British Thomson-Houston Co./Clayton.
Total b.h.p.: 800.
Engine: Paxman 16-cyl. YHXL " V "-type pressure charged by two Napier exhaust gas-driven turbo chargers. 800 b.h.p. at 1,250 r.p.m.
Transmission: **Electric.** Four B.T.H. nose-suspended traction motors with single reduction gear drive.
Weight: 68 tons.
Driving Wheels: 3' 3¼".
Maximum tractive effort: **37,500 lb.**

D8200	D8210	D8220	D8230
D8201	D8211	D8221	D8231
D8202	D8212	D8222	D8232
D8203	D8213	D8223	D8233
D8204	D8214	D8224	D8234
D8205	D8215	D8225	D8235
D8206	D8216	D8226	D8236
D8207	D8217	D8227	
D8208	D8218	D8228	
D8209	D8219	D8229	

Bo-Bo   " 1 "

Introduced: 1958.
Locomotive manufacturer: North British
  Locomotive Co.
Total b.h.p.: 800.
Engine: Paxman 16-cyl. type 16YHXL
  of 800 b.h.p. at 1,250 r.p.m.
Transmission: **Electric.** Four G.E.C.
  axle-hung nose-suspended traction
  motors.
Weight: 68 tons.
Driving Wheels: 3' 7".
Maximum tractive effort: 42,000 lb.

D8400	D8403	D8406	D8408
D8401	D8404	D8407	D8409
D8402	D8405		

Co-Co   5P/5F

Introduced: 1947.
Locomotive manufacturer: Derby Works,
  B.R.
Total b.h.p.: 1,600.
Engine: English Electric Co. 16-cyl. of
  1,600 b.h.p. at 750 r.p.m. (continuous
  rating).
Transmission: **Electric.** Six nose-
  suspended motors, single reduction
  gear drive.
Weight: 127 tons 13 cwt.
Driving Wheels: 3' 6".
Maximum tractive effort: 41,400 lb.

10000	10001	Total 2

I Co-Co I   { 10201/2 5P/5F }   { 10203 6P/6F }

Introduced: { 1951
            { 1954*
Locomotive manufacturer: Ashford
  Works, B.R.
Total b.h.p.:   { 1,750
             { 2,000*
Engine: English Electric Co. 16-cyl.
  1,750 b.h.p. (2,000 b.h.p.)*
Transmission: **Electric.** Six nose-
  suspended, axle-hung d.c. motors of
  260 h.p. (1-hour rating).
Weight: { 135 tons.
         { 132 tons.*
Driving Wheels: 3' 7".
Maximum tractive effort: { 48,000 lb.
                          { 50,000 lb.*

10201	10202	*10203
		Total 3

Bo-Bo   3P/3P

Introduced: 1950.
Locomotive manufacturer: North British
  Locomotive Co.
Total b.h.p.: 827.
Engine: Davey Paxman type RPHXL.
  16-cyl., 827 b.h.p. at 1,250 r.p.m.
Transmission: **Electric.** Four British
  Thomson - Houston Co. nose-sus-
  pended motors, single reduction gear
  drive.
Weight: 69 tons 16 cwt.
Driving Wheels: 3' 6".
Maximum tractive effort: 34,500 lb.

10800	Total 1

0-6-0   Shunter

Introduced: 1950.
Locomotive manufacturer: Ashford
  Works, B.R.
Total b.h.p.: 500.
Engine: Davey Paxman type 12RPH
  " V " 12-cyl. 500 b.h.p. at 1,250 r.p.m.
Transmission: **Mechanical** with S.S.S.
  Powerflow three-speed gearbox and
  Vulcan-Sinclair scoop-control fluid
  coupling.
Weight: 49 tons 9 cwt.
Driving Wheels: 4' 6".
Maximum tractive effort: 33,500 lb. (in
  low gear).

11001	Total 1

0-6-0   Shunter

Introduced: 1936.
Locomotive manufacturer: English Electric for L.M.S.
Total b.h.p.: 350.
Engine: English Electric 6-cyl. 350 b.h.p.
Transmission: **Electric.** Two nose-suspended motors, single reduction gear drive.
Weight: 51 tons.
Driving Wheels: 4′ 0½″.
Maximum tractive effort: 30,000 lb.

12000	12001	**Total 2**

0-6-0   Shunter

Introduced: 1939.
Locomotive manufacturer: Derby Works, B.R.
Total b.h.p.: 350.
Engine: English Electric, 6-cyl. 350 b.h.p.
Transmission: **Electric.** Single motor; jackshaft drive.
Weight: 54 tons 16 cwt.
Driving Wheels: 4′ 3″.
Maximum tractive effort: 33,000 lb.

12003	12011	12019	12027
12004	12012	12020	12028
12005	12013	12021	12029
12006	12014	12022	12030
12007	12015	12023	12031
12008	12016	12024	12032
12009	12017	12025	
12010	12018	12026	

Total 30

0-6-0   Shunter

Introduced: 1945.
Locomotive manufacturer: Derby Works, B.R.
Total b.h.p.: 350.
Engine: English Electric, 6-cyl. 350 b.h.p.
Transmission: **Electric.** Two 135 h.p. nose-suspended motors, double reduction gear drive.
Weight: 47 tons 5 cwt.
Driving Wheels: 4′ 0½″.
Maximum tractive effort: 35,000 lb.
Classified **DEJ3** by the E. & N.E.R.

12033	12060	12087	12114
12034	12061	12088	12115
12035	12062	12089	12116
12036	12063	12090	12117
12037	12064	12091	12118
12038	12065	12092	12119
12039	12066	12093	12120
12040	12067	12094	12121
12041	12068	12095	12122
12042	12069	12096	12123
12043	12070	12097	12124
12044	12071	12098	12125
12045	12072	12099	12126
12046	12073	12100	12127
12047	12074	12101	12128
12048	12075	12102	12129
12049	12076	12103	12130
12050	12077	12104	12131
12051	12078	12105	12132
12052	12079	12106	12133
12053	12080	12107	12134
12054	12081	12108	12135
12055	12082	12109	12136
12056	12083	12110	12137
12057	12084	12111	12138
12058	12085	12112	
12059	12086	12113	

Total 106

0-6-0   Shunter

Introduced: 1944.
Locomotive manufacturer: Doncaster Works, B.R.
Total b.h.p.: 350.
Engine: English Electric, 6-cyl. 350 b.h.p.
Transmission: **Electric.** Two 135 h.p. nose-suspended motors, double reduction gear drive.
Weight: 50 tons.
Driving Wheels: 4′ 0″.
Maximum tractive effort: 32,000 lb.
Classified **DEJ1** by the E. & N.E.R.

15000	15001	15002	15003

Total 4

0-6-0 Shunter

Introduced: 1949.
Locomotive manufacturer: Doncaster Works, B.R.
Total b.h.p.: 360.
Engine: Petter SS4 4-cyl. 360 b.h.p.
Transmission: **Electric.** Two 135 h.p. nose-suspended traction motors, double reduction gear drive.
Weight: 51 tons.
Driving Wheels: 4′ 0″.
Maximum tractive effort: 32,000 lb.
Classified **DEJ2** by the E. & N.E.R.

15004   **Total 1**

0-6-0 Shunter

Introduced: 1936.
Locomotive manufacturer: English Electric for G.W.R.
Total b.h.p.: 350.
Engine: English Electric, 6-cyl. 350 b.h.p.
Transmission: **Electric.** Two nose-suspended motors, single reduction gear drive.
Weight: 51 tons 10 cwt.
Driving Wheels: 4′ 1″.
Maximum tractive effort: 30,000 lb.

15100   **Total 1**

0-6-0 Shunter

Introduced: 1948.
Locomotive manufacturer: Swindon Works, B.R.
Total b.h.p.: 350.
Engine: English Electric, 6-cyl. 350 b.h.p.
Transmission: **Electric.** Two 135 h.p. nose-suspended motors, double reduction gear drive.
Weight: 50 tons.
Driving Wheels: 4′ 0½″.
Maximum tractive effort: 33,500 lb.

15101	15103	15105
15102	15104	15106 **Total 6**

0-6-0 Shunter

Introduced: 1937.
Locomotive manufacturer: Ashford Works, B.R.
Total b.h.p.: 350.
Engine: English Electric, 6-cyl. 350 b.h.p.
Transmission: **Electric.** Two nose-suspended motors, single reduction gear drive.
Weight: 55 tons 5 cwt.
Driving Wheels: 4′ 6″.
Maximum tractive effort: 30,000 lb.

15201   15202   15203   **Total 3**

0-6-0 Shunter

Introduced: 1949.
Locomotive manufacturer: Ashford Works, B.R.
Total b.h.p.: 350.
Engine: English Electric, 6-cyl. 350 b.h.p.
Transmission: **Electric.** Two 135 h.p. nose-suspended motors, double reduction gear drive.
Weight: 45 tons.
Driving Wheels: 4′ 6″.
Maximum tractive effort: 24,000 lb.

15211	15218	15225	15232
15212	15219	15226	15233
15213	15220	15227	15234
15214	15221	15228	15235
15215	15222	15229	15236
15216	15223	15230	
15217	15224	15231	

Total 26

Co-Co   "Deltic"

NOTE: British Railways are providing facilities for road tests of this locomotive, which remains the property of the manufacturer, and is not included in B.R. stock. An order has been placed for 22 of these locomotives to work on the E., N.E. & Scottish Regions.

Introduced: 1955.
Locomotive manufacturer: English Electric.
Total b.h.p.: 3,300.
Engines: Two Napier "Deltic" 18-cyl. engines of 1,650 b.h.p.
Transmission: **Electric.** Six axle-hung nose-suspended traction motors.
Weight: 106 tons.
Driving Wheels: 3′ 7″.
Maximum tractive effort: 60,000 lb.

AIA-AIA   Gas Turbine

Introduced: 1949.
Locomotive manufacturer: Swiss Locomotive & Machine Works, Winterthur.
Total b.h.p.: 2,500.
Engine: Brown-Boveri 2,500 b.h.p. Gas Turbine.
Transmission: **Electric.** Four frame-mounted traction motors driving through spring drive.
Weight: 115 tons.
Driving Wheels: 4′ 0½″.
Maximum tractive effort: 60,000 lb.

18000

SERVICE LOCOMOTIVES

Western Region

0-4-0

Introduced: 1957.
Locomotive manufacturer: Ruston & Hornsby.
Total b.h.p.: 88.
Engine: Ruston & Hornsby 4-cyl. type of 83 b.h.p.
Transmission: **Mechanical.** Chain driven from gearbox.
Weight: 17 tons.
Wheel Diameter: 3′ 0″.
Maximum tractive effort: 9,500 lb.

20

0-6-0

Introduced: 1953.
Locomotive Manufacturer: Ruston & Hornsby.
Total b.h.p.: 165.
Engine: Ruston & Hornsby 6-cyl. type of 165 b.h.p.
Transmission: **Electric.** One B.T.H. nose-suspended traction motor.
Weight: 30 tons.
Driving Wheels: 3′ 2½″.
Maximum tractive effort: 17,000 lb.

PWM650

Southern Region

0-4-0

Introduced: 1947.
Locomotive manufacturer: John Fowler & Co.
Total b.h.p.: 150.
Engine: Fowler.
Transmission: **Mechanical.** Four-speed gearbox.
Weight: 29 tons.
Driving Wheels: 3′ 3″.
Maximum tractive effort: 15,000 lb.
DS600

0-6-0

Introduced: 1947.
Locomotive manufacturer: Drewry.
Total b.h.p.: 204.
Engine: Gardner 8L3 of 204 b.h.p.
Transmission: **Mechanical.** Five-speed gearbox.
Weight: 24 tons 15 cwt.
Driving Wheels: 3′ 3″.
Maximum tractive effort: 16,850 lb.
DS1173

London Midland Region

0-4-0

Introduced: 1936.
Locomotive manufacturer: John Fowler & Co.
Total b.h.p.: 88.
Engine: Ruston & Hornsby 6-cyl. type VQ of 88 b.h.p.
Transmission: **Mechanical.** Four-speed constant mesh gearbox with multiple disc dry clutch manually operated.
Weight: 25 tons.
Driving Wheels: 3′ 0″.
Maximum tractive effort: 8,940 lb.
ED1

0-4-0

Introduced: 1936.
Locomotive manufacturer: John Fowler & Co.
Total b.h.p.: 150.
Engine: Fowler type 4C vertical of 150 b.h.p. at 1,000 r.p.m. (1 hr. rating).
Transmission: **Mechanical.** Four-speed gearbox.
Weight: 29 tons.
Driving Wheels: 3′ 3″.
Maximum tractive effort: 15,000 lb.

| ED2 | ED4 | ED5 | ED6 |
| ED3 | | | |

0-4-0

Introduced: 1955.
Locomotive manufacturer: John Fowler & Co.
Total b.h.p.: 150.
Engine: Fowler 4-cyl. type C of 150 b.h.p.
Transmission: **Mechanical.** Three-lobe synchromesh gearbox with multiple disc dry clutch manually operated.
Weight: 29 tons.
Driving Wheels: 3′ 3″.
Maximum tractive effort: 15,000 lb.
ED7

0-4-0

Introduced: 1958.
Locomotive manufacturer: Ruston & Hornsby.
Total b.h.p.:
Engine: Ruston type 4YCL.
Transmission: **Mechanical.** Chain drive.
Weight: 8 tons 4 cwt.
Driving Wheels: 2′ 6″.
Maximum tractive effort: 4,200 lb.
Gauge: 3′ 0″.
ED10

Eastern Region

0-4-0

Introduced: 1950.
Locomotive manufacturer: Hibberd & Co.
Total b.h.p.: 52.
Engine: English National 4-cyl. Gas type. DA4 of 52 b.h.p. at 1,250 r.p.m.
Transmission: **Mechanical.** Spur-type three-speed gearbox with roller chains.
Weight: 11 tons.
Driving Wheels:
Maximum tractive effort:
52 (11104)

0-4-0

Introduced: 1955.
Locomotive manufacturer: Ruston & Hornsby.
Total b.h.p.: 88.
Engine: Ruston & Hornsby Mark 4V vertical 4-cyl. of 88 b.h.p.
Transmission: **Mechanical.**
Weight: 17 tons.
Driving Wheels: 3′ 0″.
Maximum tractive effort: 9,500 lb.
56

0-4-0

Introduced: 1958.
Locomotive manufacturer: Andrew Barclay.
Total b.h.p.: 150.
Engine:
Transmission: **Mechanical.**
Weight:
Driving Wheels:
Maximum tractive effort:
81

North Eastern Region

0-6-0

Introduced: 1958.
Locomotive manufacturer: Swindon Works, B.R.
Total b.h.p.: 200.
Engine: Gardner type 8L3 of 204 b.h.p. at 1,200 r.p.m
Transmission: **Mechanical.** Wilson-Drewry Director air-operated epicyclic gearbox. R.F.11 Spiral Bevel reverse/final drive unit.
Weight: 30 tons 4 cwt.
Driving Wheels: 3′ 7″.
Maximum tractive effort: 15,300 lb.

| 91 | 92 |

DIESEL MULTIPLE UNITS

The numbers of diesel cars have been checked to December 27th, 1958

Unless otherwise stated, all multiple-unit trains are gangwayed within each set, with guard's and luggage compartment at the inner end of motor brake coaches, and seating is in open saloons with centre and/or end doors. The letter L in the headings indicates an open vehicle fitted with toilet facilities ; K indicates a side corridor vehicle with toilet. Two standard lengths of underframe are in use, namely 56 ft. 11 in. and 63 ft. 5 in. but the actual body lengths vary by a few inches for the same type of underframe. The dimensions shown are the length over body and the overall width.

Several of the types listed are sub-divided by reason of detail or mechanical differences. For example, a certain number of cars in a class may have a different seating arrangement or a different make of engine but are otherwise similar to the main batch. Such differences are noted in the heading to the class and given a reference mark by which the relevant dimensions or details and the cars concerned can be identified. The type of set in which each class is formed is shown at the head of the details for that class.

Motor Brake Second
(TWIN UNITS)

Built by: **Derby Works, B.R.**
Engines: Two B.U.T. (Leyland) 6-cyl. horizontal type of 150 b.h.p.
 *Two Rolls Royce 8-cyl. horizontal type of 238 b.h.p.
 †Two B.U.T. (Leyland) 6-cyl. horizontal type of 230 b.h.p.
Transmission: **Mechanical.** Cardan shaft and freewheel to four-speed epicyclic gearbox and further cardan shaft to final drive.
 ***Hydraulic.** Torque converter.
 †**Mechanical.** Cardan shaft and free wheel to Self Changing Gears Ltd. automatic four-speed gearbox and further cardan shaft to final drive.
Body: 64′ 6″ × 9′ 3″.
Weight: { 35 tons 10 cwt.
 { 37 tons 10 cwt.†
Seats 2nd: 62.

E50000*	E50007	E50014
E50001	E50008	E50015
E50002	E50009	E50016
E50003	E50010	E50017
E50004	E50011	E50018
E50005	E50012	E50019
E50006	E50013	E50020

E50021	E50031	E50041
E50022	E50032	E50042
E50023	E50033	E50043
E50024	E50034	E50044
E50025	E50035	E50045
E50026	E50036	E50046
E50027	E50037	E50047
E50028	E50038	E50048
E50029	E50039	E50049†
E50030	E50040	

Cars 50001–48 are to be equipped with 230 h.p. B.U.T. engines shortly.

Motor Brake Second
(W.R. THREE-CAR SUBURBAN)

Built by: **Derby Works, B.R.**
Engines: Two B.U.T. (Leyland) 6-cyl. horizontal type of 150 b.h.p.
Transmission: **Mechanical.** Cardan shaft and freewheel to four-speed epicyclic gearbox and further cardan shaft to final drive.
Body: 64′ 0″ × 9′ 3″. Non-gangwayed, side doors to each seating bay.
Weight: 35 tons 10 cwt.
Seats 2nd: 65.

W50050	W50064	W50078
W50051	W50065	W50079
W50052	W50066	W50080
W50053	W50067	W50081
W50054	W50068	W50082
W50055	W50069	W50083
W50056	W50070	W50084
W50057	W50071	W50085
W50058	W50072	W50086
W50059	W50073	W50087
W50060	W50074	W50088
W50061	W50075	W50089
W50062	W50076	W50090
W50063	W50077	W50091

Motor Second

(W.R. THREE-CAR SUBURBAN)

Built by: **Derby Works, B.R.**
Engines: Two B.U.T. (Leyland) 6-cyl. horizontal type of 150 b.h.p.
Transmission: **Mechanical.** Cardan shaft and freewheel to four-speed epicyclic gearbox and further cardan shaft to final drive.
Body: 64′ 0″ × 9′ 3″. Non-gangwayed, side doors to each seating bay.
Weight: 35 tons 10 cwt.
Seats 2nd: 95.

W50092	W50106	W50120
W50093	W50107	W50121
W50094	W50108	W50122
W50095	W50109	W50123
W50096	W50110	W50124
W50097	W50111	W50125
W50098	W50112	W50126
W50099	W50113	W50127
W50100	W50114	W50128
W50101	W50115	W50129
W50102	W50116	W50130
W50103	W50117	W50131
W50104	W50118	W50132
W50105	W50119	W50133

Motor Brake Second

(TWIN UNITS)

Built by: **Metropolitan Cammell.**
Engines: Two Rolls-Royce 6-cyl. horizontal type of 180 b.h.p.
*Two Rolls Royce 6-cyl. type supercharged to 230 b.h.p.
Transmission: **Mechanical.** Cardan shaft and freewheel to four-speed epicyclic gearbox and further cardan shaft to final drive.
Body: 57′ 0″ × 9′ 3″.
Weight: 33 tons.
Seats 2nd: 52.

M50134	M50136*	M50137
M50135		

Motor Composite (L)

(N.E. FOUR-CAR UNITS)

Built by: **Metropolitan Cammell.**
Engines: Two B.U.T. (A.E.C.) 6-cyl. horizontal type of 150 b.h.p.
Transmission: **Mechanical.** Cardan shaft and freewheel to four-speed epicyclic gearbox and further cardan shaft to final drive.
Body: 57′ 0″ × 9′ 3″.
Weight: 32 tons.
Seats 1st: 12.
*   2nd:* 45.

E50138	E50143	E50148
E50139	E50144	E50149
E50140	E50145	E50150
E50141	E50146	E50151
E50142	E50147	

Motor Brake Second

(TWIN UNITS)

Built by: **Metropolitan Cammell.**
Engines: Two B.U.T. (A.E.C.) 6-cyl. horizontal type of 150 b.h.p.
Transmission: **Mechanical.** Cardan shaft and freewheel to four-speed epicyclic gearbox and further cardan shaft to final drive.
Body: 57′ 0″ × 9′ 3″.
Weight: 32 tons.
Seats 2nd:

E50152	E50154	E50156
E50153	E50155	E50157

Motor Composite (L)
(TWIN UNITS)

Built by: **Metropolitan Cammell.**
Engines: Two B.U.T. (A.E.C.) 6-cyl.
horizontal type of 150 b.h.p.
Transmission: **Mechanical.** Cardan
shaft and freewheel to four-speed
epicyclic gearbox and further cardan
shaft to final drive.
Body: 57' 0" × 9' 3".
Weight: 32 tons.
Seats 1st: 12.
2nd: 53.

E50158	E50160	E50162
E50159	E50161	E50163

Motor Brake Second
(TWIN UNITS)
For Details see E50152-7

E50164	E50166	E50167
E50165		

Motor Composite (L)
(TWIN UNITS)
For Details see E50158-63

E50168	E50170	E50171
E50169		

Motor Composite (L)
(N.E. FOUR-CAR UNITS)

Built by: **Metropolitan Cammell.**
Engines: B.U.T. (A.E.C.) 6-cyl. horizontal type of 150 b.h.p.
Transmission: **Mechanical.** Cardan
shaft and freewheel to four-speed
epicyclic gearbox and further cardan
shaft to final drive.
Body: 57' 0" × 9' 3".
Weight: 32 tons.
Seats 1st: 12.
2nd: 53.

E50172	E50182	E50191
E50174	E50183	E50192
E50175	E50184	E50193
E50176	E50185	E50194
E50177	E50186	E50195
E50178	E50187	E50196
E50179	E50188	E50197
E50180	E50189	
E50181	E50190	

Motor Brake Second
(TWIN UNITS)

Built by: **Metropolitan Cammell.**
Engines: Two B.U.T. (A.E.C.) 6-cyl.
horizontal type of 150 b.h.p.
Transmission: **Mechanical.** Cardan
shaft and freewheel to four-speed
epicyclic gearbox and further cardan
shaft to final drive.
Body: 57' 0" × 9' 3".
Weight: 32 tons.
Seats 2nd: 52

E50198	E50210	E50222
E50199	E50211	E50223
E50200	E50212	E50224
E50201	E50213	E50225
E50202	E50214	E50225
E50203	E50215	E50227
E50204	E50216	E50223
E50205	E50217	E50229
E50206	E50218	E50230
E50207	E50219	E50231
E50208	E50220	E50232
E50209	E50221	E50233

Motor Composite (L)
(N.E. FOUR-CAR UNITS)
For Details see E50138-45

E50234	E50238	E50242
E50235	E50239	E50243
E50236	E50240	E50244
E50237	E50241	E50245

Motor Brake Second
(TWIN UNITS)

Built by: **Metropolitan Cammell.**
Engines: Two B.U.T. (A.E.C.) 6-cyl.
horizontal type of 150 b.h.p.
Transmission: **Mechanical.** Cardan
shaft and freewheel to four-speed
epicyclic gearbox and further cardan
shaft to final drive.
Body: 57' 0" × 9' 3".
Weight: 31 tons 10 **cwt.**
Seats 2nd: 44

E50246	E50247	E50248

Motor Brake Second
(TWIN UNITS)

Built by: **Metropolitan Cammell.**
Engines: Two B.U.T. (A.E.C.) 6-cyl. horizontal type of 150 b.h.p.
Transmission: **Mechanical.** Cardan shaft and freewheel to four-speed epicyclic gearbox and further cardan shaft to final drive.
Body: 57′ 0″ × 9′ 3″.
Weight: 31 tons 10 cwt.
Seats 2nd: 52.

E50250	E50254	E50258
E50251	E50255	E50259
E50252	E50256	
E50253	E50257	

Motor Composite (L)
(TWIN UNITS)

Built by: **Metropolitan Cammell.**
Engines: Two B.U.T. (A.E.C.) 6-cyl. horizontal type of 150 b.h.p.
Transmission: **Mechanical.** Cardan shaft and freewheel to four-speed epicyclic gearbox and further cardan shaft to final drive.
Body: 57′ 0″ × 9′ 3″.
Weight: 31 tons 10 cwt.
Seats 1st: 12
2nd: 53.

E50260	E50264	E50268
E50261	E50265	E50269
E50262	E50266	
E50263	E50267	

Motor Composite (L)
(N.E. THREE-CAR UNITS)

Built by: **Metropolitan Cammell.**
Engines: Two Rolls Royce 6-cyl. horizontal type of 180 b.h.p.
Transmission: **Mechanical.** Cardan shaft and freewheel to four-speed epicyclic gearbox and further cardan shaft to final drive.
Weight:
Seats 1st: 12.
2nd: 53.

E50270	E50274	E50278
E50271	E50275	E50279
E50272	E50276	
E50273	E50277	

Motor Brake Second
(N.E. THREE-CAR UNITS)

Built by: **Metropolitan Cammell.**
Engine: Rolls Royce 6-cyl. horizontal type of 180 b.h.p.
Transmission: **Mechanical.** Cardan shaft and freewheel to four-speed epicyclic gearbox and further cardan shaft to final drive.
Body: 57′ 0″ × 9′ 3″.
Weight: 33 tons.
Seats 2nd: 52.

E50280	E50285	E50290
E50281	E50286	E50291
E50282	E50287	E50292
E50283	E50288	
E50284	E50289	

Motor Brake Second
(TWIN UNITS)

Built by: **Metropolitan Cammell.**
Engines: Two B.U.T. (A.E.C.) 6-cyl. horizontal type of 150 b.h.p.
Transmission: **Mechanical.** Cardan shaft and freewheel to four-speed epicyclic gearbox and further cardan shaft to final drive.
Body: 57′ 0″ × 9′ 3″.
Weight:
Seats 2nd:

E50293	E50295	E50296
E50294		

Motor Brake Second
(L.M. THREE-CAR UNITS)

Built by: **Metropolitan Cammell.**
Engines: Two B.U.T. 6-cyl. horizontal type of 150 b.h.p.
Transmission: **Mechanical.** Cardan shaft and freewheel to four-speed epicyclic gearbox and further cardan shaft to final drive.
Body: 57′ 0″ × 9′ 3″.
Weight:
Seats 2nd: 52.

M50303	M50309	M50315
M50304	M50310	M50316
M50305	M50311	M50317
M50306	M50312	M50318
M50307	M50313	M50319
M50308	M50314	M50320

Motor Composite (L)
(L.M. THREE-CAR UNITS)

Built by: **Metropolitan Cammell.**
Engines: Two B.U.T. 6-cyl. horizontal type of 150 b.h.p.
Transmission: **Mechanical.** Cardan shaft and freewheel to four-speed epicyclic gearbox and further cardan shaft to final drive.
Body: 57′ 0″ × 9′ 3″.
Weight:
Seats 1st: 12.
2nd: 53.

M50321	M50327	M50333
M50322	M50328	M50334
M50323	M50329	M50335
M50324	M50330	M50336
M50325	M50331	M50337
M50326	M50332	M50338

Motor Brake Second
(TWIN UNITS)

Built by: **Cravens.**
Engines: Two B.U.T. (Leyland) (A.E.C.*) 6-cyl. horizontal type of 150 b.h.p.
Transmission: **Mechanical.** Cardan shaft and freewheel to four-speed epicyclic gearbox and further cardan shaft to final drive.
Body: 57′ 6″ × 9′ 3″.
Weight: 30 tons.
Seats 2nd: 52.

E50359	E50371*	E50383*
E50360	E50372*	E50384*
E50361	E50373*	E50385*
E50362	E50374*	E50386*
E50363	E50375*	E50387*
E50364	E50376*	E50388*
E50365	E50377*	E50389*
E50366	E50378*	M50390*
E50367	E50379*	M50391*
E50368	E50380*	M50392*
E50369	E50381*	M50393*
E50370	E50382*	M50394*

Motor Brake Second
(TWIN UNITS)

Built by: **Gloucester R.C. & W. Co.**
Engines: Two B.U.T. (A.E.C.) 6-cyl. horizontal type of 150 b.h.p.
Transmission: **Mechanical.** Cardan shaft and freewheel to four-speed epicyclic gearbox and further cardan shaft to final drive.
Body: 57′ 6″ × 9′ 3″.
Weight: 30 tons 5 cwt.
Seats 2nd: 52.

SC50339	SC50346	M50353
SC50340	SC50347	M50354
SC50341	SC50348	M50355
SC50342	SC50349	M50356
SC50343	M50350	M50357
SC50344	M50351	M50358*
SC50345	M50352	

* Fitted with C.A.V. Ltd. automatic gear change equipment.

Motor Brake Second
(TWIN UNITS)

Built by: **Park Royal Vehicles.**
Engines: Two B.U.T. (A.E.C.) 6-cyl. horizontal type of 150 b.h.p.
Transmission: **Mechanical.** Cardan shaft and freewheel to four-speed epicyclic gearbox and further cardan shaft to final drive.
Body: 57′ 6″ × 9′ 3″.
Weight: 33 tons 8 cwt.
Seats 2nd: 52.

M50395	M50402	M50409
M50396	M50403	M50410
M50397	M50404	M50411
M50398	M50405	M50412
M50399	M50406	M50413
M50400	M50407	M50414
M50401	M50408	

Motor Brake Second

(TWIN UNITS)

Built by: **D. Wickham & Co. Ltd.**
Engines: Two B.U.T. (Leyland) 6-cyl. horizontal type of 150 b.h.p.
Transmission: **Mechanical.** Cardan shaft and freewheel to four-speed epicyclic gearbox and further cardan shaft to final drive.
Body: 57' 0" × 9' 3".
Weight: 27 tons 10 cwt.
Seats 2nd: 59.

E50415	E50417	E50419
E50416	E50418	

Motor Brake Second

(L.M. THREE-CAR UNITS)

Built by: **Birmingham C. & W. Co.**
Engines: Two B.U.T. (Leyland) 6-cyl. horizontal type of 150 b.h.p.
Transmission: **Mechanical.** Cardan shaft and freewheel to four-speed epicyclic gearbox and further cardan shaft to final drive.
Body: 57' 6" × 9' 3".
Weight: 31 tons.
Seats 2nd: 52.

M50420	M50422	M50423
M50421		

Motor Composite (L)

(L.M. THREE-CAR UNITS)

Built by: **Birmingham C. & W. Co.**
Engines: Two B.U.T. (Leyland) 6-cyl. horizontal type of 150 b.h.p.
Transmission: **Mechanical.** Cardan shaft and freewheel to four-speed epicyclic gearbox and further cardan shaft to final drive.
Body: 57' 6" × 9' 3".
Weight: 31 tons.
Seats 1st: 12.
2nd: 54.

M50424	M50426	M50427
M50425		

Motor Brake Second

(L.M. THREE-CAR UNITS)
For Details see M50420-3

M50428	M50446	M50464
M50429	M50447	M50465
M50430	M50448	M50466
M50431	M50449	M50467
M50432	M50450	M50468
M50433	M50451	M50469
M50434	M50452	M50470
M50435	M50453	M50471
M50436	M50454	M50472
M50437	M50455	M50473
M50438	M50456	M50474
M50439	M50457	M50475
M50440	M50458	M50476
M50441	M50459	M50477
M50442	M50460	M50478
M50443	M50461	M50479
M50444	M50462	
M50445	M50463	

Motor Composite (L)

(L.M. THREE-CAR UNITS)
For Details see M50424-7.

M50480	M50498	M50516
M50481	M50499	M50517
M50482	M50500	M50518
M50483	M50501	M50519
M50484	M50502	M50520
M50485	M50503	M50521
M50486	M50504	M50522
M50487	M50505	M50523
M50488	M50506	M50524
M50489	M50507	M50525
M50490	M50508	M50526
M50491	M50509	M50527
M50492	M50510	M50528
M50493	M50511	M50529
M50494	M50512	M50530
M50495	M50513	M50531
M50496	M50514	
M50497	M50515	

Motor Brake Second

(TWIN UNITS)

Built by: **Birmingham C. & W. Co.**
Engines: Two B.U.T. (Leyland) 6-cyl.
 horizontal type of 150 b.h.p.
Transmission: **Mechanical.** Cardan
 shaft and freewheel to four-speed
 epicyclic gearbox and further cardan
 shaft to final drive.
Body: 57′ 6″ × 9′ 3″.
Weight: 31 tons.
Seats 2nd: 52.

M50532	M50536	M50540
M50533	M50537	M50541
M50534	M50538	
M50535	M50539	

Motor Composite (L)

(N.E. FOUR-CAR UNITS)

Built by: **Birmingham C. & W. Co.**
Engines: Two B.U.T. (Leyland) 6-cyl.
 horizontal type of 150 b.h.p.
Transmission: **Mechanical.** Cardan
 shaft and freewheel to four-speed
 epicyclic gearbox and further cardan
 shaft to final drive.
Body: 57′ 6″ × 9′ 3″.
Weight: 31 tons.
Seats 1st: 12.
 2nd: 51.

E50542	E50559	E50576
E50543	E50560	E50577
E50544	E50561	E50578
E50545	E50562	E50579
E50546	E50563	E50580
E50547	E50564	E50581
E50548	E50565	E50582
E50549	E50566	E50583
E50550	E50567	E50584
E50551	E50568	E50585
E50552	E50569	E50586
E50553	E50570	E50587
E50554	E50571	E50589
E50555	E50572	E50590
E50556	E50573	E50591
E50557	E50574	E50592
E50558	E50575	

Motor Brake Second

(TWIN UNITS)

Built by: **Birmingham C. & W Co.**
Engines: Two B.U.T. (Leyland) 6-cyl.
 horizontal type of 150 b.h.p.
Transmission: **Mechanical.** Cardan
 shaft and freewheel to four-speed
 epicyclic gearbox and further cardan
 shaft to final drive.
Body: 57′ 6″ × 9′ 3″
Weight: 31 tons.
Seats 2nd: 52.

E50594	E50596	E50598
E50595	E50597	

Motor Brake Second

(TWIN UNITS OR N.E. THREE-CAR UNITS*)

Built by: **Derby Works, B.R.**
Engines: Two B.U.T. (A.E.C.) 6-cyl.
 horizontal type of 150 b.h.p.
Transmission: **Mechanical.** Cardan
 shaft and freewheel to four-speed
 epicyclic gearbox and further cardan
 shaft to final drive.
Body: 57′ 6″ × 9′ 2″.
Weight: 27 tons.
Seats 2nd: 52

E50599	E50610	E50621*
E50600	E50611	E50622*
E50601	E50612	E50623*
E50602	E50613	E50624*
E50603	E50614	M50625
E50604	E50615	M50626
E50605	E50616	M50627
E50606	E50617	M50628
E50607	E50618	M50629
E50608	E50619	
E50609	E50620*	

Motor Composite (L)

(N.E. THREE AND FOUR-CAR UNITS)

Built by: **Derby Works, B.R.**
Engines: Two B.U.T. (A.E.C.) 6-cyl.
 horizontal type of 150 b.h.p.
Transmission: **Mechanical.** Cardan
 shaft and freewheel to four-speed
 epicyclic gearbox and further cardan
 shaft to final drive.
Body: 57′ 6″ × 9′ 2″
Weight:
Seats 1st:
 2nd:

E50630	E50636	E50642
E50631	E50637	E50643
E50632	E50638	E50644
E50633	E50639	E50645
E50634	E50640	E50646
E50635	E50641	

Motor Second (L)

(W.R. THREE-CAR CROSS-COUNTRY)

Built by: **Swindon Works B.R.**
Engines: Two B.U.T. 6-cyl. horizontal type of 150 b.h.p.
Transmission: **Mechanical.** Cardan shaft and freewheel to four-speed epicyclic gearbox and further cardan shaft to final drive.
Body: 64′ 6″ × 9′ 3″.
Weight: 36 tons 10 cwt.
Seats 2nd: 68.

W50647	W50664	W50681
W50648	W50665	W50682
W50649	W50666	W50683
W50650	W50667	W50684
W50651	W50668	W50685
W50652	W50669	W50686
W50653	W50670	W50687
W50654	W50671	W50688
W50655	W50672	W50689
W50656	W50673	W50690
W50657	W50674	W50691
W50658	W50675	W50692
W50659	W50676	W50693
W50660	W50677	W50694
W50661	W50678	W50695
W50662	W50679	
W50663	W50680	

Motor Brake Composite

(W.R. THREE CAR CROSS-COUNTRY)

Built by: **Swindon Works B.R.**
Engines: Two B.U.T. 6-cyl. horizontal type of 150 b.p.h.
Transmission: **Mechanical.** Cardan shaft and freewheel to four-speed epicyclic gearbox and further cardan shaft to final drive.
Body: 64′ 6″ × 9′ 3″.
Weight: 36 tons 7 cwt.
Seats 1st: 18.
 2nd: 16.

W50696	W50713	W50730
W50697	W50714	W50731
W50698	W50715	W50732
W50699	W50716	W50733
W50700	W50717	W50734
W50701	W50718	W50735
W50702	W50719	W50736
W50703	W50720	W50737
W50704	W50721	W50738
W50705	W50722	W50739
W50706	W50723	W50740
W50707	W50724	W50741
W50708	W50725	W50742
W50709	W50726	W50743
W50710	W50727	W50744
W50711	W50728	
W50712	W50729	

Motor Composite (L)

(N.E. THREE-CAR UNITS)

Built by: **Metropolitan Cammell.**
Engines: Two Rolls Royce 6-cyl. horizontal type of 180 b.h.p.
Transmission: **Mechanical.** Cardan shaft and freewheel to four-speed epicyclic gearbox and further cardan shaft to final drive.
Body: 57′ 0″ × 9′ 3″.
Weight:
Seats 1st: 12.
 2nd: 53.

E50745	E50746	E50747

Motor Composite (L)

(N.E. FOUR-CAR UNITS)

Built by: **Metropolitan Cammell.**
Engines: Two B.U.T. (A.E.C.) 6-cyl. horizontal type of 150 b.h.p.
Transmission: **Mechanical.** Cardan shaft and freewheel to four-speed epicyclic gearbox and further cardan shaft to final drive.
Body: 57′ 0″ × 9′ 3″.
Weight:
Seats 1st:
 2nd:

E50748	E50750	E50751
E50749		

Motor Brake Second
(L.M. THREE-CAR UNITS)

Built by: **Cravens.**
Engines: Two B.U.T. (Leyland) 6-cyl. horizontal type of 150 b.h.p.
Transmission: **Mechanical.** Cardan shaft and freewheel to four-speed epicyclic gearbox and further cardan shaft to final drive.
Body: 57′ 6″ × 9′ 3″.
Weight: 30 tons.
Seats 2nd: 52.

M50752	M50759	M50766
M50753	M50760	M50767
M50754	M50761	M50768
M50755	M50762	M50769
M50756	M50763	M50770
M50757	M50764	
M50758	M50765	

Motor Brake Second
(TWIN UNITS)

Built by: **Cravens.**
Engines: Two B.U.T. (A.E.C.) 6-cyl. horizontal type of 150 b.h.p.
Transmission: **Mechanical.** Cardan shaft and freewheel to four-speed epicyclic gearbox and further cardan shaft to final drive.
Body: 57′ 6″ × 9′ 3″.
Weight: 30 tons.
Seats 2nd: 52.

M50771	M50776	M50781
M50772	M50777	M50782
M50773	M50778	M50783
M50774	M50779	M50784
M50775	M50780	

Motor Composite (L)
(L.M. THREE-CAR UNITS)

Built by: **Cravens.**
Engines: Two B.U.T. (Leyland) 6-cyl. horizontal type of 150 b.h.p.
Transmission: **Mechanical.** Cardan shaft and freewheel to four-speed epicyclic gearbox and further cardan shaft to final drive.
Body: 57′ 6″ × 9′ 3″.
Weight: 30 tons.
Seats 1st: 12.
   2nd: 51.

M50785	M50792	M50799
M50786	M50793	M50800
M50787	M50794	M50801
M50788	M50795	M50802
M50789	M50796	M50803
M50790	M50797	
M50791	M50798	

Motor Composite (L)
(TWIN UNITS)

Built by: **Cravens.**
Engines: Two B.U.T. (A.E.C.) 6-cyl. horizontal type of 150 b.h.p.
Transmission: **Mechanical.** Cardan shaft and freewheel to four-speed epicyclic gearbox and further cardan shaft to final drive.
Body: 57′ 6″ × 9′ 3″.
Weight: 30 tons.
Seats 1st: 12.
   2nd: 51.

M50804	M50809	M50814
M50805	M50810	M50815
M50806	M50811	M50816
M50807	M50812	M50817
M50808	M50813	

Motor Brake Second
(W.R. THREE-CAR SUBURBAN)
For Details see W50050-91

W50818	W50836	W50854
W50819	W50837	W50855
W50820	W50838	W50856
W50821	W50839	W50857
W50822	W50840	W50858
W50823	W50841	W50859
W50824	W50842	W50860
W50825	W50843	W50861
W50826	W50844	W50862
W50827	W50845	W50863
W50828	W50846	W50864
W50829	W50847	W50865
W50830	W50848	W50866
W50831	W50849	W50867
W50832	W50850	W50868
W50833	W50851	W50869
W50834	W50852	W50870
W50835	W50853	

Motor Second
W.R. THREE-CAR SUBURBAN)
For Details see W50092-50133

W50871	W50889	W50907
W50872	W50890	W50908
W50873	W50891	W50909
W50874	W50892	W50910
W50875	W50893	W50911
W50876	W50894	W50912
W50877	W50895	W50913
W50878	W50896	W50914
W50879	W50897	W50915
W50880	W50898	W50916
W50881	W50899	W50917
W50882	W50900	W50918
W50883	W50901	W50919
W50884	W50902	W50920
W50885	W50903	W50921
W50886	W50904	W50922
W50887	W50905	W50923
W50888	W50906	

Motor Brake Second
(TWIN UNITS)
Built by: **Derby Works, B.R.**
Engines: Two B.U.T. (A.E.C.) 6-cyl. horizontal type of 150 b.h.p.
Transmission: **Mechanical.** Cardan shaft and freewheel to four-speed epicyclic gearbox and further cardan shaft to final drive.
Body: 57' 6" × 9' 2".
Weight:
Seats 2nd:

M50938	M50943	M50948
M50939	M50944	M50951
M50940	M50945	M50952
M50941	M50946	
M50942	M50947	

Motor Second
(E.R. THREE-CAR SUBURBAN)
Built by: **Derby Works, B.R.**
Engines: Two Rolls Royce horizontal type of 238 b.h.p.
Transmission: **Mechanical.** Cardan shaft and freewheel to four-speed epicyclic gearbox and further cardan shaft to final drive.
Body: 64' 0" × 9' 3". Non-gangwayed, side doors to each seating bay.
Weight: 35 tons 10 cwt.
Seats 2nd: 95.

E50988	E50995	E51002
E50989	E50996	E51003
E50990	E50997	E51004
E50991	E50998	E51005
E50992	E50999	E51006
E50993	E51000	E51007
E50994	E51001	

Motor Brake Composite
(W.R. THREE-CAR CROSS-COUNTRY)
Built by: **Gloucester R.C. & W. Co.**
Engines: Two B.U.T. 6-cyl. horizontal type of 150 b.h.p.
Transmission: **Mechanical.** Cardan shaft and freewheel to four-speed epicyclic gearbox and further cardan shaft to final drive.
Body: 64' 6" × 9' 3".
Weight: 36 tons 19 cwt.
Seats 1st: 18.
    2nd: 16.

W51052	W51056	W51060
W51053	W51057	W51061
W51054	W51058	W51062
W51055	W51059	W51063

Motor Second (L)
(W.R. THREE-CAR CROSS-COUNTRY)
Built by: **Gloucester R.C. & W. Co.**
Engines: Two B.U.T. 6-cyl. horizontal type of 150 b.h.p.
Transmission: **Mechanical.** Cardan shaft and freewheel to four-speed epicyclic gearbox and further cardan shaft to final drive.
Body: 64' 6" × 9' 3".
Weight: 37 tons 14 cwt.
Seats 2nd: 68.

W51080	W51084	W51088
W51081	W51085	W51089
W51082	W51086	W51090
W51083	W51087	W51091

Motor Brake Second
(TWIN UNITS)
For Details see SC50339-M50358

SC51108	SC51115	SC51122
SC51109	SC51116	SC51123
SC51110	SC51117	SC51124
SC51111	SC51118	SC51125
SC51112	SC51119	SC51126
SC51113	SC51120	SC51127
SC51114	SC51121	

Motor Brake Second
(W.R. THREE-CAR SUBURBAN)
For Details see W50050-91

W51128	W51133	W51138
W51129	W51134	W51139
W51130	W51135	W51140
W51131	W51136	
W51132	W51137	

Motor Second
(W.R. THREE-CAR SUBURBAN)
For Details see W50092-50133

W51141	W51146	W51151
W51142	W51147	W51152
W51143	W51148	W51153
W51144	W51149	
W51145	W51150	

Motor Brake Second
(E.R. THREE-CAR SUBURBAN)

Builty by: **Derby Works, B.R.**
Engines: Two Rolls Royce horizontal type of 238 b.h.p.
Transmission: **Mechanical.** Cardan shaft and freewheel to four-speed epicyclic gearbox and further cardan shaft to final drive.
Body: 64' 0" × 9' 3". Non-gangwayed, side doors to each seating bay.
Weight: 35 tons 10 cwt.
Seats 2nd: 65.

E51154	E51161	E51168
E51155	E51162	E51169
E51156	E51163	E51170
E51157	E51164	E51171
E51158	E51165	E51172
E51159	E51166	E51173
E51160	E51167	

Motor Brake Second
(TWIN UNITS)

Built by: **Metropolitan Cammell.**
Engines: Two B.U.T. (A.E.C.) 6-cyl. horizontal type of 150 b.h.p.
Transmission: **Mechanical.** Cardan shaft and freewheel to four-speed epicyclic gearbox and further cardan shaft to final drive.
Body: 57' 0" × 9' 3".
Weight: 32 tons.
Seats 2nd: 52.

M51174	M51196	E51218
M51175	M51197	E51219
M51176	M51198	E51220
M51177	M51199	E51221
M51178	M51200	E51222
M51179	M51201	E51223
M51180	M51202	SC51224
M51181	M51203	SC51225
M51182	E51204	SC51226
M51183	E51205	SC51227
M51184	E51206	SC51228
M51185	E51207	SC51229
M51186	E51208	SC51230
M51187	E51209	SC51231
M51188	E51210	SC51232
M51189	E51211	SC51233
M51190	E51212	SC51234
M51191	E51213	SC51235
M51192	E51214	SC51236
M51193	E51215	SC51237
M51194	E51216	SC51238
M51195	E51217	SC51239

SC51240	SC51245	SC51250
SC51241	SC51246	SC51251
SC51242	SC51247	SC51252
SC51243	SC51248	SC51253
SC51244	SC51249	

Motor Brake Second
(TWIN UNITS)

Built by: **Cravens.**
Engines: Two B.U.T. (A.E.C.) 6-cyl. horizontal type of 150 b.h.p.
Transmission: **Mechanical.** Cardan shaft and freewheel to four-speed epicyclic gearbox and further cardan shaft to final drive.
Body: 57′ 6″ × 9′ 3″.
Weight: 30 tons.
Seats 2nd: 52.

E51254	E51270	E51286
E51255	E51271	E51287
E51256	E51272	E51288
E51257	E51273	E51289
E51258	E51274	E51290
E51259	E51275	E51291
E51260	E51276	E51292
E51261	E51277	E51293
E51262	E51278	E51294
E51263	E51279	E51295
E51264	E51280	E51296
E51265	E51281	E51297
E51266	E51282	E51298
E51267	E51283	E51299
E51268	E51284	E51300
E51269	E51285	

Motor Brake Second
(TWIN AND FOUR-CAR* UNITS)

Built by: **Metropolitan Cammell.**
Engines: Two B.U.T. (A.E.C.) 6-cyl. horizontal type of 150 b.h.p.
Transmission: **Mechanical.** Cardan shaft and freewheel to four-speed epicyclic gearbox and further cardan shaft to final drive.
Body: 57′ 0″ × 9′ 3″.
Weight:
Seats 2nd:

E51425	E51435*	E51436*
E51426		

Motor Brake Second
(TWIN UNITS)

Built by: **Cravens.**
Engines: Two B.U.T. (A.E.C.) 6-cyl. horizontal type of 150 b.h.p.
Transmission: **Mechanical.** Cardan shaft and freewheel to four-speed epicyclic gearbox and further cardan shaft to final drive.
Body: 57′ 6″ × 9′ 3″.
Weight:
Seats 2nd:

E51471	E51472	SC51473

Motor Composite (L)
(TWIN AND FOUR-CAR* UNITS)

Built by: **Metropolitan Cammell.**
Engines: Two B.U.T. (A.E.C.) 6-cyl.
* horizontal type of 150 b.h.p.
Transmission: **Mechanical.** Cardan shaft and freewheel to four-speed epicyclic gearbox and further cardan shaft to final drive.
Body: 57′ 0″ × 9′ 3″.
Weight:
Seats 1st:
2nd:

E51495	E51505*	E51506*
E51496		

Motor Brake Second
(SINGLE UNITS)

Built by: **Gloucester R.C. & W. Co.**
Engines: Two B.U.T. (A.E.C.) 6-cyl. horizontal type of 150 b.h.p.
Transmission: **Mechanical.** Cardan shaft and freewheel to four-speed epicyclic gearbox and further cardan shaft to final drive.
Body: 64′ 6″ × 9′ 3″.
Non-gangwayed, side doors to each seating bay.
Weight: 35 tons.
Seats 2nd: 65.

W55000	W55007	W55014
W55001	W55008	W55015
W55002	W55009	W55016
W55003	W55010	W55017
W55004	W55011	W55018
W55005	W55012	W55019
W55006	W55013	

Motor Parcels Van

Built by: **Cravens.**
Engines: Two B.U.T. (A.E.C.) 6-cyl. horizontal type of 150 b.h.p.
Transmission: **Mechanical.** Cardan shaft and freewheel to four-speed epicyclic gearbox and further cardan shaft to final drive.
Body: 57' 6" × 9' 3".
Weight: 30 tons.

M55997	M55998	M55999

Driving Trailer
Composite (L)
(TWIN UNITS)

Built by: **Derby Works B.R.**
Body: 64' 6" × 9' 3".
Weight: 29 tons 10 cwt.
Seats 1st: 12.
2nd: 62.

E56000	E56017	E56034
E56001	E56018	E56035
E56002	E56019	E56036
E56003	E56020	E56037
E56004	E56021	E56038
E56005	E56022	E56039
E56006	E56023	E56040
E56007	E56024	E56041
E56008	E56025	E56042
E56009	E56026	E56043
E56010	E56027	E56044
E56011	E56028	E56045
E56012	E56029	E56046
E56013	E56030	E56047
E56014	E56031	E56048
E56015	E56032	E56049
E56016	E56033	

Driving Trailer
Composite (L)
(TWIN UNITS)

Built by: **Metropolitan Cammell.**
Body: 57' 0" × 9' 3".
Weight: 24 tons 4 cwt.
Seats 1st: 12.
2nd: 53.

E56050	E56065	E56080
E56051	E56066	E56081
E56052	E56067	E56082
E56053	E56068	E56083
E56054	E56069	E56084
E56055	E56070	E56085
E56056	E56071	E56086
E56057	E56072	E56087
E56058	E56073	E56088
E56059	E56074	E56089
E56060	E56075	M56090
E56061	E56076	M56091
E56062	E56077	M56092
E56063	E56078	M56093
E56064	E56079	

Driving Trailer
Composite (L)
(TWIN UNITS)

Built by: **Gloucester R. C. & W. Co.**
Body: 57' 6" × 9' 3".
Weight: 24 tons 15 cwt.
Seats 1st: 12.
2nd: 54.

SC56094	SC56101	M56108
SC56095	SC56102	M56109
SC56096	SC56103	M56110
SC56097	SC56104	M56111
SC56098	M56105	M56112
SC56099	M56106	M56113
SC56100	M56107	

Driving Trailer
Composite (L)
(TWIN UNITS)

Built by: **Cravens.**
Body: 57′ 6″ × 9′ 3″.
Weight: 23 tons.
Seats 1st: 12.
    2nd: 51.
       54*.

E56114	E56126	E56138
E56115	E56127	E56139
E56116	E56128	E56140
E56117	E56129	E56141
E56118	E56130	E56142
E56119	E56131	E56143
E56120	E56132	E56144
E56121	E56133	M56145*
E56122	E56134	M56146*
E56123	E56135	M56147*
E56124	E56136	M56148*
E56125	E56137	M56149*

Driving Trailer
Composite (L)
(TWIN UNITS)

Built by: **Park Royal Vehicles.**
Body: 57′ 6″ × 9′ 3″.
Weight: 26 tons 7 cwt.
Seats 1st: 16.
    2nd: 48.

M56150	M56157	M56164
M56151	M56158	M56165
M56152	M56159	M56166
M56153	M56160	M56167
M56154	M56161	M56168
M56155	M56162	M56169
M56156	M56163	

Driving Trailer
Composite (L)
(TWIN UNITS)

Built by: **D. Wickham & Co. Ltd.**
Body: 57′ 0″ × 9′ 3″.
Weight: 20 tons 10 cwt.
Seats 1st: 16.
    2nd: 50.

E56170	E56172	E56174
E56171	E56173	

Driving Trailer
Composite (L)
(TWIN UNITS)

Built by: **Birmingham R.C. & W. Co.**
Body: 57′ 6″ × 9′ 3″.
Weight:
Seats 1st: 12.
    2nd: 54.

M56175	M56179	M56183
M56176	M56180	M56184
M56177	M56181	
M56178	M56182	

Driving Trailer
Composite (L)
(TWIN UNITS)

Built by: **Birmingham R.C. & W. Co.**
Body: 57′ 6″ × 9′ 3″.
Weight:
Seats 1st: 12.
    2nd: 51.

E56185	E56187	E56189
E56186	E56188	

Driving Trailer
Composite (L)
(TWIN UNITS)

Built by: **Derby Works, B.R.**
Body: 57′ 6″ × 9′ 2″.
Weight: 21 tons.
Seats 1st: 12
    2nd: 53

E56190	E56199	E56208
E56191	E56200	E56209
E56192	E56201	E56210
E56193	E56202	M56211
E56194	E56203	M56212
E56195	E56204	M56213
E56196	E56205	M56214
E56197	E56206	M56215
E56198	E56207	

Driving Trailer
Composite (L)
(TWIN UNITS)

Built by: **Metropolitan Cammell.**
Body: 57′ 0″ × 9′ 3″.
Weight:
Seats 1st: 12.
    2nd: 45.

E56218	E56219	E56220

Driving Trailer Composite (L)
(TWIN UNITS)

Built by: **Derby Works, B.R.**
Body: 57' 6" × 9' 2".
Weight:
Seats 1st:
2nd:

M56221	M56226	M56231
M56222	M56227	M56232
M56223	M56228	M56233
M56224	M56229	M56234
M56225	M56230	M56235

Driving Trailer Second
(For use with Single Unit cars Nos. W55000, etc.)

Built by: **Gloucester R.C. & W. Co.**
Body: 64' 0" × 9' 3".
  Non-gangwayed, side doors to each seating bay.
Weight:
Seats 2nd: 95.

W56291	W56294	W56297
W56292	W56295	W56298
W56293	W56296	W56299

Driving Trailer Composite (L)
(TWIN UNITS)
For Details see SC56094-M56113

SC56300	SC56307	SC56314
SC56301	SC56308	SC56315
SC56302	SC56309	SC56316
SC56303	SC56310	SC56317
SC56304	SC56311	SC56318
SC56305	SC56312	SC56319
SC56306	SC56313	

Driving Trailer Composite (L)
(TWIN UNITS)

Built by: **Metropolitan Cammell.**
Body: 57' 0" × 9' 3".
Weight: 24 tons 4 cwt.
Seats 1st: 12.
2nd: 53.

M56332	M56359	SC56386
M56333	M56360	SC56387
M56334	M56361	SC56388
M56335	E56362	SC56389
M56336	E56363	SC56390
M56337	E56364	SC56391
M56338	E56365	SC56392
M56339	E56366	SC56393
M56340	E56367	SC56394
M56341	E56368	SC56395
M56342	E56369	SC56396
M56343	E56370	SC56397
M56344	E56371	SC56398
M56345	E56372	SC56399
M56346	E56373	SC56400
M56347	E56374	SC56401
M56348	E56375	SC56402
M56349	E56376	SC56403
M56350	E56377	SC56404
M56351	E56378	SC56405
M56352	E56379	SC56406
M56353	E56380	SC56407
M56354	E56381	SC56408
M56355	SC56382	SC56409
M56356	SC56383	SC56410
M56357	SC56384	SC56411
M56358	SC56385	

Driving Trailer Composite (L)

Built by: **Cravens.**
Body: 57' 6" × 9' 3".
Weight: 23 tons.
Seats 1st: 12.
2nd: 51.

E56412	E56423	E56434
E56413	E56424	E56435
E56414	E56425	E56436
E56415	E56426	E56437
E56416	E56427	E56438
E56417	E56428	E56439
E56418	E56429	E56440
E56419	E56430	E56441
E56420	E56431	E56442
E56421	E56432	E56443
E56422	E56433	E56444

E56445	E56451	E56457
E56446	E56452	E56458
E56447	E56453	E56459
E56448	E56454	E56460
E56449	E56455	E56461
E56450	E56456	E56462

Trailer Second (L)

(N.E. FOUR-CAR UNITS)

Built by: **Metropolitan Cammell.**
Body: 57′ 0″ × 9′ 3″.
Weight: 25 tons.
Seats 2nd: 61.

E59042	E59045	E59048
E59043	E59046	
E59044	E59047	

Trailer Composite

(W.R. THREE-CAR SUBURBAN)

Built by: **Derby Works B.R.**
Body: 63′ 8¾″ × 9′ 3″. Non-gangwayed, side doors to each seating bay.
Weight: 28 tons 10 cwt.
Seats 1st: 28.
    2nd: 74.

W59000	W59011	W59022
W59001	W59012	W59023
W59002	W59013	W59024
W59003	W59014	W59025
W59004	W59015	W59026
W59005	W59016	W59027
W59006	W59017	W59028
W59007	W59018	W59029
W59008	W59019	W59030
W59009	W59020	W59031
W59010	W59021	

Trailer Brake Second (L)

(N.E. FOUR-CAR UNITS)

Built by: **Metropolitan Cammell.**
Body: 57′ 0″ × 9′ 3″.
Weight: 25 tons.
Seats 2nd: 45.

E59049	E59052	E59055
E59050	E59053	
E59051	E59054	

Trailer Second (L)

(N.E. FOUR-CAR UNITS)

Built by: **Metropolitan Cammell.**
Body: 57′ 0″ × 9′ 3″.
Weight: 25 tons.
Seats 2nd: 71.

E59060	E59065	E59070
E59061	E59066	E59071
E59062	E59067	E59072
E59063	E59068	
E59064	E59069	

Trailer Second

(W.R. THREE-CAR SUBURBAN)

Built by: **Derby Works B.R.**
Body: 63′ 8¾″ × 9′ 3″. Non-gangwayed, side doors to each seating bay.
Weight: 28 tons 10 cwt.
Seats 2nd: 106.

W59032	W59036	W59040
W59033	W59037	W59041
W59034	W59038	
W59035	W59039	

Trailer Brake Second

(N.E. FOUR-CAR UNITS)

Built by: **Metropolitan Cammell.**
Body: 57′ 0″ × 9′ 3″.
Weight: 25 tons.
Seats 2nd: 53.

E59073	E59078	E59083
E59074	E59079	E59084
E59075	E59080	E59085
E59076	E59081	
E59077	E59082	

Trailer Second (L)
(N.E. FOUR-CAR UNITS)
For Details see E59042-8

E59086	E59088	E59090
E59087	E59089	E59091

Trailer Brake Second (L)
(N.E. FOUR-CAR UNITS)
For Details see E59049-55

E59092	E59094	E59096
E59093	E59095	E59097

Trailer Second (L)
(N.E. THREE-CAR UNITS)
Built by: **Metropolitan Cammell.**
Body: 57′ 0″ × 9′ 3″.
Weight: 24 tons 10 cwt.
Seats 2nd: 75.

E59100	E59104	E59108
E59101	E59105	E59109
E59102	E59106	
E59103	E59107	

Trailer Brake Second (L)
(N.E. THREE-CAR UNITS)
Built by: **Metropolitan Cammell.**
Body: 57′ 0″ × 9′ 3″.
Weight:
Seats 2nd:

E59112	E59113

Trailer Second (L)
(L.M. THREE-CAR UNITS)
Built by: **Metropolitan Cammell.**
Body: 57′ 0″ × 9′ 3″.
Weight:
Seats 2nd: 71.

M59114	M59120	M59126
M59115	M59121	M59127
M59116	M59122	M59128
M59117	M59123	M59129
M59118	M59124	M59130
M59119	M59125	M59131

Trailer Composite (L)
(L.M. THREE-CAR UNITS)
Built by: **Birmingham R. C. & W. Co.**
Body: 57′ 0″ × 9′ 3″.
Weight: 24 tons.
Seats 1st: 12.
　　　2nd: 54.

M59132	M59151	M59170
M59133	M59152	M59171
M59134	M59153	M59172
M59135	M59154	M59173
M59136	M59155	M59174
M59137	M59156	M59175
M59138	M59157	M59176
M59139	M59158	M59177
M59140	M59159	M59178
M59141	M59160	M59179
M59142	M59161	M59180
M59143	M59162	M59181
M59144	M59163	M59182
M59145	M59164	M59183
M59146	M59165	M59184
M59147	M59166	M59185
M59148	M59167	M59186
M59149	M59168	M59187
M59150	M59169	

Trailer Second (L)
(N.E. FOUR-CAR UNITS)
Built by: **Birmingham R.C. & W. Co.**
Body: 57′ 0″ × 9′ 3″.
Weight:
Seats 2nd: 69

E59188	E59195	E59202
E59189	E59196	E59203
E59190	E59197	E59204
E59191	E59198	E59205
E59192	E59199	E59206
E59193	E59200	E59207
E59194	E59201	E59208

Trailer Brake Second (L)
(N.E. FOUR-CAR UNITS)
Built by: **Birmingham R.C. & W. Co.**
Body: 57′ 0″ × 9′ 3″.
Weight:
Seats 2nd: 51

E59209	E59216	E59223
E59210	E59217	E59224
E59211	E59218	E59225
E59212	E59219	E59226
E59213	E59220	E59227
E59214	E59221	E59228
E59215	E59222	E59229

Trailer Second (L)
(N.E. FOUR-CAR UNITS)
For Details see E59188–E59208

E59230	E59232	E59233
E59231		

Trailer Brake Second (L)
(N.E. FOUR-CAR UNITS)
For Details see E59209–29

E59240	E59242	E59243
E59241		

Trailer Brake Second (L)
(N.E. FOUR-CAR UNITS)
Built by: **Derby Works, B.R.**
Body: 57′ 6″ × 9′ 2″.
Weight:
Seats 2nd:

E59245	E59247	E59249
E59246	E59248	E59250

Trailer Buffet Second (L)
(W.R. THREE-CAR CROSS-COUNTRY)
Built by: **Swindon Works B.R.**
Body: 64′ 6″ × 9′ 3″.
Open second with small buffet and counter at one end.
Weight: 30 tons 12 cwt.
Seats 2nd: 60.
Buffet: 4.

W59255	W59271	W59287
W59256	W59272	W59288
W59257	W59273	W59289
W59258	W59274	W59290
W59259	W59275	W59291
W59260	W59276	W59292
W59261	W59277	W59293
W59262	W59278	W59294
W59263	W59279	W59295
W59264	W59280	W59296
W59265	W59281	W59297
W59266	W59282	W59298
W59267	W59283	W59299
W59268	W59284	W59300
W59269	W59285	W59301
W59270	W59286	

Trailer Second (L)
(N.E. THREE-CAR UNITS)
Built by: **Metropolitan Cammell**
Body: 57′ 0″ × 9′ 3″.
Weight: 24 tons 10 cwt.
Seats 2nd: 75.

E59302	E59303	E59304

Trailer Second (L)
(N.E. FOUR-CAR UNITS)
Built by: **Metropolitan Cammell.**
Body: 57′ 0″ × 9′ 3″.
Weight:
Seats 2nd:

E59305	E59306

Trailer Second (L)
or Trailer Composite (L)*
(L.M. THREE-CAR UNITS)
Built by: **Cravens.**
Body: 57′ 6″ × 9′ 3″.
Weight: 23 tons.
Seats 2nd: 69.
   1st: 12*
   2nd: 51*

M59307*	M59314	M59321*
M59308	M59315	M59322*
M59309	M59316*	M59323
M59310*	M59317*	M59324
M59311	M59318*	M59325
M59312	M59319	
M59313	M59320*	

Trailer Composite
(W.R. THREE-CAR SUBURBAN)
For Details see W59000-31

W59326	W59343	W59360
W59327	W59344	W59361
W59328	W59345	W59362
W59329	W59346	W59363
W59330	W59347	W59364
W59331	W59348	W59365
W59332	W59349	W59366
W59333	W59350	W59367
W59334	W59351	W59368
W59335	W59352	W59369
W59336	W59353	W59370
W59337	W59354	W59371
W59338	W59355	W59372
W59339	W59356	W59373
W59340	W59357	W59374
W59341	W59358	W59375
W59342	W59359	W59376

Trailer Second (L)
(N.E. THREE AND FOUR-CAR UNITS)
Built by: Derby Works, B.R.
Body: 57′ 6″ × 9′ 2″.
Weight:
Seats 2nd:

E59380	E59384	E59388
E59381	E59385	E59389
E59382	E59386	E59390
E59383	E59387	

Trailer Buffet Second (L)
(W.R. THREE-CAR CROSS-COUNTRY)
Built by: Gloucester R.C. & W. Co.
Body: 64′ 6″ × 9′ 3″.
Open second with small buffet and counter at one end.
Weight:
Seats 2nd: 60 or 64.

W59413	W59417	W59421
W59414	W59418	W59422
W59415	W59419	
W59416	W59420	

Trailer Composite
(W.R. THREE-CAR SUBURBAN)
For Details see W59000-31

W59438	W59442	W59446
W59439	W59443	W59447
W59440	W59444	W59448
W59441	W59445	

Trailer Second
(E.R. THREE-CAR SUBURBAN)
Built by: Derby Works, B.R.
Body: 63′ 8¾″ × 9′ 3″. Non-gangwayed, side doors to each seating bay.
Weight: 28 tons 10 cwt.
Seats 2nd: 106.

E59449	E59456	E59463
E59450	E59457	E59464
E59451	E59458	E59465
E59452	E59459	E59466
E59453	E59460	E59467
E59454	E59461	E59468
E59455	E59462	

Trailer Composite (L)
(Two of these cars in a four-car unit)
(N.E. FOUR-CAR UNITS)
Built by: Metropolitan Cammell.
Body: 57′ 0″ × 9′ 3″.
Weight:
Seats 1st:
  2nd:

E59523	E59525	E59526
E59524		

215

Motor Brake Second
(S.R. HASTINGS UNITS)
Unit numbers 1001–7*
             1011–9†
             1031–7‡

Built by: **Eastleigh Works B.R.**
Engine: English Electric 4-cyl. type 4SRKT Mark II of 500 b.h.p. at 850 r.p.m.
Transmission: **Electric.** Two nose-suspended axle-hung traction motors.
Body: 58′ 0″ × 8′ 2½″ *
      64′ 6″ × 8′ 2½″ †‡
  Guard's, luggage compartment, engine room and full width driving compartment at outer end of car.
Weight: 54 tons 2 cwt.*
        55 tons 0 cwt.†‡
Seats 2nd: 22*
         30‡

S60000*	S60016†	S60032‡
S60001*	S60017†	S60033‡
S60002*	S60018†	S60034‡
S60003*	S60019†	S60035‡
S60004*	S60020†	S60036‡
S60005*	S60021†	S60037‡
S60006*	S60022†	S60038‡
S60007*	S60023†	S60039‡
S60008*	S60024†	S60040‡
S60009*	S60025†	S60041‡
S60010*	S60026†	S60042‡
S60011*	S60027†	S60043‡
S60012*	S60028†	S60044‡
S60013*	S60029†	S60045‡
S60014†	S60030†	
S60015†	S60031†	

Motor Brake Second
(S.R. TWIN UNITS)
Unit numbers 1101–22
Built by: **Eastleigh Works, B.R.**
Engine: English Electric 4-cyl. type 4SRKT Mark II of 600 b.h.p. at 850 r.p.m.
Transmission: **Electric.** Two nose-suspended axle-hung traction motors.
Body: 64′ 0″ × 9′ 3″.
  Guard's, luggage compartment, engine room and full width driving compartment at outer end of car. Non-gangwayed, side door to each seating bay.
Weight: 56 tons 0 cwt.
Seats 2nd: 52.

S60100	S60108	S60116
S60101	S60109	S60117
S60102	S60110	S60118
S60103	S60111	S60119
S60104	S60112	S60120
S60105	S60113	S60121
S60106	S60114	
S60107	S60115	

Trailer Second (L)
(S.R. HASTINGS UNITS)
Unit numbers 1001–7*
             1011–9†
             1031–7‡

Built by: **Eastleigh Works, B.R.**
Body: 58′ 0″ × 8′ 2½″.*
      64′ 6″ × 8′ 2½″†‡.
Weight: 29 tons.*
        30 tons.†‡
Seats 2nd: 52*
        60†‡

S60500*	S60521†	S60542†
S60501*	S60522†	S60543†
S60502*	S60523†	S60544†
S60503*	S60524†	S60545†
S60504*	S60525†	S60546†
S60505*	S60526†	S60547†
S60506*	S60527†	S60548‡
S60507*	S60528†	S60549‡
S60508*	S60529†	S60550‡
S60509*	S60530†	S60551‡
S60510*	S60531†	S60552‡
S60511*	S60532†	S60553‡
S60512*	S60533†	S60554‡
S60513*	S60534†	S60555‡
S60514*	S60535†	S60556‡
S60515*	S60536†	S60557‡
S60516*	S60537†	S60558‡
S60517*	S60538†	S60559‡
S60518*	S60539†	S60560‡
S60519*	S60540†	S60561‡
S60520*	S60541†	

Trailer First (K)
(S.R. HASTINGS UNITS)
Unit numbers 1001–7*
              1011–9†
              1031–7‡

Built by: **Eastleigh Works, B.R.**
Body: 58' 0" × 8' 2½"*
      64' 6" × 8' 2½"†‡
    Side corridor with seven* (eight†‡)
first class compartments with side
door to each compartment.
Weight: 30 tons*
       31 tons †‡
Seats 1st: 42*
       48†‡

S60700*	S60708†	S60716‡
S60701*	S60709†	S60717‡
S60702*	S60710†	S60718‡
S60703*	S60711†	S60719‡
S60704*	S60712†	S60720‡
S60705*	S60713†	S60721‡
S60706*	S60714†	S60722‡
S60707†	S60715†	

Trailer Buffet
(S.R. HASTINGS UNITS)
Unit numbers 1031–7
Built by: **Eastleigh Works B.R.**
Body: 64' 6" × 8' 2½".
    Buffet with kitchen and bar; self-
contained seating saloon.
Weight: 35 tons.
Seats: 21.

S60750	S60753	S60756
S60751	S60754	
S60752	S60755	

Driving Trailer Composite (L)
(S.R. TWIN UNITS)
Unit numbers 1101–22
Built by: **Eastleigh Works, B.R.**
Body: 64' 0" × 9' 3".
    Non-gangwayed, side door to each
seating bay or compartment. 5-bay
2nd saloon and 2 1st compartments
with intermediate lavatories, also a
2nd class compartment next to driving
compartment.
Weight: 32 tons 0 cwt.
Seats 1st: 13.
      2nd: 62.

S60800	S60808	S60816
S60801	S60809	S60817
S60802	S60810	S60818
S60803	S60811	S60819
S60804	S60812	S60820
S60805	S60813	S60821
S60806	S60814	
S60807	S60815	

Motor Brake Second
(TWIN UNITS)
Built by: **Derby Works B.R.**
Engines: Two B.U.T. (Leyland) 6-cyl.
horizontal type of 125 b.h.p.
Transmission: **Hydro-Mechanical.**
Lysholm Smith (Leyland) torque
converter to final drive.
Body: 57' 6" × 9' 2".
Weight: 26 tons.
Seats 2nd: 61.

E79000	E79003	E79006
E79001	E79004	E79007
E79002	E79005	

Motor Brake Second
(TWIN UNITS)
Built by: **Derby Works B.R.**
Engines: Two B.U.T. (A.E.C.) 6-cyl.
horizontal type of 150 b.h.p.
Transmission: **Mechanical.** Cardan
shaft and freewheel to four-speed
epicyclic gearbox and further cardan
shaft to final drive.
Body: 57' 6" × 9' 2".
Weight: 27 tons.
Seats 2nd: 61.
        56*.

M79008	E79021*	E79034*
M79009	E79022*	E79035*
M79010	E79023*	E79036*
M79011	E79024*	E79037*
M79012	E79025*	E79038*
M79013	E79026*	E79039*
M79014	E79027*	E79040*
M79015	E79028*	E79041*
M79016	E79029*	E79042*
M79017	E79030*	E79043*
M79018	E79031*	E79044*
M79019	E79032*	E79045*
M79020	E79033*	E79046*

Motor Brake Second
(TWIN UNITS)

Built by: **Metropolitan Cammell.**
Engines: Two B.U.T. (A.E.C.) 6-cyl. horizontal type of 150 b.h.p.
Transmission: **Mechanical.** Cardan shaft and freewheel to four-speed epicyclic gearbox and further cardan shaft to final drive.
Body: 57′ 0″ × 9′ 3″.
Weight: 31 tons 10 cwts.
Seats 2nd: 57.
　　　　　53*.

E79047	E79060	E79073
E79048	E79061	E79074
E79049	E79062	E79075
E79050	E79063	M79076*
E79051	E79064	M79077*
E79052	E79065	M79078*
E79053	E79066	M79079*
E79054	E79067	M79080*
E79055	E79068	M79081*
E79056	E79069	M79082*
E79057	E79070	
E79058	E79071	
E79059	E79072	

Motor Brake Second (L)
(INTER-CITY UNITS)

Built by: **Swindon Works B.R.**
Engines: Two B.U.T. (A.E.C.) 6-cyl. horizontal type of 150 b.h.p.
Transmission: **Mechanical.** Cardan shaft and freewheel to four-speed epicyclic gearbox and further cardan shaft to final drive.
Body: 64′ 6″ × 9′ 3″.
Guard's and luggage compartment at outer end. Two types of car: " leading "* with full width driving compartment, gangwayed at inner end only; " intermediate "† with side driving compartment, gangwayed at both ends.
Weight: 38 tons.
Seats 2nd: 52.

W79083†	W79093*	SC79103*
W79084†	W79094*	SC79104*
W79085†	SC79095†	SC79105*
W79086†	SC79096*	SC79106*
W79087†	SC79097*	SC79107*
W79088†	SC79098*	SC79108*
W79089†	SC79099*	SC79109*
W79090†	SC79100*	SC79110*
W79091*	SC79101*	SC79111*
W79092*	SC79102*	

Motor Brake Second
(TWIN UNITS)

Built by: **Derby Works B.R.**
Engines: Two B.U.T. 6-cyl. horizontal type of 150 b.h.p.

Transmission: **Mechanical.** Cardan shaft and freewheel to four-speed epicyclic gearbox and further cardan shaft to final drive.

Body: 57′ 6″ × 9′ 2″.

Weight: 27 tons.

Seats 2nd: 52.

M79118	M79129	E79140
M79119	M79130	M79141
M79120	M79131	M79142
M79121	M79132	M79143
M79122	M79133	M79144
M79123	M79134	M79145
M79124	M79135*	M79146
M79125	M79136	M79147
M79126	E79137	M79148
M79127	E79138	M79149
M79128	E79139	

* Fitted with Self Changing Gears Ltd. automatic four-speed gearbox.

Motor Second
(N.E. FOUR-CAR UNITS)

Built by: **Derby Works B.R.**
Engines: **Two B.U.T. (A.E.C.) 6-cyl.** horizontal type of 150 b.h.p.
Transmission: **Mechanical.** Cardan shaft and freewheel to four-speed epicyclic gearbox and further cardan shaft to final drive.
Body: 57' 6" × 9' 2".
Weight: 27 tons.
Seats 2nd: 64.

E79150	E79152	E79154
E79151	E79153	

Motor Second (L)
(INTER-CITY UNITS)

Built by: **Swindon Works B.R.**
Engines: **Two B.U.T. (A.E.C.) 6-cyl.** horizontal type of 150 b.h.p.
Transmission: **Mechanical.** Cardan shaft and freewheel to four-speed Wilson gearbox and further cardan shaft to final drive.
Body: 64' 6" × 9' 3".
Gangwayed both ends. Side driving compartment at one end.
Weight: 39 tons 3 cwt.
Seats 2nd: 64.

SC79155	SC79160	SC79165
SC79156	SC79161	SC79166
SC79157	SC79162	SC79167
SC79158	SC79163	SC79168
SC79159	SC79164	

Motor Brake Second
(TWIN UNITS)
For Details see M79118-49

M79169	M79174	M79179
M79170	M79175	M79180
M79171	M79176	M79181
M79172	M79177	
M79173	M79178	

Motor Brake Second
(TWIN UNITS)
For Details see M79008-20

M79184	M79186	M79188
M79185	M79187	

Motor Composite (L)
(TWIN UNITS)

Built by: **Derby Works B.R.**
Engines: **Two B.U.T. (A.E.C.) 6-cyl.** horizontal type of 150 b.h.p.
Transmission: **Mechanical.** Cardan shaft and freewheel to four-speed epicyclic gearbox and further cardan shaft to final drive.
Body: 57' 6" × 9' 2".
Weight: 27 tons.
Seats 1st: 16.
    2nd: 53.

M79189	M79191	M79193
M79190	M79192	

Driving Trailer Composite (L)
(TWIN UNITS)

Built by: **Derby Works B.R.**
Body: 57' 6" × 9' 2".
Weight: 20 tons.
Seats 1st: 16.
    2nd: 53.

E79250	E79255	E79260
E79251	E79256	E79261
E79252	E79257	E79262
E79253	E79258	
E79254	E79259	

Driving Trailer Second (L)
(TWIN UNITS)

Built by: **Metropolitan Cammell.**
Body: 57' 0" × 9' 3".
Weight: 25 tons.
Seats 2nd: 71.

E79263	E79273	E79283
E79264	E79274	E79284
E79265	E79275	E79285
E79266	E79276	E79286
E79267	E79277	E79287
E79268	E79278	E79288
E79269	E79279	E79289
E79270	E79280	E79290
E79271	E79281	E79291
E79272	E79282	

Trailer Brake Second (L)

(N.E. FOUR-CAR UNITS)

Built by: **Derby Works B.R.**
Body: 57' 6" × 9' 2".
Weight: 20 tons 10 cwt.
Seats 2nd: 45.

E79325	E79327	E79329
E79326	E79328	

Trailer Second (L)

(N.E. FOUR-CAR UNITS)

Built by: **Derby Works B.R.**
Body: 57' 6" × 9' 2".
Weight: 20 tons 10 cwt.
Seats 2nd: 61.

E79400	E79402	E79404
E79401	E79403	

Trailer Buffet First (K)

(INTER-CITY UNITS)

Built by: **Swindon Works B.R.**
Body: 64' 6" × 9' 3".
 Side corridor with three first class
 compartments. Buffet with kitchen,
 bar and saloon.
Weight: 34 tons.
Seats 1st: 18.
 Buffet: 12.

W79440	SC79443	SC79446
W79441	SC79444	SC79447
SC79442	SC79445	

Trailer First (K)

(INTER-CITY UNITS)

Built by: **Swindon Works B.R.**
Body: 64' 6" × 9' 3".
 Side corridor with seven first class
 compartments and end doors.

Weight: 33 tons 9 cwt.
Seats 1st: 42.

W79470	SC79475	SC79480
W79471	SC79476	SC79481
W79472	SC79477	SC79482
W79473	SC79478	
SC79474	SC79479	

Motor Composite (L)

(TWIN UNITS)

Built by: **Derby Works B.R.**
Engines: Two B.U.T. (Leyland) 6-cyl.
 horizontal type of 125 b.h.p.
Transmission: **Hydro-Mechanical.**
 Lysholm Smith (Leyland) torque
 converter to final drive.
Body: 57' 6" × 9' 2".
Weight:
Seats 1st: 16.
 2nd: 53.

E79500	E79503	E79506
E79501	E79504	E79507
E79502	E79505	

Motor Composite

(N.E. FOUR-CAR UNITS)

Built by: **Derby Works B.R.**
Engines: Two B.U.T. (A.E.C.) 6-cyl.
 horizontal type of 150 b.h.p.
Transmission: **Mechanical.** Cardan
 shaft and freewheel to four-speed
 epicyclic gearbox and further cardan
 shaft to final drive.
Body: 57' 6" × 9' 2".
Weight: 26 tons 10 cwt.
Seats 1st: 20.
 2nd: 36.

E79508	E79510	E79512
E79509	E79511	

Driving Trailer Composite (L)
(TWIN UNITS)

Built by: **Derby Works B.R.**
Body: 57' 6" × 9' 2".
Weight: 21 tons.
Seats 1st: 9.
16*.
2nd: 53.

M79600	M79609	E79618*
M79601	M79610	E79619*
M79602	M79611	E79620*
M79603	M79612	E79621*
M79604	E79613*	E79622*
M79605	E79614*	E79623*
M79606	E79615*	E79624*
M79607	E79616*	E79625*
M79608	E79617*	

Driving Trailer Composite (L)
(TWIN UNITS)

Built by: **Metropolitan Cammell.**
Body: 57' 0" × 9' 3".
Weight:
Seats 1st: 12.
2nd: 53.

M79626	M79629	M79632
M79627	M79630	
M79628	M79631	

Driving Trailer Composite (L)
(TWIN UNITS)
For Details see M79600-E79625

M79639	M79643	M79647
M79640	M79644	M79648
M79641	M79645	M79649†
M79642	M79646	M79650

†This vehicle has been fitted internally for use as an inspection saloon including a pantry, and is not in public service.

M79651	M79663	M79675
M79652	M79664	M79676
M79653	M79665	M79677
M79654	M79666	M79678
M79655	M79667	M79679
M79656	M79668	M79680
M79657	M79669	M79681
E79658*	M79670	M79682
E79659*	M79671	M79683
E79660*	M79672	M79684
E79661*	M79673	
M79662	M79674	

> For reasons of clarity the 4-wheel units below are not in strict numerical order.

Motor Second
(FOUR-WHEEL UNITS)

Built by: **British United Traction Co.**
Engine: B.U.T. (A.E.C.) 6-cyl. horizontal type of 125 b.h.p.
Transmission: **Mechanical.** Cardan shaft and freewheel to four-speed epicyclic gearbox and further cardan shaft to final drive.
Body: 37' 6" × 9' 0'. Non-gangwayed. Driving compartment at each end.
Weight: 15 tons 0 cwt.
Seats 2nd: 34.

M79740	M79745	M79748

Motor Brake Second
(FOUR-WHEEL UNITS)

Built by: **British United Traction Co.**
Engine: B.U.T. (A.E.C.) 6-cyl. horizontal type of 125 b.h.p.
Transmission: **Mechanical.** Cardan shaft and freewheel to four-speed

epicyclic gearbox and further cardan shaft to final drive.
Body: 37' 6" × 9' 0". Non-gangwayed. Driving compartment at each end.
Weight: 15 tons 0 cwt.
Seats 2nd: 28.

M79742	M79744	M79750
M79743		

Trailer Second

(FOUR-WHEEL UNITS)

Built by: **British United Traction Co.**
Body: 37' 6" × 9' 0". Non-gangwayed.
Weight: 10 tons 10 cwt.
Seats 2nd: 48.

M79741	M79747	M79749
M79746		

Motor Brake Second

(SINGLE UNITS)

Built by: **Derby Works B.R.**
Engine: Two B.U.T. (A.E.C.) 6-cyl. horizontal type of 150 b.h.p.
Transmission: **Mechanical.** Cardan shaft and freewheel to four-speed epicyclic gearbox and further cardan shaft to final drive.
Body: 57' 6" × 9' 2". Driving compartment at each end. Non-gangwayed.
Weight: 27 tons.
Seats 2nd: 52.

M79900	M79901

Four-Wheel Railbus

Built by: **Bristol/E.C.W.**
Engine: Gardner 6.H.L.W 6-cyl. type of 112 b.h.p. at 1,700 r.p.m.
Transmission: **Mechanical.** Cardan shaft and freewheel to Self-Changing Gears Ltd. five-speed epicyclic gearbox and further cardan shaft to final drive.
Body: 42' 4" × 9' 3". Non-gangwayed.
Weight: 13 tons 10 cwt.
Seats 2nd: 56.

SC79958	SC79959

Four-Wheel Railbus

Built by: **Waggon and Maschinenbau.**
Engine: Buessing 150 b.h.p. at 1,900 r.p.m.
Transmission: **Mechanical.** Cardan shaft to ZF electro-magnetic six-speed gearbox.
Body: 41' 10". × 8' 8 5/16". Non-gangwayed
Weight: 15 tons.
Seats 2nd: 56.

E79960	E79962	E79964
E79961	E79963	

Four-Wheel Railbus

Built by: **D. Wickham & Co.**
Engine: Meadows 6-cyl. type 6HDT500 of 105 b.h.p. at 1,800 r.p.m.
Transmission: **Mechanical.** Freeborn-Wickham disc and ring coupling driving Self-Changing Gears Ltd. four-speed epicyclic gearbox and cardan shaft to final drive.
Body: 38' 0" × 9' 0". Non-gangwayed.
Weight: 11 tons 5 cwt.
Seats 2nd: 44.

SC79965	SC79967	SC79969
SC79966	SC79968	

Four-Wheel Railbus

Built by: **Park Royal Vehicles.**
Engine: B.U.T. (A.E.C.) 6-cyl. horizontal type of 150 b.h.p.
Transmission: **Mechanical.** Cardan shaft and freewheel to Self-Changing Gears Ltd. four-speed epicyclic gearbox and further cardan shaft to final drive.
Body: 42' 0" × 9' 3". Non-gangwayed.
Weight: 15 tons.
Seats 2nd: 50.

SC79970	M79972	SC79974
M79971	M79973	

Four-Wheel Railbus

Built by: **A.C. Cars Ltd.**
Engine: B.U.T. (A.E.C.) 6-cyl. horizontal type of 150 b.h.p.
Transmission: **Mechanical.** Cardan shaft and freewheel to four-speed epicyclic gearbox and further cardan shaft to final drive.
Body: 36' 0" × 8' 11".
Weight: 11 tons.
Seats 2nd: 46.

W79975	W79977	SC79979
W79976	W79978	

Experimental Unit

This unit is not in public service but is undergoing trials. The two coaches were converted from former L.M.S. steam-hauled Open Brake Thirds and the motor bogies were recovered from withdrawn Euston-Watford electric units.

Engine: Ruston-Paxman type 6ZHHL of 450 b.h.p. in each coach.
Transmission: Electric.
Body: 57' 0" × 9' 3".
Weight: 51 tons 10 cwt.
Seats: —

9821   9828

G.W.R. Railcars

Car No.	Date	Engines	Total b.h.p.	Seats 2nd.
5/7	1935	2	242	70
8	1936	2	242	70
13–15	1936	2	242	70
17*	1936	2	242	—
19–32†	1940	2	210	48
33, 38‡	1942	4	420	92
34*	1941	2	210	—

* Parcels cars.
‡ Twin-coach unit with buffet facilities. Adjoining statistics apply per 2-car unit.
† These cars may work in pairs with an additional ordinary coach between.

W5W	W17W	W24W	W30W
W7W	W19W	W25W	W31W
W8W	W20W	W26W	W32W
W13W	W21W	W27W	W33W
W14W	W22W	W28W	W34W
W15W	W23W	W29W	W38W

Battery Electric Railcar Motor Brake Second
(TWIN UNIT)

Built by: **Derby/Cowlairs Works, B.R.**
Electrical Equipment : Two 100 kW Siemens-Schuckert nose-suspended traction motors powered by 216 lead-acid cell batteries of 1070 amp/hour capacity.
Body: 57' 6" × 9' 2".
Weight: 37 tons 10 cwt.
Seats 2nd: 52

SC79998

Battery Electric Railcar Driving Trailer Composite
(TWIN UNIT)

Built by: **Derby/Cowlairs Works, B.R.**
Body: 57' 6" × 9' 2".
Weight: 32 tons 10 cwt.
Seats 1st: 12   *2nd:* 53

SC79999

COUPLING OF DIESEL TRAINS

Although several multiple-unit diesel sets can be coupled together and driven by one man in the leading cab, for various reasons it is not possible for all types of diesel unit to work together. In order to distinguish cars that can run together all have painted under the left and right headlights a colour code symbol. This is repeated at the inner end of the car in similar positions and a miniature symbol also appears on the plug socket covers. Only units bearing the same symbol can be coupled together.

RED TRIANGLE

79000 series Derby " lightweight " cars with Leyland Hydro-Mechanical (Torque Converters) Nos. 79000–7, 79500–7

YELLOW DIAMOND

79000 series

Derby " lightweight " cars

Metropolitan-Cammell cars

50000 series

Cravens Parcels cars Nos. M55997–9

WHITE CIRCLE

79000 series

Swindon-built " Inter-City " cars

BLUE SQUARE

All 50000 series cars with B.U.T. engines except Cravens Parcels cars and Derby " heavyweight " cars E50000–49, E56000–49

BLUE SQUARE WITH CREAM STRIPE

50000 series

Derby " heavyweight " cars E50000–49, E56000–49

ORANGE STAR

Derby heavyweight cars with Rolls Royce 238 b.h.p. engines numbered in the E50988/59449/51154 series

ELECTRIC STOCK
LOCOMOTIVES

AIA-AIA

Introduced: 1958.
Locomotive manufacturer: Metropolitan-Vickers.
Total h.p.: 2,500.
Equipment: Four 625 h.p. Metropolitan-Vickers nose-suspended traction motors.
Weight: 109 tons.
Driving Wheels: 3' 8".
Maximum Tractive effort: 40,000 lb.
System: 25 kV. a.c. Overhead.
(Rebuilt from former Gas Turbine Loco. No. 18100.)

E1000

Bo-Bo

Introduced: 1958.
Locomotive manufacturer: B.R., Doncaster.
Total h.p.: 2,552.
Equipment: Motor generator booster set and four 638 h.p. English Electric spring-borne traction motors driving through S.L.M. flexible drive.
Weight: 77 tons.
Driving Wheels: 4' 0".
Maximum tractive effort: 43,000 lb.
System: 750 V. d.c. 3rd rail or overhead.

E5000	E5004	E5008	E5012
E5001	E5005	E5009	
E5002	E5006	E5010	
E5003	E5007	E5011	

Co-Co   Class CC

Introduced: { 1941.
           { 1948.*
Locomotive manufacturer: B.R., Ashford.
Total h.p.: 1,470.
Equipment: Motor generator booster set and six 245 h.p. English Electric nose-suspended traction motors.
Weight: { 99 tons 14 cwt.
        { 104 tons 14 cwt.*
Driving Wheels: 3' 6".
Maximum tractive effort: { 40,000 lb.
                 { 45,000 lb.*
System: 630–750 V. d.c. 3rd rail or overhead.

20001	20002	20003*

Bo-Bo   Class EM1

Introduced: { 1941.*
           { 1950.
Locomotive manufacturer: B.R., Doncaster.
Total h.p.: 1,868.
Equipment: Four 467 h.p. Metropolitan-Vickers nose-suspended traction motors.
Weight: 87 tons 18 cwt.
Driving Wheels: 4' 2".
Maximum tractive effort: 45,000 lb.
System: 1,500 V. d.c. Overhead.

26000* Tommy			
26001	26016	26031	26046
26002	26017	26032	26047
26003	26018	26033	26048
26004	26019	26034	26049
26005	26020	26035	26050
26006	26021	26036	26051
26007	26022	26037	26052
26008	26023	26038	26053
26009	26024	26039	26054
26010	26025	26040	26055
26011	26026	26041	26056
26012	26027	26042	26057
26013	26028	26043	
26014	26029	26044	
26015	26030	26045	

Bo-Bo   Class ES1

Introduced: 1902.
Locomotive manufacturer: Brush Traction.
Total h.p.:
Equipment: Four B.T.H. nose-suspended traction motors.
Weight: 46 tons.
Driving Wheels:
Maximum tractive effort: 25,000 lb.
System: 630 V. d.c. Overhead and 3rd rail.

26500	26501

Co-Co   Class EM2

Introduced: 1954.
Locomotive manufacturer: B.R., Gorton.
Total h.p.: 2,490.
Equipment: Six 415 h.p. Metropolitan-Vickers nose-suspended traction motors.
Weight: 102 tons.
Driving Wheels: 4' 2".
Maximum tractive effort: 45,000 lb.
System: 1,500 V. d.c. Overhead.

27000	27002	27004	27006
27001	27003	27005	

Service Locomotives

Eastern Region

Bo-Bo   Class EB1

Introduced: 1946.
Locomotive manufacturer:
Total h.p.:
Equipment:
Weight: 74 tons 8 cwt.
Driving Wheels: 4' 0".
Maximum tractive effort: 37,600 lb.
System: 1,500 V. d.c. Overhead.

100 (26510)

Southern Region

DS 74	DS 75

EASTERN & NORTH EASTERN ELECTRIC UNIT NUMBERS

LIVERPOOL ST.–SOUTHEND 4-CAR ELECTRIC TRAIN UNITS

01s	05s	09s	13s	17s	21s	25s	29s
02s	06s	10s	14s	18s	22s	26s	30s
03s	07s	11s	15s	19s	23s	27s	31s
04s	08s	12s	16s	20s	24s	28s	32s

LIVERPOOL ST.–SHENFIELD 3-CAR ELECTRIC TRAIN UNITS

Note: Units prefixed "0XX" have been re-equipped in readiness for 25 kV. a.c. working.

01	11	021	31	041	51	61	071	81	91
02	12	22	32	42	052	62	72	82	92
03	13	23	33	43	53	63	073	83	
04	14	24	34	44	54	64	74	084	
05	15	025	035	45	55	65	75	85	
06	16	26	36	046	056	66	76	86	
007	017	27	37	047	57	67	77	87	
08	18	28	38	48	58	068	78	88	
09	19	29	39	049	59	69	79	89	
10	20	30	40	50	60	70	80	90	

*FENCHURCH ST.–SHOEBURYNESS 4-CAR ELECTRIC TRAIN UNITS

201	213	225	236	247	258	269	280	291	302
202	214	226	237	248	259	270	281	292	303
203	215	227	238	249	260	271	282	293	304
204	216	228	239	250	261	272	283	294	305
205	217	229	240	251	262	273	284	295	306
206	218	230	241	252	263	274	285	296	307
207	219	231	242	253	264	275	286	297	308
208	220	232	243	254	265	276	287	298	309
209	221	233	244	255	266	277	288	299	310
210	222	234	245	256	267	278	289	300	311
211	223	235	246	257	268	279	290	301	312
212	224								

* Until required for the L.T. & S. line in 1961 these units may be seen on the Manchester–Crewe and Clacton or Walton-on-Naze–Colchester lines; also on the Liverpool St.–Chelmsford, Southend lines after conversion to the 25 kV. a.c. system.

GRIMSBY–IMMINGHAM ELECTRIC TRAMS

1	5	14	17	20	23	26	29	32
3	11	15	18	21	24	27	30	33
4	12	16	19	22	25	28	31	

SOUTH TYNESIDE ELECTRIC MOTOR COACHES

E65311	E65314	E65317	E65320	E65323
E65312	E65315	E65318	E65321	E65324
E65313	E65316	E65319	E65322	E65325

Motor Parcels Van E68000

NORTH TYNESIDE ELECTRIC TWIN-UNIT MOTOR COACHES

E29101E	E29113E	E29124E	E29135E	E29146E	E29157E
E29102E	E29114E	E29125E	E29136E	E29147E	E29158E
E29103E	E29115E	E29126E	E29137E	E29148E	E29159E
E29104E	E29116E	E29127E	E29138E	E29149E	E29160E
E29105E	E29117E	E29128E	E29139E	E29150E	E29161E
E29106E	E29118E	E29129E	E29140E	E29151E	E29162E
E29107E	E29119E	E29130E	E29141E	E29152E	E29163E
E29108E	E29120E	E29131E	E29142E	E29153E	E29164E
E29109E	E29121E	E29132E	E29143E	E29154E	
E29110E	E29122E	E29133E	E29144E	E29155E	
E29111E	E29123E	E29134E	E29145E	E29156E	

Motor Coaches		Motor Parcels Vans	
E29165E	E29166E	E29467E	E29468E

L.M. ELECTRIC MOTOR COACH NUMBERS

LONDON DISTRICT

OPEN STOCK			M28267M	M28281M	M28292M
M28000M	M28246M	M28258M	M28269M	M28282M	M28294M
M28224M	M28248M	M28259M	M28270M	M28283M	M28295M
M28225M	M28249M	M28260M	M28272M	M28284M	M28296M
M28226M	M28252M	M28261M	M28273M	M28285M	M28297M
M28228M	M28253M	M28262M	M28274M	M28286M	M28298M
M28229M	M28254M	M28263M	M28275M	M28287M	M28299M
M28230M	M28255M	M28264M	M28277M	M28288M	
M28237M	M28256M	M28265M	M28279M	M28289M	
M28242M	M28257M	M28266M	M28280M	M28290M	

COMPARTMENT STOCK			M28013M	M28018M	M28022M
M28001M	M28005M	M28009M	M28014M	M28019M	M28023M
M28002M	M28006M	M28010M	M28015M	M28020M	M28024M
M28003M	M28007M	M28011M	M28016M	M28021M	M28025M
M28004M	M28008M	M28012M	M28017M		

			M61160	M61170	M61180
M61133	M61142	M61151	M61161	M61171	M61181
M61134	M61143	M61152	M61162	M61172	M61182
M61135	M61144	M61153	M61163	M61173	M61183
M61136	M61145	M61154	M61164	M61174	M61184
M61137	M61146	M61155	M61165	M61175	M61185
M61138	M61147	M61156	M61166	M61176	M61186
M61139	M61148	M61157	M61167	M61177	M61187
M61140	M61149	M61158	M61168	M61178	M61188
M61141	M61150	M61159	M61169	M61179	M61189

LIVERPOOL–SOUTHPORT

COMPARTMENT STOCK

M28301M	M28303M	M28305M	M28307M	M28309M	M28310M
M28302M	M28304M	M28306M	M28308M		

OPEN STOCK

M28311M	M28323M	M28334M	M28345M	M28354M	M28362M
M28312M	M28324M	M28335M	M28347M	M28355M	M28363M
M28313M	M28325M	M28336M	M28348M	M28356M	M28364M
M28314M	M28326M	M28337M	M28349M	M28357M	M28365M
M28315M	M28327M	M28338M	M28350M	M28358M	M28366M
M28316M	M28328M	M28339M	M28351M	M28359M	M28367M
M28317M	M28329M	M28340M	M28352M	M28360M	M28368M
M28318M	M28330M	M28341M	M28353M	M28361M	M28369M
M28319M	M28331M	M28342M			
M28321M	M28332M	M28343M			
M28322M	M28333M	M28344M			

BAGGAGE CARS

M28496M	M28497M

WIRRAL & MERSEY

M28371M	M28379M	M28387M	M28394M	M28678M	M28685M
M28372M	M28380M	M28388M	M28672M	M28679M	M28686M
M28373M	M28381M	M28389M	M28673M	M28680M	M28687M
M28374M	M28382M	M28390M	M28674M	M28681M	M28688M
M28375M	M28383M	M28391M	M28675M	M28682M	M28689M
M28376M	M28384M	M28392M	M28676M	M28683M	M28690M
M28377M	M28385M	M28393M	M28677M	M28684M	
M28378M	M28386M				

MANCHESTER–BURY

M28500M	M28506M	M28512M	M28518M	M28525M	M28531M
M28501M	M28507M	M28513M	M28519M	M28526M	M28532M
M28502M	M28508M	M28514M	M28521M	M28527M	M28533M
M28503M	M28509M	M28515M	M28522M	M28528M	M28534M
M28504M	M28510M	M28516M	M28523M	M28529M	M28535M
M28505M	M28511M	M28517M	M28524M	M28530M	M28537M

LANCASTER–MORECAMBE–HEYSHAM

M28219M	M28221M
M28220M	M28222M

MANCHESTER, S. JUNCT. & ALTRINCHAM

M28571M	M28579M	M28587M
M28572M	M28580M	M28588M
M28573M	M28581M	M28589M
M28574M	M28582M	M28590M
M28575M	M28583M	M28591M
M28576M	M28584M	M28592M
M28577M	M28585M	M28593M
M28578M	M28586M	M28594M

MANCHESTER–GLOSSOP–HADFIELD

M59401E	M59403E	M59405E	M59407E
M59402E	M59404E	M59406E	M59408E

SOUTHERN REGION ELECTRIC UNIT NUMBERS

(Number to be seen on front and rear of each set)

TWO-CAR NON-CORRIDOR MOTOR UNITS

Motor Brake Second, Driving Trailer Composite.

(2-NOL.)

1813	1822	1832	1844
1814	1824	1834	1845
1815	1825	1836	1846
1816	1826	1837	1847
1817	1827	1839	1848
1818	1829	1840	1849
1820	1830	1841	1850
1821	1831	1842	

TWO-CAR MOTOR LAVATORY UNITS

Motor Lavatory Brake Second, Driving Trailer Lavatory Composite.

(2-BIL.)

2001†	2005†	2009†	2013
2002†	2006†	2010†	2015
2003†	2007†	2011	2016
2004†	2008†	2012	2017

2018	2043	2068	2093
2019	2044	2069*	2094
2020	2045	2070	2095
2021	2046	2071	2096
2022	2047	2072	2097
2023	2048	2073	2098
2024	2049	2074	2099
2025	2050	2075	2100*
2026	2051	2076	2101
2027	2052	2077	2103
2028	2053	2078	2104
2029	2054	2079	2105
2030	2055	2080	2106
2031	2056*	2081	2107
2032	2057	2082	2108
2033	2058	2083	2109
2034	2059	2084	2110
2035	2060	2085	2111
2036	2061	2086	2112
2037	2062	2087	2113
2038	2063	2088*	2114
2039	2064	2089	2115
2040	2065	2090	2116
2041	2066	2091	2117
2042	2067	2092	2118

2120	2128	2137	2145
2121	2129	2138	2146
2122	2130	2139	2147
2123	2132	2140	2148
2124	2133*	2141	2149
2125	2134	2142	2150
2126	2135	2143	2151
2127	2136	2144	2152

† 88 2nd seats instead of 84 and all-electric control gear.

* BIL Motor Coach and HAL trailer.

TWO-CAR MOTOR LAVATORY UNITS

Motor Brake Second, Driving Trailer Lavatory Composite.

(2-HAL.)

2601	2626	2652	2677
2602	2627	2653	2678
2603	2628	2654	2679
2604	2629	2655	2681
2605	2630	2656	2682
2606	2631	2657	2683
2607	2632	2658	2684
2608	2633	2659	2685
2609	2634	2660	2686
2610	2635	2661	2687
2611	2636	2662	2688
2612	2637	2663	2689
2613	2638	2664	2690
2614	2639	2665	2691
2615	2640	2666	2692
2616	2641	2667	2693
2617	2642	2668	2694
2618	2643	2669	2695
2619	2644	2670	2696
2620	2645	2671	2697
2621	2647	2672	2698
2622	2648	2673	2699
2623	2649	2674	2700
2624	2650	2675	
2625	2651	2676	

FOUR-CAR MOTOR LAVATORY UNITS

Motor Brake Second, Composite, Lavatory Composite, Motor Brake Second.

(4-LAV.)

2921	2930	2939	2948
2922	2931	2940	2949
2923	2932	2941	2950
2924	2933	2942	2951
2925	2934	2943	2952
2926*	2935	2944	2953
2927	2936	2945	2954†
2928	2937	2946	2955†
2929	2938	2947	

* One motor coach with electro-pneumatic control gear.

† With electro-pneumatic control gear.

SIX-CAR MOTOR CORRIDOR UNITS (with Pullman Car)

Gangwayed within set

Motor Brake Second, Second, Composite, Composite Pullman, Composite, Motor Brake Second.

(6-PUL.)

3001	3007	3013	3019
3002	3008	3014	3020
3003	3009	3015	3041*
3004	3010	3016	3042*
3005	3011	3017	3043*
3006	3012	3018	

* Ex- " 6-CIT " Units. Trailers (except Pullman) formerly Firsts.

SIX-CAR MOTOR CORRIDOR UNITS (with Pantry Car)

Gangwayed within set

Motor Brake Second, Second, First, Pantry First, Second, Motor Brake Second.

(6-PAN.)

3021	3025	3029	3034
3022	3026	3030	3035
3023	3027	3031	3036
3024	3028	3033	3037

FIVE-CAR PULLMAN MOTOR UNITS

(For " Brighton Belle " Service)

All-Pullman
Gangwayed within set.
Motor Second, Second, First, First, Motor Second.

(5-BEL.)

3051	3052	3053

FOUR-CAR KITCHEN CORRIDOR MOTOR UNITS

Gangwayed throughout.
Motor Brake Second, First (and First Dining), Kitchen Second Dining, Motor Brake Second.

(4-RES.)

3054	3059	3065	3069
3055	3061	3066	3070
3056	3062	3067	3071
3057	3064	3068	3072*

*Kitchen Second rebuilt as Buffet Car.

FOUR-CAR BUFFET CORRIDOR MOTOR UNITS

Gangwayed throughout.
Motor Brake Second, Composite, Buffet, Motor Brake Second.

(4-BUF.)

3073	3077	3080	3083
3074	3078	3081	3084
3075	3079	3082	3085
3076			

FOUR-CAR CORRIDOR MOTOR UNITS

Gangwayed throughout.
Motor Brake Second, Second, Composite, Motor Brake Second.

(4-COR.)

3101	3116	3131	3145
3102	3117	3132	3146
3103	3118	3133	3147
3104	3119	3134	3148
3105	3120	3135	3149
3106	3121	3136	3150
3107	3122	3137	3151
3108	3123	3138	3152
3109	3124	3139	3153
3110	3125	3140	3154
3111	3126	3141	3155
3112	3127	3142	3156
3113	3128	3143	3157
3114	3129	3144	3158
3115	3130		

FOUR-CAR DOUBLE DECK SUBURBAN UNITS

Motor Brake Second, 2 Trailer Seconds, Motor Brake Second.

(4-DD.)

4001	4002

FOUR-CAR NON-CORRIDOR SUBURBAN UNITS

See table for formation.

(4-SUB.)

4101	4115	4129	4289
4102	4116	4130	4290
4103	4117	4277	4291
4104	4118	4278	4292
4105	4119	4279	4293
4106	4120	4280	4294
4107	4121	4281	4295
4108	4122	4282	4296
4109	4123	4283	4297
4110	4124	4284	4298
4111	4125	4285	4299
4112	4126	4286	4301
4113	4127	4287	4302
4114	4128	4288	4303

4304	4351	4510	4652
4305	4352	4511	4653
4306	4353	4512	4654
4307	4354	4513	4655
4308	4355	4514	4656
4309	4356	4515	4657
4310	4357	4516	4658
4311	4358	4517	4659
4312	4359	4601	4660
4313	4360	4602	4661
4314	4361	4603	4662
4315	4362	4604	4663
4316	4363	4605	4664
4317	4364	4606	4665
4318	4365	4607	4666
4319	4366	4621	4667
4320	4367	4622	4668
4321	4368	4623	4669
4322	4369	4624	4670
4323	4370	4625	4671
4324	4371	4626	4672
4325	4372	4627	4673
4326	4373	4628	4674
4327	4374	4629	4675
4328	4375	4630	4676
4329	4376	4631	4677
4330	4377	4632	4678
4331	4378	4633	4679
4332	4379	4634	4680
4333	4380	4635	4681
4334	4381	4636	4682
4335	4382	4637	4683
4336	4383	4638	4684
4337	4384	4639	4685
4338	4385	4640	4686
4339	4386	4641	4687
4340	4387	4642	4688
4341	4501	4643	4689
4342	4502	4644	4690
4343	4503	4645	4691
4344	4504	4646	4692
4345	4505	4647	4693
4346	4506	4648	4694
4347	4507	4649	4695
4348	4508	4650	4696
4349	4509	4651	4697

4698	4713	4728	4743
4699	4714	4729	4744
4700	4715	4730	4745
4701	4716	4731	4746
4702	4717	4732	4747
4703	4718	4733	4748
4704	4719	4734	4749
4705	4720	4735	4750
4706	4721	4736	4751
4707	4722	4737	4752
4708	4723	4738	4753
4709	4724	4739	4754
4710	4725	4740	
4711	4726	4741	
4712	4727	4742	

FOUR-CAR NON-CORRIDOR SUBURBAN UNITS

See table for formation.

(4-EPB)

5001	5027	5052	5124
5002	5028	5053	5125
5003	5029	5101	5126
5004	5030	5102	5127
5005	5031	5103	5128
5006	5032	5104	5129
5007	5033	5105	5130
5008	5034	5106	5131
5009	5035	5107	5132
5010	5036	5108	5133
5011	5037	5109	5134
5012	5038	5110	5135
5013	5039	5111	5136
5014	5040	5112	5137
5015	5041	5113	5138
5016	5042	5114	5139
5017	5043	5115	5140
5018	5044	5116	5141
5019	5045	5117	5142
5020	5046	5118	5143
5021	5047	5119	5144
5022	5048	5120	5145
5024	5049	5121	5146
5025	5050	5122	5147
5026	5051	5123	5148

5149	5177	5206	5234
5150	5178	5207	5235
5151	5179	5208	5236
5152	5180	5209	5237
5153	5181	5210	5238
5154	5182	5211	5239
5155	5183	5212	5240
5156	5184	5213	5241
5157	5185	5214	5242
5158	5186	5215	5243
5159	5187	5216	5244
5160	5188	5217	5245
5161	5189	5218	5246
5162	5190	5219	5247
5163	5191	5220	5248
5164	5192	5221	5249
5165	5193	5222	5250
5166	5194	5223	5251
5167	5195	5224	5252
5168	5196	5225	5253
5169	5197	5226	5254
5170	5198	5227	5255
5171	5199	5228	5256
5172	5200	5229	5257
5173	5201	5230	5258
5174	5202	5231	5259
5175	5203	5232	5260
5176	5205	5233	

TWO-CAR NON-CORRIDOR SUBURBAN UNITS

(B.R. Standard design)

Motor Brake Saloon Second, Driving Trailer Second (part Saloon).

(2-EPB)

5701	5721	5741	5761
5702	5722	5742	5762
5703	5723	5743	5763
5704	5724	5744	5764
5705	5725	5745	5765
5706	5726	5746	5767
5707	5727	5747	5768
5708	5728	5748	5769
5709	5729	5749	5770
5710	5730	5750	5771
5711	5731	5751	5772
5712	5732	5752	5773
5713	5733	5753	5774
5714	5734	5754	5775
5715	5735	5755	5776
5716	5736	5756	5777
5717	5737	5757	5778
5718	5738	5758	5779
5719	5739	5759	
5720	5740	5760	

TWO-CAR MOTOR LAVATORY UNITS

(B.R. Standard design)

Motor Brake Saloon Second, Driving Trailer Lavatory Composite (part Saloon).

(2-HAP.)

6001	6012	6023	6034
6002	6013	6024	6035
6003	6014	6025	6036
6004	6015	6026	6037
6005	6016	6027	6038
6006	6017	6028	6039
6007	6018	6029	6040
6008	6019	6030	6041
6009	6020	6031	6042
6010	6021	6032	6043
6011	6022	6033	6044

TWO-CAR MOTOR LAVATORY UNITS

Motor Brake Saloon Second, Driving Trailer Lavatory Composite.

(2-HAP.)

5601	5610	5619	5628
5602	5611	5620	5629
5603	5612	5621	5630
5604	5613	5622	5631
5605	5614	5623	5632
5606	5615	5624	5633
5607	5616	5625	5634
5608	5617	5626	5635
5609	5618	5627	5636

6045	6060	6075	6090
6046	6061	6076	6091
6047	6062	6077	6092
6048	6063	6078	6093
6049	6064	6079	6094
6050	6065	6080	6095
6051	6066	6081	6096
6052	6067	6082	6097
6053	6068	6083	6098
6054	6069	6084	6099
6055	6070	6085	6100
6056	6071	6086	6101
6057	6072	6087	6102
6058	6073	6088	6103
6059	6074	6089	6104

FOUR-CAR CORRIDOR BUFFET UNITS

(B.R. Standard design)

Gangwayed throughout.

Motor Brake Second, Composite, Buffet, Motor Brake Second.

(4-BEP.)

7001	7004	7007	7010
7002	7005	7008	7011
7003	7006	7009	7012

N.B.—These units are still being delivered.

FOUR-CAR CORRIDOR UNITS

(B.R. Standard design)

Gangwayed throughout.

Motor Brake Second, Composite, Second, Motor Brake Second.

(4-CEP.)

7101	7115	7129	7143
7102	7116	7130	7144
7103	7117	7131	7145
7104	7118	7132	7146
7105	7119	7133	7147
7106	7120	7134	7148
7107	7121	7135	7149
7108	7122	7136	7150
7109	7123	7137	7151
7110	7124	7138	7152
7111	7125	7139	7153
7112	7126	7140	
7113	7127	7141	
7114	7128	7142	

N.B.—These units are still being delivered.

WATERLOO AND CITY LINE MOTOR COACH NOS.

51	54	57	60
52	55	58	61
53	56	59	62

FOUR–CAR SUBURBAN (4–SUB & 4–EPB) UNITS

Make-up, Seating Capacity, etc.

Unit Nos.	Type	Motor Coaches	Trailer Coaches	Seating Capacity
4101– 4110	All-Steel Built 1941/5	9 compt.	1 10 compt. 1 11 compt.	468
4111– 4120	All-Steel Built 1946	8 compt.	1 9 compt. 1 10 compt.	420
4121– 4130	All-Steel Built 1946	Semi-Saloon	1 Semi-Saloon 1 9 compt.	382

4277–4299	All-Steel Built 1948–9	Saloon	1 1	Saloon 10 compt.	386
4300–25	Augmented W-Section Built 1925	7 compt.	1 1	9 compt. All-Steel* 10 compt.	350 338*
4326–38 4340–49 51–4	Augmented E-Section Built 1925/6	8 compt.	1 1	9 compt. All-Steel 10 compt.	370
4339	Augmented E-Section Built 1925/6	1–7 compt. 1–8 compt.	1 1	9 compt. All-Steel 10 compt.	360
4355–4363	All-Steel Built 1947/8	8 compt.	2	10 compt.	432
4364–4376	All-Steel Built 1947/8	8 compt.	1 1	9 compt. 10 compt.	420
4377	All-Steel Built 1947	8 compt.	1 1	9 compt. Saloon	402
4378–4387	All-Steel Built 1948	Saloon	1 1	Saloon 10 compt.	386
4501–17	Reformed L.B.S.C.R. converted S.R. (4501/11 have one or two converted ex-L.S.–W.R. coaches)	1–7 compt. 1–8 compt.† († 7-compt. on unit 4501)	2	10 compt.	350 340†
4601–4607	All-Steel bodies on original or new underframes Rebuilt 1949/50	Semi-Saloon	2	10 compt.	404
4621–4666		Saloon	1 1	Saloon 10 compt.*	386*
4667–4754	New all-steel bodies (1950–7) on original underframes	Saloon	1 1	Saloon 10 compt.	386
5001–53, 5101–5260		Saloon	1 1	Saloon 10 compt.*	386*

*Except units **4313**, **4688/96**, **4723/8/33/9**, **5005**, **5220**, which have 9 compt. trailers thus reducing the number of seats by 12.

GLASGOW UNDERGROUND

Motor Coach Nos.

1	6	14	17	21	25	29	57
2	11	15	18	23	27	30	58
3	12	16	20	24	28	55	59
						56	60

SWANSEA & MUMBLES
Tramcar Nos.

| 1 2 | 3 4 | 5 6 | 7 8 | 9 10 | 11 12 | 13 |

BRIGHTON CORPORATION—VOLK'S ELECTRIC RAILWAY

Car No.	Seating Capacity	Sides	H.P. of Motor
1	40	Open	Approximately 7
2	40	Open	,,
3	40	Sliding Doors	,,
4	40	,, ,,	,,
5	40	,, ,,	,,
6	40	,, ,,	,,
7	40	,, ,,	,,
8	36	Open	,, 10/12
9	36	Open	,, ,,

Cars Nos. 8 and 9 were originally trailers purchased from Southend, and the truck were reconstructed and motorised by Brighton Corporation Transport.

MANX ELECTRIC RAILWAY

No.	Seating Capacity	Type	No.	Seating Capacity	Type
1	36	Saloon*	20	48	Saloon
2	36	Saloon*	21	48	Saloon
5	36	Saloon	22	48	Saloon
6	36	Saloon	25	56	Open
7	36	Saloon	26	56	Open
9	36	Saloon	27	56	Open
14	56	Open	28	56	Open
15	56	Open	29	56	Open
16	56	Open	30	56	Open
17	56	Open	31	56	Open
18	56	Open	32	56	Open
19	48	Saloon	33	56	Open

* With open front end.

NOTES ON THE USE OF THIS BOOK

The *ABC Locoshed Book* is not designed to be used on its own, but as a companion to the *ABC of British Railways Locomotives*. As it is difficult to include shed allocations in the latter without harm to the format which has proved popular with *ABC* users, this all-in-one *Locoshed Book* was instituted wherein the number of *all* British Railways locomotives are listed with the code number of the shed to which each engine is allocated.

1. No details of wheel arrangements, dimensions or locomotive names are provided in the *Locoshed Book*. All these details are readily ascertained from the *ABC of British Railways Locomotives*, as follows :

PART I	Locomotives Nos. 1–9999	
PART II	„	10000–39999
PART III	„	40000–59999
PART IV	„	60000–99999

and the *ABC of British Railways Diesels*

In <u>this</u> publication named locomotives are indicated by an asterisk.

2. Against each locomotive in this booklet is shown the code of its home shed, which the locomotive carries on a small plate at the bottom of the smokebox door. A key to the British Railways shed code is found on pp. 4–9.

3. Sub-sheds, which are not given a special code number by British Railways are included in this list, but locomotives allocated to them carry the shed code of the parent depot, whose number appears immediately above them in the list of shed codes. Sheds listed in bold type are chief sheds of a motive power district.

4. Locomotives not given a shed code were on order, under construction or not yet allocated at the time of compilation.

5. All locomotives solely employed on service or departmental work, whether numbered in the British Railways or in individual departmental series, are listed on page 89.

6. The shed allocations given in this booklet are as they were reported to the following dates :—E. & N.E.R. to April 11th, 1959 ; L.M.R. to March 21st, 1959 ; Sc.R. to February 14th, 1959 : S.R. to May 1st, 1959 ; W.R. to March 21st, 1959.

SHED ALLOCATIONS OF
BRITISH RAILWAYS LOCOMOTIVES

IN NUMERICAL ORDER

7 *	89C	1152	87K	1466	83A	1631	85B
8 *	89C	1338	83B	1467	85B	1632	85B
9 *	89C	1361	83D	1468	83C	1633	87F
822	89A	1362	83B	1470	83A	1634	87C
823	89A	1363	83D	1471	83C	1635	84J
		1364	83D	1472	85B	1636	89C
		1365	82C	1473	14D	1637	87H
1000 *	82A	1366	83B	1474	71G	1638	87F
1001 *	87H	1367	71G	1500	81A	1639	85B
1002 *	83G	1368	71G	1501	81C	1640	87C
1003 *	84G	1369	82C	1502	81E	1641	87D
1004 *	82C	1370	71G	1503	81A	1642	85B
1005 *	82A	1371	82C	1504	81A	1643	87F
1006 *	83G	1407	81D	1505	81A	1644	87F
1007 *	83F	1409	82A	1506	86B	1645	87A
1008 *	83G	1410	82C	1507	86B	1646	60C
1009 *	82A	1412	82A	1508	86C	1647	87C
1010 *	83D	1419	83E	1509	86A	1648	87C
1011 *	82A	1420	81C	1601	87H	1649	60C
1012 *	82C	1421	83D	1602	89A	1650	83D
1013 *	84G	1424	85B	1603	89A	1651	87F
1014 *	82A	1426	85B	1604	89A	1652	87D
1015 *	83D	1427	85B	1605	85B	1653	86A
1016 *	84G	1428	85B	1606	87F	1654	87F
1017 *	82A	1431	81C	1607	87F	1655	87F
1018 *	83G	1432	89A	1608	83A	1656	86A
1019 *	82C	1433	82C	1609	87F	1657	85C
1020 *	87H	1434	83D	1610	88E	1658	82C
1021 *	83D	1435	81F	1611	87H	1659	84J
1022 *	84G	1438	82C	1612	87F	1660	84J
1023 *	83F	1440	83C	1613	87F	1661	85A
1024 *	82A	1441	85B	1614	87F	1662	85C
1025 *	84G	1442	81F	1615	87F	1663	84K
1026 *	84G	1444	81D	1616	85B	1664	83E
1027 *	87H	1445	85C	1617	85C	1665	87F
1028 *	82A	1447	81F	1618	84K	1666	87F
1029 *	87H	1448	81B	1619	84F	1667	85C
1101	87C	1449	89C	1620	88E	1668	83B
1102	87C	1450	81B	1621	84F	1669	84K
1103	87C	1451	83C	1622	87F	2012	6C
1104	87C	1452	83A	1623	85B	2069	6C
1105	87C	1453	71G	1624	83E	2200	89C
1106	87C	1454	82A	1625	85C	2201	89C
1142	84G	1455	85C	1626	83E	2202	89C
1143	87C	1458	89A	1627	85B	2203	82C
1144	87D	1462	83C	1628	87F	2204	89C
1145	87C	1463	82A	1629	85A	2205	82B
1151	87C	1464	82C	1630	85B	2206	85A

2207	85B	2268	82D	2841	84B	2899	83D
2208	87H	2270	84C	2842	86A	3103	86A
2209	85A	2271	89C	2843	83D	3200	89A
2210	84G	2272	87G	2844	87E	3201	84K
2211	84C	2273	87H	2845	86A	3202	89A
2212	81D	2274	87G	2846	83A	3203	85B
2213	82B	2275	89A	2847	86E	3204	84K
2214	81E	2276	81A	2848	86G	3205	85A
2215	82E	2277	82B	2849	84E	3206	81E
2216	87G	2278	87J	2850	84B	3207	84K
2217	89C	2280	89C	2851	84E	3208	89A
2218	86A	2281	89C	2852	82C	3209	89A
2219	89A	2282	81A	2853	84F	3210	81E
2220	87H	2283	87H	2854	85B	3211	81E
2221	81E	2284	87E	2855	84J	3212	81E
2222	81A	2285	89C	2856	84E	3213	85A
2223	87J	2286	89C	2857	84B	3214	85A
2224	87G	2287	89B	2858	86A	3215	82B
2225	89B	2288	87H	2859	84B	3216	85A
2226	87E	2289	84G	2860	86E	3217	85A
2227	86A	2290	87G	2861	86E	3218	85A
2228	87H	2291	85B	2862	86E	3219	81D
2229	87H	2292	86E	2863	86J	3400	84G
2230	84C	2293	82C	2864	86C	3401	88A
2231	86E	2294	89A	2865	82C	3402	88A
2232	89C	2295	85C	2866	86G	3403	88A
2233	89C	2296	86G	2867	86E	3404	88A
2234	84C	2297	84C	2868	86A	3405	88A
2235	83B	2298	89C	2869	86E	3406	88A
2236	89A	2299	81D	2870	86J	3407	88A
2237	89C	2803	86G	2871	84J	3408	88A
2238	84E	2804	84F	2872	86E	3409	88A
2239	89A	2805	83A	2873	86E	3440 *	82C
2240	81E	2806	86E	2874	86C	3600	89A
2241	85C	2807	83A	2875	83A	3601	85D
2242	85C	2808	87F	2876	86J	3602	84G
2243	85A	2809	83D	2877	86C	3603	82B
2244	89C	2810	86J	2878	84J	3604	82B
2245	81D	2811	82D	2879	82C	3605	85A
2246	81E	2813	86J	2880	81F	3606	83C
2247	85A	2815	86E	2881	83A	3607	85A
2248	85B	2816	84C	2882	84E	3608	81B
2249	85C	2818	82C	2883	86E	3609	85B
2250	82B	2819	81E	2884	86G	3610	86J
2251	87H	2821	87E	2885	84E	3611	87A
2252	81E	2822	83B	2886	84E	3612	86D
2253	85B	2823	84F	2887	86E	3613	87B
2255	89C	2824	87F	2888	84B	3614	82D
2256	84C	2826	86E	2889	86C	3615	84A
2257	84E	2831	86J	2890	84C	3616	86F
2259	87H	2832	86E	2891	86C	3617	86D
2260	89C	2834	86C	2892	86E	3618	81C
2261	82B	2835	82C	2893	86E	3619	84D
2262	81D	2836	81F	2894	86A	3620	81C
2264	89C	2837	86E	2895	86C	3621	87A
2265	82B	2838	86E	2896	86E	3622	81E
2266	85C	2839	86A	2897	84E	3623	82B
2267	84E	2840	84J	2898	86A	3624	84D

3625	84E	3683	86H	3742	82F	3801	86C
3626	84H	3684	82C	3743	84F	3802	84B
3627	86F	3685	86G	3744	84H	3803	85B
3628	86G	3686	83D	3745	84F	3804	86A
3629	82D	3687	87A	3746	82C	3805	86A
3630	6E	3688	81A	3747	86H	3806	86A
3631	84D	3689	84J	3748	82A	3807	86A
3632	82B	3690	86F	3749	84K	3808	86A
3633	87C	3691	86A	3750	81C	3809	86C
3634	86A	3692	82B	3751	81E	3810	86C
3635	83E	3693	84E	3752	87F	3811	87F
3636	86A	3694	87K	3753	86J	3812	86E
3637	87J	3695	86J	3754	81A	3813	84B
3638	89B	3696	82D	3755	86C	3814	81F
3639	87H	3697	81B	3756	84A	3815	86G
3640	86G	3698	84B	3757	87A	3816	86C
3641	87D	3699	86J	3758	82B	3817	86C
3642	87F	3700	86K	3759	82A	3818	86C
3643	82B	3701	87E	3760	84K	3819	82D
3644	86D	3702	83F	3761	87F	3820	84B
3645	82C	3703	86G	3762	87B	3821	86F
3646	84C	3704	81C	3763	82C	3822	86G
3647	86H	3705	83E	3764	82B	3823	81F
3648	81A	3706	89B	3765	82B	3824	86G
3649	84F	3707	88E	3766	87A	3825	84F
3650	82B	3708	86G	3767	89B	3826	86G
3651	86G	3709	81E	3768	87E	3827	86A
3652	86B	3710	84G	3769	84G	3828	84J
3653	81E	3711	82C	3770	89B	3829	84B
3654	87H	3712	86A	3771	87F	3830	86A
3655	86J	3713	87E	3772	86A	3831	84E
3656	86D	3714	86A	3773	82B	3832	86A
3657	84E	3715	81C	3774	87A	3833	86A
3658	84F	3716	86J	3775	85A	3834	83A
3659	83A	3717	86G	3776	82B	3835	86C
3660	84E	3718	87B	3777	87F	3836	81C
3661	87F	3719	87F	3778	84A	3837	84B
3662	86A	3720	82A	3779	86G	3838	86E
3663	86B	3721	81E	3780	82C	3839	84E
3664	84A	3722	81F	3781	87C	3840	83A
3665	6E	3723	81D	3782	84G	3841	83A
3666	82C	3724	82C	3783	88E	3842	86C
3667	84F	3725	85A	3784	82B	3843	86C
3668	86F	3726	82B	3785	87E	3844	86E
3669	83B	3727	88A	3786	6E	3845	86C
3670	86C	3728	85C	3787	83D	3846	84B
3671	72C	3729	84F	3788	84G	3847	86E
3672	88A	3730	88E	3789	89A	3848	85B
3673	84E	3731	82B	3790	83D	3849	87E
3674	86B	3732	84H	3791	87B	3850	86J
3675	83D	3733	72C	3792	84A	3851	87F
3676	6E	3734	88E	3793	83C	3852	86E
3677	82A	3735	82D	3794	84A	3853	86A
3678	87E	3736	83B	3795	82B	3854	86G
3679	87C	3737	71G	3796	83A	3855	86C
3680	88D	3738	81D	3797	87E	3856	84C
3681	88D	3739	82C	3798	86A	3857	81F
3682	82C	3741	87A	3799	81C	3858	84C
				3800	86A		

3859	86G	4123	85B	4207	86C	4279	87A
3860	86C	4124	85A	4208	86D	4280	86B
3861	84B	4125	81F	4211	86A	4281	87A
3862	83D	4126	84E	4212	84G	4282	87A
3863	84B	4127	86E	4213	87F	4283	86A
3864	83A	4128	83B	4214	86B	4284	87A
3865	84B	4129	82C	4215	86E	4285	86H
3866	86E	4130	86E	4217	86E	4286	86A
4037 *	83A	4131	82B	4218	86F	4287	86H
4073 *	86C	4132	87H	4221	87A	4288	87A
4074 *	87E	4133	71G	4222	86F	4289	86E
4075 *	82A	4134	87G	4223	87F	4290	86A
4076 *	87E	4135	86G	4225	86C	4291	86H
4077 *	83D	4136	83G	4227	86A	4292	87B
4078 *	82A	4137	86E	4228	86J	4293	87B
4079 *	82A	4140	84F	4229	86A	4294	83E
4080 *	82A	4141	85B	4230	86G	4295	87A
4081 *	82A	4142	85A	4231	86C	4296	87B
4082 *	81A	4143	88A	4232	87D	4297	86C
4083 *	83A	4144	86F	4233	86B	4298	86F
4084 *	83A	4145	83A	4235	86B	4299	87C
4085 *	85B	4146	84F	4236	86F	4358	85B
4086 *	82C	4147	81F	4237	86H	4507	71G
4087 *	83D	4148	81F	4238	86B	4508	83F
4088 *	85A	4149	84C	4241	86F	4536	82D
4089 *	85A	4150	83A	4242	87A	4547	83E
4090 *	81A	4151	86E	4243	86F	4549	89C
4092 *	81D	4152	85A	4246	86A	4550	87H
4093 *	87E	4153	85D	4247	86A	4552	83E
4094 *	87E	4154	85A	4248	86A	4555	82D
4095 *	83G	4155	84E	4250	86H	4556	87H
4096 *	81A	4156	86E	4251	86F	4557	87H
4097 *	87E	4157	83B	4252	86D	4558	87H
4098 *	83A	4158	84H	4253	86B	4559	83E
4099 *	87E	4159	83B	4254	86C	4560	89C
4100	85B	4160	88A	4255	86J	4561	83A
4101	85B	4161	84A	4256	87B	4562	71G
4102	82C	4162	84D	4257	86J	4563	83G
4103	84D	4163	82A	4258	86B	4564	83E
4104	84F	4164	86E	4259	86B	4565	83E
4105	83A	4165	85B	4260	87F	4566	83G
4106	87E	4166	71G	4261	86J	4567	82D
4107	87E	4167	83E	4262	86J	4569	83E
4108	83A	4168	84F	4263	86F	4570	83G
4109	85A	4169	87A	4264	87A	4571	83D
4110	84H	4170	84E	4265	87B	4573	85B
4111	84E	4171	84D	4266	86C	4574	83F
4112	84D	4172	84E	4267	86A	4575	89C
4113	85A	4173	84F	4268	86D	4577	83G
4114	85D	4174	83A	4269	86F	4585	83E
4115	85C	4175	85D	4270	86C	4587	83F
4116	85B	4176	83A	4271	86C	4588	83G
4117	83C	4177	83A	4272	86J	4589	83C
4118	84D	4178	83A	4273	86D	4591	83D
4119	86E	4179	83A	4274	86F	4592	83D
4120	84H	4201	86B	4275	87A	4593	86G
4121	86F	4203	86A	4276	86B	4594	87H
4122	87H	4206	83E	4277	86H	4600	86G
				4278	87B		

4601	73H	4659	85C	4908 *	83G	4967 *	83A
4602	6E	4660	82B	4909 *	82B	4968 *	84G
4603	82B	4661	81D	4910 *	87E	4969 *	81E
4604	83B	4662	86D	4912 *	84G	4970 *	83B
4605	84H	4663	83B	4913 *	84G	4971 *	83B
4606	81B	4664	85A	4914 *	82B	4972 *	82C
4607	82D	4665	81D	4915 *	81E	4973 *	86C
4608	81C	4666	87C	4916 *	86A	4974 *	84E
4609	81D	4667	88C	4917 *	82D	4975 *	83A
4610	73H	4668	86G	4918 *	84G	4976 *	83G
4611	86A	4669	86F	4919 *	81A	4977 *	81D
4612	82C	4670	81D	4920 *	83A	4978 *	83B
4613	85A	4671	86A	4921 *	81F	4979 *	81F
4614	85A	4672	70A	4922 *	82A	4980 *	82B
4615	81A	4673	81C	4923 *	87E	4981 *	87J
4616	73H	4674	86D	4924 *	84C	4982 *	84E
4617	84J	4675	86F	4925 *	81C	4983 *	87G
4618	88C	4676	87K	4926 *	86G	4984 *	84B
4619	82A	4677	87J	4927 *	82A	4985 *	83B
4620	86D	4678	85C	4928 *	83D	4986 *	84A
4621	87A	4679	83D	4929 *	85B	4987 *	81D
4622	86C	4680	85B	4930 *	83B	4988 *	82A
4623	84G	4681	87B	4931 *	83G	4989 *	81D
4624	71G	4682	86B	4932 *	83B	4990 *	84A
4625	85A	4683	84K	4933 *	82D	4991 *	83B
4626	73H	4684	87B	4934 *	81C	4992 *	83C
4627	86H	4685	86H	4935 *	87G	4993 *	81D
4628	85B	4686	70A	4936 *	83A	4994 *	81E
4629	85A	4687	84F	4937 *	87E	4995 *	81F
4630	73H	4688	82B	4938 *	81F	4996 *	81C
4631	73H	4689	71G	4939 *	81E	4997 *	84B
4632	88C	4690	88D	4940 *	83B	4998 *	81D
4633	86C	4691	87F	4941 *	87F	4999 *	86C
4634	70A	4692	70A	4942 *	84C	5000 *	82C
4635	88D	4693	84G	4943 *	86G	5001 *	84G
4636	82D	4694	87C	4944 *	83C	5002 *	82C
4637	86D	4695	87B	4945 *	82D	5003 *	83A
4638	81B	4696	84F	4946 *	86C	5004 *	87E
4639	86G	4697	82C	4947 *	82A	5005 *	82C
4640	87B	4698	70A	4948 *	83C	5006 *	87G
4641	81D	4699	87H	4949 *	82B	5007 *	82C
4642	86G	4700	83G	4950 *	83G	5008 *	81A
4643	86B	4701	81A	4951 *	84B	5009 *	82C
4644	81A	4702	81A	4952 *	85A	5010 *	81D
4645	84J	4703	82B	4953 *	82C	5011 *	83A
4646	84F	4704	81A	4954 *	81F	5012 *	81F
4647	82D	4705	83D	4955 *	83A	5013 *	87E
4648	84E	4706	82B	4956 *	86C	5014 *	81A
4649	81E	4707	81C	4957 *	84B	5015 *	82A
4650	81B	4708	81A	4958 *	87G	5016 *	87E
4651	82C	4900 *	81A	4959 *	81E	5017 *	85B
4652	86H	4901 *	84A	4960 *	83C	5018 *	81D
4653	87A	4902 *	81F	4961 *	81D	5019 *	84A
4654	87H	4903 *	81F	4962 *	81D	5020 *	83G
4655	82B	4904 *	84G	4963 *	84B	5021 *	83D
4656	72C	4905 *	83A	4964 *	84C	5022 *	84A
4657	85C	4906 *	83E	4965 *	81E	5023 *	82C
4658	83D	4907 *	81C	4966 *	84B	5024 *	83A

5025 * 81F	5084 * 81A	5196	83A	5254	87B
5026 * 84A	5085 * 82A	5197	82A	5255	86A
5027 * 81A	5087 * 81A	5198	85B	5256	86A
5028 * 83D	5088 * 84A	5199	84F	5257	86B
5029 * 85A	5089 * 84A	5200	86B	5258	86J
5030 * 87G	5090 * 82A	5201	86A	5259	86A
5031 * 84A	5091 * 87E	5202	86B	5260	86C
5032 * 83A	5092 * 82A	5203	87F	5261	86C
5033 * 81F	5093 * 81A	5204	87F	5262	87D
5034 * 81A	5094 * 85B	5205	86A	5263	86J
5035 * 81A	5095 * 86C	5206	86H	5264	87B
5036 * 81D	5096 * 82A	5207	86C	5306	82C
5037 * 85A	5097 * 84G	5208	86F	5311	82A
5038 * 84G	5098 * 83D	5209	87F	5318	86G
5039 * 87E	5099 * 86C	5210	87D	5319	84G
5040 * 81A	5101	84D	5211	87D	5321	86G
5041 * 87E	5102	87A	5212	86E	5322	81D
5042 * 85A	5103	86G	5213	87F	5324	81D
5043 * 81A	5104	82B	5214	87F	5326	81E
5044 * 81A	5106	83D	5215	87F	5330	86G
5045 * 84A	5110	85D	5216	87B	5331	84G
5046 * 84A	5148	83D	5217	86A	5332	87F
5047 * 84A	5150	83A	5218	86C	5333	85D
5048 * 82A	5151	84A	5219	87F	5336	86E
5049 * 83A	5152	84C	5220	87B	5337	84C
5050 * 84G	5153	83A	5221	87B	5339	83C
5051 * 87E	5154	83A	5222	87A	5341	87F
5052 * 81A	5155	86E	5223	87F	5345	86G
5053 * 83A	5158	83A	5224	86E	5350	85C
5054 * 82A	5163	84E	5225	87A	5351	82C
5055 * 83A	5164	83A	5226	85C	5353	87G
5056 * 81A	5166	86E	5227	86A	5355	85D
5057 * 82A	5167	84H	5228	86A	5356	82B
5058 * 83D	5169	86E	5229	86A	5357	87H
5059 * 84A	5170	84C	5230	87F	5358	82D
5060 * 81A	5173	86A	5231	86B	5361	87D
5061 * 81D	5174	6E	5232	87D	5369	84E
5062 * 82A	5175	83D	5233	86A	5370	84E
5063 * 84A	5176	84F	5234	86A	5375	84C
5064 * 82C	5177	85B	5235	86B	5376	83F
5065 * 81A	5178	83A	5236	86E	5378	84E
5066 * 81A	5179	85A	5237	86J	5380	81E
5067 * 87G	5180	87H	5238	86A	5381	86G
5068 * 82C	5181	86E	5239	87A	5382	86E
5069 * 83D	5182	85B	5240	87D	5384	71G
5070 * 84A	5183	83A	5241	86H	5385	82B
5071 * 85A	5184	84D	5242	87A	5393	82B
5072 * 84A	5185	83B	5243	85C	5396	85D
5073 * 82A	5186	82A	5244	86B	5399	6E
5074 * 81A	5187	84A	5245	85C	5400	89A
5075 * 83D	5188	86A	5246	87A	5407	84C
5076 * 82A	5189	84F	5247	87F	5409	14D
5077 * 87E	5190	81F	5248	87F	5410	81C
5078 * 82A	5191	86E	5249	87F	5412	83C
5079 * 83A	5192	84E	5250	86B	5414	82D
5080 * 87G	5193	83E	5251	86A	5416	82D
5081 * 85A	5194	85B	5252	86B	5417	85B
5082 * 81A	5195	83A	5253	86E	5418	85B

5420	84C	5563	72C	5648	88A	5713	87J
5421	85B	5564	86G	5649	86J	5717	81A
5422	89A	5565	89C	5650	88D	5720	87A
5423	82D	5567	83D	5651	84K	5721	83B
5424	84C	5568	86H	5652	88D	5726	89A
5500	83F	5569	83D	5653	88F	5727	86C
5503	83B	5570	89C	5654	88F	5728	87K
5504	83B	5571	83B	5655	88D	5731	87C
5508	82D	5572	83D	5656	87E	5734	86B
5509	82C	5573	83A	5657	86A	5737	81E
5510	82C	5600	88F	5658	84E	5738	87B
5511	83D	5601	88E	5659	86G	5740	86B
5514	85B	5602	86C	5660	88D	5744	81E
5515	83F	5603	88D	5661	88D	5745	84E
5516	86H	5604	87B	5662	88D	5746	81E
5518	85D	5605	88D	5663	88A	5747	86B
5519	83E	5606	84K	5664	88D	5748	87H
5520	87H	5607	88F	5665	88F	5749	86C
5521	83B	5608	88F	5666	88D	5750	86G
5523	83E	5609	88C	5667	88C	5753	81C
5524	83G	5610	88F	5668	88F	5754	84F
5525	83B	5611	88F	5669	88A	5755	81B
5526	82D	5612	87F	5670	88D	5756	86G
5527	87H	5613	88F	5671	88D	5757	82D
5528	82C	5614	88C	5672	88D	5758	86B
5529	82A	5615	88C	5673	87E	5759	86G
5530	82A	5616	87D	5674	88A	5761	87K
5531	83D	5617	88E	5675	88A	5763	85B
5532	82C	5618	88E	5676	88F	5764	81A
5533	83F	5619	88C	5677	88D	5766	81B
5534	86F	5620	86E	5678	88F	5768	86B
5536	82A	5621	88C	5679	86E	5769	82B
5537	83F	5622	88C	5680	88E	5770	87B
5538	85B	5623	88E	5681	88D	5771	82D
5539	83E	5624	86J	5682	88E	5773	87K
5540	82C	5625	86G	5683	88A	5774	84J
5541	89C	5626	88D	5684	88F	5775	86G
5542	82D	5627	88E	5685	86C	5776	86C
5543	83B	5628	87D	5686	88E	5778	87A
5544	86H	5629	86F	5687	88F	5779	83B
5545	86F	5630	88D	5688	87B	5780	83B
5546	83C	5631	87E	5689	82D	5783	81E
5547	82C	5632	88F	5690	84G	5784	71G
5548	72C	5633	86J	5691	88F	5787	87B
5549	87H	5634	84G	5692	88A	5788	86D
5550	87H	5635	88D	5693	88F	5789	86G
5551	83E	5636	88D	5694	88F	5791	84G
5552	83F	5637	88F	5695	88F	5793	87K
5553	89C	5638	86G	5696	88D	5794	86H
5554	82D	5639	81E	5697	81E	5795	84F
5555	86F	5640	88A	5698	86J	5798	83B
5556	89C	5641	88E	5699	88E	5799	81C
5557	83E	5642	82B	5702	87F	5804	82C
5558	83A	5643	88E	5704	87C	5809	89C
5559	83F	5644	88E	5705	87F	5815	82C
5560	87H	5645	86G	5706	86F	5818	81F
5561	82A	5646	88F	5708	86D	5900 *	84A
5562	83F	5647	81E	5709	86A	5901 *	81D

5902 * 87F	5960 * 81F	6018 * 81A	6147 81C
5903 * 87H	5961 * 87F	6019 * 81A	6148 81C
5904 * 82B	5962 * 86C	6020 * 84A	6149 81A
5905 * 87J	5963 * 82D	6021 * 83D	6150 81B
5906 * 81D	5964 * 82C	6022 * 81A	6151 81B
5907 * 81D	5965 * 84B	6023 * 81A	6152 81B
5908 * 87J	5966 * 81F	6024 * 81A	6153 81D
5909 * 87F	5967 * 83A	6025 * 83D	6154 81B
5910 * 86C	5968 * 84G	6026 * 83D	6155 86E
5911 * 86C	5969 * 82B	6027 * 83D	6156 81C
5912 * 84E	5970 * 86C	6028 * 81A	6157 81C
5913 * 87E	5971 * 85A	6029 * 83D	6158 81A
5914 * 85B	5972 * 83D	6101 81D	6159 81A
5915 * 81D	5973 * 81D	6102 81D	6160 84E
5916 * 84B	5974 * 82D	6103 81D	6161 81D
5917 * 85A	5975 * 82D	6104 81D	6162 81D
5918 * 81C	5976 * 81A	6105 87H	6163 81F
5919 * 84B	5977 * 81D	6106 81F	6164 81B
5920 * 83A	5978 * 82C	6107 82A	6165 81C
5921 * 84C	5979 * 81D	6108 81B	6166 86E
5922 * 82C	5980 * 85A	6109 81A	6167 81B
5923 * 81A	5981 * 82C	6110 81A	6168 81A
5924 * 82B	5982 * 81D	6111 81A	6169 81C
5925 * 81C	5983 * 82C	6112 81F	6300 83F
5926 * 84A	5984 * 85A	6113 81A	6301 83D
5927 * 84E	5985 * 84B	6114 81D	6302 81D
5928 * 87J	5986 * 82C	6115 81B	6303 84G
5929 * 81A	5987 * 81A	6116 84E	6304 85B
5930 * 84C	5988 * 87E	6117 81B	6305 87G
5931 * 81A	5989 * 84C	6118 86E	6306 87H
5932 * 81A	5990 * 87E	6119 86E	6307 82C
5933 * 81C	5991 * 84B	6120 81A	6308 86C
5934 * 83G	5992 * 83B	6121 81A	6309 82C
5935 * 82B	5993 * 81D	6122 81B	6310 87F
5936 * 81A	5994 * 85A	6123 81B	6311 84C
5937 * 87G	5995 * 84B	6124 81B	6312 82B
5938 * 87G	5996 * 81C	6125 81C	6313 81D
5939 * 81A	5997 * 82C	6126 81B	6314 85D
5940 * 81A	5998 * 85C	6127 81B	6316 84J
5941 * 81A	5999 * 83B	6128 81C	6317 84F
5942 * 81D	6000 * 81A	6129 81D	6319 83D
5943 * 81E	6001 * 84A	6130 81D	6320 82D
5944 * 84B	6002 * 81A	6131 81D	6323 83B
5945 * 82D	6003 * 81A	6132 81A	6324 81D
5946 * 86C	6004 * 83D	6133 81B	6325 86E
5947 * 84C	6005 * 84A	6134 81D	6326 86C
5948 * 86G	6006 * 84A	6135 81A	6327 82B
5949 * 82A	6007 * 83D	6136 81B	6329 87G
5950 * 82A	6008 * 84A	6137 85B	6330 85B
5951 * 85B	6009 * 81A	6138 81F	6331 84C
5952 * 85A	6010 * 83D	6139 84E	6332 84F
5953 * 87F	6011 * 84A	6140 81D	6333 86C
5954 * 81A	6012 * 81A	6141 81A	6334 82C
5955 * 87E	6013 * 81A	6142 81A	6335 89C
5956 * 85A	6014 * 84A	6143 81B	6336 82C
5957 * 81D	6015 * 81A	6144 81A	6337 83B
5958 * 81A	6016 * 83D	6145 81A	6338 86E
5959 * 83C	6017 * 84A	6146 81B	6339 84J

6340	84F	6402	83D	6626	88A	6684	88A
6341	82B	6403	84F	6627	81D	6685	86G
6342	89A	6404	89A	6628	86J	6686	87B
6343	83B	6405	84J	6629	86H	6687	86J
6344	71G	6406	83D	6630	82B	6688	87E
6345	6E	6408	82D	6631	84E	6689	88A
6346	82E	6410	86J	6632	84J	6690	85B
6347	87J	6411	88A	6633	88A	6691	87B
6348	86A	6412	86A	6634	86G	6692	84F
6349	84F	6413	86J	6635	88A	6693	86G
6350	82E	6414	83D	6636	86G	6694	84J
6351	82B	6415	85B	6637	88C	6695	87E
6352	86C	6416	88D	6638	88A	6696	84J
6353	84B	6417	86A	6639	82C	6697	84D
6356	82B	6418	84A	6640	84B	6698	84G
6357	84E	6419	83D	6641	88C	6699	88A
6358	82D	6420	83D	6642	86E	6700	87K
6359	85C	6421	83D	6643	88C	6701	87B
6360	83A	6422	84A	6644	86H	6702	86B
6361	86J	6424	86G	6645	84B	6707	86B
6362	86E	6425	86A	6646	84F	6711	86B
6363	82A	6426	86A	6647	88A	6712	87K
6364	83B	6429	84J	6648	88A	6714	87K
6365	85B	6430	86E	6649	87E	6719	87C
6366	82C	6431	86J	6650	87A	6720	87K
6367	84F	6433	88D	6651	86J	6724	86B
6368	86G	6434	88A	6652	86J	6725	86B
6369	86E	6435	88E	6653	86H	6728	86B
6370	86A	6436	88D	6654	81D	6729	86B
6371	89C	6437	86J	6655	81D	6735	88B
6372	83B	6438	88E	6656	82B	6738	87K
6373	85B	6439	86K	6657	84D	6739	86B
6374	82B	6600	86C	6658	88C	6741	82C
6375	83B	6601	82B	6659	88A	6742	86B
6376	82E	6602	87B	6660	88A	6743	86B
6377	87G	6603	88A	6661	86J	6745	86B
6378	89C	6604	84F	6662	87D	6749	87K
6379	81E	6605	86J	6663	86H	6750	86B
6380	6E	6606	88A	6664	81F	6751	86B
6381	85B	6607	83A	6665	83A	6752	88C
6382	85D	6608	83A	6666	86E	6753	87K
6384	86E	6609	84F	6667	84F	6754	88C
6385	83C	6610	84K	6668	84E	6755	86B
6386	86E	6611	84J	6669	85B	6756	86B
6387	84C	6612	88A	6670	82B	6757	86B
6388	81E	6613	87A	6671	86J	6758	82C
6389	87H	6614	83A	6672	86E	6759	86B
6390	83B	6615	83C	6673	86F	6760	86B
6391	82C	6616	87B	6674	84F	6761	87B
6392	89C	6617	84J	6675	86G	6762	87C
6393	87G	6618	88A	6676	86F	6763	87K
6394	85B	6619	88F	6677	84F	6764	86B
6395	84G	6620	87B	6678	84F	6765	88C
6397	83E	6621	86H	6679	85D	6766	87C
6398	83B	6622	86J	6680	87E	6767	87K
6399	84E	6623	87B	6681	82B	6768	87K
6400	86G	6624	88A	6682	88A	6769	82C
6401	84F	6625	82D	6683	84F	6770	87K

6772 86B	6850 * 83D	6928 * 86G	6986 * 82B
6773 88C	6851 * 85A	6929 * 84C	6987 * 84F
6774 87K	6852 * 82B	6930 * 84F	6988 * 83D
6775 88C	6853 * 84E	6931 * 83E	6989 * 85C
6776 87K	6854 * 81F	6932 * 86C	6990 * 81A
6777 87K	6855 * 83F	6933 * 83A	6991 * 81C
6778 87K	6856 * 85A	6934 * 84B	6992 * 85C
6779 87K	6857 * 84B	6935 * 86C	6993 * 82C
6800 * 83G	6858 * 81F	6936 * 86C	6994 * 82D
6801 * 83G	6859 * 83A	6937 * 81F	6995 * 83B
6802 * 86G	6860 * 83G	6938 * 83A	6996 * 81E
6803 * 84F	6861 * 84E	6939 * 86C	6997 * 82A
6804 * 82B	6862 * 84B	6940 * 83A	6998 * 84G
6805 * 83F	6863 * 83D	6941 * 83D	6999 * 86C
6806 * 84B	6864 * 81F	6942 * 81A	7000 * 83A
6807 * 85A	6865 * 86A	6943 * 86C	7001 * 81A
6808 * 83G	6866 * 84E	6944 * 84G	7002 * 87E
6809 * 82B	6867 * 86G	6945 * 82D	7003 * 82A
6810 * 87F	6868 * 83B	6946 * 86G	7004 * 81A
6811 * 82B	6869 * 82B	6947 * 85A	7005 * 85A
6812 * 86G	6870 * 83G	6948 * 85A	7006 * 83D
6813 * 83A	6871 * 83D	6949 * 84C	7007 * 85A
6814 * 83E	6872 * 86G	6950 * 85A	7008 * 81A
6815 * 83B	6873 * 83D	6951 * 82B	7009 * 87E
6816 * 83G	6874 * 83B	6952 * 81E	7010 * 81A
6817 * 84B	6875 * 83G	6953 * 81D	7011 * 82A
6818 * 87F	6876 * 82B	6954 * 82A	7012 * 87E
6819 * 86G	6877 * 85A	6955 * 82D	7013 * 81A
6820 * 85A	6878 * 82B	6956 * 84G	7014 * 82A
6821 * 81F	6879 * 83F	6957 * 82A	7015 * 82A
6822 * 81F	6900 * 82A	6958 * 86C	7016 * 87E
6823 * 83F	6901 * 86C	6959 * 81A	7017 * 81A
6824 * 83G	6902 * 82C	6960 * 81D	7018 * 82A
6825 * 83G	6903 * 86G	6961 * 81A	7019 * 82A
6826 * 83G	6904 * 84E	6962 * 81A	7020 * 81A
6827 * 82B	6905 * 87E	6963 * 86C	7021 * 87G
6828 * 83F	6906 * 84C	6964 * 86C	7022 * 83D
6829 * 83A	6907 * 84B	6965 * 83C	7023 * 86C
6830 * 82B	6908 * 82A	6966 * 81A	7024 * 81A
6831 * 82B	6909 * 87J	6967 * 81C	7025 * 81A
6832 * 83F	6910 * 81E	6968 * 81D	7026 * 84A
6833 * 82B	6911 * 83F	6969 * 81E	7027 * 81A
6834 * 82B	6912 * 87E	6970 * 81F	7028 * 87E
6835 * 82B	6913 * 83D	6971 * 84E	7029 * 83A
6836 * 83A	6914 * 71G	6972 * 82A	7030 * 81A
6837 * 83G	6915 * 81E	6973 * 81A	7031 * 83D
6838 * 86A	6916 * 84G	6974 * 81A	7032 * 81A
6839 * 84B	6917 * 85B	6975 * 84A	7033 * 81A
6840 * 86G	6918 * 87E	6976 * 84C	7034 * 82A
6841 * 82B	6919 * 82A	6977 * 82B	7035 * 87E
6842 * 81A	6920 * 81A	6978 * 81A	7036 * 81A
6843 * 87F	6921 * 83D	6979 * 84C	7037 * 82C
6844 * 87F	6922 * 81F	6980 * 84F	7200 87E
6845 * 83G	6923 * 81D	6981 * 82A	7201 86G
6846 * 82B	6924 * 81D	6982 * 82A	7202 88A
6847 * 86A	6925 * 84B	6983 * 81E	7203 87F
6848 * 81F	6926 * 84G	6984 * 85A	7204 86G
6849 * 83D	6927 * 81F	6985 * 85B	7205 88A

7206	86G	7310	84J	7431	84J	7745	87F
7207	87E	7311	83C	7432	84F	7746	86F
7208	86E	7312	85B	7433	84J	7747	87J
7209	87E	7313	84J	7434	89A	7748	82D
7210	86G	7314	87F	7435	84F	7749	82B
7211	87F	7315	84C	7436	83B	7751	88C
7212	86A	7316	83C	7437	85C	7752	86F
7213	86G	7317	84E	7439	87C	7753	86F
7214	86J	7318	87H	7440	84J	7755	86A
7215	87D	7319	85A	7441	84F	7756	87D
7216	86J	7320	87F	7442	84J	7757	87A
7217	87E	7321	87F	7443	84J	7758	87B
7218	86A	7322	86E	7444	87G	7759	84B
7219	86A	7323	82B	7445	83A	7760	81F
7220	86G	7324	81E	7446	83E	7761	84C
7221	86J	7325	86G	7447	84F	7762	6E
7222	86A	7326	85C	7448	84F	7763	84E
7223	86E	7327	81E	7449	84F	7764	86E
7224	87E	7328	86E	7700	85B	7765	87F
7225	87D	7329	84G	7701	87A	7766	88C
7226	87D	7332	86C	7702	84D	7767	87A
7227	86C	7333	83D	7703	86B	7768	86A
7228	87F	7334	86G	7704	87D	7769	87A
7229	86A	7335	83D	7705	81E	7770	86F
7230	87E	7336	84G	7706	87B	7771	86A
7231	86A	7338	85A	7707	85A	7772	81E
7232	87F	7339	84B	7708	81D	7773	86J
7233	86A	7340	87H	7709	83E	7774	86A
7234	86A	7341	84B	7712	86G	7775	86C
7235	87F	7400	87G	7713	84E	7776	87F
7236	87E	7401	85C	7715	83E	7777	85A
7237	86E	7402	87G	7716	83C	7778	86F
7238	81F	7403	84J	7717	88C	7780	71G
7239	81F	7404	81F	7718	87F	7781	86A
7240	86A	7405	89A	7719	82B	7782	71G
7241	88C	7406	89C	7720	86J	7783	82B
7242	88A	7407	87G	7721	86K	7784	82D
7243	86A	7408	87K	7722	81A	7785	87F
7244	87B	7409	84J	7723	85B	7786	87A
7245	86A	7410	89A	7724	86G	7787	86A
7246	86G	7411	81F	7725	86F	7788	81D
7247	84B	7412	81F	7726	88E	7789	86E
7248	87D	7413	82C	7727	82D	7790	82B
7249	87B	7414	84J	7728	82B	7791	81A
7250	86A	7417	89C	7729	82B	7793	87C
7251	86G	7418	82C	7731	81C	7794	82C
7252	88C	7419	87G	7732	86F	7796	86G
7253	86A	7420	84E	7733	88E	7797	84G
7300	82D	7421	82C	7734	81A	7798	86F
7301	82B	7422	87G	7735	84E	7799	87A
7302	82D	7423	86J	7736	86A	7800 *	89A
7303	71G	7424	82C	7737	87A	7801 *	89A
7304	83B	7425	87G	7739	87A	7802 *	89C
7305	84C	7426	85C	7740	86G	7803 *	89C
7306	87H	7427	82C	7741	85B	7804 *	87G
7307	87F	7428	84J	7742	87A	7805 *	86C
7308	84C	7429	84F	7743	87A	7806 *	89C
7309	84G	7430	84F	7744	88E	7807 *	89A

7808 * 85B	8106	85A	8455	88A	8714	82B
7809 * 85B	8107	87H	8456	81C	8715	87A
7810 * 85B	8108	84E	8457	86C	8716	86G
7811 * 84G	8109	84D	8458	81E	8717	85B
7812 * 83D	8400	85F	8459	81A	8718	85D
7813 * 83D	8401	85F	8460	88A	8719	83E
7814 * 89C	8402	85F	8461	82C	8720	87F
7815 * 85B	8403	85F	8462	84B	8721	86F
7816 * 83E	8404	85F	8463	87E	8722	85C
7817 * 84J	8405	85F	8464	86C	8723	86C
7818 * 84B	8406	85F	8465	82C	8724	87C
7819 * 89A	8407	87B	8466	86C	8725	82E
7820 * 83D	8408	87D	8467	87F	8726	84A
7821 * 84E	8409	83G	8468	84E	8727	84J
7822 * 89A	8410	87B	8469	88A	8728	86C
7823 * 83F	8411	84A	8470	88A	8729	6E
7824 * 87G	8412	83F	8471	88A	8730	6E
7825 * 87G	8413	81C	8472	82C	8731	85B
7826 * 87G	8414	87D	8473	83G	8732	87A
7827 * 89A	8415	84E	8474	87F	8733	83E
7828 * 84G	8416	87B	8475	87D	8734	84K
7829 * 87G	8418	87B	8476	87D	8735	88E
7900 * 81F	8419	88C	8477	87F	8736	87F
7901 * 82A	8420	88A	8478	88A	8737	85A
7902 * 81A	8421	83F	8479	82B	8738	87H
7903 * 81A	8422	83D	8480	85A	8739	87H
7904 * 81A	8423	87D	8481	88A	8740	86F
7905 * 83D	8424	81F	8482	82D	8741	82A
7906 * 81D	8425	84A	8483	87D	8742	84F
7907 * 82A	8426	84A	8484	86C	8743	85B
7908 * 84E	8427	85A	8485	83E	8744	82D
7909 * 82D	8428	84B	8486	83F	8745	72C
7910 * 81C	8429	86H	8487	85B	8746	82B
7911 * 81F	8430	81D	8488	85B	8747	82B
7912 * 84E	8431	87D	8489	86H	8748	86F
7913 * 86C	8432	81F	8490	87B	8749	87F
7914 * 81D	8433	82C	8491	82B	8750	81C
7915 * 84B	8434	81A	8492	82B	8751	81A
7916 * 83A	8435	81E	8493	86A	8752	81C
7917 * 82D	8436	86H	8494	86H	8753	81A
7918 * 84E	8437	86H	8495	86A	8754	81A
7919 * 81D	8438	88A	8496	85A	8756	81A
7920 * 85A	8439	86C	8497	86F	8757	81A
7921 * 84G	8440	86A	8498	86A	8759	81A
7922 * 84G	8441	86C	8499	86A	8760	81A
7923 * 81C	8442	87A	8700	84E	8761	81A
7924 * 82D	8443	87D	8701	85D	8762	81A
7925 * 83G	8444	86J	8702	83E	8763	81A
7926 * 85B	8445	86J	8704	84F	8764	81A
7927 * 81A	8446	88C	8705	86H	8765	81A
7928 * 85A	8447	86C	8706	87K	8766	86A
7929 * 82B	8448	86F	8707	86G	8767	81A
	8449	84G	8708	87F	8768	81A
8100 84D	8450	87D	8709	6E	8769	81A
8101 85D	8451	82B	8710	86A	8770	81A
8102 87G	8452	84C	8711	86A	8771	81A
8103 87G	8453	86A	8712	86F	8772	81A
8104 87A	8454	87B	8713	84E	8773	81A

8774	81C	9422	81C	9480	85A	9638	88D
8775	87A	9423	81A	9481	82A	9639	84H
8776	86C	9424	81B	9482	86A	9640	81F
8777	87G	9425	88C	9483	87B	9641	81C
8778	86H	9426	86C	9484	87E	9642	82B
8779	82C	9427	86A	9485	87D	9643	88D
8780	88C	9428	84A	9486	85A	9644	86A
8781	85C	9429	85A	9487	83A	9645	87C
8782	87A	9430	87A	9488	82A	9646	83B
8783	82C	9431	87D	9489	87D	9647	83B
8784	87A	9432	84E	9490	86A	9648	86C
8785	87F	9433	83D	9491	87D	9649	86F
8786	86H	9434	83F	9492	85B	9650	86G
8787	85C	9435	84A	9493	86C	9651	82G
8788	87E	9436	87E	9494	86C	9652	87F
8789	87E	9437	86C	9495	82B	9653	81F
8790	82B	9438	85B	9496	84A	9654	81F
8791	84J	9439	83C	9497	83C	9655	83E
8792	84F	9440	83A	9498	84G	9656	84G
8793	82C	9441	85B	9499	82B	9657	84G
8794	87E	9442	87B	9600	82C	9658	81A
8795	82B	9443	86C	9601	82B	9659	81A
8796	84A	9444	87B	9602	87J	9660	86F
8797	84F	9445	85B	9603	86C	9661	81A
8798	84A	9446	87A	9604	82C	9662	86A
8799	71G	9447	87B	9605	82C	9663	83B
		9448	87A	9606	87G	9664	86A
9004	84J	9449	84C	9607	86J	9665	85C
9005	89A	9450	81F	9608	83B	9666	87J
9014	84J	9451	86F	9609	86F	9667	86A
9015	89C	9452	87A	9610	84K	9668	82D
9017	89C	9453	86C	9611	81F	9669	84J
9018	84J	9454	87B	9612	82D	9670	83B
9308	84G	9455	85A	9613	84F	9671	83B
9309	81D	9456	87B	9614	84E	9672	82C
9315	82C	9457	87B	9615	82D	9673	83E
9400	81A	9458	86H	9616	86A	9674	86A
9401	85A	9459	86H	9617	87B	9675	88D
9402	81D	9460	86H	9618	88D	9676	88D
9403	81F	9461	86C	9619	86E	9677	87J
9404	81D	9462	83A	9620	71G	9678	83A
9405	81C	9463	81B	9621	84J	9679	88A
9406	81B	9464	85P	9622	88E	9680	84E
9407	81E	9465	87F	9623	82A	9681	89A
9408	84B	9466	85A	9624	84F	9682	84E
9409	81C	9467	83D	9625	87D	9700	81A
9410	81A	9468	86A	9626	82A	9701	81A
9411	81A	9469	81C	9627	87A	9702	81A
9412	81A	9470	84G	9628	82D	9703	81A
9413	81C	9471	85B	9629	83C	9704	81A
9414	81A	9472	84G	9630	84H	9705	81A
9415	81B	9473	87A	9631	88D	9706	81A
9416	81A	9474	83C	9632	71H	9707	81A
9417	81C	9475	85B	9633	83A	9709	81A
9418	81A	9476	82C	9634	87B	9710	81A
9419	81A	9477	86C	9635	84E	9711	83D
9420	81A	9478	87A	9636	84F	9712	86J
9421	81B	9479	81A	9637	87E	9713	86C

W.R. Diesel Railcars

5	85A	17	84D	24	82B	30	81D
7	84F	19	85B	25	82B	31	81C
8	84F	20	85A	26	85A	32	85A
13	84F	21	81C	27	81C	33	81D
14	84F	22	85A	28	82B	34	81C
15	84F	23	85A	29	85A	33	81D

9714	87H	9736	87B	9758	81A	9781	81B
9715	87E	9737	87B	9759	86C	9782	84F
9716	83D	9738	87E	9760	87J	9783	87A
9717	85C	9739	84B	9761	87A	9784	81A
9718	83B	9740	82C	9762	82D	9785	87B
9719	84F	9741	84H	9763	81D	9786	87A
9720	82C	9742	87B	9764	72C	9787	87G
9721	82C	9743	87F	9765	83C	9788	87F
9722	81B	9744	87C	9766	87B	9789	81C
9723	86C	9745	86A	9767	84F	9790	82C
9724	84E	9746	86A	9768	84B	9791	81D
9725	81A	9747	88D	9769	82B	9792	87A
9726	81C	9748	83G	9770	70A	9793	84J
9727	84E	9749	81D	9771	82A	9794	6E
9728	6E	9750	87A	9772	82A	9795	82C
9729	82A	9751	81A	9773	82C	9796	86G
9730	86G	9752	84B	9774	84H	9797	86G
9731	86J	9753	84E	9775	87E	9798	84E
9732	72C	9754	81A	9776	88D	9799	87B
9733	84E	9755	83E	9777	87E		
9734	87A	9756	87A	9778	86C		
9735	87B	9757	83B	9779	87A		
				9780	86D		

Diesel Locomotives at present numbered 11100-11719 and 13000-13336 are being re-numbered as under.

Present No.	New No.
11100-3	D2200-3
11105-15	D2204-14
11116-20	D2500-4
11121-35	D2215-29
11136-43	D2550-7
11144-8	D2505-9
11149-60	D2230-41
11161-76	D2558-73
11177-86	D2400-9
11187-11209	D2000-22
11212-29	D2242-59
11500-8	D2950-8
11700-19	D2700-19
13000-13336	D3000-D3336

D1 D826

D1 *	D59	D117	D226
D2 *	D60	D118	D227
D3 *	D61	D119	D228
D4 *	D62	D120	D229
D5 *	D63	D121	D230
D6 *	D64	D122	D231
D7 *	D65	D123	D232
D8 *	D66	D124	D233
D9 *	D67	D125	D234
D10 *	D68	D126	D235
D11	D69	D127	D236
D12	D70	D128	D237
D13	D71	D129	D238
D14	D72	D130	D239
D15	D73	D131	D240
D16	D74	D132	D241
D17	D75	D133	D242
D18	D76	D134	D243
D19	D77	D135	D244
D20	D78	D136	D245
D21	D79	D137	D246
D22	D80	D138	D247
D23	D81	D139	D248
D24	D82	D140	D249
D25	D83	D141	
D26	D84	D142	D600 * 83D
D27	D85	D143	D601 * 83D
D28	D86	D144	D602 * 83D
D29	D87	D145	D603 * 83D
D30	D88	D146	D604 * 83D
D31	D89	D147	
D32	D90		D800 * 83D
D33	D91		D801 * 83D
D34	D92	D200 30A	D802 * 83D
D35	D93	D201 34B	D803 * 83D
D36	D94	D202 30A	D804 *
D37	D95	D203 30A	D805 *
D38	D96	D204 30A	D806 *
D39	D97	D205 30A	D807 *
D40	D98	D206 34B	D808 *
D41	D99	D207 34B	D809 *
D42	D100	D208 34B	D810 *
D43	D101	D209 34B	D811 *
D44	D102	D210	D812 *
D45	D103	D211	D813 *
D46	D104	D212	D814 *
D47	D105	D213	D815 *
D48	D106	D214	D816 *
D49	D107	D215	D817 *
D50	D108	D216	D818 *
D51	D109	D217	D819 *
D52	D110	D218	D820 *
D53	D111	D219	D821 *
D54	D112	D220	D822 *
D55	D113	D221	D823 *
D56	D114	D222	D824 *
D57	D115	D223	D825 *
D58	D116	D224	D826 *
		D225	

24

D827 *	D1018	D2053	53A	D2216	30A
D828 *	D1019	D2054	53A	D2217	30A
D829 *	D1020	D2055		D2218	6B
D830 *	D1021	D2056		D2219	32A
D831 *		D2057		D2220	6B
D832 *	D2000	34D	D2058		D2221	5B
D833 *	D2001	34C	D2059		D2222	32B
D834 *	D2002	34C	D2060		D2223	30A
D835 *	D2003	34D	D2061		D2224	30A
D836 *	D2004	31A	D2062		D2225	30A
D837 *	D2005	31A	D2063		D2226	30A
D838 *	D2006	31A	D2064		D2227	30A
D839 *	D2007	31A	D2065		D2228	30A
D840 *	D2008	31A	D2066		D2229	30A
D841 *	D2009	31A	D2067		D2230	51C
D842 *	D2010	31A	D2068		D2231	51C
D843 *	D2011	31C	D2069		D2232	51C
D844 *	D2012	31C	D2070		D2233	40B
D845 *	D2013	31C	D2071		D2234	40B
D846 *	D2014	31C	D2072		D2235	40B
D847 *	D2015	31C	D2073		D2236	5B
D848 *	D2016	31A	D2074		D2237	31F
D849 *	D2017	31A	D2075		D2238	31F
D850 *	D2018	34D	D2076		D2239	31F
D851 *	D2019	34D	D2077		D2240	31B
D852 *	D2020	40B	D2078		D2241	40F
D853 *	D2021	40B	D2079		D2242	50B
D854 *	D2022	40B	D2080		D2243	50B
D855 *	D2023	40F	D2081		D2244	50B
D856 *	D2024	40F	D2082	75A	D2245	50B
D857 *	D2025	40F	D2083	73C	D2246	50B
D858 *	D2026	40A	D2084	73F	D2247	52F
D859 *	D2027	40A	D2085	71A	D2248	52F
D860 ☆	D2028	31A	D2086		D2249	52F
D861 *	D2029	31A	D2087		D2250	73H
D862 *	D2030	31B	D2088		D2251	73C
D863 *	D2031	31B			D2252	71A
D864 *	D2032	32A			D2253	73F
D865 *	D2033	32A			D2254	71A
	D2034	32A			D2255	83H
D1000	D2035	32A			D2256	73C
D1001	D2036	32A			D2257	83H
D1002	D2037	32A			D2258	83H
D1003	D2038	32A	D2200	30A	D2259	83H
D1004	D2039	32A	D2201	31B	D2260	56G
D1005	D2040	32B	D2202	31B	D2261	56G
D1006	D2041	32B	D2203	32E	D2262	55G
D1007	D2042		D2204	51C	D2263	55G
D1008	D2043		D2205	51C	D2264	56G
D1009	D2044	52F	D2206	51C	D2265	56G
D1010	D2045	52F	D2207	40B	D2266	55D
D1011	D2046	52F	D2208	30A	D2267	55D
D1012	D2047	52B	D2209	30A	D2268	55D
D1013	D2048	52A	D2210	32A	D2269	55E
D1014	D2049	52C	D2211	30A	D2270	55E
D1015	D2050	52B	D2212	32D	D2271	55A
D1016	D2051	53A	D2213	5B	D2272	55A
D1017	D2052	53A	D2214	32A	D2273	55A
			D2215	30A		

D2400	40B	D2570	32C	D2739	63B	D3025	84E
D2401	40F	D2571	32D	D2740	63B	D3026	84E
D2402	40F	D2572	32B	D2741	63B	D3027	84E
D2403	40B	D2573	32A	D2742	63B	D3028	84E
D2404	40A	D2574	68C	D2743	62C	D3029	84E
D2405	40A	D2575	68C	D2744		D3030	81A
D2406	40A	D2576	62A			D3031	81A
D2407	40A	D2577	62A			D3032	81A
D2408	40A	D2578	62A			D3033	81A
D2409	40F	D2579	62A			D3034	84B
D2410	60A	D2580	62A	D2900	1D	D3035	84B
D2411	60A	D2581	62A	D2901	1D	D3036	84B
D2412	60A	D2582	62A	D2902	1D	D3037	84B
D2413	60A	D2583	62A	D2903	1D	D3038	84B
D2414	61C	D2584	62A	D2904	14A	D3039	84B
D2415	61C	D2585		D2905	1D	D3040	70B
D2416	61A			D2906	1D	D3041	70B
D2417	61A			D2907	1D	D3042	70B
D2418	61A			D2908	2A	D3043	73F
D2419	61A	D2700	51C	D2909	2A	D3044	73F
D2420	61A	D2701	5!C	D2910	2A	D3045	73F
D2421	61A	D2702	51C	D2950	32B	D3046	75C
D2422	61A	D2703	64E	D2951	32B	D3047	75C
D2423	61A	D2704	62C	D2952	32B	D3048	75C
D2424		D2705	64A	D2953	30A	D3049	75C
		D2706	64A	D2954	30A	D3050	1A
		D2707	62C	D2955	30A	D3051	1A
		D2708	62B	D2956	30A	D3052	1A
		D2709	62B	D2957	30A	D3053	2A
D2500	6C	D2710	62B	D2958	30A	D3054	2A
D2501	6C	D2711	62B			D3055	2A
D2502	6C	D2712	62B			D3056	15A
D2503	6C	D2713	62B			D3057	15A
D2504	6C	D2714	62B			D3058	15A
D2505	6C	D2715	62B			D3059	15A
D2506	6C	D2716	62B	D3000	82B	D3060	41F
D2507	6C	D2717	62C	D3001	82B	D3061	41F
D2508	6C	D2718	62C	D3002	82B	D3062	41F
D2509	6C	D2719	64A	D3003	82B	D3063	41F
D2550	30F	D2720	64A	D3004	84E	D3064	41F
D2551	30F	D2721	64A	D3005	67C	D3065	31B
D2552	30F	D2722	64A	D3006	67C	D3066	2F
D2553	32A	D2723	64A	D3007	67B	D3067	2F
D2554	30F	D2724	65F	D3008	67B	D3068	2F
D2555	32B	D2725	64A	D3009	67B	D3069	2F
D2556	32B	D2726	64A	D3010	71A	D3070	53A
D2557	32B	D2727	64A	D3011	71A	D3071	53A
D2558	32A	D2728	64A	D3012	71A	D3072	53A
D2559	32A	D2729	64A	D3013	71A	D3073	53A
D2560	32B	D2730	64A	D3014	71A	D3074	53A
D2561	32B	D2731	64A	D3015	1A	D3075	53A
D2562	32A	D2732	64A	D3016	1A	D3076	53A
D2563	32A	D2733	65G	D3017	1A	D3077	53A
D2564	32B	D2734	65G	D3018	1A	D3078	53A
D2565	32A	D2735	65G	D3019	8C	D3079	53A
D2566	32A	D2736	65G	D3020	3D	D3080	53A
D2567	32A	D2737	65G	D3021	3C	D3081	53A
D2568	32C	D2738	65G	D3022	14A	D3082	21A
D2569	32A			D3023	14A		
				D3024	14A		

D3547	61B	D3605	81A	D3663	41A	D3721	73C
D3548	61B	D3606	88B	D3664	41A	D3722	
D3549	61B	D3607	88B	D3665	71A	D3723	
D3550	61B	D3608	30A	D3666	71A	D3724	
D3551	61B	D3609	30A	D3667	71A	D3725	
D3552	61A	D3610	31A	D3668	71A	D3726	
D3553	61A	D3611	31A	D3669	75C	D3727	
D3554	64F	D3612	36E	D3670	73F	D3728	64A
D3555	64F	D3613	36E	D3671	73C	D3729	64A
D3556	64E	D3614	36E	D3672	51A	D3730	64A
D3557	64E	D3615	36E	D3673	52C	D3731	64A
D3558	64E	D3616	36E	D3674	52C	D3732	64A
D3559	64E	D3617	36E	D3675	53E	D3733	64A
D3560	64B	D3618	36E	D3676	53E	D3734	
D3561	64B	D3619	36E	D3677	51A	D3735	
D3562	65C	D3620	36E	D3678	52C	D3736	
D3563	67C	D3621	36E	D3679	52F	D3737	
D3564	67C	D3622	36A	D3680	30F	D3738	
D3565	12A	D3623	36A	D3681	30A	D3739	
D3566	12A	D3624	40E	D3682	30A	D3740	
D3567	12A	D3625	40E	D3683	30A	D3741	
D3568	17B	D3626	40E	D3684	30A	D3742	
D3569	17B	D3627	40E	D3685	41A	D3743	
D3570	17B	D3628	40E	D3686	41A	D3744	
D3571	17B	D3629	40E	D3687	34A	D3745	
D3572	17B	D3630	40E	D3688	34A	D3746	
D3573	14D	D3631	30A	D3689	34A	D3747	
D3574	41B	D3632	30A	D3690	34B	D3748	
D3575	41B	D3633	30A	D3691	34B	D3749	
D3576	18A	D3634		D3692	34B	D3750	
D3577	18A	D3635		D3693	34B	D3751	
D3578	8A	D3636	30A	D3694	41A	D3752	
D3579	8A	D3637	40B	D3695		D3753	
D3580	11B	D3638	36C	D3696		D3754	
D3581	24K	D3639	36C	D3697		D3755	
D3582	21A	D3640	36C	D3698		D3756	
D3583	5B	D3641	36C	D3699		D3757	
D3584	5B	D3642	36C	D3700		D3758	
D3585	17B	D3643	36C	D3701		D3759	
D3586	17B	D3644	36C	D3702		D3760	
D3587	17B	D3645	36C	D3703		D3761	
D3588	26A	D3646	36C	D3704		D3762	
D3589	26A	D3647	36C	D3705		D3763	
D3590	26A	D3648	36C	D3706		D3764	
D3591	26A	D3649	36A	D3707		D3765	
D3592	26A	D3650	36A	D3708		D3766	
D3593	88B	D3651	36A	D3709		D3767	
D3594	88B	D3652	55C	D3710		D3768	
D3595	88B	D3653	55C	D3711		D3769	
D3596	88B	D3654	55B	D3712		D3770	
D3597	81A	D3655	55B	D3713		D3771	
D3598	81A	D3656	55F	D3714		D3772	
D3599	81A	D3657	55F	D3715		D3773	
D3600	81A	D3658	55F	D3716		D3774	
D3601	81A	D3659	41A	D3717		D3775	
D3602	81A	D3660	41A	D3718		D3776	
D3603	88B	D3661	41A	D3719	73C	D3777	
D3604	81A	D3662	41B	D3720	73C	D3778	

D3779		D5005	73C	D5063		D5308	34B
D3780		D5006	73C	D5064		D5309	34B
D3781		D5007	73C	D5065		D5310	34B
D3782		D5008	73C	D5066		D5311	34B
D3783		D5009	73C	D5067		D5312	34B
D3784		D5010	73C	D5068		D5313	34B
D3785		D5011	73C	D5069		D5314	34B
D3786		D5012	73C	D5070		D5315	34B
D3787		D5013	73C	D5071		D5316	34B
D3788		D5014	73C	D5072		D5317	34B
D3789		D5015		D5073		D5318	34B
D3790		D5016		D5074		D5319	34B
D3791		D5017		D5075		D5320	Leith Cen.
D3792		D5018		D5076		D5321	
D3793		D5019		D5077		D5322	
D3794		D5020		D5078		D5323	
D3795		D5021		D5079		D5324	
D3796		D5022		D5080		D5325	
D3797		D5023		D5081		D5326	
D3798		D5024		D5082		D5327	
D3799		D5025		D5083		D5328	
D3800		D5026		D5084		D5329	
D3801		D5027		D5085		D5330	
D3802		D5028		D5086		D5331	
D3803	82B	D5029		D5087		D5332	
D3804	82B	D5030		D5088		D5333	
D3805	82B	D5031		D5089		D5334	
D3806	82B	D5032		D5090		D5335	
D3807	86B	D5033		D5091		D5336	
D3808	86B	D5034		D5092		D5337	
D3809	86B	D5035		D5093		D5338	
D3810	86B	D5036		D5094		D5339	
D3811	86B	D5037		D5095		D5340	
D3812	86B	D5038		D5096		D5341	
D3813	86B	D5039		D5097		D5342	
D3814	86B	D5040		D5098		D5343	
D3815	86B	D5041		D5099		D5344	
D3816	86B	D5042		D5100		D5345	
D3817	86B	D5043		D5101		D5346	
D3818	86B	D5044		D5102			
D3819		D5045		D5103		D5500	30A
D3820		D5046		D5104		D5501	30A
D3821		D5047		D5105		D5502	32B
D3822		D5048		D5106		D5503	30A
D3823		D5049		D5107		D5504	30A
D3824		D5050		D5108		D5505	30A
D3825		D5051		D5109		D5506	30A
D3826		D5052		D5110		D5507	31B
D3827		D5053		D5111		D5508	31B
D3828		D5054		D5112		D5509	30A
D3829		D5055		D5113		D5510	31B
D3830		D5056		D5300	34B	D5511	30A
D3831		D5057		D5301	34B	D5512	30A
D5000	73C	D5058		D5302	34B	D5513	30A
D5001	73C	D5059		D5303	Leith Cen.	D5514	30A
D5002	73C	D5060		D5304	34B	D5515	31B
D5003	73C	D5061		D5305	34B	D5516	30A
D5004	73C	D5062		D5306	34B	D5517	30A
				D5307	34B	D5518	31B

D5519	31B	D5577		D6121		D6320
D5520	30A	D5578		D6122		D6321
D5521	32B	D5579		D6123		D6322
D5522	30A			D6124		D6323
D5523	30A	D5700	17A	D6125		D6324
D5524	30A	D5701	17A	D6126		D6325
D5525	31B	D5702	17A	D6127		D6326
D5526	30A	D5703	17A	D6128		D6327
D5527		D5704	17A	D6129		D6328
D5528		D5705	17A	D6130		D6329
D5529		D5706	17A	D6131		D6330
D5530		D5707	17A	D6132		D6331
D5531		D5708	17A	D6133		D6332
D5532		D5709	17A	D6134		D6333
D5533		D5710	17A	D6135		D6334
D5534		D5711	17A	D6136		D6335
D5535		D5712	17A	D6137		D6336
D5536		D5713	17A	D6138		D6337
D5537		D5714	17A	D6139		D6338
D5538		D5715		D6140		D6339
D5539		D5716		D6141		D6340
D5540		D5717		D6142		D6341
D5541		D5718		D6143		D6342
D5542		D5719		D6144		D6343
D5543				D6145		D6344
D5544		D5900		D6146		D6345
D5545		D5901		D6147		D6346
D5546		D5902		D6148		D6347
D5547		D5903	34B	D6149		D6348
D5548		D5904		D6150		D6349
D5549		D5905		D6151		D6350
D5550		D5906		D6152		D6351
D5551		D5907		D6153		D6352
D5552		D5908		D6154		D6353
D5553		D5909		D6155		
D5554				D6156		D6500
D5555				D6157		D6501
D5556		D6100	34B			D6502
D5557		D6101	34B			D6503
D5558		D6102	34B	D6300	83D	D6504
D5559		D6103		D6301	83D	D6505
D5560		D6104	34B	D6302	83D	D6506
D5561		D6105	34B	D6303		D6507
D5562		D6106	34B	D6304		D6508
D5563		D6107	34B	D6305		D6509
D5564		D6108	34B	D6306		D6510
D5565		D6109	34B	D6307		D6511
D5566		D6110		D6308		D6512
D5567		D6111		D6309		D6513
D5568		D6112		D6310		D6514
D5569		D6113		D6311		D6515
D5570		D6114		D6312		D6516
D5571		D6115		D6313		D6517
D5572		D6116		D6314		D6518
D5573		D6117		D6315		D6519
D5574		D6118		D6316		D6520
D5575		D6119		D6317		D6521
D5576		D6120		D6318		D6522
				D6319		

D6523		D8014	1D	11001	75C	12056	3C
D6524		D8015	1D			12057	2A
D6525		D8016	1D			12058	14A
D6526		D8017	1D	12000	5B	12059	21A
D6527		D8018	1D	12001	5B	12060	21A
D6528		D8019	1D	12003	5B	12061	21A
D6529				12004	5B	12062	21A
D6530				12005	5B	12063	14A
D6531				12006	18A	12064	14A
D6532		D8200	1D	12007	8C	12065	14A
D6533		D8201	1D	12008	8C	12066	21A
D6534		D8202	1D	12009	5B	12067	14A
D6535		D8203	1D	12010	5B	12068	14A
D6536		D8204	1D	12011	5B	12069	1D
D6537		D8205	1D	12012	5B	12070	1A
D6538		D8206	1D	12013	53	12071	8F
D6539		D8207	1D	12014	8C	12072	14A
D6540		D3208	18A	12015	8C	12073	1A
D6541		D8209	1D	12016	8C	12074	1A
D6542		D8210		12017	8C	12075	1A
D6543		D8211		12018	5B	12076	1A
D6544		D8212		12019	5B	12077	21A
D6545		D8213		12020	5B	12078	1A
D6546		D8214		12021	5B	12079	12A
D6547		D8215		12022	5B	12080	12A
D6548		D8216		12023	5B	12081	8C
D6549		D8217		12024	8C	12082	8C
D6550		D8218		12025	5B	12083	12A
D6551		D8219		12026	8C	12084	12C
D6552		D8220		12027	8C	12085	12C
D6553		D8221		12028	8C	12086	12C
D6554		D8222		12029	8C	12087	12A
D6555		D8223		12030	5B	12088	3D
D6556		D8224		12031	5B	12089	3D
D6557		D8225		12032	5B	12090	3D
D6558		D8226		12033	17A	12091	3A
D6559				12034	17A	12092	3A
D6560				12035	21A	12093	3B
D6561				12036	6A	12094	3B
D6562		D3400	30A	12037	6A	12095	3D
D6563		D8401	30A	12038	18A	12096	16A
D6564		D8402	30A	12039	21A	12097	16A
		D8403	30A	12040	21A	12098	16A
		D8404	30A	12041	21A	12099	8F
D8000	5B	D8405	30A	12042	21A	12100	1A
D8001	5B	D8406	30A	12043	21A	12101	1A
D8002	5B	D8407	30A	12044	21A	12102	8F
D8003	5B	D8408	30A	12045	2A	12103	30A
D8004	5B	D8409	30A	12046	2A	12104	30A
D8005	1D			12047	2A	12105	30A
D8006	1D			12048	2A	12106	30A
D8007	1D	10000	1B	12049	16A	12107	30A
D8008	1D	10001	1B	12050	16A	12108	30A
D8009	1D	10201	1B	12051	16A	12109	30A
D8010	1D	10202	1B	12052	16A	12110	30A
D8011	1D	10203	1B	12053	2A	12111	30A
D8012	1D	10800	2A	12054	2A	12112	34B
D8013	1D			12055	18A	12113	53C

32

12114	53C	15227	73F	26028	Reddish	30039	70F
12115	53C	15228	73F	26029	Reddish	30040	71B
12116	53C	15229	73C	26030	Reddish	30043	70B
12117	53C	15230	82B	26031	Reddish	30044	72A
12118	53C	15231	71A	26032	Reddish	30045	72A
12119	53C	15232	71A	26033	Reddish	30047	75D
12120	53C	15233	71A	26034	Reddish	30048	75D
12121	53C	15234	71A	26035	Reddish	30049	75D
12122	53C	15235	71A	26036	Reddish	30050	75D
12123	40B	15236	71A	26037	Reddish	30051	75D
12124	40B			26038	Reddish	30052	75A
12125	40B			26039	Reddish	30053	75A
12126	40B	18000	81A	26040	Reddish	30055	75A
12127	30A			26041	Reddish	30056	75A
12128	30A			26042	Reddish	30057	71B
12129	34B	E1000		26043	Reddish	30058	71B
12130	30A			26044	Reddish	30059	71B
12131	34B			26045	Reddish	30060	71B
12132	30A	E5000	73A	26046 *	Reddish	30061	711
12133	40B	E5001	73A	26047	Reddish	30062	711
12134	31B	E5002	73A	26048	Reddish	30063	711
12135	40B	E5003	73A	26049	Reddish	30064	711
12136	31B	E5004	73A	26050	Reddish	30065	711
12137	34B			26051	Reddish	30066	711
12138	34B			26052	Reddish	30067	711
		20001	73A	26053	Reddish	30068	711
		20002	73A	26054	Reddish	30069	711
15000	31B	20003	73A	26055	Reddish	30070	711
15001	31B			26056	Reddish	30071	711
15002	31B			26057	Reddish	30072	711
15003	31B	26000 *	Reddish			30073	711
15004	34E	26001	Reddish	26500	52B	30074	711
15100	82B	26002	Reddish	26501	52B	30083	71A
15101	88B	26003	Reddish			30084	73H
15102	88B	26004	Reddish			30088	71A
15103	88B	26005	Reddish	27000	Reddish	30089	70C
15104	88B	26006	Reddish	27001	Reddish	30093	71A
15105	88B	26007	Reddish	27002	Reddish	30096	71A
15106	88B	26008	Reddish	27003	Reddish	30102	71B
15201	75C	26009	Reddish	27004	Reddish	30104	71B
15202	73C	26010	Reddish	27005	Reddish	30105	71B
15203	75C	26011	Reddish	27006	Reddish	30106	71B
15211	75C	26012	Reddish			30107	71B
15212	75C	26013	Reddish			30108	71B
15213	75C	26014	Reddish	30021	72A	30109	75A
15214	75C	26015	Reddish	30023	72A	30110	75A
15215	75C	26016	Reddish	30024	72A	30111	71B
15216	73C	26017	Reddish	30025	72A	30112	71B
15217	75A	26018	Reddish	30026	70C	30117	71A
15218	73C	26019	Reddish	30027	72A	30120	71A
15219	73C	26020	Reddish	30028	71A	30123	70A
15220	73F	26021	Reddish	30029	71A	30124	70C
15221	73C	26022	Reddish	30030	71A	30125	71A
15222	73C	26023	Reddish	30031	75A	30127	71B
15223	73C	26024	Reddish	30032	70B	30128	71B
15224	73F	26025	Reddish	30033	71A	30129	72C
15225	73C	26026	Reddish	30034	83H	30130	71A
15226	73C	26027	Reddish	30035	83H	30131	72C
				30036	83H		

33

30132	70C	30339	70B	30517	70B	30706	71B
30133	70A	30346	70B	30518	70B	30707	71B
30177	70B	30349	70C	30519	70B	30709	72A
30179	70B	30350	70C	30520	70B	30711	72A
30182	72A	30352	70B	30521	70A	30715	72A
30183	83H	30355	70B	30522	70A	30717	72A
30192	83H	30357	70F	30523	70A	30718	70A
30193	83H	30368	70D	30524	70A	30719	70A
30199	72A	30374	72A	30530	71A	30724	70C
30200	72F	30375	71A	30531	71A	30726	72A
30212	71A	30377	71A	30532	71A	30729	72B
30223	71A	30378	71A	30533	75C	30732	70B
30225	83H	30379	71A	30534	75C	30763	* 70A
30229	71A	30448	* 72B	30535	71A	30764	* 71B
30232	72A	30449	* 72B	30536	71A	30765	* 70D
30236	72F	30450	* 72B	30537	75C	30767	* 73A
30238	70C	30451	* 72B	30538	75C	30768	* 73A
30241	70A	30452	* 72B	30539	71B	30769	* 73A
30245	70A	30453	* 72B	30540	75C	30770	* 71A
30246	70C	30456	* 70D	30541	71B	30771	* 71B
30247	72E	30457	* 70A	30542	71A	30772	* 71B
30248	70A	30473	71A	30543	71A	30773	* 71A
30249	70A	30474	71A	30544	75D	30774	* 70A
30251	72E	30475	71A	30545	75D	30775	* 73H
30253	72E	30476	71A	30546	75D	30777	* 73H
30254	72E	30477	71A	30547	75D	30778	* 70A
30255	72E	30479	71A	30548	71B	30779	* 70A
30256	72E	30480	71A	30549	75C	30780	* 71B
30258	70D	30481	71A	30567	70B	30781	* 71B
30266	72B	30482	70A	30582	72A	30782	* 71B
30274	71B	30484	70A	30583	72A	30783	* 71B
30277	70C	30486	70A	30584	72A	30784	* 71A
30287	71A	30489	70A	30585	72F	30785	* 71A
30288	71A	30491	70A	30586	72F	30788	* 71A
30289	71A	30493	70B	30587	72F	30789	* 71A
30300	71A	30494	70B	30667	72A	30790	* 71A
30301	72B	30495	70B	30668	72A	30791	* 71A
30306	71A	30496	70B	30669	72A	30793	* 73A
30308	70C	30497	70B	30670	72A	30794	* 70D
30309	72B	30498	70B	30671	72E	30795	* 73A
30310	71B	30499	70B	30673	72B	30796	* 73C
30313	71A	30500	70B	30674	72B	30797	* 73H
30315	72B	30501	70B	30676	72A	30798	* 73H
30316	71A	30502	70B	30687	70B	30799	* 73B
30317	72A	30503	70B	30689	70B	30800	* 73B
30318	71B	30504	70B	30690	71B	30802	* 73A
30319	70A	30505	70B	30691	72A	30803	* 73A
30320	70A	30506	70B	30692	72B	30804	* 73H
30321	70A	30507	70B	30693	70C	30805	* 73H
30323	72A	30508	70B	30694	70A	30806	* 73C
30324	71B	30509	70B	30695	71B	30823	72B
30325	70C	30510	70B	30696	70B	30824	72B
30326	70C	30511	70B	30697	70C	30825	72B
30327	72A	30512	70B	30698	70C	30826	72B
30328	71A	30513	70B	30699	70A	30827	72B
30331	72B	30514	70B	30700	70C	30828	72B
30335	72B	30515	70B	30701	70A	30829	72B
30338	70A	30516	70B	30702	72A		

30830	72B	30924 *	73B	31221	73F	31405	73F
30831	72B	30925 *	73B	31223	73F	31406	73F
30832	72B	30926 *	73B	31227	73D	31407	73F
30833	70B	30927 *	73B	31229	73D	31408	73A
30834	70B	30928 *	73B	31239	73J	31409	73A
30835	75B	30929 *	73B	31242	73E	31410	73A
30836	75B	30930 *	73B	31243	73H	31411	73A
30837	75B	30931 *	73B	31244	73J	31412	73A
30838	70B	30932 *	73B	31245	73G	31413	73A
30839	70B	30933 *	73B	31246	73F	31414	73A
30840	70B	30934 *	73B	31247	73B	31425	73H
30841	72A	30935 *	73B	31252	73G	31430	73H
30842	72A	30936 *	73B	31253	73C	31434	73H
30843	72A	30937 *	73A	31255	73E	31470	73J
30844	72A	30938 *	73A	31256	73E	31480	73B
30845	72A	30939 *	73A	31258	73H	31481	73E
30846	72A	30950	72A	31259	73J	31487	73J
30847	72B	30951	73F	31261	73A	31489	73J
30850 *	71A	30952	73F	31263	73F	31492	73J
30851 *	71A	30953	72A	31265	73A	31494	73E
30852 *	71A	30954	72B	31266	73J	31495	73D
30853 *	71A	30955	72A	31267	73B	31497	73B
30854 *	71A	30956	72A	31268	73E	31498	73C
30855 *	71A	30957	72A	31269	75E	31500	73G
30856 *	71A			31270	73J	31503	73E
30857 *	71A			31271	73G	31505	73E
30858 *	71A	31004	73G	31272	73J	31507	73B
30859 *	71A	31005	73F	31276	73J	31509	73E
30860 *	71B	31010	73H	31278	75F	31510	73D
30861 *	71A	31019	73A	31279	73J	31512	73D
30862 *	71A	31027	73H	31280	73J	31517	73J
30863 *	71A	31033	73C	31287	73C	31518	73D
30864 *	71B	31037	73D	31293	73B	31519	73F
30865 *	71B	31047	73H	31295	73J	31520	73F
30900 *	75A	31048	73A	31297	73D	31521	75F
30901 *	70A	31054	73C	31298	73E	31522	73F
30902 *	70A	31061	73C	31305	73B	31523	73J
30903 *	70A	31065	73H	31306	73B	31530	75E
30904 *	70D	31067	73A	31307	73F	31533	73A
30905 *	70D	31068	73B	31308	73D	31540	73B
30906 *	70A	31071	73B	31310	75F	31542	73H
30907 *	70A	31086	73B	31317	73H	31543	73J
30908 *	70A	31102	73B	31319	73F	31544	75F
30909 *	73A	31107	73H	31322	73D	31545	73A
30910 *	73G	31112	73D	31323	73H	31548	73D
30911 *	73G	31113	73H	31324	73G	31550	73A
30912 *	73G	31128	73H	31325	75A	31551	73A
30913 *	73G	31145	73A	31326	73G	31552	73A
30914 *	73G	31150	75E	31327	75F	31553	73B
30915 *	73G	31161	73D	31328	73H	31554	75F
30916 *	73G	31162	75E	31329	75F	31556	75A
30917 *	73G	31164	73J	31337	73H	31558	73A
30918 *	73G	31174	73H	31370	73A	31573	73C
30919 *	73G	31177	73J	31400	73F	31575	73A
30920 *	73G	31191	73H	31401	73F	31576	73D
30921 *	73G	31193	73J	31402	73F	31578	73A
30922 *	73G	31218	73F	31403	73F	31579	73D
30923 *	70D	31219	73F	31404	73F	31581	73A

31583	73A	31725	73C	31809	70F	31867	75B
31584	73A	31727	73F	31810	73A	31868	75B
31588	73J	31735	73B	31811	73A	31869	75B
31589	73F	31739	73B	31812	73A	31870	73B
31590	73J	31741	73B	31813	72B	31871	73B
31592	73G	31743	73A	31814	72B	31872	73B
31610	72C	31749	73A	31815	73D	31873	73B
31611	70D	31753	73H	31816	73D	31874	73B
31612	70C	31754	73H	31817	75B	31875	73B
31613	72C	31755	73H	31818	73H	31876	73C
31614	71B	31756	73F	31819	73H	31877	73C
31615	71B	31757	73F	31820	73H	31878	73C
31616	70C	31758	73F	31821	73H	31879	73C
31617	70A	31759	73F	31822	73C	31880	73C
31618	71A	31760	73J	31823	73B	31890	73B
31619	71A	31762	73J	31824	73B	31891	73B
31620	71A	31763	73J	31825	73B	31892	73E
31621	70A	31764	73G	31826	73B	31893	73E
31622	70C	31765	73E	31827	73B	31894	73A
31623	72C	31766	73E	31828	73B	31895	73A
31624	70A	31768	73J	31829	73B	31896	73J
31625	70C	31770	73J	31830	72A	31897	73A
31626	72C	31771	73J	31831	72A	31898	73A
31627	70C	31773	73J	31832	72A	31899	73B
31628	70C	31775	73G	31833	72A	31900	73B
31629	71A	31776	75A	31834	72A	31901	73B
31630	70C	31777	75A	31835	72A	31902	73B
31631	70C	31778	75A	31836	72A	31903	73E
31632	71B	31779	73G	31837	72A	31904	73A
31633	72C	31780	73G	31838	72A	31905	73A
31634	70A	31781	73G	31839	72A	31906	73A
31635	70C	31782	73F	31840	72A	31907	73A
31636	70C	31783	73B	31841	72A	31908	73J
31637	70C	31784	73B	31842	72A	31909	73J
31638	70F	31785	73D	31843	72A	31910	73J
31639	71A	31786	73D	31844	72A	31911	73C
31682	73D	31787	73D	31845	72A	31912	73C
31683	73D	31788	73H	31846	72A	31913	73C
31684	73D	31789	73H	31847	72A	31914	73A
31686	73C	31790	72A	31848	73F	31915	73A
31688	73C	31791	72A	31849	72A	31916	73C
31689	73C	31792	71A	31850	73E	31917	75C
31690	73C	31793	71A	31851	73B	31918	75C
31691	73C	31794	71A	31852	73E	31919	75C
31692	73C	31795	71A	31853	73B	31920	75C
31693	73C	31796	70A	31854	73F	31921	73A
31694	73C	31797	70C	31855	73C	31922	73C
31695	73C	31798	70C	31856	73C	31923	73C
31714	73E	31799	70C	31857	73C	31924	73C
31715	73E	31800	70C	31858	73C	31925	73C
31716	73J	31801	71A	31859	73C		
31717	73B	31802	71A	31860	73C		
31719	73A	31803	71A	31861	73C	32100	73A
31720	73D	31804	70F	31862	75B	32101	71I
31721	73C	31805	70F	31863	75B	32102	73A
31722	70C	31806	70D	31864	75B	32103	73A
31723	70C	31807	70C	31865	75B	32104	73B
31724	73A	31808	71A	31866	75B	32105	73B

32106	73A	32463	75D	32541	75D	33003	70C
32107	73B	32468	75A	32543	73A	33004	70C
32108	71I	32469	75D	32544	75C	33005	70C
32109	71I	32470	75D	32545	75C	33006	70B
32151	71I	32471	73B	32546	75C	33007	70B
32165	75C	32472	73B	32547	73A	33008	70B
32166	75C	32473	73B	32548	70F	33009	70B
32337	70F	32474	73B	32549	70F	33010	70B
32338	75A	32475	75A	32550	70F	33011	70B
32339	75A	32479	70F	32551	73B	33012	70B
32340	75A	32480	75A	32552	73B	33013	70B
32341	75A	32484	75A	32553	73B	33014	73C
32342	75A	32487	70A	32554	73B	33015	70A
32343	75A	32491	71A	32556	71A	33016	70B
32344	75E	32494	75A	32557	73B	33017	70A
32345	75E	32495	70F	32559	71A	33018	70B
32346	75E	32497	70A	32562	75A	33019	70C
32347	75E	32498	70A	32563	70A	33020	71A
32348	75E	32500	70A	32564	73B	33021	71A
32349	70F	32503	75A	32565	73B	33022	70C
32350	75E	32504	75A	32577	75A	33023	71A
32351	75E	32505	70C	32578	73J	33024	73J
32352	75E	32506	70C	32579	71A	33025	70C
32353	75E	32508	75A	32580	73J	33026	70B
32408	73B	32509	70F	32581	75F	33027	70B
32410	73B	32510	71A	32635	75A	33028	73J
32415	73B	32512	75A	32636	73F	33029	73J
32416	75C	32515	75A	32640	70F	33030	73J
32417	73B	32517	75F	32646	70F	33031	73J
32418	73B	32519	75A	32650	70F	33032	73J
32437	70B	32521	75C	32655	75A	33033	73J
32438	70B	32522	75D	32661	70F	33034	73J
32441	75A	32523	75E	32662	75A	33035	73J
32442	75A	32525	73B	32670	75A	33036	73J
32443	75C	32526	75D	32677	70F	33037	73C
32444	75C	32527	75E	32678	70F	33038	70A
32445	75C	32528	75E	32689	71I	33039	73C
32446	75C	32529	75E	32694	70F	33040	73C
32447	75C	32532	75E	32697	72A		
32448	75C	32534	75E				
32449	75A	32535	75E				
32450	75B	32536	75E				
32451	75B	32538	73B	33001	70C	34001 *	73B
32456	73J	32539	73B	33002	70C	34002 *	72A
						34003 *	73B

Isle of Wight Locomotives

3 * 70H	20 * 70H	27 * 70H	33 * 70H
4 * 70H	21 * 70H	28 * 70H	35 * 70H
14 * 70H	22 * 70H	29 * 70H	36 * 70H
16 * 70H	24 * 70H	30 * 70H	
17 * 70H	25 * 70H	31 * 70H	
18 * 70H	26 * 70H	32 * 70H	

34004 * 73B	34062 * 72A	35006 * 72B	40032 14B
34005 * 73B	34063 * 72A	35007 * 72B	40033 14B
34006 * 70A	34064 * 70A	35008 * 72A	40034 14B
34007 * 70A	34065 * 70A	35009 * 72A	40035 14B
34008 * 75A	34066 * 73A	35010 * 71B	40036 14B
34009 * 70A	34067 * 73A	35011 * 72A	40037 14C
34010 * 70A	34068 * 73A	35012 * 70A	40038 14B
34011 * 72A	34069 * 72A	35013 * 72A	40039 14C
34012 * 73B	34070 * 73H	35014 * 70A	40040 14B
34013 * 73B	34071 * 73H	35015 * 73A	40041 24L
34014 * 73B	34072 * 72A	35016 * 70A	40042 1A
34015 * 72A	34073 * 73H	35017 * 70A	40043 1A
34016 * 73G	34074 * 72A	35018 * 70A	40044 1A
34017 * 73G	34075 * 72A	35019 * 70A	40045 1A
34018 * 70A	34076 * 72A	35020 * 70A	40046 1A
34019 * 75A	34077 * 73A	35021 * 71B	40047 1A
34020 * 70A	34078 * 73G	35022 * 71B	40048 6G
34021 * 73G	34079 * 72A	35023 * 72A	40049 67B
34022 * 73G	34080 * 72A	35024 * 71B	40050 1A
34023 * 72A	34081 * 72A	35025 * 71B	40051 1A
34024 * 72A	34082 * 73H	35026 * 72A	40052 9E
34025 * 73G	34083 * 73H	35027 * 71B	40053 1A
34026 * 73G	34084 * 73H	35028 * 73A	40054 62B
34027 * 73G	34085 * 73A	35029 * 70A	40055 9E
34028 * 71B	34086 * 73A	35030 * 70A	40056 9F
34029 * 70A	34087 * 73A		40057 9F
34030 * 72A	34088 * 73A		40058 6G
34031 * 70A	34089 * 73A		40059 9F
34032 * 72A	34090 * 70A		40060 1A
34033 * 72A	34091 * 73A	40001 9F	40061 9F
34034 * 72A	34092 * 73A	40002 WW	40062 26A
34035 * 72A	34093 * 70A	40003 1A	40063 26A
34036 * 72A	34094 * 70A	40004 16C	40064 1A
34037 * 73G	34095 * 70A	40006 WW	40065 26A
34038 * 72A	34096 * 72A	40007 1A	40066 1A
34039 * 71B	34097 * 75A	40008 6G	40067 9F
34040 * 71B	34098 * 75A	40009 9E	40068 1A
34041 * 71B	34099 * 75A	40010 1A	40069 1A
34042 * 71B	34100 * 73A	40011 61C	40070 1A
34043 * 71B	34101 * 73A	40012 21A	40071 6H
34044 * 71B	34102 * 71B	40013 26A	40072 24E
34045 * 71B	34103 * 73H	40014 26A	40073 6G
34046 * 71B	34104 * 72A	40015 26A	40074 56C
34047 * 70A	34105 * 71B	40016 1A	40075 55E
34048 * 71B	34106 * 72A	40017 9E	40076 9A
34049 * 72B	34107 * 71B	40018 9E	40077 9A
34050 * 72B	34108 * 72A	40019 1A	40078 9A
34051 * 72B	34109 * 72A	40020 14E	40079 16C
34052 * 72B	34110 * 72A	40021 14B	40080 3A
34053 * 72B		40022 14C	40081 24L
34054 * 72B		40023 14A	40082 55D
34055 * 72B		40024 14C	40083 3A
34056 * 72B		40025 14C	40084 9A
34057 * 72A		40026 14C	40085 84K
34058 * 72A	35001 * 73A	40027 14B	40086 84K
34059 * 72B	35002 * 71B	40028 14B	40087 2B
34060 * 72A	35003 * 72A	40029 14B	40088 9E
34061 * 72A	35004 * 72B	40030 14B	40089 9F
	35005 * 70A	40031 14B	

40090	27C	40148	41C	40206	3D	40585	16A
40091	86G	40149	21A	40207	2B	40586	24G
40092	14B	40150	60D	40208	9E	40587	27D
40093	9A	40151	68B	40209	6C	40588	27A
40094	9F	40152	65D	40332	82E	40589	6K
40095	6G	40153	65D	40396	17B	40590	67C
40096	16C	40154	65D	40402	15C	40592	67B
40097	9E	40155	56A	40411	16A	40593	67B
40098	86K	40156	8B	40412	17A	40594	67A
40099	24E	40157	2B	40416	17A	40595	67C
40100	14B	40158	65D	40421	16A	40596	67A
40101	6C	40159	65D	40439	21B	40597	67B
40102	6C	40160	14B	40443	21A	40598	67A
40103	24E	40161	86K	40452	15C	40599	67A
40104	2B	40162	24D	40453	17B	40600	61C
40105	9E	40163	24D	40454	16A	40601	82F
40106	6E	40164	24E	40487	16A	40602	12A
40107	9A	40165	15E	40489	85E	40603	61A
40108	3E	40166	24E	40491	55A	40604	61A
40109	24E	40167	15E	40493	16A	40605	67B
40110	84K	40168	16C	40501	82E	40606	67D
40111	14B	40169	56A	40502	16A	40607	67D
40112	56C	40170	68B	40504	16A	40608	67B
40113	9F	40171	86K	40511	21A	40609	67B
40114	56C	40172	14B	40513	17A	40610	67C
40115	21A	40173	3A	40534	16A	40611	68C
40116	6E	40174	24E	40536	17A	40612	67B
40117	56A	40175	16C	40537	82E	40613	12A
40118	3E	40176	65D	40538	17A	40614	68B
40119	14B	40177	65D	40540	85E	40615	12A
40120	24D	40178	HW	40542	16A	40616	68C
40121	6C	40179	55E	40543	15C	40617	61B
40122	9A	40180	3D	40548	14B	40618	61B
40123	6G	40181	55D	40550	16A	40619	67B
40124	9F	40182	15E	40552	55A	40620	67A
40125	8B	40183	24D	40557	16A	40621	61A
40126	84K	40184	16C	40563	82G	40622	61C
40127	27F	40185	6H	40564	82G	40623	68C
40128	6G	40186	65D	40565	24K	40624	67D
40129	3E	40187	65D	40566	68C	40625	67D
40130	6G	40188	65D	40567	14B	40626	67D
40131	6C	40189	65D	40568	21B	40627	67A
40132	6H	40190	56C	40569	82G	40628	12B
40133	6G	40191	27C	40570	67B	40629	12B
40134	8D	40192	24C	40571	67B	40630	55E
40135	2B	40193	55A	40572	67B	40631	26F
40136	6H	40194	27C	40573	67B	40632	16A
40137	8D	40195	27C	40574	67C	40633	17B
40138	2B	40196	27C	40575	67C	40634	82G
40139	56A	40197	27C	40576	68B	40635	6G
40140	55A	40198	27C	40577	68B	40636	67A
40141	9E	40199	27C	40578	67D	40637	67A
40142	14B	40200	65D	40579	67D	40638	67D
40143	8D	40201	8D	40580	14B	40640	67C
40144	21B	40202	6C	40581	55D	40641	67A
40145	86G	40203	27F	40582	14B	40642	67A
40146	16C	40204	2B	40583	5C	40643	67B
40147	56E	40205	84K	40584	55C	40644	67B

40645	67B	41062	17A	41249	82A	41307	72A
40646	5C	41063	55F	41250	56F	41308	73E
40647	67C	41101	24J	41251	50F	41309	73E
40648	61A	41120	6G	41252	50A	41310	73E
40649	67A	41123	85E	41253	56F	41311	73E
40650	61A	41157	17A	41254	55C	41312	73E
40651	12A	41158	6A	41255	55C	41313	73E
40652	5A	41162	2A	41256	55C	41314	72E
40653	5A	41168	3E	41257	55F	41315	83H
40654	11A	41200	6H	41258	55C	41316	83H
40655	5A	41201	86K	41259	55C	41317	83H
40656	12B	41202	82A	41260	24F	41318	72A
40657	24K	41203	82A	41261	24F	41319	75F
40658	6A	41204	86K	41262	56F	41320	2E
40659	5A	41205	24F	41263	56F	41321	9G
40660	5A	41206	26E	41264	56A	41322	6G
40661	67B	41207	82E	41265	50F	41323	6G
40663	61A	41208	82E	41266	56F	41324	6C
40664	67C	41209	41C	41267	55A	41325	55F
40665	67B	41210	8B	41268	27A	41326	55F
40666	67D	41211	8G	41269	27A	41327	24G
40667	67D	41212	5A	41270	14D	41328	17B
40668	67D	41213	8B	41271	14E	41329	14D
40669	67D	41214	2A	41272	14D	41528	41E
40670	67C	41215	6D	41273	55F	41529	41E
40671	26F	41216	6K	41274	55D	41531	41E
40672	1C	41217	9A	41275	1E	41532	17B
40673	3A	41218	2E	41276	6K	41533	41E
40674	9A	41219	2E	41277	17B	41535	85E
40675	6G	41220	5A	41278	2A	41536	17B
40677	24K	41221	9A	41279	3B	41537	85E
40678	5C	41222	1E	41280	14E	41661	53E
40679	5A	41223	1C	41281	55D	41702	9G
40680	27D	41224	1C	41282	55D	41708	41E
40681	27D	41225	3B	41283	24F	41712	16C
40682	17A	41226	6G	41284	14D	41726	17A
40683	24K	41227	84D	41285	84D	41734	41E
40684	27A	41228	84D	41286	8G	41739	41E
40685	24H	41229	5A	41287	26F	41754	17A
40686	67B	41230	6H	41288	8G	41763	41E
40687	67B	41231	84K	41289	8G	41769	41E
40688	67B	41232	84K	41290	73A	41773	17A
40689	67B	41233	6H	41291	73A	41795	41B
40690	55A	41234	6H	41292	73A	41797	53E
40691	18C	41235	6G	41293	71A	41804	41E
40692	3A	41236	6G	41294	72E	41835	41D
40693	9A	41237	6G	41295	72E	41844	16C
40694	24K	41238	6G	41296	82F	41847	17A
40695	11A	41239	6H	41297	72E	41855	53E
40696	82F	41240	82E	41298	72E	41857	41B
40697	82F	41241	82F	41299	73B	41875	41D
40698	82F	41242	82F	41300	73B	41878	17B
40699	6G	41243	82F	41301	73B	41879	82E
40700	82F	41244	6G	41302	83H	41900	85E
40907	41C	41245	41C	41303	73B	41901	1C
40925	17A	41246	41C	41304	82F	41902	2A
40936	3E	41247	50B	41305	71A	41903	24J
		41248	82G	41306	72A	41904	24J

41905	9D	42093	55F	42151	56E	42209	67D
41906	9D	42094	56E	42152	56D	42210	67D
41907	9A	42095	73H	42153	24A	42211	67D
41908	9A	42096	73F	42154	24D	42212	67D
41909	2A	42097	73F	42155	8A	42213	68D
41947	18A	42098	73F	42156	14B	42214	68D
41949	31F	42099	73F	42157	14D	42215	68D
41969	31F	42100	73F	42158	24C	42216	64D
41975	31F	42101	75F	42159	14C	42217	64D
41981	33A	42102	75F	42160	15C	42218	33C
		42103	75F	42161	16A	42219	33C
		42104	75F	42162	64D	42220	33C
		42105	75F	42163	64D	42221	33C
		42106	75F	42164	66C'	42222	14D
		42107	56F	42165	66C	42223	33C
42050	9E	42108	56F	42166	66C	42224	33C
42051	24H	42109	56F	42167	66C	42225	14D
42052	55A	42110	24A	42168	63A	42226	33A
42053	17C	42111	18C	42169	63A	42227	33A
42054	21A	42112	27E	42170	66A	42228	17C
42055	66A	42113	27E	42171	66A	42229	67A
42056	66A	42114	26E	42172	66A	42230	14D
42057	66A	42115	26E	42173	64D	42231	14D
42058	66A	42116	56F	42174	17A	42232	14D
42059	66A	42117	1A	42175	66D	42233	11A
42060	66A	42118	1A	42176	66D	42234	1A
42061	2A	42119	8F	42177	64D	42235	8F
42062	2A	42120	8F	42178	14B	42236	66D
42063	26A	42121	8A	42179	11A	42237	14B
42064	9E	42122	67A	42180	27D	42238	67A
42065	9E	42123	67A	42181	17A	42239	66A
42066	75A	42124	67D	42182	15C	42240	66D
42067	75A	42125	66B	42183	27F	42241	66A
42068	75E	42126	66B	42184	17A	42242	66A
42069	75E	42127	66B	42185	16A	42243	66A
42070	75E	42128	66C	42186	18C	42244	66A
42071	75E	42129	66C	42187	24B	42245	66A
42072	55F	42130	68D	42188	56F	42246	66A
42073	56F	42131	67C	42189	56F	42247	67A
42074	73H	42132	24H	42190	67A	42248	14D
42075	73H	42133	14C	42191	67A	42249	14D
42076	73H	42134	14C	42192	68D	42250	14D
42077	73H	42135	24J	42193	67A	42251	14D
42078	73H	42136	24J	42194	67C	42252	14D
42079	73H	42137	15C	42195	67C	42253	14D
42080	73B	42138	55A	42196	67C	42254	33A
42081	73B	42139	55F	42197	67C	42255	33A
42082	73B	42140	16A	42198	63B	42256	14D
42083	50A	42141	55F	42199	63B	42257	33A
42084	56F	42142	64D	42200	66B	42258	66D
42085	50A	42143	66A	42201	67C	42259	66D
42086	73B	42144	66A	42202	67C	42260	66D
42087	73A	42145	64D	42203	66B	42261	66D
42088	73A	42146	27F	42204	66D	42262	66D
42089	73A	42147	24D	42205	68D	42263	66D
42090	73A	42148	24E	42206	65B	42264	66D
42091	73A	42149	56E	42207	65B	42265	66D
42092	73H	42150	56E	42208	66B	42266	66D

42267	3E	42324	56D	42382	9C	42440	12A
42268	66A	42325	14B	42383	21A	42441	8A
42269	60B	42326	17A	42384	55G	42442	26F
42270	64C	42327	21A	42385	87K	42443	5D
42271	63A	42328	9G	42386	8E	42444	26D
42272	64C	42329	14B	42387	87K	42445	27F
42273	64C	42330	15C	42388	87K	42446	15F
42274	66A	42331	15C	42389	5C	42447	6C
42275	66A	42332	11A	42390	87K	42448	27F
42276	66A	42333	16D	42391	9B	42449	12B
42277	66A	42334	14B	42392	11A	42450	14D
42278	24H	42335	14C	42393	11D	42451	26A
42279	14D	42336	9E	42394	87K	42452	9E
42280	24B	42337	21A	42395	84G	42453	14D
42281	14D	42338	14B	42396	11D	42454	5D
42282	14D	42339	16D	42397	9C	42455	26D
42283	14D	42340	21A	42398	9A	42456	8F
42284	14D	42341	14C	42399	9A	42457	11C
42285	56D	42342	14B	42400	5C	42458	26F
42286	24C	42343	9B	42401	11A	42459	8A
42287	26A	42344	5D	42402	11A	42460	26D
42288	26A	42345	11C	42403	11D	42461	24E
42289	26C	42346	5D	42404	11D	42462	8F
42290	27C	42347	5C	42405	56E	42463	1A
42291	14D	42348	9C	42406	56D	42464	11C
42292	27C	42349	27F	42407	56D	42465	8F
42293	27C	42350	1A	42408	55G	42466	9E
42294	24A	42351	1A	42409	55G	42467	1E
42295	24A	42352	27F	42410	11D	42468	26F
42296	24C	42353	2E	42411	56F	42469	9E
42297	27D	42354	9B	42412	55G	42470	3D
42298	24C	42355	9C	42413	55G	42471	8F
42299	27D	42356	8E	42414	55G	42472	26C
42300	14C	42357	9B	42415	6D	42473	27D
42301	11C	42358	5F	42416	9A	42474	24B
42302	14C	42359	1A	42417	6D	42475	27D
42303	6D	42360	1A	42418	84G	42476	24C
42304	1A	42361	16D	42419	9E	42477	50D
42305	87K	42362	84G	42420	84G	42478	26F
42306	9D	42363	9C	42421	5D	42479	9E
42307	87K	42364	11A	42422	1A	42480	24A
42308	6D	42365	1A	42423	8E	42481	24C
42309	5C	42366	1A	42424	11D	42482	1A
42310	55G	42367	1A	42425	5C	42483	24D
42311	56E	42368	1A	42426	12B	42484	24H
42312	55G	42369	9A	42427	11A	42485	24D
42313	11C	42370	9D	42428	3B	42486	17C
42314	11C	42371	9D	42429	9G	42487	1A
42315	5D	42372	84G	42430	1A	42488	3E
42316	9B	42373	18C	42431	6A	42489	1A
42317	11C	42374	9G	42432	24L	42490	18C
42318	9C	42375	5F	42433	24A	42491	24H
42319	8E	42376	11A	42434	24C	42492	24H
42320	84G	42377	55G	42435	27C	42493	6C
42321	1A	42378	5D	42436	53E	42494	26F
42322	9B	42379	9B	42437	14D	42500	33C
42323	5D	42380	56E	42438	24B	42501	33C
		42381	9A	42439	24B		

42502	33C	42558	24D	42616	3D	42674	3E
42503	33C	42559	24D	42617	14B	42675	9E
42504	33C	42560	9G	42618	14D	42676	9E
42505	33C	42561	26F	42619	24A	42677	5A
42506	33C	42562	5C	42620	24A	42678	33C
42507	33C	42563	26F	42621	27C	42679	33C
42508	33C	42564	8A	42622	56F	42680	14C
42509	33C	42565	26C	42623	26A	42681	33C
42510	33C	42566	84D	42624	26A	42682	14B
42511	33C	42567	5D	42625	24E	42683	9E
42512	33C	42568	14D	42626	26C	42684	33C
42513	33C	42569	27D	42627	1A	42685	14B
42514	33C	42570	8A	42628	9E	42686	14C
42515	33C	42571	8F	42629	14D	42687	33C
42516	33C	42572	8F	42630	26C	42688	68D
42517	33C	42573	2A	42631	27D	42689	66B
42518	33C	42574	26F	42632	27D	42690	63B
42519	33C	42575	5A	42633	26C	42691	62B
42520	33C	42576	1A	42634	24C	42692	62B
42521	33C	42577	2A	42635	26C	42693	63B
42522	33C	42578	5A	42636	16A	42694	65D
42523	33C	42579	1A	42637	27C	42695	66A
42524	33C	42580	27F	42638	24E	42696	66B
42525	33C	42581	11A	42639	50D	42697	67D
42526	33C	42582	5D	42640	27D	42698	66D
42527	33C	42583	8A	42641	27D	42699	66B
42528	33C	42584	27F	42642	27D	42700	26D
42529	33C	42585	1A	42643	24A	42701	26A
42530	33C	42586	1A	42644	27D	42702	55F
42531	33C	42587	14B	42645	26B	42703	26A
42532	33C	42588	14D	42646	26B	42704	26A
42533	33C	42589	24J	42647	26B	42705	26A
42534	33C	42590	5D	42648	24H	42706	24B
42535	33C	42591	24L	42649	56F	42707	26A
42536	33C	42592	27D	42650	56F	42708	26A
42537	27C	42593	5D	42651	26A	42709	26A
42538	1A	42594	12B	42652	26C	42710	26A
42539	12B	42595	14D	42653	26C	42711	27B
42540	14B	42596	27F	42654	26C	42712	26D
42541	2A	42597	6C	42655	26C	42713	55C
42542	12A	42598	27F	42656	26C	42714	26A
42543	5D	42599	6C	42657	26E	42715	26A
42544	6A	42600	5D	42658	3D	42716	24B
42545	26C	42601	3E	42659	5D	42717	24B
42546	24B	42602	8A	42660	26A	42718	24D
42547	24B	42603	5D	42661	24A	42719	26D
42548	26A	42604	1A	42662	26F	42720	12A
42549	26A	42605	5F	42663	5D	42721	27B
42550	26D	42606	8B	42664	12B	42722	24D
42551	26E	42607	8B	42665	5F	42723	26B
42552	3D	42608	6C	42666	8F	42724	26B
42553	50D	42609	5D	42667	5D	42725	26B
42554	27D	42610	14B	42668	5D	42726	26A
42555	24B	42611	1A	42669	2A	42727	26A
42556	14D	42612	27F	42670	5D	42728	26A
42557	27D	42613	11C	42671	5D	42729	24D
		42614	27D	42672	5D	42730	26D
		42615	2E	42673	2A	42731	26D

42732	24F	42790	21A	42848	9A	42906	12A
42733	26A	42791	21A	42849	8C	42907	12A
42734	26B	42792	17C	42850	66C	42908	68B
42735	66C	42793	12A	42851	24J	42909	68B
42736	65F	42794	41B	42852	1A	42910	67C
42737	65F	42795	55A	42853	3A	42911	67D
42738	66C	42796	24D	42854	9B	42912	67D
42739	67C	42797	41B	42855	17B	42913	68B
42740	66D	42798	55A	42856	6C	42914	67C
42741	66D	42799	17B	42857	21A	42915	68B
42742	67D	42800	63A	42858	9A	42916	67C
42743	67B	42801	63A	42859	1A	42917	67C
42744	67B	42802	65F	42860	26B	42918	68B
42745	67C	42803	65F	42861	56A	42919	68B
42746	66C	42804	12A	42862	56A	42920	3D
42747	1A	42805	67C	42863	56A	42921	3A
42748	12A	42806	67D	42864	27B	42922	17B
42749	68C	42807	64C	42865	55C	42923	9A
42750	26A	42808	67C	42866	55C	42924	9A
42751	12A	42809	67C	42867	24F	42925	9A
42752	12A	42810	24J	42868	26B	42926	5B
42753	26B	42811	5B	42869	24B	42927	67C
42754	17C	42812	1A	42870	1A	42928	24J
42755	26B	42813	21A	42871	26A	42929	3D
42756	17B	42814	9A	42872	16D	42930	9A
42757	12A	42815	5B	42873	17C	42931	1A
42758	21A	42816	21A	42874	17C	42932	9B
42759	17B	42817	2B	42875	12A	42933	5B
42760	17C	42818	17B	42876	12A	42934	9A
42761	21A	42819	26B	42877	12A	42935	5B
42762	55F	42820	26D	42878	27B	42936	9A
42763	17B	42821	24D	42879	67C	42937	5B
42764	15B	42822	17B	42880	66C	42938	9A
42765	24F	42823	21A	42881	12A	42939	5B
42766	55C	42824	17B	42882	12A	42940	3D
42767	17B	42825	17B	42883	12A	42941	6C
42768	17C	42826	17B	42884	12A	42942	9D
42769	16D	42827	21A	42885	1A	42943	9D
42770	55F	42828	24B	42886	9D	42944	1A
42771	55A	42829	17B	42887	9A	42945	6B
42772	9A	42830	12A	42888	6C	42946	5A
42773	9B	42831	12A	42889	9A	42947	3D
42774	55A	42832	12A	42890	21A	42948	5B
42775	21A	42833	12A	42891	2B	42949	5B
42776	5B	42834	12A	42892	8C	42950	5B
42777	5B	42835	12A	42893	24J	42951	3D
42778	6C	42836	12A	42894	6C	42952	5B
42779	3A	42837	12A	42895	24J	42953	5B
42780	65F	42838	26B	42896	17B	42954	5A
42781	2B	42839	17B	42897	16D	42955	5A
42782	3A	42840	24F	42898	24B	42956	5B
42783	2B	42841	24F	42899	12A	42957	3D
42784	16D	42842	24F	42900	21A	42958	5A
42785	5B	42843	24F	42901	26A	42959	53
42786	9A	42844	24F	42902	17C	42960	6B
42787	5B	42845	27B	42903	21A	42961	5A
42788	21A	42846	21A	42904	41B	42962	5B
42789	55C	42847	16D	42905	12A		

42963	5A	43031	14A	43089	31C	43147	40F
42964	5B	43032	41C	43090	31C	43148	30A
42965	6B	43033	21B	43091	40F	43149	30A
42966	5A	43034	2B	43092	40F	43150	30A
42967	6B	43035	11D	43093	40F	43151	30A
42968	5A	43036	21A	43094	31C	43152	30E
42969	6C	43037	41D	43095	40F	43153	30E
42970	6C	43038	55B	43096	50C	43154	40E
42971	6B	43039	55A	43097	50C	43155	40E
42972	5B	43040	21B	43098	50C	43156	32A
42973	6B	43041	21A	43099	53A	43157	40F
42974	3D	43042	15B	43100	56F	43158	40E
42975	1A	43043	55A	43101	56B	43159	40F
42976	6B	43044	55B	43102	51L	43160	32A
42977	6C	43045	24J	43103	53A	43161	32A
42978	6C	43046	21A	43104	40F	43174	41B
42979	3D	43047	21A	43105	30A	43178	55F
42980	5B	43048	15B	43106	2F	43183	55E
42981	6B	43049	21A	43107	40F	43185	8G
42982	6C	43050	51A	43108	40F	43187	9G
42983	5B	43051	50C	43109	40F	43188	17B
42984	5B	43052	50C	43110	40F	43189	3A
		43053	53A	43111	40F	43192	9B
		43054	50C	43112	24J	43194	82G
		43055	55A	43113	24J	43200	17A
		43056	55A	43114	55E	43203	41B
		43057	50C	43115	24J	43205	15C
43000	2B	43058	40F	43116	55E	43207	9G
43001	2B	43059	40F	43117	55A	43210	21A
43002	2B	43060	40F	43118	14A	43211	9E
43003	2B	43061	40F	43119	14C	43212	9F
43004	11B	43062	40F	43120	14A	43213	8G
43005	2B	43063	2F	43121	14A	43214	21A
43006	11B	43064	40F	43122	53A	43216	82G
43007	2B	43065	40F	43123	50C	43218	82G
43008	11B	43066	40F	43124	55A	43219	21A
43009	11B	43067	34E	43125	50C	43222	41B
43010	21A	43068	40F	43126	56E	43223	21A
43011	11D	43069	53A	43127	31F	43225	41D
43012	21B	43070	55F	43128	51C	43233	55D
43013	21A	43071	50C	43129	51A	43234	41E
43014	55B	43072	51L	43130	55A	43235	18B
43015	51C	43073	51E	43131	53A	43237	8B
43016	55F	43074	55E	43132	65E	43240	24L
43017	21A	43075	56B	43133	65E	43241	12A
43018	24J	43076	53A	43134	65E	43242	21A
43019	14A	43077	53A	43135	65A	43243	41B
43020	2B	43078	53A	43136	65A	43245	9F
43021	24J	43079	53A	43137	65A	43247	17B
43022	8G	43080	40F	43138	64F	43248	82G
43023	2B	43081	34E	43139	12C	43249	15B
43024	2B	43082	34E	43140	65B	43250	55D
43025	11B	43083	40F	43141	64G	43251	18A
43026	2B	43084	34E	43142	40F	43253	21A
43027	21B	43085	40F	43143	40F	43254	41B
43028	11D	43086	34E	43144	30A	43256	17B
43029	11D	43087	31A	43145	32A	43257	24J
43030	55F	43088	34E	43146	32A	43258	8G

43261	15C	43410	9B	43615	8B	43762	85F
43263	21B	43411	15C	43618	6K	43763	9G
43266	18B	43427	82G	43619	8B	43766	14E
43267	55D	43428	14E	43620	21A	43773	9G
43268	9D	43429	17C	43621	17B	43778	17C
43271	24J	43431	41B	43622	12A	43784	55F
43277	15C	43433	21A	43623	17B	43785	14E
43278	9D	43435	21A	43624	15B	43789	55D
43282	8B	43436	82G	43627	21A	43793	18A
43284	21A	43440	14E	43629	15C	43799	15C
43287	16B	43444	82E	43630	9G	43800	41B
43294	8G	43446	55D	43634	41B	43808	14E
43295	24J	43449	55E	43637	41B	43809	17B
43305	9B	43453	18A	43638	9G	43812	21A
43306	17A	43456	55B	43639	55E	43814	41D
43307	41B	43457	9G	43644	21A	43822	3A
43308	8B	43459	17A	43645	85E	43825	18B
43309	18A	43464	5B	43650	18A	43826	18A
43314	8B	43468	21A	43651	8B	43828	41E
43315	17A	43474	14E	43652	17B	43829	14E
43318	17A	43482	21A	43657	8B	43832	18A
43321	55E	43484	21A	43658	17A	43836	9D
43324	17A	43490	21A	43660	41D	43839	17B
43325	1C	43496	17C	43664	41D	43840	17A
43326	15C	43499	18A	43665	14E	43841	1E
43327	17B	43502	24J	43668	21B	43842	9D
43329	9D	43506	8G	43669	41B	43843	17B
43330	2F	43507	21A	43673	21A	43844	41B
43333	15B	43509	55E	43674	21A	43845	18A
43335	41B	43510	17A	43675	21B	43846	9E
43337	85E	43514	12A	43678	12A	43848	66A
43339	21A	43515	41E	43679	17B	43849	66A
43340	17B	43520	85E	43680	21A	43850	18B
43342	17C	43521	21B	43681	55B	43853	85E
43344	82E	43523	21B	43682	82F	43854	15D
43355	21A	43529	14E	43687	21B	43855	21B
43359	21B	43531	14E	43693	21A	43856	16A
43361	41D	43538	9D	43705	56D	43858	21A
43368	17A	43548	17A	43709	17B	43859	16A
43369	41D	43558	9F	43711	41E	43860	18A
43370	17C	43562	9D	43714	55E	43861	15A
43371	41D	43565	14E	43715	41B	43863	41E
43373	85E	43570	17B	43721	15B	43864	5D
43374	21A	43572	9F	43727	17A	43865	18A
43378	6K	43574	17B	43728	15C	43866	18B
43379	21A	43579	56F	43729	41E	43868	11B
43381	21A	43580	9E	43731	41B	43869	41E
43386	41E	43583	21B	43734	82E	43870	17B
43387	8B	43584	17A	43735	17A	43871	55B
43388	41B	43585	24H	43737	55B	43872	41B
43389	2F	43586	55F	43749	41B	43873	14C
43394	2F	43587	9E	43750	17C	43876	15D
43395	41D	43593	82E	43751	41B	43877	5F
43398	8B	43594	21A	43753	41D	43878	21A
43399	2E	43599	21A	43754	85E	43880	17B
43400	9E			43756	24H	43881	17A
43405	15C			43759	17C	43882	41B
43406	41B	43605	41E	43760	3A	43883	66B
		43608	17B				

43884	66B	43960	24G	44028	55B	44086	11A

43884	66B	43960	24G	44028	55B	44086	11A
43885	16B	43961	9F	44029	14A	44037	41B
43886	41E	43962	16A	44030	16A	44088	41E
43887	85E	43963	21A	44031	17A	44089	41D
43888	16A	43964	14B	44032	5D	44090	9F
43893	24G	43965	21A	44033	16A	44091	21A
43896	12B	43966	18B	44034	15C	44092	21A
43897	24D	43967	85E	44035	85E	44093	5D
43899	67A	43968	55B	44036	41D	44094	55B
43900	41E	43969	17A	44037	41D	44095	16A
43902	12A	43971	14C	44038	27E	44096	82F
43903	16B	43972	16A	44039	41B	44097	31F
43904	11A	43973	3E	44040	27E	44098	55E
43905	14A	43975	15D	44041	24G	44099	55E
43906	55D	43976	17B	44042	17A	44100	17B
43907	16B	43977	15A	44043	14C	44101	17C
43908	6B	43979	15A	44044	55B	44102	82G
43910	27F	43981	6K	44045	85E	44103	15D
43911	21A	43982	17C	44046	17C	44104	41E
43913	24G	43983	21A	44047	17B	44105	24G
43914	55D	43985	21A	44048	17A	44106	18A
43915	27F	43986	21A	44049	17A	44107	55D
43917	16A	43987	55B	44050	17C	44108	21A
43918	16A	43988	9E	44051	14A	44109	15D
43919	15C	43989	17B	44052	14B	44110	31F
43920	41E	43990	18A	44053	18C	44111	41D
43921	18A	43991	17A	44054	18C	44112	17A
43922	12A	43994	18A	44055	55F	44113	15D
43923	16B	43995	15A	44056	56D	44114	9G
43924	85E	43996	67A	44057	3E	44115	3E
43925	17A	43997	18C	44058	1A	44116	1A
43926	82E	43998	17B	44059	9B	44117	6B
43928	16A	43999	24G	44060	12B	44118	16B
43929	15A	44000	24G	44061	9A	44119	24G
43930	17A	44001	67A	44062	56F	44120	3D
43931	55B	44002	41D	44063	5E	44121	12B
43932	21A	44003	55D	44064	2A	44122	18C
43933	16B	44004	21A	44065	6B	44123	85E
43934	14A	44005	16B	44066	41E	44124	17B
43935	14A	44007	24G	44067	5E	44125	5E
43937	15C	44008	12A	44068	5D	44126	12B
43938	21A	44009	12A	44069	8F	44127	27F
43939	21A	44010	41E	44070	41E	44128	41D
43940	21A	44011	66D	44071	41D	44129	41E
43942	55D	44012	18A	44072	1E	44130	18B
43944	55F	44013	21A	44073	6B	44131	16A
43945	9F	44014	27E	44074	5D	44132	16A
43947	14A	44015	9F	44075	9B	44133	18C
43948	17B	44016	12B	44076	2E	44134	17C
43949	21A	44018	16A	44077	5D	44135	82G
43950	17C	44019	56A	44078	9G	44136	18C
43951	21A	44020	17A	44079	5E	44137	21A
43952	27D	44021	16A	44080	9E	44138	21A
43953	17B	44022	26A	44081	12B	44139	16A
43954	16A	44023	16B	44082	41D	44140	18A
43955	17A	44025	9G	44083	11D	44141	55D
43957	31F	44026	21A	44084	21A	44142	17A
43958	16A	44027	3B	44085	15D	44143	21A

44144	9F	44203	21A	44261	9F	44319	67A
44146	82F	44204	16A	44262	17C	44320	65F
44147	41E	44205	41E	44263	21A	44321	18B
44148	15D	44206	41D	44264	85E	44322	66A
44149	24H	44207	55B	44265	41B	44323	67C
44150	18B	44208	1A	44266	8G	44324	12A
44151	16A	44209	85E	44267	41E	44325	67B
44152	31F	44210	14B	44268	16B	44326	12B
44153	55B	44211	21A	44269	82E	44327	17C
44154	27F	44212	41B	44270	14B	44328	63A
44155	8E	44213	21A	44271	5D	44329	67C
44156	15D	44214	17A	44272	85E	44330	67C
44157	12C	44215	16A	44273	31F	44331	67C
44158	16A	44216	55F	44274	55D	44332	17B
44159	67D	44217	18C	44275	9E	44333	21A
44160	21A	44218	27E	44276	24H	44334	17A
44161	18A	44219	2E	44277	24G	44335	55B
44162	18C	44220	24G	44278	15D	44336	55E
44163	17C	44221	27D	44279	15D	44337	55E
44165	21A	44222	24G	44280	8F	44338	55E
44166	15D	44223	16A	44281	67B	44339	9D
44167	85E	44224	18A	44282	24H	44340	9B
44168	17B	44225	27D	44283	66A	44341	8E
44169	17A	44226	21A	44284	18A	44342	5E
44170	55E	44227	21A	44285	18B	44343	11B
44171	21A	44228	14A	44286	9F	44344	5B
44172	17C	44229	18B	44287	41B	44345	11D
44173	18B	44230	21A	44288	18C	44346	12B
44174	41B	44231	15C	44289	18B	44347	11A
44175	15A	44232	27F	44290	55D	44348	1C
44176	17A	44233	18B	44291	27E	44349	9A
44177	17A	44234	65F	44292	11B	44350	8G
44178	18A	44235	14B	44293	27F	44351	11A
44179	21A	44236	9F	44294	14B	44352	5E
44180	15D	44237	8B	44295	17A	44353	2E
44181	12A	44238	55B	44296	85E	44354	5E
44182	15A	44239	31F	44297	14A	44355	82E
44183	12A	44240	27D	44298	14B	44356	8B
44184	21A	44241	17B	44299	27E	44357	5F
44185	21A	44242	2E	44300	8G	44358	5D
44186	5B	44243	14B	44301	5D	44359	5B
44187	21A	44244	18C	44302	3D	44360	11B
44188	27E	44245	41D	44303	8F	44361	9F
44189	67A	44246	5D,	44304	17A	44362	18B
44190	16B	44247	31F	44305	6H	44363	CW
44191	18B	44248	16A	44306	24L	44364	1E
44192	8G	44249	41E	44307	5D	44365	11B
44193	66A	44250	9F	44308	5D	44366	11A
44194	65B	44251	66A	44309	5D	44367	6K
44195	16A	44252	16C	44310	5D	44368	55B
44196	66C	44253	63A	44311	26A	44369	17A
44197	24G	44254	63A	44312	67B	44370	1E
44198	67A	44255	65J	44313	16A	44371	41E
44199	65B	44256	66A	44314	63A	44372	1A
44200	18A	44257	63A	44315	12A	44373	CW
44201	21A	44258	63A	44316	17B	44374	CW
44202	16B	44259	14A	44317	8G	44375	8E
		44260	15D	44318	66A	44376	18A

44377	5D	44435	17B	44493	6B	44551	17B
44378	9F	44436	17B	44494	27F	44552	17B
44379	9F	44437	41B	44495	11B	44553	82E
44380	17A	44438	8F	44496	5D	44554	9F
44381	14B	44439	3B	44497	1A	44555	16A
44382	9B	44440	1C	44498	5D	44556	17C
44383	5D	44441	16C	44499	5D	44557	82G
44384	8B	44442	1C	44500	9F	44558	82F
44385	5B	44443	11A	44501	9F	44559	82F
44386	5E	44444	3E	44502	5E	44560	82F
44387	9F	44445	6H	44503	5E	44561	82F
44388	15F	44446	55D	44504	5F	44562	17B
44389	6G	44447	1E	44505	11B	44563	14B
44390	11B	44448	3A	44506	3E	44564	17C
44391	2E	44449	11B	44507	5D	44565	17C
44392	9E	44450	5E	44508	5D	44566	17C
44393	5D	44451	1A	44509	31F	44567	85E
44394	16A	44452	5E	44510	24L	44568	41B
44395	2A	44453	5E	44511	11A	44569	82E
44396	27F	44454	24L	44512	3A	44570	55B
44397	1E	44455	5D	44513	5D	44571	21B
44398	24D	44456	8E	44514	3E	44572	15D
44399	24L	44457	41B	44515	21A	44573	41B
44400	16A	44458	55E	44516	21B	44574	15A
44401	16A	44459	5D	44517	3D	44575	15A
44402	9E	44460	24D	44518	31F	44576	41D
44403	15C	44461	11B	44519	31F	44577	16A
44404	41E	44462	27E	44520	21A	44578	16A
44405	5E	44463	21A	44521	31F	44579	24H
44406	21A	44464	27D	44522	31F	44580	21A
44407	9F	44465	17A	44523	82F	44581	14A
44408	55E	44466	82E	44524	2E	44582	55D
44409	17A	44467	55B	44525	6G	44583	21A
44410	18C	44468	24G	44526	17B	44584	55B
44411	82E	44469	24L	44527	17B	44585	16A
44412	16A	44470	16B	44528	17B	44586	55B
44413	21A	44471	27E	44529	14A	44587	27F
44414	16A	44472	16A	44530	14A	44588	17C
44415	16C	44473	5D	44531	14B	44589	27F
44416	16C	44474	56D	44532	14B	44590	41E
44417	82G	44475	41E	44533	16A	44591	17B
44418	16B	44476	31F	44534	82E	44592	5B
44419	17A	44477	41B	44535	41B	44593	5D
44420	17A	44478	5D	44536	82E	44594	11A
44421	9F	44479	24D	44537	82E	44595	5B
44422	82F	44480	16A	44538	17B	44596	12B
44423	15C	44481	27E	44539	15D	44597	17B
44424	82E	44482	41E	44540	17A	44598	18B
44425	17A	44483	24D	44541	17B	44599	17B
44426	41B	44484	5D	44542	17B	44600	17B
44427	18A	44485	56D	44543	26A	44601	17A
44428	17A	44486	27D	44544	27D	44602	17C
44429	17C	44487	11A	44545	17A	44603	18C
44430	18B	44488	3A	44546	16A	44604	55E
44431	24G	44489	27F	44547	41B	44605	27E
44432	5D	44490	3E	44548	5D	44606	41E
44433	17B	44491	2E	44549	11B	44658	14B
44434	17B	44492	3D	44550	55D	44659	21A

44660	21A	44718	60A	44775	21A	44833	2A
44661	6J	44719	60A	44776	21A	44834	5B
44662	55A	44720	63A	44777	14A	44835	84G
44663	14B	44721	63A	44778	24E	44836	2A
44664	21A	44722	60A	44779	24E	44837	11A
44665	9E	44723	60A	44780	24B	44838	1A
44666	21A	44724	60A	44781	26B	44839	17A
44667	15C	44725	12A	44782	26B	44840	3E
44668	12A	44726	12A	44783	60A	44841	21A
44669	12A	44727	12A	44784	60A	44842	21A
44670	12A	44728	27C	44785	60A	44843	15C
44671	12A	44729	27C	44786	65B	44844	3D
44672	12A	44730	24E	44787	65A	44845	26A
44673	12A	44731	24E	44788	60A	44846	14B
44674	12A	44732	24E	44789	60A	44847	14D
44675	12A	44733	24E	44790	12A	44848	15C
44676	12A	44734	26A	44791	67A	44849	55A
44677	65B	44735	26A	44792	12A	44850	66B
44678	5A	44736	26A	44793	64D	44851	17A
44679	5A	44737	24E	44794	61B	44852	55A
44680	5A	44738	6G	44795	12A	44853	55A
44681	5B	44739	6G	44796	63A	44854	55A
44682	5A	44740	6G	44797	63A	44855	14B
44683	5A	44741	9A	44798	60A	44856	17A
44684	5A	44742	9A	44799	60A	44857	55A
44685	5A	44743	27A	44800	6B	44858	16A
44686	9A	44744	27A	44801	63A	44859	21A
44687	9A	44745	27A	44802	6J	44860	2A
44688	17A	44746	9A	44803	26A	44861	16A
44689	24A	44747	26F	44804	21A	44862	2A
44690	15C	44748	9A	44805	21A	44863	2A
44691	14D	44749	9A	44806	16A	44864	6G
44692	24A	44750	9A	44807	3E	44865	6G
44693	56F	44751	9A	44808	26F	44866	2A
44694	56F	44752	9A	44809	9E	44867	2A
44695	56F	44753	55A	44810	14B	44868	5B
44696	26A	44754	55A	44811	15C	44869	1A
44697	26A	44755	55A	44812	14B	44870	2A
44698	63A	44756	55A	44813	21A	44871	5B
44699	63A	44757	55A	44814	21A	44872	3D
44700	64D	44758	5A	44815	15C	44873	3A
44701	64D	44759	5A	44816	14A	44874	24L
44702	65A	44760	5A	44817	14B	44875	1A
44703	61B	44761	5A	44818	17A	44876	3D
44704	63A	44762	5A	44819	14D	44877	12A
44705	63A	44763	5A	44820	63A	44878	12A
44706	67A	44764	5A	44821	14B	44879	63A
44707	65A	44765	5A	44822	14B	44880	65B
44708	26F	44766	5A	44823	26B	44831	65B
44709	24L	44767	27A	44824	56F	44882	12A
44710	6A	44768	8A	44825	14B	44883	12A
44711	2E	44769	8A	44826	55A	44884	12A
44712	2E	44770	12B	44827	9A	44885	63A
44713	5B	44771	1A	44828	55A	44886	12A
44714	5A	44772	8A	44829	3B	44887	27C
44715	2A	44773	8A	44830	14D	44888	21A
44716	2A	44774	14A	44831	2A	44889	24A
44717	9E			44832	5B	44890	26A

44891	26A	44949	24B	45003	5B	45061	27C
44892	24L	44950	24E	45004	5A	45062	14A
44893	26A	44951	56F	45005	8A	45063	55C
44894	26A	44952	64D	45006	14D	45064	1A
44895	26A	44953	64D	45007	67A	45065	3D
44896	55C	44954	62B	45008	66B	45066	60A
44897	3D	44955	64D	45009	66B	45067	5B
44898	12A	44956	65A	45010	67B	45068	24A
44899	12A	44957	65A	45011	66B	45069	8A
44900	12A	44958	12A	45012	12A	45070	12B
44901	12A	44959	63A	45013	12A	45071	3E
44902	12A	44960	63A	45014	24L	45072	24L
44903	12A	44961	63A	45015	3B	45073	5A
44904	24L	44962	21A	45016	63B	45074	5B
44905	24L	44963	21A	45017	24L	45075	55C
44906	8A	44964	21A	45018	12A	45076	26A
44907	8A	44965	21A	45019	24L	45077	24E
44908	65A	44966	21A	45020	1E	45078	24A
44909	2A	44967	65A	45021	5A	45079	55C
44910	6A	44968	65A	45022	64C	45080	55C
44911	6A	44969	66B	45023	64C	45081	12A
44912	56F	44970	65A	45024	1A	45082	12A
44913	6H	44971	6B	45025	12B	45083	12A
44914	3A	44972	65J	45026	8F	45084	63B
44915	2A	44973	65J	45027	1A	45085	66B
44916	1A	44974	65J	45028	6B	45086	64C
44917	6C	44975	65J	45029	66B	45087	64D
44918	16A	44976	65J	45030	64C	45088	16A
44919	21A	44977	65J	45031	26A	45089	1E
44920	21A	44978	63A	45032	8A	45090	60A
44921	63A	44979	63A	45033	5A	45091	2E
44922	65B	44980	63A	45034	3E	45092	8F
44923	65B	44981	21B	45035	8B	45093	5A
44924	63A	44982	24E	45036	64C	45094	3D
44925	63A	44983	55A	45037	24L	45095	26F
44926	24E	44984	14E	45038	3E	45096	24K
44927	24E	44985	14B	45039	8A	45097	24L
44928	27A	44986	6J	45040	21A	45098	60A
44929	26B	44987	26B	45041	6A	45099	66B
44930	24E	44988	24E	45042	6A	45100	12A
44931	63A	44989	27C	45043	6B	45101	26A
44932	26B	44990	56F	45044	5B	45102	26A
44933	26A	44991	60A	45045	5B	45103	26A
44934	26A	44992	60A	45046	24L	45104	26A
44935	6G	44993	12A	45047	63A	45105	26A
44936	12B	44994	64C	45048	5B	45106	12B
44937	9A	44995	68B	45049	63B	45107	24F
44938	2A	44996	65A	45050	2E	45108	5B
44939	12B	44997	63A	45051	3A	45109	9A
44940	24B	44998	63A	45052	3E	45110	6J
44941	14A	44999	63A	45053	63A	45111	9A
44942	3D			45054	24L	45112	12B
44943	55A			45055	6B	45113	5A
44944	16A			45056	6J	45114	3A
44945	21A			45057	8F	45115	65B
44946	56F	45000	5B	45058	3D	45116	26B
44947	24E	45001	6B	45059	14A	45117	60A
44948	24B	45002	5B	45060	5B	45118	12A

45119	65B	45177	65B	45235	5A	45292	2E
45120	12A	45178	65B	45236	11A	45293	12B
45121	66B	45179	60A	45237	2E	45294	26F
45122	12A	45180	6G	45238	14A	45295	12B
45123	60A	45181	8A	45239	9E	45296	12B
45124	60A	45182	26F	45240	5A	45297	12B
45125	68C	45183	64C	45241	24L	45298	84G
45126	12A	45184	1E	45242	8A	45299	5B
45127	64C	45185	12B	45243	5A	45300	5B
45128	5B	45186	21A	45244	12B	45301	5B
45129	26F	45187	1A	45245	64D	45302	9A
45130	6B	45188	5B	45246	12B	45303	24L
45131	5B	45189	5A	45247	6B	45304	26F
45132	3D	45190	84G	45248	12B	45305	5A
45133	26F	45191	2E	45249	8A	45306	24L
45134	5B	45192	60A	45250	5A	45307	2E
45135	8F	45193	24L	45251	67A	45308	3E
45136	60B	45194	67A	45252	8B	45309	66B
45137	14E	45195	1E	45253	16A	45310	3B
45138	12A	45196	8B	45254	5A	45311	5A
45139	14E	45197	12B	45255	8B	45312	6A
45140	12B	45198	5B	45256	8A	45313	8F
45141	11A	45199	26F	45257	5A	45314	8F
45142	5B	45200	24E	45258	12B	45315	12B
45143	84G	45201	24E	45259	12B	45316	12B
45144	6H	45202	26A	45260	14D	45317	12B
45145	84G	45203	26A	45261	26B	45318	24E
45146	2A	45204	55C	45262	27F	45319	60A
45147	2E	45205	24B	45263	16A	45320	60A
45148	5A	45206	24F	45264	15C	45321	8B
45149	5B	45207	56F	45265	21A	45322	3D
45150	9A	45208	56F	45266	67B	45323	12B
45151	66B	45209	24B	45267	14E	45324	1A
45152	66B	45210	27A	45268	21A	45325	6B
45153	65B	45211	55C	45269	21A	45326	24L
45154 *	26A	45212	24F	45270	5B	45327	24L
45155	64C	45213	63B	45271	8B	45328	8B
45156 *	26A	45214	63B	45272	21A	45329	12B
45157 *	65B	45215	14D	45273	55A	45330	12A
45158 *	65B	45216	27A	45274	14A	45331	1E
45159	65B	45217	27F	45275	6B	45332	24K
45160	67A	45218	27C	45276	8A	45333	21A
45161	67A	45219	56F	45277	14B	45334	12A
45162	61B	45220	26A	45278	1A	45335	14A
45163	12A	45221	14E	45279	14B	45336	26A
45164	62B	45222	2E	45280	21A	45337	26B
45165	63A	45223	26B	45281	84G	45338	26B
45166	64D	45224	26A	45282	5A	45339	6A
45167	61B	45225	26A	45283	84G	45340	24K
45168	63A	45226	24A	45284	26A	45341	26A
45169	68B	45227	24A	45285	14B	45342	14E
45170	63A	45228	27C	45286	12B	45343	8A
45171	63A	45229	24B	45287	3B	45344	12B
45172	63A	45230	24L	45288	1A	45345	6B
45173	64D	45231	3D	45289	5A	45346	27F
45174	64D	45232	26A	45290	26A	45347	8F
45175	64D	45233	26A	45291	24L	45348	5A
45176	66B	45234	26B			45349	3D

45350	1A	45408	8F	45466	12A	45524 *	12B
45351	12B	45409	2E	45467	63B	45525 *	8A
45352	26F	45410	8A	45468	65B	45526 *	12B
45353	3D	45411	26F	45469	61B	45527 *	8A
45354	8B	45412	12B	45470	63A	45528	5A
45355	65B	45413	8A	45471	65B	45529 *	5A
45356	65B	45414	12B	45472	63A	45530 *	9A
45357	63B	45415	24A	45473	63A	45531 *	8A
45358	65B	45416	14D	45474	63A	45532 *	1B
45359	63B	45417	6H	45475	63A	45533 *	12B
45360	60A	45418	3D	45476	60A	45534 *	8A
45361	60A	45419	3A	45477	60A	45535 *	8A
45362	67A	45420	26F	45478	60A	45536 *	9A
45363	12A	45421	8A	45479	60A	45537 *	12B
45364	12A	45422	84G	45480	68B	45538 *	24K
45365	63A	45423	8A	45481	12A	45539 *	8A
45366	63A	45424	26F	45482	65B	45540 *	9A
45367	63A	45425	8F	45483	63A	45541 *	12B
45368	12B	45426	9A	45484	66B	45542	24K
45369	5A	45427	24L	45485	66B	45543 *	9A
45370	3D	45428	55A	45486	62B	45544	8A
45371	12B	45429	6J	45487	63B	45545 *	5A
45372	1A	45430	3D	45488	63A	45546 *	5A
45373	5A	45431	12B	45489	67A	45547	1A
45374	1A	45432	68B	45490	67A	45548 *	5A
45375	1A	45433	66B	45491	12A	45549	8A
45376	8A	45434	5A	45492	63A	45550	8A
45377	26F	45435	26A	45493	2A	45551	12B
45378	26F	45436	24E	45494	12B	45552 *	8A
45379	5A	45437	12B	45495	8B	45553 *	5A
45380	8A	45438	12B	45496	63A	45554 *	8A
45381	1A	45439	3B	45497	63A	45555 *	3B
45382	6J	45440	26F	45498	66B	45556 *	5A
45383	11A	45441	6J	45499	65B	45557 *	14B
45384	62B	45442	26F	45500 *	1A	45558 *	26F
45385	3A	45443	65B	45501 *	5A	45559 *	26F
45386	11A	45444	27F	45502 *	12B	45560 *	8A
45387	1A	45445	12B	45503 *	5A	45561 *	14B
45388	1E	45446	5A	45504 *	82E	45562 *	55A
45389	63B	45447	14B	45505 *	9A	45563 *	26F
45390	5A	45448	3D	45506 *	82E	45564 *	55A
45391	5B	45449	8F	45507 *	12B	45565 *	55A
45392	2E	45450	26B	45508	12B	45566 *	55A
45393	1E	45451	12B	45509 *	26A	45567 *	8A
45394	12B	45452	63A	45510	1A	45568 *	55A
45395	3B	45453	60A	45511 *	1A	45569 *	55A
45396	63B	45454	24K	45512 *	12B	45570 *	41C
45397	12B	45455	12A	45513	12B	45571 *	24E
45398	8A	45456	67D	45514 *	1B	45572 *	82E
45399	8A	45457	67D	45515 *	8A	45573 *	55A
45400	63B	45458	63A	45516 *	8A	45574 *	24E
45401	8A	45459	63A	45517	27A	45575 *	14B
45402	12B	45460	60A	45518 *	8A	45576 *	41C
45403	5B	45461	60A	45519 *	82E	45577 *	B2E
45404	1A	45462	66B	45520 *	9A	45578 *	9A
45405	3B	45463	63A	45521 *	8A	45579 *	14B
45406	84G	45464	24E	45522 *	1B	45580 *	24E
45407	14B	45465	63A	45523 *	1B	45581 *	55C

45582 * 24K	45641 * 16A	45699 * 82E	46109 * 55A
45583 * 8A	45642 * 26A	45700 * 26A	46110 * 5A
45584 * 24E	45643 * 5A	45701 * 26A	46111 * 9A
45585 * 14B	45644 * 9A	45702 * 26A	46112 * 55A
45586 * 8A	45645 * 26F	45703 * 5A	46113 * 55A
45587 * 9A	45646 * 55C	45704 * 12A	46114 * 8A
45588 * 12B	45647 * 3B	45705 * 24E	46115 * 9A
45589 * 55A	45648 * 17A	45706 * 26A	46116 * 5A
45590 * 41C	45649 * 14B	45707 * 67A	46117 * 55A
45591 * 5A	45650 * 16A	45708 * 55C	46118 * 5A
45592 * 1B	45651 * 82E	45709 * 3B	46119 * 8A
45593 * 12B	45652 * 14B	45710 * 26A	46120 * 5A
45594 * 41C	45653 * 24E	45711 * 67A	46121 * 66A
45595 * 9A	45654 * 41C	45712 * 9E	46122 * 9A
45596 * 8A	45655 * 5A	45713 * 12A	46123 * 8A
45597 * 55A	45656 * 41C	45714 * 12A	46124 * 8A
45598 * 14B	45657 * 12A	45715 * 12A	46125 * 5A
45599 * 12B	45658 * 55A	45716 * 12A	46126 * 12B
45600 * 26F	45659 * 55A	45717 * 27A	46127 * 6J
45601 * 1B	45660 * 82E	45718 * 12A	46128 * 5A
45602 * 41C	45661 * 26A	45719 * 27A	46129 * 5A
45603 * 1A	45662 * 82E	45720 * 67A	46130 * 14B
45604 * 5A	45663 * 17A	45721 * 5A	46131 * 9A
45605 * 5A	45664 * 41C	45722 * 1B	46132 * 8A
45606 * 1B	45665 * 67A	45723 * 12B	46133 * 14B
45607 * 41C	45666 * 5A	45724 * 12A	46134 * 5A
45608 * 55A	45667 * 16A	45725 * 41C	46135 * 5A
45609 * 41C	45668 * 26F	45726 * 5A	46136 * 12B
45610 * 17A	45669 * 1B	45727 * 63A	46137 * 9A
45611 * 16A	45670 * 8A	45728 * 12A	46138 * 5A
45612 * 14B	45671 * 9A	45729 * 12A	46139 * 1B
45613 * 6E	45672 * 12B	45730 * 12A	46140 * 9A
45614 * 14B	45673 * 63A	45731 * 12A	46141 * 12B
45615 * 14B	45674 * 5A	45732 * 12A	46142 * 8A
45616 * 14B	45675 * 55A	45733 * 8A	46143 * 9A
45617 * 12B	45676 * 1B	45734 * 3B	46144 * 1B
45618 * 14B	45677 * 67A	45735 * 1B	46145 * 55A
45619 * 55A	45678 * 8A	45736 * 5A	46146 * 1B
45620 * 16A	45679 * 12A	45737 * 3B	46147 * 8A
45621 * 67A	45680 * 9A	45738 * 3B	46148 * 14B
45622 * 14B	45681 * 8A	45739 * 55A	46149 * 6J
45623 * 5A	45682 * 82E	45740 * 1A	46150 * 5A
45624 * 6E	45683 * 41C	45741 * 3B	46151 * 5A
45625 * 5A	45684 * 5A	45742 * 3B	46152 * 5A
45626 * 17A	45685 * 82E		46153 * 9A
45627 * 17A	45686 * 1B		46154 * 1B
45628 * 14B	45687 * 67A		46155 * 8A
45629 * 5A	45688 * 3B		46156 * 8A
45630 * 5A	45689 * 5A		46157 * 5A
45631 * 9A	45690 * 82E		46158 * 9A
45632 * 6E	45691 * 12A		46159 * 5A
45633 * 24K	45692 * 63A		46160 * 9A
45634 * 5A	45693 * 67A	46100 * 1B	46161 * 1B
45635 * 26A	45694 * 55A	46101 * 5A	46162 * 1B
45636 * 16A	45695 * 55C	46102 * 66A	46163 * 5A
45638 * 9A	45696 * 12A	46103 * 14B	46164 * 8A
45639 * 55A	45697 * 12A	46104 * 66A	46165 * 12B
45640 * 12A	45698 * 27A	46105 * 66A	46166 * 9A
		46106 * 9A	
		46107 * 66A	
		46108 * 9A	

46167 * 12B	46404 15B	46462 64A	46520 89B
46168 * 1B	46405 27B	46463 62B	46521 89B
46169 * 9A	46406 26D	46464 62B	46522 89B
46170 * 1B	46407 53E	46465 31A	46523 89A
46200 * 8A	46408 53E	46466 31A	46524 89A
46201 * 66A	46409 53E	46467 31A	46525 82B
46203 * 8A	46410 24J	46468 30E	46526 89A
46204 * 8A	46411 26A	46469 30E	46527 89A
46205 * 5A	46412 27B	46470 12D	
46206 * 5A	46413 56A	46471 51J	
46207 * 8A	46414 26D	46472 2A	
46208 * 8A	46415 53E	46473 51A	
46209 * 8A	46416 26D	46474 51A	
46210 * 66A	46417 26D	46475 51A	47000 17A
46211 * 8A	46418 26A	46476 52D	47001 27A
46212 * 5A	46419 26A	46477 51A	47002 27A
46220 * 5A	46420 2A	46478 51E	47003 18C
46221 * 5A	46421 3A	46479 51A	47004 18C
46222 * 66A	46422 8F	46480 50A	47005 6C
46223 * 66A	46423 3D	46481 50A	47006 6A
46224 * 66A	46424 1A	46482 51F	47007 17C
46225 * 5A	46425 3A	46483 56F	47008 24K
46226 * 12B	46426 24J	46484 26A	47009 6C
46227 * 66A	46427 3D	46485 26B	47160 6C
46228 * 5A	46428 8F	46486 26B	47161 24F
46229 * 1B	46429 5D	46487 26A	47162 64A
46230 * 66A	46430 5D	46488 11B	47163 64C
46231 * 66A	46431 1C	46489 11B	47164 6C
46232 * 66A	46432 11B	46490 3A	47165 24F
46233 * 5A	46433 11B	46491 11B	47166 6F
46234 * 5A	46434 8F	46492 3D	47167 66D
46235 * 5A	46435 56A	46493 55A	47168 66D
46236 * 12B	46436 26D	46494 41C	47169 66D
46237 * 12B	46437 26A	46495 15B	47190 82F
46238 * 12B	46438 56A	46496 15B	47191 82F
46239 * 1B	46439 27B	46497 17A	47200 14B
46240 * 1B	46440 17A	46498 55A	47201 24A
46241 * 5A	46441 24J	46499 17A	47202 14B
46242 * 1B	46442 24G	46500 17A	47203 15E
46243 * 5A	46443 17A	46501 16C	47204 14B
46244 * 12B	46444 15B	46502 17A	47205 14B
46245 * 1B	46445 6K	46503 89A	47207 26A
46246 * 5A	46446 2A	46504 89A	47209 14B
46247 * 1B	46447 11B	46505 89A	47210 14A
46248 * 5A	46448 8F	46506 82B	47211 14A
46249 * 5A	46449 12B	46507 89A	47212 14B
46250 * 12B	46450 41B	46508 89B	47213 15C
46251 * 5A	46451 41B	46509 89A	47214 14A
46252 * 5A	46452 24G	46510 89A	47216 14A
46253 * 5A	46453 55A	46511 89A	47217 26A
46254 * 1B	46454 15C	46512 89A	47218 18C
46255 * 12B	46455 11B	46513 89A	47221 41E
46256 * 1B	46456 11B	46514 89A	47223 18A
46257 * 12B	46457 12B	46515 89A	47224 26A
46400 41C	46458 1A	46516 89B	47225 27E
46401 85E	46459 3A	46517 82B	47226 14A
46402 17A	46460 61A	46518 89B	47228 27E
46403 15B	46461 64A	46519 89B	47229 14B

47230	27A	47304	1B	47362	8B	47420	55A
47231	17B	47305	27B	47363	3B	47421	50A
47235	27E	47306	30A	47364	26F	47422	85E
47236	17B	47307	1B	47365	26F	47423	18C
47238	24J	47308	85F	47366	8G	47424	41E
47239	50A	47309	26F	47367	27F	47425	27B
47241	14B	47310	1B	47368	6J	47426	41E
47247	18A	47311	30A	47369	9A	47427	24G
47248	14A	47312	33A	47370	5D	47428	24G
47250	15C	47313	15C	47371	6A	47429	16D
47254	50A	47314	8C	47372	6G	47430	26F
47255	56F	47315	1A	47373	24L	47431	6C
47257	17B	47316	82F	47374	6A	47432	14A
47259	27B	47317	24L	47375	6A	47433	14A
47260	14B	47318	2E	47376	8B	47434	14A
47261	14C	47319	24K	47377	12B	47435	14A
47262	33A	47320	27F	47378	26F	47436	50A
47263	41E	47321	6J	47379	56E	47437	14B
47264	14E	47322	11A	47380	5D	47438	50D
47265	15A	47323	11A	47381	24J	47439	6J
47266	56F	47324	6C	47382	3A	47440	26A
47267	9A	47325	27F	47383	6A	47441	15C
47268	8B	47326	12B	47384	5B	47442	15C
47269	2A	47327	27F	47385	3A	47443	56B
47270	5D	47328	33A	47386	24B	47444	8G
47271	56A	47329	67A	47387	8B	47445	5E
47272	18C	47330	5B	47388	8C	47446	56F
47273	15A	47331	66C	47389	6A	47447	17C
47274	15C	47332	12A	47390	11B	47448	50A
47275	82F	47333	82E	47391	CW	47449	15D
47276	85F	47334	50A	47392	9B	47450	5B
47277	16A	47335	56D	47393	8G	47451	5D
47278	18C	47336	9B	47394	6G	47452	8G
47279	14E	47337	12B	47395	9A	47453	8G
47280	5B	47338	6C	47396	3A	47454	24G
47281	5D	47339	24L	47397	3B	47455	41E
47282	30A	47340	12B	47398	3B	47457	17C
47283	14B	47341	9A	47399	26F	47458	16D
47284	26F	47342	24L	47400	9A	47459	17C
47285	2B	47343	9A	47401	26F	47460	17C
47286	WW	47344	5D	47402	8A	47461	17C
47287	11A	47345	9A	47403	50A	47462	50D
47288	12B	47346	9B	47404	8A	47463	56A
47289	9B	47347	9A	47405	56F	47464	17B
47290	11B	47348	1B	47406	24L	47465	82F
47291	9A	47349	3A	47407	8A	47466	18B
47292	12B	47350	6K	47408	12B	47467	5B
47293	24K	47351	33A	47409	24L	47468	24J
47294	3A	47352	8B	47410	24L	47469	24J
47295	12B	47353	8A	47411	8A	47470	24J
47296	3A	47354	3A	47412	1A	47471	24J
47297	6A	47355	1C	47413	24K	47472	24K
47298	8G	47356	9A	47414	5B	47473	3B
47299	56E	47357	8B	47415	12B	47474	3A
47300	31F	47358	12A	47416	8A	47475	5C
47301	27A	47359	5C	47417	85E	47476	6J
47302	1B	47360	24K	47418	50A	47477	27A
47303	27A	47361	11B	47419	55F	47478	87K

47479	87K	47537	12A	47596	5D	47656	8A
47480	27A	47538	56A	47597	8A	47657	8B
47481	87K	47539	85E	47598	5E	47658	5D
47482	1A	47540	12A	47599	5D	47659	8B
47483	1A	47541	66A	47600	6A	47660	17A
47484	33A	47542	82G	47601	9B	47661	5B
47485	17B	47543	15C	47602	12B	47662	11B
47486	1A	47544	82E	47603	8B	47664	5B
47487	8A	47545	41E	47604	11B	47665	5C
47488	8A	47546	26A	47605	11A	47666	12B
47489	8A	47547	26A	47606	5E	47667	12A
47490	8D	47548	41B	47607	50A	47668	1B
47491	26F	47549	14E	47608	5B	47669	1B
47492	12B	47550	82E	47609	5D	47670	5B
47493	8C	47551	18A	47610	5D	47671	1B
47494	3E	47552	82E	47611	27F	47672	26F
47495	1B	47554	14C	47612	8C	47673	9A
47496	82F	47555	33A	47614	12B	47674	6C
47497	6C	47556	50A	47615	6B	47675	11A
47498	8A	47557	82F	47616	8D	47676	11A
47499	2E	47558	6H	47618	5B	47677	6C
47500	1E	47559	1A	47619	41E	47678	82E
47501	1A	47560	8C	47620	41E	47679	17C
47502	17B	47561	3E	47621	26F	47680	5B
47503	11A	47562	24A	47622	6F	47681	27E
47504	6A	47563	17A	47623	85E		
47505	11A	47564	11A	47624	41B		
47506	85E	47565	6C	47625	41E	48000	16A
47507	6C	47566	8A	47626	41E	48001	16C
47508	56E	47567	56A	47627	6C	48002	21A
47509	56E	47568	55C	47628	6F	48003	16B
47510	56A	47569	55C	47629	17A	48004	16B
47511	6H	47570	55C	47630	41E	48005	17A
47512	33A	47571	56A	47631	6G	48006	16B
47513	41B	47572	56A	47632	56B	48007	15C
47514	1B	47573	56A	47633	5E	48008	16B
47515	12A	47574	26B	47634	50C	48009	16B
47516	5B	47575	24B	47635	56F	48010	15C
47517	11A	47576	24B	47636	41B	48011	41D
47518	11A	47577	24B	47637	41E	48012	2A
47519	8A	47578	26B	47638	16D	48016	2B
47520	11A	47579	26B	47639	24J	48017	8E
47521	1E	47580	56A	47640	56B	48018	2A
47522	1B	47581	50D	47641	17B	48020	2B
47523	5B	47582	56A	47642	14B	48024	16C
47524	5B	47583	26B	47643	17B	48026	41D
47525	11B	47584	26D	47644	14B	48027	15C
47526	5B	47585	26B	47645	14B	48029	16B
47527	12A	47586	24B	47646	6B	48033	14A
47528	9A	47587	5D	47647	5D	48035	2A
47529	1B	47588	5C	47648	5D	48036	1A
47530	6C	47589	5B	47649	5C	48037	41E
47531	11A	47590	5C	47650	6B	48039	8C
47532	24J	47591	8B	47651	8C	48045	8E
47533	15C	47592	CW	47652	8B	48046	8E
47534	15C	47593	11B	47653	5C	48050	15B
47535	18C	47594	2B	47654	8B	48053	15D
47536	66A	47595	5E	47655	27E	48054	8C

48055	55B	48122	1A	48180	14A	48258	2B
48056	17C	48123	55D	48181	41D	48259	6B
48057	18B	48124	15B	48182	17B	48260	6C
48060	18B	48125	18C	48183	18A	48261	16A
48061	15C	48126	55B	48184	18A	48262	5B
48062	14A	48127	18B	48185	18A	48263	5B
48063	17C	48128	18A	48186	18A	48264	8C
48064	16A	48129	1A	48187	18A	48265	56D
48065	18C	48130	55D	48188	8B	48266	15C
48067	55A	48131	2A	48189	41B	48267	16B
48069	15B	48132	14A	48190	9F	48268	9D
48070	55D	48133	15C	48191	9F	48269	2E
48073	16B	48134	1A	48192	17C	48270	17A
48074	1A	48135	8E	48193	16B	48271	18A
48075	41D	48136	2A	48194	18A	48272	16C
48076	55B	48137	16B	48195	18A	48273	9E
48077	2B	48138	41D	48196	18A	48274	56D
48078	55D	48139	8E	48197	18A	48275	9A
48079	17A	48140	41D	48198	9F	48276	55B
48080	56F	48141	15B	48199	41E	48277	16C
48081	16B	48142	15B	48200	41E	48278	9D
48082	18C	48143	15B	48201	18A	48279	16A
48083	17A	48144	41B	48202	56D	48280	8A
48084	55B	48145	18A	48203	2A	48281	55D
48085	2A	48146	55D	48204	18B	48282	16C
48088	16C	48147	2E	48205	18C	48283	55A
48089	18C	48148	26A	48206	8C	48284	18A
48090	2E	48149	15C	48207	1E	48285	15B
48092	16B	48150	41D	48208	9F	48286	16A
48093	55D	48151	8A	48209	41D	48287	5B
48094	8B	48152	8A	48210	41E	48288	9E
48095	18C	48153	17A	48211	15C	48289	5B
48096	16B	48154	2B	48212	18C	48290	2E
48097	16B	48155	8E	48213	41E	48291	5B
48098	16B	48156	16C	48214	16B	48292	5B
48099	18A	48157	55A	48215	16B	48293	17A
48100	16B	48158	55A	48216	41D	48294	5B
48101	21A	48159	55A	48217	16A	48295	8E
48102	16B	48160	55B	48218	16A	48296	8B
48103	41E	48161	9F	48219	17B	48297	8E
48104	55A	48162	55D	48220	21A	48301	15B
48105	21A	48163	14A	48221	18A	48302	17A
48106	8B	48164	41E	48222	55D	48303	6E
48107	15C	48165	9A	48223	16B	48304	18A
48108	16A	48166	8D	48224	16B	48305	2E
48109	14A	48167	17B	48225	16B	48306	18A
48110	84G	48168	17A	48246	6B	48307	84G
48111	5B	48169	55D	48247	8B	48308	8D
48112	18B	48170	16A	48248	5B	48309	87K
48113	55D	48171	1A	48249	8A	48310	3A
48114	16B	48172	84G	48250	3A	48311	55B
48115	26A	48173	2A	48251	5B	48312	2B
48116	18C	48174	5B	48252	5B	48313	15B
48117	16A	48175	8D	48253	6F	48314	18A
48118	18A	48176	41D	48254	8E	48315	21A
48119	16C	48177	16A	48255	5B	48316	9F
48120	6C	48178	41B	48256	5B	48317	9F
48121	17A	48179	41B	48257	5B	48318	8A

48319	18A	48377	16A	48435	2B	48507	18A
48320	2B	48378	15A	48436	82B	48508	41D
48321	12A	48379	16B	48437	2A	48509	8A
48322	9D	48380	15B	48438	84G	48510	17A
48323	8C	48381	14A	48439	55D	48511	8C
48324	18A	48382	15D	48440	1A	48512	8A
48325	1A	48383	16B	48441	8B	48513	8A
48326	8D	48384	18A	48442	16C	48514	3A
48327	9F	48385	15A	48443	55A	48515	41E
48328	84G	48386	15A	48444	6E	48516	5B
48329	9F	48387	18A	48445	2E	48517	18A
48330	87K	48388	21A	48446	1E	48518	1A
48331	41E	48389	9A	48447	16C	48519	9D
48332	18A	48390	17A	48448	6C	48520	8B
48333	18A	48391	41D	48449	2B	48521	8E
48334	16B	48392	16B	48450	82B	48522	8C
48335	1A	48393	16B	43451	9D	48523	21A
48336	21A	48394	56F	48452	87K	48524	87K
48337	55D	48395	16B	48453	3A	48525	87K
48338	18A	48396	41D	48454	55A	48526	2A
48339	21A	48397	41D	48455	6C	48527	18C
48340	8E	48398	2B	48456	2B	48528	16B
48341	41E	48399	55A	48457	8A	48529	5B
48342	21A	48400	87K	48458	6B	48530	18A
48343	2B	48401	17B	48459	82B	48531	8B
48344	6E	48402	6E	48460	84G	48532	55D
48345	2B	48403	17A	48461	87K	48533	41E
48346	41E	48404	82B	48462	8E	48534	2E
48347	84G	48405	16C	48463	87K	48535	1E
48348	8B	48406	9F	48464	12A	48536	12A
48349	6C	48407	41D	48465	9A	48537	55D
48350	18A	48408	6E	48466	55D	48538	18A
48351	21A	48409	87K	48467	15B	48539	41E
48352	55B	48410	82B	48468	84G	48540	55D
48353	18B	48411	5B	48469	82B	48541	16C
48354	84G	48412	6E	48470	87K	48542	55D
48355	15B	48413	16B	48471	6E	48543	9F
48356	15B	48414	14A	48472	12A	48544	1E
48357	56D	48415	6E	48473	55D	48545	18A
48358	55B	48416	1A	48474	84G	48546	41E
48359	18C	48417	6E	48475	82B	48547	18C
48360	2E	48418	6E	48476	1A	48548	5B
48361	18A	48419	87K	48477	3A	48549	1E
48362	18A	48420	82B	48478	84G	48550	1E
48363	18A	48421	9D	48479	8A	48551	1A
48364	18C	48422	2E	48490	18A	48552	16B
48365	2A	48423	2A	48491	26A	48553	26A
48366	3A	48424	6E	48492	15A	48554	8D
48367	18A	48425	8D	48493	2E	48555	8E
48368	8E	48426	8E	48494	18C	48556	3A
48369	84G	48427	2A	48495	14A	48557	9F
48370	18A	48428	9A	48500	9A	48558	8D
48371	18C	48429	9F	48501	9F	48559	2A
48372	26A	48430	6E	48502	8D	48600	1A
48373	8B	48431	82B	48503	9F	48601	1A
48374	15A	48432	17C	48504	8A	48602	3A
48375	3A	48433	8A	48505	9D	48603	1A
48376	14A	48434	82B	48506	8D	48604	18A

48605	8E	48663	41E	48721	55B	48915	8F
48606	18A	48664	55D	48722	3A	48922	5B
48607	18A	48665	1A	48723	2B	48926	26F
48608	55D	48666	16A	48724	84G	48927	2B
48609	15B	48667	6F	48725	3A	48930	3A
48610	1E	48668	2A	48726	3D	48932	9D
48611	15B	48669	21A	48727	3A	48942	8C
48612	12A	48670	55D	48728	18A	48943	5C
48613	9F	48671	15A	48729	1A	48944	8C
48614	16A	48672	18A	48730	87K	48950	3B
48615	18A	48673	16B	48731	9F	48951	1E
48616	18A	48674	3A	48732	87K	48953	1E
48617	15A	48675	16A	48733	3A	48964	3A
48618	41E	48676	9F	48734	5B		
48619	15D	48677	9F	48735	87K		
48620	18A	48678	15A	48736	15A		
48621	16C	48679	9D	48737	87K		
48622	55B	48680	9A	48738	84G	49002	2B
48623	2B	48681	18A	48739	84G	49007	8F
48624	1A	48682	9F	48740	9D	49008	8C
48625	15A	48683	8B	48741	9E	49009	8F
48626	5B	48684	6C	48742	8E	49010	9B
48627	15A	48685	18A	48743	5B	49018	8F
48628	1A	48686	2B	48744	9A	49020	8F
48629	1A	48687	21A	48745	26A	49021	3A
48630	5B	48688	1E	48746	8B	49023	8F
48631	8C	48689	55D	48747	8C	49025	8F
48632	1A	48690	15B	48748	16A	49027	26F
48633	5B	48691	6C	48749	8D	49034	26F
48634	9F	48692	5B	48750	14A	49037	3B
48635	16A	48693	5B	48751	2B	49044	3B
48636	18A	48694	18A	48752	3D	49045	3A
48637	18A	48695	15A	48753	8D	49048	5B
48638	14A	48696	16A	48754	1E	49049	8F
48639	16A	48697	8D	48755	3A	49061	1E
48640	18A	48698	18A	48756	12A	49063	3A
48641	55B	48699	15A	48757	2A	49064	86K
48642	41B	48700	21A	48758	12A	49070	1A
48643	16C	48701	16C	48759	15B	49077	3A
48644	15A	48702	56F	48760	87K	49078	1A
48645	15B	48703	55B	48761	87K	49079	8F
48646	2A	48704	15B	48762	3A	49081	5C
48647	21A	48705	3A	48763	16A	49082	8A
48648	1A	48706	87K	48764	1A	49087	26F
48649	1A	48707	84G	48765	41B	49093	1E
48650	18B	48708	12A	48766	3A	49094	1E
48651	15A	48709	8D	48767	3A	49099	3A
48652	55B	48710	55D	48768	87K	49104	24K
48653	16A	48711	8E	48769	3A	49105	2E
48654	17C	48712	9D	48770	16B	49106	3A
48655	5B	48713	3A	48771	8D	49112	2B
48656	1A	48714	8B	48772	41E	49114	3A
48657	1A	48715	8B	48773	66A	49115	5C
48658	2B	48716	26A	48774	66A	49116	8A
48659	5B	48717	8E	48775	66A	49119	26F
48660	84G	48718	3D	48895	3D	49120	2B
48661	18B	48719	3D	48898	1E	49122	1A
48662	18A	48720	26A	48905	8F		

60

49125	3A	49310	1E	49421	26F	50781	27C
49126	5C	49311	8F	49422	8F	50795	55F
49129	8F	49313	3A	49423	9D	50850	26C
49130	24L	49314	2B	49424	8C	51204	26B
49132	8A	49315	9D	49425	2B	51206	27A
49134	8C	49321	8F	49426	26F	51207	26B
49137	8A	49323	26F	49427	8A	51217	82E
49139	8F	49327	3A	49428	9A	51218	8D
49141	24K	49328	3A	49429	8A	51221	82E
49142	2B	49335	26F	49430	2B	51222	53E
49143	8C	49340	26F	49431	2B	51227	27A
49144	2B	49342	2B	49432	2B	51229	27A
49147	26F	49343	3A	49433	8C	51231	27A
49149	26F	49344	1A	49434	8A	51232	27A
49150	8F	49348	9D	49435	8A	51237	27A
49153	8C	49350	2B	49436	8F	51241	53E
49154	8F	49352	8F	49437	8A	51244	53E
49155	8F	49355	8A	49438	8F	51246	27A
49158	5B	49357	5C	49439	9A	51253	27A
49160	8F	49361	3A	49440	2B	51319	9G
49164	1A	49366	8A	49441	2B	51336	24F
49173	8A	49373	3A	49442	2A	51343	26A
49181	2B	49375	8A	49443	1E	51358	56D
49191	9B	49377	2A	49444	15F	51371	26A
49196	24K	49378	8F	49445	8A	51408	26C
49198	5C	49381	8F	49446	5C	51412	CW
49199	26F	49382	24K	49447	15F	51413	26B
49200	8A	49386	26F	49448	8G	51419	24F
49203	8F	49387	3A	49449	24L	51429	HW
49209	26F	49391	9D	49450	1E	51441	8G
49210	9D	49392	8A	49451	8C	51444	CW
49216	3A	49394	8A	49452	3B	51445	8A
49224	8A	49395	9D	49453	9B	51446	CW
49228	8F	49396	24K	49454	5B	51458	26A
49229	5B	49397	8C	49505	26B	51484	9G
49234	26F	49398	8C	49508	26A	51486	26C
49240	3B	49399	8A	49509	26B	51496	26B
49243	84G	49400	9D	49511	26A	51497	26A
49245	2A	49401	8F	49515	26A	51498	26C
49246	3A	49402	8F	49544	26C	51524	24F
49249	26F	49403	1E	49578	26B	51537	27B
49252	24L	49404	8A	49582	27B	51544	27A
49262	8G	49405	8A	49586	26A		
49266	2A	49406	8C	49592	26A		
49267	8F	49407	5B	49618	26C		
49268	8F	49408	8F	49624	26A		
49270	2B	49409	86K	49627	26B		
49275	3A	49410	5C	49637	27D		
49277	1A	49411	3B	49640	27B		
49278	3A	49412	8A	49662	26C	52044	56A
49281	9D	49413	1A	49667	26A	52089	56D
49287	1E	49414	2B	49668	26B	52093	CW
49288	8G	49415	2B	49674	26C	52095	24B
49289	1E	49416	8A			52108	26A
49293	2B	49417	5B			52119	6K
49304	8G	49418	9B			52121	56D
49306	8C	49419	8A	50721	27A	52129	26D
49308	3A	49420	8C	50746	27C	52133	56A
						52135	27B

52139	56D	52464	CW	54495	60C	55232	68B
52140	26A	52466	26E	54496	60A	55233	64C
52141	26A	52515	56D	54497	66D	55234	68D
52154	53E	52523	26C	54498	66D	55235	67A
52161	26A	52526	24B	54499	63A	55236	60A
52162	6K	52527	26D	54500	63A	55237	66A
52171	27B			54501	65B	55238	65F
52179	24B			54502	68B	55239	66A
52182	24C			54503	63A	55240	68C
52183	26E			54504	63B	55260	68D
52201	26F			54505	64D	55261	64D
52207	5B	53800	82F	54506	66D	55262	67C
52218	CW	53801	82F	54507	68B	55263	63D
52225	CW	53802	82F	54508	68C	55264	67B
52230	26A	53803	82F			55265	66A
52232	8C	53804	82F			55266	67A
52240	26E	53805	82F			55267	66D
52244	53E	53806	82F			55268	66A
52248	26E	53807	82F			55269	60E
52252	53E	53808	82F	55124	68B		
52260	27B	53809	82F	55126	63D		
52269	26E	53810	82F	55165	64B		
52270	26A			55167	66A		
52271	26A			55169	66A		
52275	26A			55173	60B		
52278	26A			55185	61C		
52289	26D	54461	64D	55189	66A		
52290	24C	54462	66B	55195	63B		
52305	53E	54463	60A	55198	60A	56025	RW
52311	27B	54464	66B	55199	60A	56027	CW
52312	CW	54465	66B	55200	63A	56029	65D
52319	53E	54466	60B	55201	66A	56031	66D
52322	26E	54467	63A	55202	64C	56032	CW
52341	26A	54468	66D	55203	67B	56035	66D
52345	5B	54469	63A	55204	65F	56038	60A
52348	26C	54470	60C	55206	67A	56039	65G
52351	56E	54471	60E	55207	66A	56151	65B
52355	56A	54472	60E	55208	63D	56153	66A
52378	27B	54473	60E	55209	63A	56154	66A
52389	26C	54474	65B	55210	64C	56156	67A
52393	26C	54475	67B	55211	67B	56158	66A
52400	56E	54476	63B	55214	65F	56159	66A
52410	26E	54477	64D	55215	63D	56160	66A
52411	56E	54478	64C	55216	60A	56163	66D
52413	56F	54479	66D	55217	62A	56165	66D
52415	26C	54480	60C	55218	63A	56166	66D
52429	24C	54482	60B	55219	67A	56167	66D
52431	26A	54483	65B	55220	63D	56168	65G
52438	8C	54484	60B	55221	61C	56169	65B
52441	CW	54485	63A	55222	63B	56170	66D
52443	26D	54486	63A	55223	66A	56171	65D
52445	24C	54487	60A	55224	66A	56172	65E
52452	56E	54488	60B	55225	67A	56173	66D
52455	26A	54489	63A	55226	60A	56232	63B
52456	24C	54490	64D	55227	60A	56235	12A
52458	24C	54491	60D	55228	66A	56239	66A
52459	CW	54492	68C	55229	64C	56240	61B
52461	56F	54493	60A	55230	63A	56241	66A
		54494	63A	55231	67C	56242	66C

56246	63A	56364	67A	57274	67D	57375	68C
56252	67C	56365	63B	57275	66A	57377	66B
56256	66C	56367	66B	57276	63B	57378	68B
56259	67D	56368	67B	57278	66B	57383	67B
56260	66A	56370	65B	57279	67C	57384	66C
56264	66B	56371	66C	57284	67B	57385	64D
56266	66A	56372	67C	57285	65F	57386	64D
56269	66B	56373	12A	57287	65F	57389	66A
56278	61B	56374	12A	57288	66A	57392	67C
56279	67A	56376	65F	57291	66B	57398	66C
56285	66B			57292	66A	57404	66B
56286	66C			57295	67B	57407	66C
56287	66C			57296	65D	57411	65B
56289	65B			57299	66B	57414	66B
56290	63A			57300	67A	57416	66D
56291	60E			57302	68B	57417	66A
56292	66A			57303	66B	57418	66A
56295	66A			57307	66C	57419	66A
56296	66C			57309	67D	57424	63A
56298	66A			57311	65B	57426	65B
56300	60A			57314	65D	57429	65D
56302	68C			57317	66A	57431	66C
56304	66A	57232	63B	57319	66A	57432	66A
56305	60A	57233	63B	57321	66C	57434	65B
56308	66C	57236	67B	57324	63B	57435	66B
56309	66C	57237	66B	57325	66B	57436	66B
56310	68B	57238	68C	57326	66B	57441	63C
56312	64C	57239	66A	57328	66B	57444	66A
56313	64C	57240	65B	57329	68B	57445	68C
56316	12A	57241	67A	57331	67B	57446	66C
56318	66A	57242	66C	57335	66C	57447	66C
56321	66C	57243	63B	57336	65D	57448	66A
56322	66A	57244	66C	57338	65F	57451	64D
56324	66A	57245	65D	57339	63B	57461	66B
56325	61B	57246	63B	57340	68C	57462	66B
56326	61B	57247	66B	57341	65D	57463	66A
56327	68B	57249	67A	57345	63A	57465	66A
56331	63A	57250	66C	57347	66A	57470	65D
56332	12A	57251	65B	57348	67D	57472	65D
56333	12A	57252	63B	57349	68B	57473	63A
56335	66A	57253	65B	57350	65B	57550	64C
56336	65D	57254	65D	57353	67B	57552	66D
56337	66B	57256	66B	57354	67C	57553	66A
56338	66B	57257	63B	57355	67D	57554	65D
56340	12A	57258	65B	57356	67D	57555	66A
56341	60A	57259	65G	57357	67D	57557	65B
56343	63B	57261	65B	57359	67A	57558	65B
56344	67C	57262	67C	57360	66A	57559	64C
56347	63A	57263	67D	57361	66A	57560	64C
56348	61C	57264	63B	57362	68B	57562	67B
56349	66A	57265	65F	57363	66B	57563	66A
56352	67D	57266	67D	57364	67C	57564	66A
56356	66B	57267	66B	57365	66A	57565	64C
56359	63A	57268	66A	57366	65F	57566	67D
56360	66C	57269	65B	57367	66A	57568	68D
56361	67A	57270	66B	57369	66A	57569	67C
56362	66C	57271	66A	57370	66C	57570	67B
56363	67C	57273	65D	57373	65B	57571	63D

63

57572	67B	57650	67B	58167	21B	60006 *	34A
57575	60A	57651	67B	58168	21A	60007 *	34A
57576	63B	57652	65D	58169	3A	60008 *	34A
57577	67B	57653	12A	58170	41D	60009 *	64B
57579	67D	57654	64C	58171	6A	60010 *	34A
57580	67C	57655	64D	58173	18A	60011 *	64B
57581	66A	57658	67C	58174	3A	60012 *	64B
57583	64D	57659	64D	58175	16A	60013 *	34A
57585	60D	57661	60A	58177	11A	60014 *	34A
57586	60B	57663	66C	58178	3E	60015 *	34A
57587	60C	57665	66C	58181	3A	60016 *	52A
57590	67D	57666	66B	58182	3D	60017 *	34A
57591	60B	57667	63D	58183	3B	60018 *	52A
57592	65D	57668	66B	58185	3E	60019 *	52A
57593	66B	57669	67D	58186	17B	60020 *	52A
57594	60A	57670	64D	58190	11A	60021 *	34A
57595	66B	57671	67B	58191	55D	60022 *	34A
57596	67C	57672	67B	58197	55D	60023 *	52A
57597	60B	57673	67D	58198	41D	60024 *	64B
57599	66B	57674	66A	58199	2A	60025 *	34A
57600	68B	57679	63B	58204	3B	60026 *	34A
57601	68B	57681	66B	58209	15D	60027 *	64B
57602	68B	57682	66D	58213	9E	60028 *	34A
57603	66A	57684	67C	58214	14E	60029 *	34A
57604	64D	57686	65B	58215	12B	60030 *	34A
57605	65D	57688	66B	58217	11A	60031 *	64B
57607	65D	57689	67B	58218	2A	60032 *	34A
57608	64D	57690	66D	58219	17A	60033 *	34A
57609	66C	57691	65F	58220	3E	60034 *	34A
57611	67C			58221	11A	60035 *	64B
57612	65D			58228	17C	60036 *	50B
57613	64D	58065	40A	58246	15D	60037 *	64B
57614	67C	58086	82F	58260	55D	60038 *	52A
57615	67C	58115	11A	58261	21A	60039 *	34A
57617	65B	58116	11A	58271	5B	60040 *	52A
57618	64D	58118	3B	58279	26F	60041 *	64B
57619	66D	58119	3B	58281	3B	60042 *	52A
57620	60E	58120	11A	58283	3A	60043 *	64B
57621	68B	58122	3A	58287	6K	60044 *	34A
57622	66A	58123	11A	58291	11A	60045 *	52A
57623	68B	58124	3B	58293	6K	60046 *	36A
57625	66A	58128	17B	58295	3B	60047 *	34F
57626	64D	58130	17A	58298	15D	60048 *	34F
57627	67D	58131	14B	58305	17B	60049 *	34F
57628	67C	58132	17A	58308	2A	60050 *	34F
57630	66C	58135	5B	58850	17C	60051 *	52A
57631	65B	58137	17C			60052 *	52A
57632	60B	58138	21B			60053 *	51A
57633	67C	58143	21B			60054 *	34F
57634	61C	58144	17A			60055 *	34A
57635	64D	58146	41D			60056 *	34F
57637	67B	58148	17B			60057 *	64B
57638	66B	58153	18A			60058 *	51A
57640	67C	58158	17A			60059 *	34A
57642	63B	58160	17B	60001 *	52A	60060 *	52A
57643	67B	58163	15D	60002 *	52A	60061 *	34A
57644	67C	58165	17B	60003 *	34A	60062 *	34A
57645	64C	58166	18A	60004 *	64B	60063 *	34F
				60005 *	52A		

60064 * 36A	60122 * 36A	60517 * 52B	60834 62B
60065 * 34F	60123 * 56C	60518 * 52A	60835 * 52B
60066 * 34A	60124 * 52A	60519 * 64B	60836 64A
60067 * 36A	60125 * 36A	60520 * 34F	60837 50A
60068 * 12C	60126 * 52B	60521 * 52A	60838 62B
60069 * 52D	60127 * 52B	60522 * 50A	60839 50A
60070 * 52A	60128 * 36A	60523 * 34E	60840 64A
60071 * 52A	60129 * 52A	60524 * 50A	60841 36A
60072 * 52D	60130 * 56C	60525 * 61B	60842 15E
60073 * 52B	60131 * 56C	60526 * 50A	60843 52D
60074 * 50B	60132 * 52A	60527 * 62B	60844 62B
60075 * 52A	60133 * 56C	60528 * 62B	60845 34E
60076 * 52A	60134 * 56C	60529 * 64B	60846 52B
60077 * 52B	60135 * 52A	60530 * 64B	60847 * 50A
60078 * 52A	60136 * 36A	60531 * 61B	60848 51A
60079 * 12C	60137 * 52A	60532 * 61B	60849 36A
60080 * 52B	60138 * 50A	60533 * 34F	60850 34E
60081 * 50B	60139 * 36A	60534 * 64B	60851 61B
60082 * 52B	60140 * 50A	60535 * 64B	60852 36A
60083 * 52B	60141 * 56C	60536 * 64B	60853 34E
60084 * 50B	60142 * 52A	60537 * 64B	60854 34A
60085 * 52B	60143 * 52A	60538 * 52A	60855 50A
60086 * 50B	60144 * 36A	60539 * 52B	60856 50A
60087 * 64B	60145 * 52A	60700 36A	60857 36A
60088 * 52B	60146 * 50A	60300 * 34A	60858 31B
60089 * 64B	60147 * 52A	60801 52D	60859 56C
60090 * 64B	60148 * 56C	60802 52B	60860 * 52A
60091 * 52A	60149 * 36A	60803 31B	60861 56B
60092 * 52B	60150 * 52A	60804 62B	60862 34A
60093 * 12C	60151 * 52A	60805 52A	60863 15E
60094 * 64B	60152 * 64B	60806 52B	60864 50A
60095 * 12C	60153 * 50A	60807 52A	60865 52D
60096 * 64B	60154 * 52A	60808 52A	60866 36A
60097 * 64B	60155 * 52A	60809 * 52A	60867 34E
60098 * 64B	60156 * 36A	60810 52B	60868 52A
60099 * 64B	60157 * 36A	60811 52B	60869 34E
60100 * 64B	60158 * 36A	60812 52B	60870 36A
60101 * 64B	60159 * 64B	60813 64B	60871 34A
60102 * 36A	60160 * 64B	60814 34A	60872 * 36A
60103 * 34A	60161 * 64B	60815 2F	60873 * 64B
60104 * 36A	60162 * 64B	60816 64B	60874 34E
60105 * 34F	60500 * 34E	60817 36A	60875 34E
60106 * 34F	60501 * 50A	60818 64A	60876 50A
60107 * 34F	60502 * 50A	60819 64B	60877 50A
60108 * 36A	60503 * 50A	60820 34A	60878 50A
60109 * 34A	60504 * 34E	60821 34E	60879 15E
60110 * 34A	60505 * 34E	60822 62B	60880 36A
60111 * 34F	60506 * 34E	60823 64A	60881 36A
60112 * 36A	60507 * 64B	60824 64B	60882 64A
60113 * 36A	60508 * 34E	60825 64A	60883 64A
60114 * 36A	60509 * 64B	60826 64B	60884 56B
60115 * 52A	60510 * 64B	60827 64B	60885 56C
60116 * 52B	60511 * 52B	60828 50A	60886 52B
60117 * 56C	60512 * 50A	60829 34E	60887 50A
60118 * 56C	60513 * 34F	60830 31B	60888 61B
60119 * 36A	60514 * 34E	60831 15E	60889 36A
60120 * 56C	60515 * 50A	60832 34E	60890 2F
60121 * 50A	60516 * 52A	60833 52A	60891 52B

60892	64A	60950	34A	61020 *	56F	61079	40B
60893	34E	60951	64B	61021 *	51G	61080	53B
60894	64A	60952	52A	61022 *	52A	61081	64B
60895	50A	60953	64A	61023 *	56F	61082	40B
60896	36A	60954	50A	61024 *	51G	61083	41A
60897	34E	60955	61B	61025 *	52D	61084	50A
60398	61B	60956	36A	61026 *	40A	61085	15E
60399	36A	60957	64B	61027 *	34D	61086	50A
60900	64A	60958	64A	61028 *	15E	61087	36A
60901	52B	60959	64B	61029 *	64A	61088	40E
60902	34A	60960	50A	61030 *	51E	61089	30A
60903	34A	60961	50A	61031 *	51L	61090	34D
60904	52A	60962	52B	61032 *	51E	61091	34D
60905	36A	60963	50A	61033 *	41A	61092	40E
60906	34E	60964 *	52A	61034 *	51A	61093	34D
60907	50A	60965	64A	61035 *	50B	61094	34D
60903	34E	60966	34E	61036 *	36A	61095	31F
60909	36A	60967	52A	61037 *	51G	61096	31F
60910	52B	60968	50A	61038 *	50B	61097	34D
60911	15E	60969	64A	61039 *	56F	61098	40B
60912	34E	60970	61B	61040 *	56D	61099	64A
60913	52D	60971	64A	61041	41A	61100	52C
60914	34A	60972	61B	61042	32A	61101	62C
60915	2F	60973	61B	61043	32A	61102	62B
60916	56B	60974	50A	61044	41A	61103	62A
60917	36A	60975	50A	61045	32A	61104	31A
60918	50A	60976	52B	61046	32A	61105	41A
60919	61B	60977	50A	61047	41A	61106	15E
60920	64B	60978	52B	61048	32A	61107	36A
60921	36A	60979	52A	61049	56F	61108	64A
60922	52B	60980	64A	61050	41A	61109	30A
60923	52A	60981	50A	61051	41A	61110	56B
60924	34A	60982	50A	61052	32B	61111	30F
60925	50A	60983	34A	61053	50A	61112	41F
60926	52D			61054	32B	61113	34E
60927	64B			61055	32B	61114	36A
60928	36A			61056	32B	61115	56C
60929	52A			61058	32B	61116	14D
60930	36A	61000 *	30E	61059	32B	61117	65C
60931	64A	61001 *	32B	61060	34E	61118	62A
60932	52B	61002 *	50A	61061	51C	61119	30A
60933	64A	61003 *	30F	61062	50B	61120	36A
60934	52A	61004 *	30F	61063	15E	61121	36A
60935	36A	61005 *	30F	61064	12C	61122	36A
60936	36A	61006 *	30F	61065	53A	61123	56B
60937	64A	61007 *	64B	61066	31A	61124	36A
60938	31B	61008 *	15E	61067	65C	61125	36A
60939	50A	61009 *	40A	61068	53B	61126	36E
60940	52A	61010 *	53B	61069	50A	61127	36A
60941	50A	61011 *	56D	61070	34E	61128	36A
60942	52A	61012 *	52A	61071	50A	61129	56C
60943	36A	61013 *	56B	61072	62C	61130	40B
60944	52B	61014 *	52D	61073	34E	61131	56A
60945	52B	61015 *	56A	61074	34E	61132	62B
60946	50A	61016 *	50B	61075	34A	61133	62A
60947	52A	61017 *	56A	61076	64B	61134	62A
60948	31B	61018 *	51G	61077	14D	61135	30F
60949	52A	61019 *	52C	61078	2F	61136	14D

61137	15E	61195	40B	61253	32B	61311	30E
61138	41A	61196	36A	61254	32B	61312	32A
61139	34D	61197	65A	61255	51G	61313	41A
61140	65A	61198	51A	61256	53A	61314	31A
61141	40E	61199	52D	61257	50B	61315	41A
61142	40B	61200	34A	61258	40A	61316	41A
61143	40B	61201	15E	61259	50B	61317	32A
61144	40B	61202	40A	61260	64A	61318	40B
61145	36A	61203	31A	61261	65A	61319	51A
61146	62A	61204	31F	61262	62A	61320	56C
61147	62A	61205	31F	61263	62B	61321	51A
61148	62A	61206	14D	61264	30F	61322	52D
61149	30F	61207	34E	61265	9G	61323	31F
61150	41A	61208	36E	61266	36A	61324	61A
61151	41A	61209	40E	61267	51C	61325	40B
61152	41A	61210	34E	61268	56A	61326	36A
61153	41A	61211	36E	61269	15E	61327	41A
61154	41A	61212	36E	61270	32A	61328	40B
61155	36A	61213	36A	61271	2F	61329	30A
61156	31F	61214	56C	61272	34A	61330	62A
61157	36A	61215 *	53B	61273	51A	61331	34A
61158	36A	61216	50B	61274	51A	61332	64A
61159	40B	61217	12C	61275	51C	61333	65C
61160	32B	61218	50B	61276	51A	61334	41A
61161	9G	61219	64B	61277	62A	61335	30A
61162	41A	61220	51E	61278	62B	61336	30E
61163	40E	61221 *	64B	61279	32A	61337	50A
61164	30A	61222	12C	61280	50A	61338	51A
61165	41F	61223	32A	61281	40E	61339	56C
61166	41F	61224	51A	61282	34E	61340	65A
61167	41F	61225	36A	61283	31A	61341	64A
61168	40B	61226	30F	61284	40B	61342	65A
61169	41A	61227	30F	61285	36A	61343	62A
61170	36A	61228	32B	61286	31A	61344	65C
61171	31A	61229	51A	61287	31A	61345	61A
61172	62B	61230	56F	61288	50A	61346	61A
61173	51E	61231	36E	61289	53B	61347	61A
61174	34A	61232	30F	61290	12C	61348	31F
61175	40B	61233	30A	61291	51A	61349	61A
61176	51A	61234	30A	61292	62B	61350	61A
61177	40B	61235	32A	61293	62A	61351	64A
61178	64B	61236	31A	61294	61A	61352	64A
61179	34A	61237 *	50B	61295	56B	61353	51A
61180	62B	61238 *	52C	61296	56A	61354	64A
61181	41A	61239	12C	61297	56B	61355	65A
61182	31A	61240 *	50B	61298	15E	61356	64A
61183	41A	61241 *	52D	61299	40E	61357	64A
61184	64A	61242 *	61A	61300	30E	61358	62A
61185	40E	61243 *	65A	61301	31A	61359	64A
61186	2F	61244 *	64B	61302	34E	61360	31A
61187	14D	61245 *	64B	61303	51E	61361	30E
61188	40E	61246 *	64A	61304	53B	61362	30F
61189 *	56C	61247 *	36A	61305	53B	61363	30E
61190	40B	61248 *	40A	61306	53B	61364	34A
61191	64A	61249 *	30F	61307	64A	61365	36A
61192	2F	61250 *	36A	61308	64A	61366	40B
61193	36A	61251 *	34D	61309	56C	61367	30A
61194	41F	61252	32B	61310	56B	61368	2F

61369	15E	61427	50B	61571	32A	61753	40E
61370	30E	61428	50B	61572	32B	61754	40E
61371	31A	61429	50B	61577	31A	61755	61C
61372	30F	61430	50A	61607 *	31A	61756	40B
61373	30E	61431	50B	61608 *	31A	61758	62C
61374	40B	61432	50B	61610 *	31B	61759	34E
61375	30A	61433	50C	61611 *	32B	61760	41A
61376	15E	61434	50A	61612 *	32B	61761	41A
61377	36A	61435	50A	61613 *	31A	61762	40F
61378	30F	61436	50A	61614 *	31A	61763	40B
61379 *	40B	61437	50A	61616 *	31A	61764 *	65A
61380	15E	61438	50A	61618 *	32B	61766	40B
61381	15E	61439	50A	61620 *	31C	61767	40B
61382	51F	61440	50A	61623 *	31A	61769	65C
61383	56F	61441	50A	61625 *	32B	61770	62C
61384	30F	61442	50B	61626 *	31A	61771	40B
61385	56A	61443	50A	61627 *	31B	61772 *	65C
61386	56C	61444	50A	61629 *	32B	61773	40B
61387	51A	61445	50E	61633 *	31B	61777	34E
61388	56C	61446	50B	61636 *	32A	61778	40B
61389	34F	61447	50B	61637 *	32B	61779	61C
61390	40B	61448	50A	61639 *	31A	61780	40E
61391	34E	61449	50A	61641 *	31B	61782 *	61C
61392	34F	61450	50A	61644 *	31A	61783 *	61C
61393	34A	61451	50A	61647 *	32B	61784	65J
61394	34A	61452	50A	61651 *	31A	61785	65A
61395	12C	61453	50A	61652 *	31A	61786	65A
61396	65A	61454	50A	61653 *	31B	61787 *	65A
61397	64A	61455	50A	61654 *	32A	61788 *	65A
61398	64A	61456	50C	61656 *	32D	61789 *	61A
61399	32A	61457	50A	61657 *	31B	61790 *	61A
61400	61A	61458	50C	61658 *	30E	61791 *	65J
61401	62A	61459	50C	61659 *	32C	61792	61C
61402	62B	61460	50A	61660 *	32C	61794 *	65A
61403	62A	61461	50A	61661 *	31A	61800	36A
61404	65C	61462	50A	61662 *	30E	61801	31B
61405	40A	61463	50A	61663 *	30E	61802	40A
61406	40B	61464	50A	61664 *	32D	61803	36A
61407	62C	61465	50A	61666 *	30E	61804	2F
61408	40B	61466	50C	61668 *	30E	61805	34E
61409	40B	61467	50A	61670 *	32D	61806	40A
61410	50A	61468	50A	61672 *	32B	61807	40A
61411	50B	61469	50C	61721	62C	61808	40E
61412	50B	61470	50B	61723	40E	61809	2F
61413	50A	61471	50B	61728	41A	61810	31B
61414	50B	61472	50A	61730	40B	61811	31B
61415	50B	61473	50A	61731	40F	61812	36A
61416	50A	61475	50A	61738	40E	61813	53A
61417	50A	61476	50A	61740	40B	61814	53A
61418	50A	61477	50A	61741	61A	61815	30F
61419	50A	61478	50D	61742	40F	61816	41A
61420	50A	61514	32A	61743	40F	61817	31A
61421	50A	61530	32A	61745	40B	61818	52B
61422	50A	61533	32A	61747	41A	61819	53A
61423	50A	61535	32B	61748	40F	61820	30F
61424	50A	61546	31E	61750	40F	61821	40E
61425	50B	61564	32B	61751	40E	61822	31B
61426	50A	61568	32A	61752	40E	61823	64A

61824 2F	61882 12C	61941 53A	62001 51E
61825 41A	61883 53A	61942 30F	62002 52C
61826 32A	61884 52B	61943 41A	62003 51E
61827 31B	61885 64A	61944 40A	62004 51A
61828 40A	61886 31B	61945 53A	62005 51A
61829 36A	61887 36A	61946 31B	62006 52C
61830 34E	61888 40E	61947 40E	62007 51A
61831 31B	61889 40A	61948 31B	62008 51A
61832 9G	61890 31B	61949 32A	62009 51A
61833 40E	61891 40B	61950 40B	62010 52C
61834 31A	61892 53A	61951 30F	62011 65J
61835 31B	61893 53A	61952 52D	62012 65J
61836 41F	61894 40A	61953 32A	62013 30A
61837 40E	61895 36A	61954 31B	62014 30A
61838 2F	61896 40E	61955 64A	62015 30A
61839 41F	61897 53A	61956 40B	62016 31B
61840 31B	61898 53A	61957 32A	62017 31B
61841 2F	61899 53A	61958 32C	62018 31B
61842 2F	61900 64A	61959 32C	62019 30A
61843 2F	61901 52D	61960 40A	62020 31B
61844 52B	61902 53A	61961 36A	62021 52C
61845 31B	61903 53A	61962 52B	62022 52C
61846 53A	61904 53A	61963 30F	62023 52C
61847 53A	61905 40B	61964 36A	62024 52C
61848 40A	61906 52B	61965 53A	62025 52C
61849 31A	61907 41A	61966 40B	62026 52C
61850 41F	61908 32A	61967 64A	62027 52C
61851 12C	61909 64A	61968 64A	62028 52C
61852 40E	61910 9G	61969 52D	62029 52C
61853 2F	61911 64A	61970 32A	62030 52C
61854 52D	61912 40B	61971 32A	62031 65J
61855 64A	61913 9G	61972 31B	62032 31B
61856 16D	61914 40E	61973 32A	62033 31B
61857 53A	61915 31B	61974 40E	62034 65J
61858 12C	61916 12C	61975 16D	62035 31B
61859 40A	61917 52D	61976 31B	62036 30A
61860 31B	61918 32A	61977 30F	62037 31B
61861 31B	61919 40A	61978 34E	62038 31B
61862 30F	61920 53A	61979 34E	62039 31B
61863 30A	61921 30F	61980 16D	62040 31B
61864 34E	61922 53A	61981 32A	62041 51E
61865 9G	61923 52B	61982 40E	62042 51E
61866 40B	61924 64A	61983 64A	62043 51A
61867 41F	61925 36A	61984 52B	62044 51J
61868 41F	61926 32C	61985 52D	62045 51A
61869 52B	61927 52B	61986 52B	62046 50A
61870 40E	61928 64A	61987 52B	62047 51E
61871 53A	61929 31B	61988 64A	62048 50A
61872 53A	61930 52D	61989 32A	62049 50A
61873 40E	61931 64A	61990 64A	62050 50A
61874 53A	61932 53A	61991 64A	62051 31B
61875 52B	61933 64A	61992 64A	62052 65J
61876 64A	61934 52D	61993 * 53A	62053 30A
61877 32A	61935 53A	61994 * 65A	62054 31B
61878 64A	61936 12C	61995 * 65A	62055 31B
61879 64A	61937 12C	61996 * 65A	62056 50A
61880 31A	61938 41A	61997 * 65J	62057 50A
61881 64A	61939 32A	61998 * 65A	62058 51A
	61940 36A		

62059 51A	62661 * 41A	62747 * 12C	63379 52K
62060 52J	62662 * 41A	62753 * 50D	63380 51L
62061 50A	62663 * 41H	62759 * 50D	63381 52C
62062 50A	62664 * 41A	62760 * 53B	63382 51G
62063 50A	62665 * 41A	62762 * 50E	63383 51C
62064 51A	62666 * 41A	62763 * 50D	63384 52J
62065 51E	62667 * 41A	62765 * 50D	63385 52C
62066 31B	62668 * 41A	62770 * 50E	63386 52J
62067 31B	62669 * 41A	62785 31A	63387 52H
62068 31B	62670 * 41A		63388 51L
62069 31B	62671 * 65A		63389 51L
62070 31B	62672 * 65A		63390 52C
62418 * 62A	62673 * 65A		63391 51C
62421 * 64A	62674 * 65A		63392 51C
62426 * 63B	62675 * 65A		63393 51L
62427 * 62C	62676 * 65A		63394 52C
62436 * 62C	62677 * 62A		63395 50C
62439 * 64F	62680 * 65A		63396 51L
62467 * 62A	62681 * 65A		63397 51C
62469 * 61C	62682 * 65A	63340 51F	63398 51F
62470 * 63A	62684 * 65A	63341 51G	63399 52C
62471 * 64A	62685 * 64B	63342 52J	63400 52J
62472 * 65A	62686 * 65A	63343 51G	63401 51L
62474 * 65A	62687 * 65A	63344 51G	63402 52J
62475 * 62A	62688 * 65B	63345 52K	63403 51F
62477 * 65A	62689 * 65A	63346 52J	63404 52K
62478 * 62A	62690 * 64B	63347 51G	63405 51L
62479 * 61A	62691 * 64B	63348 50C	63406 52K
62480 * 61A	62692 * 64B	63349 51L	63407 51G
62482 * 61A	62693 * 64B	63350 52J	63408 52J
62483 * 64G	62694 * 64B	63351 51F	63409 51L
62484 * 63A	62701 * 53B	63352 52C	63410 51C
62485 * 62B	62705 * 64B	63353 51F	63411 51L
62487 * 64A	62707 * 53B	63354 52J	63412 51C
62488 * 64A	62708 * 62A	63355 51L	63413 52C
62489 * 61A	62709 * 64B	63356 52C	63414 51C
62492 * 62A	62710 * 53B	63357 52K	63415 51C
62493 * 61A	62711 * 64A	63358 52J	63416 51G
62494 * 64G	62712 * 62A	63359 52K	63417 51L
62495 * 64F	62714 * 63B	63360 51L	63418 52K
62496 * 65A	62715 * 64A	63361 51G	63419 51C
62497 * 61A	62716 * 62A	63362 52C	63420 51L
62498 * 61A	62717 * 53B	63363 52C	63421 51C
62511 32A	62718 * 64A	63364 51L	63422 51C
62517 32A	62719 * 64B	63365 52K	63423 50C
62524 32A	62720 * 53B	63366 52J	63424 51L
62529 31B	62722 * 53B	63367 51G	63425 52H
62540 32A	62723 * 53B	63368 51L	63426 51L
62544 32A	62727 * 50D	63369 51L	63427 52K
62570 32D	62728 * 62A	63370 51L	63428 51L
62589 31B	62729 * 62A	63371 51L	63429 50C
62597 31F	62733 * 62A	63372 52K	63430 51L
62604 32D	62734 * 12C	63373 51L	63431 52J
62606 31C	62738 * 50D	63374 51G	63432 51G
62612 31F	62739 * 50E	63375 51L	63433 52K
62613 31F	62740 * 50A	63376 52C	63434 52J
62618 31B	62743 * 64B	63377 52J	63435 51L
62660 * 41A	62744 * 62A	63378 52C	63436 50C

63437	52H	63592	40E	63655	36E	63717	41J
63438	51C	63593	41F	63656	41G	63718	41G
63439	52K	63594	40E	63657	40E	63719	9G
63440	51C	63595	36C	63658	41A	63720	41H
63441	52C	63596	31B	63659	41G	63721	9G
63442	51L	63597	41J	63660	36C	63722	41J
63443	51G	63598	9G	63661	41A	63723	41F
63444	52J	63599	41A	63662	36C	63724	56B
63445	51L	63600	9G	63663	31B	63725	31B
63446	51G	63601	36C	63664	41J	63726	41G
63447	51L	63602	40E	63665	41J	63727	41G
63448	50C	63603	9G	63666	41F	63728	36C
63449	50C	63604	41A	63669	41G	63730	41F
63450	50C	63605	56B	63670	31B	63731	41G
63451	50C	63606	41J	63671	36C	63732	41J
63452	51L	63607	41J	63672	41F	63733	41A
63453	52C	63608	36E	63673	41F	63734	41A
63454	51C	63609	41A	63674	40E	63735	41H
63455	52K	63610	16D	63675	40E	63736	36E
63456	52J	63611	41F	63676	16D	63737	41A
63457	51C	63612	41G	63677	36A	63738	40B
63458	52J	63613	36A	63678	31B	63739	41J
63459	51F	63614	40E	63679	41J	63740	16D
63460	52H	63615	40B	63680	41A	63741	36C
63461	52H	63616	40B	63681	9G	63742	41A
63462	52H	63617	36C	63683	41J	63743	9G
63463	52H	63618	36A	63684	41F	63744	36C
63464	52G	63619	31B	63685	41A	63746	31B
63465	52H	63621	41A	63686	9G	63747	36C
63466	52G	63622	41J	63687	31B	63748	41A
63467	52G	63623	41G	63688	36E	63749	41H
63468	52H	63624	41A	63689	16D	63750	40B
63469	52H	63626	36C	63690	36C	63752	r6D
63470	52H	63628	41F	63691	41J	63753	41F
63471	52H	63630	31B	63692	40B	63754	40E
63472	52H	63631	9G	63693	36A	63755	52H
63473	52H	63632	41J	63694	40E	63756	41F
63474	52G	63633	56B	63695	41A	63757	41F
63570	56B	63634	41J	63696	36C	63758	41J
63571	31B	63635	41J	63697	41G	63759	40B
63572	36C	63636	41J	63698	36A	63760	52H
63573	9G	63637	36E	63699	40E	63761	36C
63574	41A	63639	40E	63700	9G	63762	41H
63575	9G	63640	41A	63701	41F	63763	41G
63576	36C	63641	9G	63702	41H	63764	41F
63577	41J	63642	36C	63703	41J	63765	41J
63578	16D	63643	41J	63704	41G	63766	9G
63579	16D	63644	40B	63705	41H	63767	9G
63582	9G	63645	41A	63706	41H	63768	40E
63583	41A	63646	31B	63707	41J	63770	40E
63584	56B	63647	40E	63708	40B	63771	41A
63585	40E	63648	41H	63709	9G	63772	41H
63586	41F	63649	9G	63710	41A	63773	31B
63587	40E	63650	31B	63711	16D	63774	41F
63588	56A	63651	40E	63712	52H	63775	9G
63589	40E	63652	31B	63713	9G	63776	41J
63590	31B	63653	36C	63715	41J	63777	16D
63591	16D	63654	36C	63716	9G	63779	41F

63780	31B	63857	56A	63929	34F	63987	36E
63781	36C	63858	36A	63930	34F		
63782	36E	63859	40E	63931	34F		
63783	41A	63860	40B	63932	34F	64170	56F
63784	31B	63861	41J	63933	34F	64171	40F
63785	36E	63862	9G	63934	36A	64172	40F
63786	31B	63863	40E	63935	36A	64173	56C
63787	41H	63864	56A	63936	34F	64174	36E
63788	36C	63865	16D	63937	36E	64175	34D
63789	16D	63867	16D	63938	34F	64177	34E
63791	41F	63868	31B	63939	36A	64178	36E
63792	16D	63869	16D	63940	34F	64179	36A
63793	36C	63870	41J	63941	36A	64180	40F
63794	9G	63872	31B	63942	36A	64181	34F
63795	31B	63873	40E	63943	36A	64182	56B
63796	16D	63874	52H	63944	36E	64184	34D
63798	41F	63877	41H	63945	36E	64185	36A
63799	36C	63878	40B	63946	34F	64188	36E
63800	41J	63879	31B	63947	36E	64190	40F
63801	41H	63880	36C	63948	34F	64191	40F
63802	41G	63881	41A	63949	36E	64192	34F
63803	31B	63882	41A	63950	34F	64196	34B
63804	41H	63883	41G	63951	36A	64197	34D
63805	9G	63884	41H	63952	36A	64203	56F
63806	16D	63885	56B	63953	36A	64206	34D
63807	36C	63886	16D	63954	36A	64207	40A
63808	16D	63887	31B	63955	36A	64208	56B
63812	41F	63888	41A	63956	36A	64209	36A
63813	41F	63889	41A	63957	36A	64210	34E
63816	40E	63890	31B	63958	36A	64213	40E
63817	16D	63891	41F	63959	36E	64214	40F
63818	36E	63893	41J	63960	34F	64219	40A
63819	40B	63894	41F	63961	36E	64222	56B
63821	41A	63895	9G	63962	36A	64223	34B
63822	41A,	63897	41F	63963	36A	64224	34E
63823	56B	63898	41F	63964	36A	64226	56F
63824	41G	63899	41H	63965	36E	64228	34E
63827	41H	63900	40B	63966	34F	64229	40F
63828	41F	63901	16D	63967	36A	64231	40F
63829	41J	63902	41J	63968	36A	64232	36A
63832	41F	63904	41G	63969	36A	64233	34B
63833	41J	63906	36C	63970	36E	64234	36E
63836	41G	63907	41G	63971	41G	64235	40E
63837	40B	63908	41F	63972	36E	64236	36E
63838	16D	63911	41J	63973	36A	64237	34D
63840	41J	63912	41J	63974	36A	64238	40E
63841	41F	63913	41G	63975	36A	64239	40E
63842	41J	63914	36E	63976	36E	64240	34D
63843	41F	63915	9G	63977	36A	64241	36A
63845	41H	63917	36C	63978	36A	64245	36E
63846	41A	63920	56A	63979	36E	64246	34F
63847	41H	63922	36A	63980	36E	64247	40F
63848	9G	63923	34F	63981	36A	64250	40F
63850	41A	63924	36E	63982	36E	64251	34D
63852	41A	63925	36E	63983	36E	64253	34B
63853	41J	63926	36E	63984	36A	64254	34E
63854	16D	63927	36E	63985	36A	64256	15E
63856	52H	63928	36A	63986	36E	64257	40E

64258	36A	64373	41A	64471	66A	64540	65A
64259	36A	64375	16D	64472	65E	64541	65A
64260	40F	64376	41G	64473	65E	64542	62B
64265	34E	64377	41F	64474	62A	64543	62C
64266	34B	64379	41J	64475	62C	64544	62B
64268	56B	64382	9G	64476	62C	64545	62B
64269	40E	64383	9G	64477	66A	64546	62A
64270	36A	64384	41H	64478	12C	64547	64A
64272	34E	64385	36E	64479	64A	64548	65A
64273	40A	64386	40B	64480	62C	64549	62A
64277	56C	64387	41A	64482	64A	64550	62A
64278	40A	64389	9G	64483	64A	64551	64E
64279	34E	64393	41F	64484	64F	64552	64A
64280	36E	64394	41A	64487	62C	64553	64F
64283	36E	64395	36E	64488	62A	64554	64C
64284	40B	64396	41H	64489	64A	64555	64A
64287	36E	64397	40E	64490	64E	64556	62B
64288	9G	64402	41F	64491	64F	64557	64A
64292	41H	64403	41G	64493	62C	64558	65A
64294	9G	64404	41G	64494	64G	64559	65C
64297	9G	64405	9G	64496	62C	64560	62C
64298	9G	64406	41F	64497	64C	64561	64A
64304	9G	64407	36C	64498	65E	64562	64A
64305	40B	64417	41G	64499	12C	64563	65C
64308	36C	64418	9G	64500	64C	64564	62A
64310	9G	64419	41A	64501	64C	64565	62A
64311	9G	64420	16D	64502	64E	64566	64A
64313	41H	64421	36E	64504	64F	64567	62C
64314	41J	64423	36E	64505	62C	64568	62C
64315	36C	64425	41G	64506	64A	64569	64C
64316	41J	64427	41J	64507	65E	64570	64E
64317	41J	64428	9G	64509	64G	64571	64E
64318	40A	64429	36C	64510	64F	64572	64A
64319	36C	64430	40A	64511	66A	64573	65C
64321	36E	64433	41H	64512	64F	64574	65E
64324	41J	64434	9G	64513	62C	64575	62B
64325	40B	64435	9G	64514	65C	64576	64A
64329	41A	64437	9G	64515	64A	64577	64A
64331	9G	64438	40E	64516	62C	64578	65A
64332	41J	64439	16D	64518	64A	64579	65E
64333	41J	64440	9G	64519	64A	64580	65A
64336	41H	64441	41A	64520	65C	64581	65A
64337	9G	64442	41G	64522	62A	64582	64A
64341	9G	64443	41A	64523	64A	64583	64F
64346	41J	64444	41H	64524	64A	64584	65C
64348	40E	64445	41A	64525	62C	64585	62B
64351	36C	64446	40B	64527	64C	64586	64A
64352	41J	64447	41A	64529	64F	64587	62B
64354	41J	64450	36E	64530	62B	64588	65F
64355	40B	64451	36E	64531	65E	64589	65F
64357	9G	64452	41G	64532	64A	64590	64A
64359	16D	64460	65E	64533	64A	64591	64A
64362	41J	64461	65C	64534	65E	64592	65F
64363	9G	64462	64A	64535	64A	64593	65F
64364	41J	64463	64G	64536	64A	64594	64A
64365	36C	64466	62A	64537	64E	64595	64A
64368	9G	64468	64F	64538	64A	64596	62A
64371	40A	64470	65E	64539	64G	64597	62C

64598	62B	64659	31B	64720	56B	64778	51F
64599	64A	64660	30E	64721	36A	64779	31B
64600	62A	64661	31A	64722	36A	64780	30A
64601	64A	64663	30A	64723	36A	64781	30A
64602	62A	64664	30E	64724	32B	64782	31B
64603	64A	64665	31B	64725	50B	64783	30A
64604	62C	64666	30E	64726	40A	64784	30A
64605	64A	64667	30E	64727	9G	64785	32B
64606	64A	64668	31B	64728	40F	64786	62B
64607	64A	64669	31B	64729	40F	64787	30A
64608	64A	64670	30A	64730	50B	64788	30A
64609	65C	64671	31B	64731	32A	64789	31F
64610	65H	64673	31A	64732	56B	64790	62B
64611	65A	64674	32A	64733	12C	64791	56F
64612	64A	64675	30A	64734	40A	64792	62B
64613	64A	64676	30A	64735	40E	64793	32B
64614	64A	64677	30A	64736	41A	64794	64C
64615	62B	64678	31B	64737	36A	64795	64A
64616	62A	64679	31B	64738	9G	64796	56F
64617	62C	64680	30A	64739	16D	64797	32C
64618	62A	64681	30A	64740	9G	64798	16D
64619	62B	64682	30A	64741	40A	64799	30A
64620	62B	64683	31A	64742	9G	64800	32B
64621	65C	64684	31B	64743	9G	64801	56F
64622	65A	64685	30C	64744	9G	64802	40E
64623	65A	64686	30A	64745	9G	64803	31A
64624	64A	64687	31B	64746	41A	64804	41A
64625	64A	64689	30A	64747	16D	64805	30A
64626	65C	64690	31B	64748	9G	64806	56B
64627	62B	64691	31B	64749	56A	64807	41A
64628	65E	64692	31B	64750	30A	64808	41A
64629	62A	64693	30A	64751	40A	64809	9G
64630	62C	64694	30A	64752	32B	64810	36A
64631	62B	64695	31A	64753	9G	64811	56B
64632	65A	64696	31A	64754	56B	64812	52C
64633	65A	64697	31B	64755	40A	64813	52D
64634	64F	64698	31B	64756	51F	64814	52C
64635	62A	64699	31B	64757	56B	64815	52C
64636	64E	64700	52J	64758	50B	64816	52C
64637	64A	64701	52B	64759	36E	64817	56F
64638	65A	64702	41A	64760	56B	64818	50D
64639	65A	64703	52B	64761	32A	64819	53A
64640	31C	64704	52A	64762	40E	64820	56B
64641	32A	64705	56B	64763	40E	64821	50D
64642	31B	64706	50D	64764	31B	64822	62B
64643	32A	64707	52J	64765	30A	64823	40F
64644	32A	64708	30A	64766	30A	64824	9G
64646	31A	64709	53A	64767	30A	64825	56B
64647	31B	64710	52J	64768	30A	64826	32B
64648	31B	64711	52D	64769	31B	64827	36A
64650	30E	64712	40E	64770	31B	64828	41G
64652	30F	64713	52B	64771	31B	64829	32B
64653	30A	64714	36E	64772	31B	64830	36E
64654	31A	64715	40E	64773	30A	64831	56B
64655	30A	64716	36A	64774	31B	64832	40E
64656	30A	64717	9G	64775	30A	64833	56B
64657	30E	64718	9G	64776	30F	64834	32B
64658	31A	64719	41A	64777	30F	64835	50B

64836	56B	64894	32B	64952	33A	65158	2F
64837	56B	64895	12C	64953	33A	65166	9E
64838	36A	64896	40A	64954	33A	65169	8E
64839	56B	64897	52D	64955	16D	65177	8F
64840	56B	64898	36E	64956	33A	65184	8D
64841	32B	64899	12C	64957	33A	65192	8F
64842	52C	64900	32A	64958	33A	65194	9F
64843	52D	64901	31F	64959	40A	65198	8D
64844	52D	64902	41G	64960	40A	65210	65E
64845	50D	64903	56F	64961	40A	65211	65C
64846	52J	64904	50C	64962	33A	65214	65E
64847	50D	64905	32B	64963	64C	65216 *	66A
64848	51F	64906	36E	64964	12C	65217 *	65E
64849	52C	64907	56F	64965	33A	65218	62A
64850	50B	64908	36E	64966	40A	65221	61A
64851	52J	64909	36A	64967	36A	65222 *	64E
64852	52A	64910	53A	64968	33A	65224 *	64A
64853	52B	64911	56C	64969	56B	65227	61A
64854	52J	64912	12C	64970	36E	65228	65A
64855	50D	64913	32A	64971	53A	65229	64F
64856	52B	64914	53A	64972	36A	65230	64F
64857	50D	64915	52B	64973	30A	65232	66A
64858	52C	64916	52D	64974	40E	65233 *	64E
64859	50D	64917	52D	64975	64A	65234	64G
64860	50C	64918	56B	64976	40E	65235 *	64B
64861	50D	64919	56F	64977	40E	65237	12C
64862	51F	64920	50B	64978	51F	65239	62C
64863	50B	64921	52J	64979	56B	65241	65F
64864	52B	64922	50B	64980	40E	65243 *	64B
64865	52A	64923	52B	64981	36A	65246	65F
64866	50D	64924	52D	64982	51F	65247	61C
64867	50F	64925	52D	64983	40E	65249	65E
64868	52D	64926	52F	64984	40A	65251	61A
64869	52A	64927	51F	64985	31A	65252	62A
64870	50B	64928	50F	64986	64C	65253 *	62C
64871	52B	64929	52D	64987	36A	65257	64E
64872	56F	64930	9G	64988	40E	65258	64A
64873	30A	64931	52B			65259	64F
64874	36A	64932	12C			65260	65E
64875	9G	64933	50B			65261	64F
64876	36A	64934	50B			65265	64F
64877	12C	64935	50B			65266	65E
64878	41A	64936	52J			65267	61C
64879	56B	64937	40A			65268 *	64F
64880	12C	64938	50F			65273	65C
64881	40A	64939	52B			65275	64G
64882	36E	64940	53A			65276	64F
64883	36A	64941	52D			65277	64F
64884	12C	64942	50D			65280	64E
64885	36A	64943	50B	65033	52C	65281	62C
64886	56F	64944	50D	65070	52D	65282	64F
64887	40E	64945	52B	65099	52H	65285	65E
64888	12C	64946	64C	65110	52B	65287	65E
64889	40A	64947	53A	65131	8F	65288	64A
64890	40A	64948	12C	65133	27E	65290	64F
64891	32B	64949	52D	65134	8E	65293	12C
64892	12C	64950	62B	65138	8F	65295	65C
64893	36E	64951	33A	65140	8F	65296	65A
				65157	9E		

65297	61A	65461	31A	65567	32C	65776	51L
65300	65J	65462	32C	65570	32A	65777	51L
65303	61A	65463	30A	65576	31B	65778	51L
65304	61C	65464	30A	65577	31B	65779	51L
65305	61B	65465	30E	65578	32B	65780	52E
65306	64E	65468	30E	65580	31A	65781	52F
65307	62C	65469	32A	65581	32A	65782	51C
65309	62B	65470	30E	65582	31C	65783	52F
65310	61C	65471	32A	65583	31B	65784	52E
65311	64E	65472	30E	65584	31B	65785	52J
65312	12C	65473	30E	65586	32A	65786	52F
65313	65J	65474	31B	65588	32C	65787	51E
65315	65A	65475	31A	65589	31A	65788	51E
65316	64E	65476	30A	65645	52H	65789	52F
65317	64G	65477	31A	65656	52A	65790	51L
65318	64F	65478	32B	65662	52G	65791	52E
65319	62B	65479	34D	65663	50C	65792	52F
65320	62C	65502	31A	65666	52G	65794	52F
65321	12C	65503	30E	65670	52H	65795	52E
65323	62C	65505	30E	65685	50C	65796	52E
65325	65E	65506	30E	65687	52F	65797	52F
65327	64A	65507	32E	65691	53A	65798	52G
65329	64A	65511	30E	65693	53A	65799	52E
65330	62B	65512	32B	65695	52H	65800	52F
65331	64G	65513	32B	65698	50A	65801	52F
65333	62B	65514	30E	65700	52A	65802	52E
65334	64A	65519	32A	65702	52J	65804	52F
65335	65H	65520	31A	65706	52F	65805	51C
65338	61C	65521	31C	65712	52J	65806	52E
65339	65I	65526	31C	65713	52H	65807	52E
65341	64F	65528	31A	65714	50A	65808	52F
65342	64F	65530	31C	65720	51L	65809	52E
65343	65E	65531	30E	65726	50D	65810	52F
65344	64F	65532	31A	65727	52F	65811	52F
65345	62A	65533	31C	65728	52J	65812	52E
65346	64F	65536	30C	65731	51F	65813	52E
65361	30A	65539	30E	65732	51L	65814	52E
65388	32B	65541	31A	65735	51F	65815	52F
65389	32B	65542	32A	65736	51L	65816	51C
65420	31B	65544	31C	65737	51L	65817	52G
65424	30E	65545	30E	65741	51L	65818	51C
65434	30F	65546	30A	65743	51L	65819	52F
65440	30A	65548	30A	65745	51L	65820	51C
65443	30E	65549	31C	65747	51C	65821	52E
65445	30E	65551	32A	65751	51L	65822	52F
65446	30E	65553	32A	65753	51L	65823	52J
65448	30E	65554	31B	65755	51L	65824	52F
65449	30A	65555	30A	65756	51L	65825	52F
65450	31A	65556	31A	65757	51L	65826	52E
65451	31A	65557	32A	65760	51L	65827	50F
65452	30A	65558	32C	65761	51L	65828	52F
65453	30F	65559	32C	65762	51L	65830	51C
65454	32B	65560	32B	65763	51L	65831	52E
65455	30A	65561	32B	65768	51L	65832	52G
65457	31A	65563	30A	65769	51L	65833	52G
65458	30F	65564	30E	65772	51L	65834	52F
65459	32B	65565	31C	65773	51E	65835	52G
65460	32C	65566	32A	65774	51L	65837	52E

76

65838	52F	65902	62A	67491	62B	67650	65C
65839	52E	65903	62A	67492	64A	67651	52B
65840	52G	65904	62A	67494	64E	67652	52B
65841	52G	65905	62A	67496	62B	67653	52C
65842	52E	65906	64A	67497	64A	67654	52B
65844	50F	65907	62A	67500	65C	67655	65C
65845	50A	65908	62A	67501	62B	67656	52B
65846	51C	65909	64E	67502	62B	67657	52A
65847	52J	65910	62A	67600	65A	67658	52B
65848	50F	65911	62A	67601	65I	67659	64A
65849	50F	65912	64A	67602	65A	67660	65E
65850	52G	65913	62A	67603	65A	67661	65C
65851	52F	65914	64A	67604	65H	67662	65C
65852	52E	65915	64A	67605	65E	67663	53B
65853	51E	65916	64A	67606	64G	67664	65A
65854	52G	65917	64E	67607	65C	67665	65E
65855	51L	65918	64A	67608	65C	67666	64A
65856	52G	65919	64A	67609	65E	67667	65A
65857	52F	65920	64A	67610	64B	67668	64A
65858	52E	65921	62A	67611	65C	67669	62C
65859	51L	65922	64A	67612	65C	67670	64A
65860	51A	65923	62C	67613	65H	67671	65A
65861	50C	65924	62C	67614	64B	67672	62C
65862	52F	65925	62A	67615	65H	67673	52G
65863	52F	65926	62C	67616	65H	67674	65E
65864	52B	65927	64A	67617	64A	67675	65C
65865	51L	65928	62C	67618	65E	67676	65C
65866	51C	65929	64A	67619	65H	67677	53B
65867	52F	65930	62C	67620	64B	67678	65C
65868	51L	65931	62A	67621	65C	67679	65C
65869	52B	65932	62A	67622	65H	67680	65A
65870	51L	65933	62C	67623	65C	67681	65C
65871	52G	65934	64A	67624	64A	67682	53B
65872	52G			67625	65C	67683	52B
65873	52J			67626	65C	67684	53B
65874	50A			67627	65E	67685	52B
65875	52F			67628	65H	67686	53B
65876	52B			67629	65C	67687	52A
65877	52B			67630	65C	67688	52A
65878	52G			67631	65H	67689	52A
65879	52F			67632	65H	67690	52A
65880	52F			67633	65C	67691	52B
65881	50C			67634	52C	67701	31A
65882	52B			67635	53B	67702	30A
65883	50A	67417	9G	67636	52C	67703	30A
65884	51E	67445	41G	67637	52A	67704	30A
65885	50C	67448	41G	67638	53B	67705	32B
65886	52B	67450	9G	67639	52A	67706	30A
65887	50A	67460	65A	67640	53B	67707	32C
65888	50C	67474	65A	67641	52B	67708	30A
65889	52F	67482	65C	67642	52B	67709	30A
65890	50A	67484	62B	67643	65C	67710	32B
65891	50C	67485	65A	67644	65A	67711	32B
65892	52G	67486	62B	67645	52G	67712	31A
65893	52J	67487	65C	67646	52B	67713	31A
65894	50A	67488	64E	67647	52B	67714	32A
65900	62A	67489	64G	67648	65C	67715	30A
65901	62A	67490	62B	67649	64A	67716	30A

67717	32A	67775	32B	68034	17C	68150	50C
67718	31A	67776	34A	68035	52C	68190	61A
67719	32B	67777	51A	68036	52C	68192	61A
67720	31A	67778	30A	68037	51A	68230	53A
67721	31A	67779	34A	68038	52C	68233	51C
67722	31A	67780	34A	68039	50A	68235	51F
67723	31A	67781	9G	68040	50A	68245	51L
67724	30A	67782	9G	68041	52G	68254	51F
67725	30A	67783	34A	68042	53A	68260	51E
67726	30A	67784	34A	68043	51A	68262	52H
67727	30A	67785	34D	68044	52G	68263	52A
67728	30A	67786	32A	68045	51A	68264	53A
67729	30A	67787	34A	68046	50A	68265	52H
67730	30A	67788	40E	68047	51A	68269	51F
67731	30A	67789	2F	68048	52G	68272	51L
67732	30A	67790	34D	68049	51E	68275	50C
67733	31A	67791	34D	68050	51A	68278	52J
67734	31A	67792	34A	68051	51C	68283	52A
67735	30A	67793	34A	68052	51A	68309	50A
67736	30A	67794	34F	68053	51C	68314	52A
67737	30A	67795	9G	68054	51C	68316	52J
67738	32C	67796	9G	68055	51C	68320	64A
67739	30A	67797	34A	68056	51C	68325	64A
67740	2F	67798	9G	68057	51C	68326	65F
67741	34D	67799	40E	68058	52G	68332	62A
67742	51A	67800	34A	68059	52H	68334	62A
67743	9G			68060	51L	68335	62A
67744	34D			68061	50A	68336	65E
67745	34D			68062	51L	68338	64A
67746	34D			68063	6F	68342	64A
67747	9G	68006	17C	68064	9G	68343	65E
67748	9G	68007	51A	68065	6F	68344	65D
67749	34D	68008	51A	68066	6F	68345	65A
67750	51A	68009	40B	68067	34B	68346	62C
67751	9G	68010	52C	68068	9G	68349	65B
67752	30A	68011	53A	68069	36A	68350	62C
67753	40E	68012	9G	68070	40B	68352	65A
67754	51A	68013	17C	68071	36A	68353	62A
67755	51A	68014	52B	68072	40E	68354	64E
67756	9G	68015	51A	68073	34B	68359	51C
67757	34A	68016	52G	68074	40B	68360	53A
67758	40E	68017	51A	68075	34B	68361	53A
67759	51L	68018	40B	68076	40E	68363	53B
67760	40E	68019	52K	68077	34B	68364	51C
67761	34D	68020	36A	68078	40B	68392	50A
67762	9G	68021	51C	68079	9G	68406	51L
67763	51A	68022	36A	68080	41J	68408	52F
67764	51L	68023	51L	68095	64A	68409	53A
67765	51C	68024	51A	68100	65E	68410	51C
67766	51E	68025	51A	68101	62C	68425	53A
67767	34A	68026	41J	68104	64E	68431	50A
67768	34A	68027	51A	68108	65E	68442	65E
67769	40A	68028	40E	68110	65E	68443	65E
67770	34A	68029	52H	68114	65D	68444	65E
67771	2F	68030	17C	68117	65E	68445	65E
67772	34A	68031	52H	68119	65E	68447	65A
67773	34A	68032	50A	68123	65E	68448	64A
67774	34A	68033	34B	68124	67C	68453	62A

Part	Code	Part	Code	Part	Code	Part	Code
68454	64A	68600	30A	68696	51E	68892	51E
68456	62A	68601	40E	68697	52J	68893	40E
68457	64B	68602	40F	68698	51C	68894	34B
68458	62A	68609	31A	68701	55E	68895	56F
68459	62A	68612	30A	68702	52B	68896	34E
68467	64E	68613	30A	68703	51C	68897	51A
68468	65A	68619	30A	68704	52J	68898	51A
68470	64A	68621	36A	68705	52J	68899	32A
68471	64E	68623	41F	68706	52H	68900	56B
68472	64A	68626	34F	68707	51C	68901	56B
68477	64A	68629	40E	68708	52B	68902	56B
68479	65A	68633	30A	68709	65E	68903	34B
68481	64B	68635	34F	68711	51C	68904	56A
68497	41F	68640	32A	68713	52B	68905	32A
68498	36A	68641	32A	68714	6F	68906	34B
68499	31C	68642	32C	68715	51C	68907	34B
68500	30A	68643	30F	68716	51A	68908	56F
68501	40A	68644	30A	68717	61A	68909	51A
68502	36A	68645	32A	68718	61A	68910	56A
68507	36A	68646	30A	68719	61A	68911	56C
68508	36A	68647	30A	68720	52A	68912	56F
68510	40A	68648	30A	68721	51L	68913	56C
68513	30A	68649	30A	68722	51C	68914	56B
68520	36A	68650	30A	68723	52A	68915	56B
68522	40E	68652	30A	68724	51F	68916	56B
68524	64E	68654	36A	68725	52D	68917	34B
68526	30A	68655	30A	68726	55E	68918	34B
68528	40A	68656	32D	68727	6F	68919	56B
68530	36A	68660	30A	68728	52J	68920	34B
68535	62B	68661	34D	68729	51L	68921	34B
68538	30A	68663	30A	68730	52J	68922	56F
68542	31C	68665	30A	68731	52A	68923	56F
68543	40A	68670	53A	68732	52C	68924	32A
68545	40E	68671	6F	68733	65E	68925	56C
68549	30A	68672	53A	68734	51C	68926	34B
68550	40E	68673	53C	68736	50A	68927	40E
68552	30E	68674	52A	68737	52J	68928	34B
68554	41J	68675	52A	68738	52B	68929	34B
68556	36A	68676	53C	68739	50E	68930	34B
68557	40F	68677	50A	68740	51L	68931	34B
68560	40A	68678	52G	68741	53A	68932	56F
68563	30A	68679	51A	68742	52B	68933	56F
68565	32C	68680	52A	68743	52H	68934	51A
68566	31A	68681	55E	68744	52A	68935	56B
68569	36A	68682	52D	68745	53C	68936	34B
68570	40F	68683	51C	68747	52B	68937	56B
68571	30A	68684	51L	68749	61A	68938	56B
68573	30E	68685	51F	68750	61A	68939	56A
68575	30A	68686	50C	68751	53A	68941	51C
68577	30A	68687	50A	68752	53A	68943	56F
68578	30A	68688	51L	68753	53A	68944	56F
68579	30E	68689	51L	68754	51A	68945	34B
68581	40A	68690	51L	68824	56B	68946	34A
68587	36A	68691	51F	68834	56B	68947	56B
68591	41H	68692	51F	68846	34A	68948	50C
68596	30A	68693	52A	68869	56B	68950	40E
68599	40A	68694	52J	68875	56B	68951	51C
		68695	52J	68890	56B	68952	65A
				68891	34B		

68953	66A	69015	65C	69184	65D	69341	14D
68954	65A	69016	50A	69185	64A	69342	41G
68955	65A	69017	52J	69186	64A	69343	41G
68956	65A	69018	51F	69187	64C	69344	27E
68957	65A	69019	51L	69188	65A	69354	41G
68958	66A	69020	50A	69190	65C	69360	9G
68959	51A	69021	51A	69191	65A	69361	41A
68960	34B	69022	51A	69194	65C	69370	41G
68961	34B	69023	52C	69196	65E	69490	34A
68962	36A	69024	52C	69197	65A	69492	34A
68963	36C	69025	52C	69198	65C	69498	34A
68964	36A	69026	52C	69199	65C	69504	34A
68965	36A	69027	52A	69202	62C	69505	34B
68966	34B	69028	52B	69204	62B	69506	34A
68967	40E	69097	52A	69205	65D	69507	65C
68968	34B	69101	52H	69206	65E	69508	65C
68969	56F	69105	52H	69207	65E	69509	65C
68970	34B	69109	52A	69208	65D	69510	64G
68971	34B	69126	65D	69209	65C	69511	65D
68972	34B	69127	61B	69211	64B	69512	34A
68973	36A	69128	61B	69212	65A	69513	34B
68974	40E	69131	65A	69213	65C	69515	34A
68975	40E	69132	62A	69214	65A	69516	34F
68976	34E	69133	64A	69215	12C	69517	34A
68977	36C	69134	64A	69216	64F	69518	65E
68979	34B	69135	64A	69217	65D	69520	34A
68980	34B	69136	62B	69218	65A	69521	34A
68981	34B	69137	64E	69219	64A	69522	34B
68982	34B	69138	61B	69221	62C	69523	34A
68983	34B	69141	64A	69222	64A	69524	34A
68984	56C	69143	62A	69223	62A	69526	34A
68985	34B	69144	64A	69224	61B	69528	34A
68986	34B	69145	65E	69257	14D	69529	34A
68987	34B	69146	64A	69258	41A	69530	34B
68988	56C	69149	64A	69262	34E	69531	34C
68989	34B	69150	64A	69263	41H	69532	34A
68990	34B	69152	64A	69265	27E	69533	34B
68991	34B	69154	64A	69266	34E	69535	34A
		69155	12C	69267	34E	69536	34D
		69156	64F	69268	41G	69537	34B
		69159	64F	69274	34E	69538	34A
		69161	65C	69276	34E	69539	34A
		69163	65A	69286	41J	69540	34D
		69164	62B	69290	41A	69541	34A
69001	52A	69165	65C	69292	34E	69543	34A
69002	52G	69166	65C	69293	34E	69545	34A
69003	53C	69168	64A	69294	41A	69546	34A
69004	51A	69170	65A	69296	41A	69547	34C
69005	52A	69171	65A	69298	27E	69548	34D
69006	51L	69173	64A	69299	41J	69549	34A
69007	51F	69176	65D	69307	9G	69552	34F
69008	53A	69177	65D	69308	41F	69553	65D
69009	53C	69178	65A	69309	41H	69556	34B
69010	53C	69179	65A	69314	41A	69560	34B
69011	53C	69180	61A	69319	14D	69561	34B
69012	62A	69181	65A	69320	41G	69563	65C
69013	64A	69182	65A	69322	36E	69564	12C
69014	64A	69183	65A	69327	34E	69567	34B

69568	34A	69655	30A	69723	30A	69929	36C
69570	34A	69656	30A	69724	30A	69934	36C
69571	34C	69657	30A	69725	30A	69935	36C
69572	34B	69658	30A	69726	30A	69936	36C
69574	34A	69660	30A	69727	30E		
69575	34A	69661	30A	69728	30A		
69576	34A	69662	30A	69729	30A		
69577	34C	69663	30A	69730	30A	70000 *	32A
69578	34A	69664	30A	69732	30E	70001 *	32A
69579	34A	69665	30A	69733	30E	70002 *	32A
69580	34A	69668	30A	69800	40E	70003 *	32A
69581	34A	69670	30A	69801	9G	70004 *	9E
69582	34C	69671	30A	69803	40A	70005 *	32A
69583	34A	69672	30F	69805	40E	70006 *	32A
69584	34A	69673	30E	69806	9G	70007 *	32A
69585	34B	69674	30A	69808	40A	70008 *	32A
69586	34C	69675	30F	69809	40A	70009 *	32A
69587	34B	69677	30A	69812	40E	70010 *	32A
69588	34C	69678	30E	69813	9G	70011 *	32A
69589	34A	69679	30A	69814	34F	70012 *	32A
69591	34C	69680	30B	69817	9G	70013 *	32A
69592	34A	69681	30B	69820	40A	70014 *	9E
69593	34A	69682	30B	69821	40A	70015 *	9E
69594	34B	69683	30B	69823	9G	70016 *	86C
69596	65E	69684	30B	69825	40E	70017 *	9E
69602	30A	69685	30B	69827	34F	70018 *	86C
69603	30A	69686	30E	69829	40B	70019 *	86C
69604	30A	69687	30B	69850	52G	70020 *	86C
69611	30A	69688	30B	69852	52G	70021 *	9E
69612	30E	69690	30A	69853	52G	70022 *	86C
69613	30E	69691	30A	69854	52G	70023 *	86C
69614	30A	69692	34C	69855	52G	70024 *	86C
69615	30A	69693	30B	69856	51F	70025 *	86C
69617	30E	69694	31C	69857	52G	70026 *	86C
69618	34C	69696	30A	69858	52G	70027 *	86C
69620	30A	69697	30A	69859	52G	70028 *	86C
69621	32C	69698	34C	69860	51L	70029 *	86C
69622	30A	69699	30A	69861	50F	70030 *	32A
69626	30A	69700	30A	69867	50E	70031 *	9A
69629	34C	69701	30A	69869	51L	70032 *	9A
69630	30A	69702	30A	69870	52G	70033 *	9A
69631	34C	69704	34C	69873	52G	70034 *	32A
69632	34C	69705	30A	69874	52G	70035 *	31B
69633	30B	69706	32C	69875	52G	70036 *	32A
69636	34C	69707	32A	69877	50E	70037 *	32A
69638	34C	69708	30A	69878	52G	70038 *	32A
69640	34C	69709	30A	69880	51C	70039 *	32A
69642	30A	69710	30A	69883	52G	70040 *	32A
69645	30A	69711	30A	69885	50F	70041 *	32A
69646	30A	69712	30A	69886	50F	70042 *	9E
69647	30A	69713	30C	69887	51A	70043 *	9A
69648	34C	69714	30A	69889	52G	70044 *	55A
69649	34C	69715	30A	69894	51C	70045 *	6J
69650	34C	69718	50C	69910	50C	70046	6J
69651	30A	69719	30A	69912	50C	70047	6J
69652	30E	69720	30A	69917	52H	70048 *	6J
69653	30A	69721	30A	69921	50C	70049	6J
69654	34C	69722	30A	69928	36C	70050 *	66A

70051 *	66A	73036	84G	73094	84G	73152	65B
70052 *	66A	73037	84G	73095	84G	73153	65B
70053 *	55A	73038	6E	73096	84G	73154	65B
70054 *	55A	73039	6C	73097	84G	73155	41C
		73040	6A	73098	66A	73156	41B
		73041	73A	73099	66A	73157	17A
71000 *	5A	73042	73A	73100	67A	73158	17A
		73043	41B	73101	67A	73159	17A
		73044	26F	73102	67A	73160	55E
72000 *	66A	73045	55A	73103	67A	73161	55E
72001 *	66A	73046	41C	73104	67A	73162	55G
72002 *	66A	73047	82F	73105	65A	73163	55G
72003 *	66A	73048	41C	73106	63A	73164	55G
72004 *	66A	73049	82F	73107	63A	73165	55G
72005 *	12A	73050	82F	73108	65A	73166	55G
72006 *	12A	73051	82F	73109	65A	73167	50E
72007 *	12A	73052	82F	73110	70A	73168	50E
72008 *	12A	73053	55A	73111	70A	73169	50E
72009 *	12A	73054	82E	73112	70A	73170	50E
		73055	66A	73113	70A	73171	55A
		73056	66A	73114	70A		
		73057	66A	73115	70A		
73000	41B	73058	66A	73116	70A		
73001	82C	73059	66A	73117	70A		
73002	41D	73060	66A	73118	70A	75000	82C
73003	82E	73061	66A	73119	70A	75001	81F
73004	41C	73062	66A	73120	63A	75002	82C
73005	63A	73063	66A	73121	67A	75003	85A
73006	63A	73064	66A	73122	67A	75004	82E
73007	63A	73065	41C	73123	67A	75005	6E
73008	63A	73066	55A	73124	67A	75006	6E
73009	63A	73067	41C	73125	26F	75007	81F
73010	55A	73068	82E	73126	26F	75008	81F
73011	41C	73069	55A	73127	26F	75009	85E
73012	82C	73070	6A	73128	26F	75010	6G
73013	6E	73071	6A	73129	26F	75011	6G
73014	6E	73072	66A	73130	26F	75012	6G
73015	82E	73073	41C	73131	26F	75013	6G
73016	41C	73074	41B	73132	26F	75014	6A
73017	71G	73075	66A	73133	26F	75015	27C
73018	71G	73076	66A	73134	23F	75016	27C
73019	82F	73077	65A	73135	17A	75017	27C
73020	71G	73078	65A	73136	17A	75018	27C
73021	6E	73079	67A	73137	17A	75019	27C
73022	71G	73080	73A	73138	17A	75020	6E
73023	6E	73081	73A	73139	17A	75021	82E
73024	6E	73082	73A	73140	17A	75022	82E
73025	6E	73083	73A	73141	17A	75023	85E
73026	6E	73084	73A	73142	17A	75024	82C
73027	82C	73085	73A	73143	17A	75025	85A
73028	82F	73086	73A	73144	17A	75026	6E
73029	71G	73087	70A	73145	65B	75027	82C
73030	26F	73088	70A	73146	65B	75028	6E
73031	RT6	73089 *	70A	73147	65B	75029	82C
73032	6E	73090	84G	73148	65B	75030	1E
73033	6E	73091	84G	73149	65B	75031	6A
73034	84G	73092	84G	73150	65B	75032	6G
73035	84G	73093	84G	73151	65B	75033	6A

Part	Code	Part	Code	Part	Code	Part	Code
75034	6A	76010	71A	76068	71A	77009	66A
75035	6A	76011	71A	76069	71A	77010	53A
75036	1E	76012	71A	76070	66B	77011	52C
75037	1E	76013	71A	76071	66B	77012	50A
75038	1E	76014	71A	76072	68B	77013	50B
75039	6A	76015	71A	76073	68B	77014	52C
75040	14E	76016	71A	76074	65A	77015	67B
75041	14E	76017	71A	76075	8G	77016	67B
75042	14E	76018	71A	76076	8G	77017	67B
75043	14E	76019	71A	76077	8G	77018	67B
75044	14E	76020	12D	76078	8G	77019	67B
75045	27A	76021	51F	76079	8G		
75046	27A	76022	12D	76080	24D	78000	89C
75047	27A	76023	12D	76081	24D	78001	85A
75048	27A	76024	51F	76082	24D	78002	89C
75049	27A	76025	71A	76083	24D	78003	89C
75050	6A	76026	71A	76084	24J	78004	85C
75051	6A	76027	71A	76085	9F	78005	89C
75052	1E	76028	71A	76086	9E	78006	89C
75053	6A	76029	71A	76087	9F	78007	89C
75054	6A	76030	30A	76088	9E	78008	85A
75055	14E	76031	30A	76089	9E	78009	85A
75056	16A	76032	30A	76090	67A	78010	51J
75057	15C	76033	30A	76091	67A	78011	51J
75058	15C	76034	30A	76092	67A	78012	51J
75059	15C	76035	14D	76093	67A	78013	12D
75060	15C	76036	14D	76094	67A	78014	51J
75061	15C	76037	14D	76095	67A	78015	51J
75062	16A	76038	14D	76096	67A	78016	51F
75063	16A	76039	14D	76097	67A	78017	12D
75064	16A	76040	14D	76098	67A	78018	12D
75065	73H	76041	14D	76099	67A	78019	12D
75066	73H	76042	14D	76100	65D	78020	15B
75067	73H	76043	14D	76101	65D	78021	15B
75068	73H	76044	14D	76102	65B	78022	41C
75069	73H	76045	51F	76103	65B	78023	41C
75070	75A	76046	51F	76104	61A	78024	41C
75071	82F	76047	12D	76105	61A	78025	41C
75072	82F	76048	24G	76106	61A	78026	41D
75073	82F	76049	51F	76107	61A	78027	41D
75074	73A	76050	51F	76108	61A	78028	15B
75075	75E	76051	12D	76109	62A	78029	15C
75076	70D	76052	12D	76110	62A	78030	5A
75077	70D	76053	75B	76111	62A	78031	6D
75078	70D	76054	75B	76112	68C	78032	8D
75079	70D	76055	75B	76113	65B	78033	8D
		76056	75B	76114	65B	78034	8D
		76057	75B			78035	8D
76000	66B	76058	75B			78036	24K
76001	66B	76059	75B	77000	53A	78037	24K
76002	66B	76060	75B	77001	53B	78038	6K
76003	66B	76061	75B	77002	51F	78039	8D
76004	66B	76062	75B	77003	51F	78040	27D
76005	72B	76063	71A	77004	50B	78041	27A
76006	72B	76064	71A	77005	66C	78042	27A
76007	72B	76065	71A	77006	66C	78043	27A
76008	72B	76066	71A	77007	66C	78044	27A
76009	72B	76067	71A	77008	66A		

78045	61A	80036	IC	80094	6H	80152	75A
78046	64G	80037	IC	80095	6H	80153	75A
78047	64G	80038	IC	80096	33A	80154	75A
78048	64A	80039	IE	80097	33A		
78049	64A	80040	6A	80098	33A		
78050	66B	80041	IE	80099	33A	82000	84K
78051	66B	80042	IE	80100	33A	82001	6E
78052	60B	80043	IE	80101	33A	82002	6E
78053	61C	80044	26A	80102	33A	82003	6E
78054	61C	80045	6A	80103	33A	82004	84H
78055	6D	80046	24E	80104	33A	82005	6E
78056	6D	80047	6A	80105	33A	82006	84H
78057	6H	80048	6A	80106	66A	82007	82A
78058	6D	80049	6A	80107	66A	82008	85A
78059	6D	80050	6A	80108	66C	82009	84H
78060	27D	80051	6A	80109	66C	82010	72A
78061	27D	80052	6A	80110	66A	82011	72A
78062	27D	80053	6A	80111	61A	82012	71A
78063	27D	80054	66A	80112	61A	82013	72A
78064	27D	80055	66A	80113	61A	82014	71A
		80056	66A	80114	61A	82015	71A
		80057	66A	80115	61A	82016	71A
80000	67A	80058	66A	80116	50B	82017	72A
80001	66A	80059	14D	80117	50B	82018	72A
80002	66A	80060	26A	80118	50B	82019	72A
80003	66A	80061	26A	80119	50B	82020	84K
80004	61A	80062	6C	80120	50B	82021	84K
80005	61A	80063	6C	80121	61C	82022	72A
80006	66A	80064	IC	80122	61C	82023	72A
80007	66A	80065	IC	80123	62B	82024	72A
80008	67A	80066	IC	80124	62B	82025	72A
80009	67A	80067	IC	80125	63B	82026	50E
80010	75E	80068	IC	80126	63A	82027	50F
80011	75E	80069	33B	80127	67A	82028	50E
80012	75E	80070	33B	80128	67A	82029	50F
80013	75A	80071	33B	80129	66A	82030	85A
80014	75F	80072	33B	80130	66A	82031	84K
80015	75F	80073	33B	80131	33A	82032	6E
80016	75F	80074	33B	80132	33A	82033	82A
80017	75F	80075	33B	80133	33A	82034	6E
80018	75F	80076	33B	80134	33A	82035	82A
80019	75F	80077	33B	80135	33A	82036	6E
80020	61A	80078	33B	80136	33A	82037	84K
80021	61A	80079	33B	80137	14D	82038	85A
80022	66A	80080	33B	80138	14D	82039	82G
80023	66A	80081	IE	80139	14D	82040	82A
80024	67A	80082	IE	80140	14D	82041	82F
80025	67A	80083	14D	80141	14D	82042	82A
80026	66A	80084	IE	80142	14D	82043	82A
80027	66A	80085	IE	80143	14D	82044	82A
80028	61A	80086	6A	80144	14D		
80029	61A	80087	6H	80145	75A		
80030	67A	80088	6H	80146	75A		
80031	75A	80089	6H	80147	75A		
80032	75A	80090	6C	80148	75A		
80033	75A	80091	6A	80149	75A		
80034	IC	80092	6A	80150	75A	84000	6C
80035	IC	80093	24E	80151	75A	84001	6D
						84002	IE

84003	6C
84004	IE
84005	I4F
84006	I5A
84007	I5A
84008	I5A
84009	55D
84010	24B
84011	24D
84012	24D
84013	26E
84014	26C
84015	24G
84016	24F
84017	24F
84018	24F
84019	26C
84020	73F
84021	73F
84022	73F
84023	73F
84024	73F
84025	73G
84026	73G
84027	73G
84028	73G
84029	73G
90000	34E
90001	31B
90002	40E
90003	40B
90004	62A
90005	40E
90006	53A
90007	41H
90008	53A
90009	53A
90010	82B
90011	53A
90012	55E
90013	36C
90014	51L
90015	34E
90016	56A
90017	62C
90018	31B
90019	62A
90020	62A
90021	55E
90022	53A
90023	31B
90024	40E
90025	40E
90026	50B
90027	51L
90028	30A
90029	40B
90030	53A
90031	36C
90032	36C
90033	2F
90034	33B
90035	40B
90036	40B
90037	40E
90038	40E
90039	66A
90040	2F
90041	61B
90042	31B
90043	41J
90044	50D
90045	50B
90046	2F
90047	56A
90048	51C
90049	65A
90050	40E
90051	41J
90052	40E
90053	40E
90054	50D
90055	41H
90056	56A
90057	53A
90058	62A
90059	36C
90060	66A
90061	56A
90062	30A
90063	31F
90064	40E
90065	2F
90066	2F
90067	51C
90068	50A
90069	86A
90070	36C
90071	66B
90072	53A
90073	40E
90074	51L
90075	40E
90076	56A
90077	66A
90078	53A
90079	31B
90080	2F
90081	51L
90082	51E
90083	31B
90084	40E
90085	41H
90086	51G
90087	41H
90088	41J
90089	56A
90090	51L
90091	51L
90092	51C
90093	33B
90094	53E
90095	2F
90096	34E
90097	61B
90098	51L
90099	53A
90100	56A
90101	27B
90102	26C
90103	40E
90104	40E
90105	26A
90106	33B
90107	27B
90108	36A
90109	24B
90110	26C
90111	36C
90112	56A
90113	56E
90114	65D
90115	40E
90116	56A
90117	62A
90118	40E
90119	41F
90120	40E
90121	27D
90122	56E
90123	26E
90124	56A
90125	86C
90126	56D
90127	55C
90128	62A
90129	30A
90130	40E
90131	40B
90132	51L
90133	36C
90134	66A
90135	51A
90136	41F
90137	2F
90138	24B
90139	41F
90140	26E
90141	26E
90142	26A
90143	24B
90144	36A
90145	40B
90146	40E
90147	6B
90148	84C
90149	86A
90150	31B
90151	34E
90152	81C
90153	41F
90154	40E
90155	51E
90156	30A
90157	6B
90158	34E
90159	24B
90160	53A
90161	40E
90162	41J
90163	26A
90164	27B
90165	34E
90166	40E
90167	87G
90168	62A
90169	34E
90170	12A
90171	24B
90172	51E
90173	6C
90174	81C
90175	40B
90176	82B
90177	62C
90178	6B
90179	87G
90180	34E
90181	24B
90182	62A
90183	24B
90184	51E
90185	40E
90186	53E
90187	6B
90188	86C
90189	40E
90190	41F
90191	31B
90192	86G
90193	65D
90194	26D
90195	41F
90196	33A
90197	26A
90198	66A
90199	66A

90200	50A	90258	24C	90316	27B	90374	24A
90201	86C	90259	41J	90317	6B	90375	27B
90202	40E	90260	53E	90318	55C	90376	26A
90203	41F	90261	84G	90319	67C	90377	51E
90204	27B	90262	53E	90320	66A	90378	53A
90205	26D	90263	40B	90321	56A	90379	56A
90206	26C	90264	24B	90322	55C	90380	56A
90207	87G	90265	53E	90323	86C	90381	27B
90208	31B	90266	24C	90324	26B	90382	56A
90209	41F	90267	26C	90325	55G	90383	40B
90210	56E	90268	81C	90326	56A	90384	41F
90211	41F	90269	34E	90327	27B	90385	56A
90212	6C	90270	41F	90328	26A	90386	66B
90213	53E	90271	26A	90329	56E	90387	66A
90214	6E	90272	53A	90330	41F	90388	26A
90215	40E	90273	51L	90331	24C	90389	26A
90216	27B	90274	24B	90332	55G	90390	26A
90217	53A	90275	41J	90333	56F	90391	41H
90218	2F	90276	41H	90334	55C	90392	6C
90219	26D	90277	24C	90335	24C	90393	40B
90220	41F	90278	27B	90336	55C	90394	40E
90221	40B	90279	31B	90337	55E	90395	55C
90222	26A	90280	40B	90338	26A	90396	56A
90223	34E	90281	53E	90339	56A	90397	51G
90224	40B	90282	27B	90340	31B	90398	24C
90225	86A	90283	27B	90341	56A	90399	24A
90226	26D	90284	81F	90342	56A	90400	41F
90227	6B	90285	40B	90343	27B	90401	41F
90228	53E	90286	41F	90344	51C	90402	26E
90229	66A	90287	41J	90345	55G	90403	2F
90230	50A	90288	40E	90346	2F	90404	56A
90231	24B	90289	26A	90347	55G	90405	50A
90232	36C	90290	41F	90348	56A	90406	51A
90233	53A	90291	26A	90349	34E	90407	55C
90234	66A	90292	26B	90350	62A	90408	26D
90235	40E	90293	31B	90351	55C	90409	51L
90236	50A	90294	40B	90352	53A	90410	41F
90237	2F	90295	24C	90353	56A	90411	41J
90238	86C	90296	40E	90354	26B	90412	56E
90239	34E	90297	26C	90355	81C	90413	24C
90240	51L	90298	30A	90356	81C	90414	56A
90241	24B	90299	2F	90357	55E	90415	56A
90242	6B	90300	53E	90358	41F	90416	27B
90243	55G	90301	41F	90359	26B	90417	56A
90244	81F	90302	41J	90360	56E	90418	41H
90245	26A	90303	40E	90361	56A	90419	26D
90246	34E	90304	41F	90362	55E	90420	24B
90247	55E	90305	31B	90363	56A	90421	41F
90248	26A	90306	26E	90364	26D	90422	36C
90249	55G	90307	26B	90365	2F	90423	6B
90250	41F	90308	55C	90366	26A	90424	50A
90251	81F	90309	55E	90367	24C	90425	36C
90252	41F	90310	56E	90368	40E	90426	51L
90253	34E	90311	41F	90369	6C	90427	53A
90254	55C	90312	86C	90370	56A	90428	34E
90255	36A	90313	84C	90371	24B	90429	56A
90256	33A	90314	24B	90372	26B	90430	51E
90257	6B	90315	86G	90373	51L	90431	41J

90432	40E	90490	36C	90548	26A	90606	6B
90433	2F	90491	41F	90549	66A	90607	56A
90434	51L	90492	41J	90550	36A	90608	41F
90435	65D	90493	65D	90551	30A	90609	53A
90436	65D	90494	33B	90552	27B	90610	55E
90437	40E	90495	41F	90553	62C	90611	55D
90438	41J	90496	40E	90554	41J	90612	41F
90439	34E	90497	56A	90555	26D	90613	34E
90440	65D	90498	30A	90556	24C	90614	62A
90441	62A	90499	41F	90557	24B	90615	56A
90442	33B	90500	51L	90558	26B	90616	66A
90443	40B	90501	31F	90559	32A	90617	55E
90444	62B	90502	41H	90560	62C	90618	40E
90445	50A	90503	53A	90561	27D	90619	55G
90446	51L	90504	2F	90562	55C	90620	56A
90447	31F	90505	67C	90563	82B	90621	55G
90448	2F	90506	41F	90564	26B	90622	56D
90449	41J	90507	2F	90565	86C	90623	53A
90450	53A	90508	30A	90566	6B	90624	55G
90451	51L	90509	8F	90567	41F	90625	56A
90452	51L	90510	40B	90568	26D	90626	26D
90453	36A	90511	53A	90569	36A	90627	53A
90454	34B	90512	36C	90570	27D	90628	66B
90455	61B	90513	62A	90571	53A	90629	40E
90456	36C	90514	33B	90572	86C	90630	81C
90457	50D	90515	62B	90573	86C	90631	56A
90458	53A	90516	2F	90574	2F	90632	26B
90459	51L	90517	51L	90575	62C	90633	56A
90460	40B	90518	50D	90576	26A	90634	40E
90461	51L	90519	40E	90577	41J	90635	36A
90462	51L	90520	2F	90578	50A	90636	36A
90463	67C	90521	41F	90579	86C	90637	55E
90464	12A	90522	31B	90580	41F	90638	2F
90465	51L	90523	26A	90581	56A	90639	56A
90466	81C	90524	86C	90582	41F	90640	66A
90467	50B	90525	26E	90583	40B	90641	26C
90468	66B	90526	41F	90584	24H	90642	56D
90469	36C	90527	27B	90585	84C	90643	27B
90470	56E	90528	31F	90586	53A	90644	56A
90471	40B	90529	87G	90587	41F	90645	55C
90472	62A	90530	26A	90588	55C	90646	36C
90473	40E	90531	53E	90589	26A	90647	36C
90474	2F	90532	6B	90590	41F	90648	40B
90475	50A	90533	26A	90591	55C	90649	55C
90476	40E	90534	62A	90592	24B	90650	55C
90477	31B	90535	27B	90593	51A	90651	56A
90478	53E	90536	66A	90594	41J	90652	55E
90479	51G	90537	36A	90595	24J	90653	33A
90480	30A	90538	36A	90596	66A	90654	56A
90481	51L	90539	62A	90597	36C	90655	56D
90482	53A	90540	36C	90598	36C	90656	56A
90483	84D	90541	24C	90599	27D	90657	41J
90484	31B	90542	62C	90600	62C	90658	24C
90485	87G	90543	50A	90601	36C	90659	34E
90486	2F	90544	86A	90602	36A	90660	30A
90487	55E	90545	41J	90603	51L	90661	55D
90488	55D	90546	26B	90604	56A	90662	40E
90489	65A	90547	62C	90605	51L	90663	50B

90664	55C	90722	55E	92019	15A	92077	18A
90665	34E	90723	56D	92020	15A	92078	18A
90666	55C	90724	27B	92021	15A	92079	85F
90667	8F	90725	26C	92022	15A	92080	15A
90668	41F	90726	55C	92023	15A	92081	16D
90669	26A	90727	62C	92024	15A	92082	15A
90670	53A	90728	55C	92025	15A	92083	15A
90671	26E	90729	26C	92026	15A	92084	15A
90672	2F	90730	34E	92027	15A	92085	15A
90673	55E	90731	56D	92028	15A	92086	18A
90674	40B	90732 *	36A	92029	15A	92087	16D
90675	24C	90750	66B	92030	16D	92088	16D
90676	86A	90751	66A	92031	16D	92089	16D
90677	53A	90752	66B	92032	16D	92090	16D
90678	56D	90753	64D	92033	16D	92091	16D
90679	56A	90754	66B	92034	36C	92092	16D
90680	55G	90755	65F	92035	36C	92093	16D
90681	24C	90756	66B	92036	34E	92094	18A
90682	55E	90757	65F	92037	34E	92095	16D
90683	31B	90758	66B	92038	34E	92096	16D
90684	55C	90759	65F	92039	40B	92097	52H
90685	86C	90760	66B	92040	34E	92098	52H
90686	6E	90761	66B	92041	34E	92099	52H
90687	27B	90762	66B	92042	34E	92100	15C
90688	53A	90763	12A	92043	16D	92101	15C
90689	24C	90764	66C	92044	34E	92102	15C
90690	62A	90765	65F	92045	6F	92103	15C
90691	86C	90766	65F	92046	6F	92104	15C
90692	56A	90767	66A	92047	6F	92105	15B
90693	86C	90768	64D	92048	21A	92106	15B
90694	55G	90769	65F	92049	21A	92107	15A
90695	53A	90770	66B	92050	18A	92108	14A
90696	36A	90771	66C	92051	21A	92109	15C
90697	2F	90772	66C	92052	15A	92110	14A
90698	51A	90773	65F	92053	21A	92111	14A
90699	55C	90774	65F	92054	15A	92112	14A
90700	41F			92055	15A	92113	18B
90701	86G			92056	15A	92114	18B
90702	6B			92057	18A	92115	18B
90703	40E			92058	15A	92116	18B
90704	53A	92000	86A	92059	15A	92117	18B
90705	62A	92001	86A	92060	52H	92118	18B
90706	24J	92002	86A	92061	52H	92119	14A
90707	56D	92003	86C	92062	52H	92120	21A
90708	26E	92004	86A	92063	52H	92121	15C
90709	31B	92005	86C	92064	52H	92122	15A
90710	56A	92006	86A	92065	52H	92123	15A
90711	56F	92007	86A	92066	52H	92124	15A
90712	27B	92008	21A	92067	16D	92125	15A
90713	26B	92009	21A	92068	16D	92126	15A
90714	36C	92010	16D	92069	16D	92127	15A
90715	26A	92011	16D	92070	16D	92128	15C
90716	84G	92012	16D	92071	16D	92129	18A
90717	40E	92013	16D	92072	16D	92130	18A
90718	26D	92014	16D	92073	16D	92131	18A
90719	56A	92015	26A	92074	16D	92132	15A
90720	24C	92016	26A	92075	16D	92133	15A
90721	56D	92017	26A	92076	16D	92134	15A
		92018	15A				

92135	21A	92164	15B	92193	40B	92222	84C
92136	21A	92165	21A	92194	40B	92223	84C
92137	21A	92166	RTS	92195	40B	92224	84C
92138	21A	92167	21A	92196	40B	92225	84C
92139	21A	92168	36A	92197	36C	92226	84C
92140	34E	92169	36A	92198	36C	92227	84C
92141	34E	92170	36A	92199	36A	92228	84C
92142	34E	92171	36A	92200	36A	92229	81A
92143	34E	92172	36A	92201	36A	92230	81A
92144	34E	92173	36A	92202	40B	92231	86C
92145	34E	92174	36A	92203		92232	86C
92146	34E	92175	36A	92204		92233	86C
92147	34E	92176	36A	92205		92234	86C
92148	34E	92177	36A	92206		92235	86C
92149	34E	92178	34E	92207		92236	86C
92150	21A	92179	34E	92208		92237	86C
92151	21A	92180	34E	92209		92238	81A
92152	21A	92181	34E	92210		92239	81A
92153	18A	92182	34E	92211		92240	81A
92154	15A	92183	34E	92212		92241	81A
92155	21A	92184	36C	92213		92242	86A
92156	18A	92185	36C	92214		92243	86A
92157	21A	92186	40E	92215		92244	81A
92158	18A	92187	34E	92216		92245	81A
92159	15A	92188	34E	92217		92246	81A
92160	15B	92189	36A	92218		92247	81A
92161	26A	92190	36C	92219		92248	86A
92162	26A	92191	36A	92220		92249	86A
92163	15B	92192	36A	92221	84C	92250	84C

ALLOCATION OF SERVICE LOCOMOTIVES

Service No.	Region	B.R. No.	Type	Allocation
2* ..	E.	68858	J52	Doncaster Works.
3* ..	E.	68181	Y3	Ranskill Wagon Works.
4* ..	E.	68132	Y1	Ranskill Wagon Works.
5* ..	E.	68165	Y3	Doncaster Wagon Works.
7* ..	E.	68166	Y3	Boston Sleeper Depot.

* Numbered in E. & N.E. Region Departmental stock.

Service No.	Region	B.R. No.	Type	Allocation
8*	E.	68183	Y3	Peterborough Engineer's Yard.
9*	E.	68840	J52	Doncaster Works.
21*	E.	68162	Y3	Cambridge Engineer's Dept.
31*	E.	68382	J66	Stratford Works.
32*	E.	68370	J66	Stratford Works.
33*	E.	68129	Y4	Stratford Works.
36*	E.	68378	J66	Stratford Works.
38*	E.	68168	Y3	Lowestoft Engineer's Dept.
39*	E.	68131	Y1	Lowestoft Engineer's Dept.
40*	E.	68173	Y3	Lowestoft Engineer's Dept.
41*	E.	68177	Y3	Lowestoft Engineer's Dept.
42*	E.	68178	Y3	Cambridge Engineer's Dept.
52*	N.E.	11104	0-4-0 Diesel	West Hartlepool P.W. Depot.
54*	N.E.	68153	Y1	Darlington P.W. Depot.
56*	N.E.		0-4-0 Diesel	Hull Engineer's Dept.
57*	N.E.	68160	Y3	Faverdale Works, Darlington.
91*	N.E.		0-6-0 Diesel	
92*	N.E.		0-6-0 Diesel	
100 *	E.	26510	Bo-Bo Electric	Ilford.
C.D.3	M.		L.N.W. 0-6-0 ST	Wolverton Carriage Works.
C.D.6	M.		L.N.W. 0-6-0 ST	Wolverton Carriage Works.
C.D.7	M.		L.N.W. 0-6-0 ST	Wolverton Carriage Works.
11304	M.		L.Y.R. 0-6-0 ST	Horwich Works.
11305	M.		L.Y.R. 0-6-0 ST	Horwich Works.
11324	M.		L.Y.R. 0-6-0 ST	Horwich Works.
11368	M.		L.Y.R. 0-6-0 ST	Horwich Works.
11394	M.		L.Y.R. 0-6-0 ST	Horwich Works.
E.D.1	M.		0-4-0 Diesel	Beeston Creosote Works.
E.D.2	M.		0-4-0 Diesel	Ditton Creosote Works.
E.D.3	M.		0-4-0 Diesel	Lenton P.W. Depot.
E.D.4	M.		0-4-0 Diesel	Northampton.
E.D.5	M.		0-4-0 Diesel	Castleton P.W. Depot.
E.D.6	M.		0-4-0 Diesel	Castleton P.W. Depot.
E.D.7	M.		0-4-0 Diesel	Fazakerley.
E.D.10	M.		0-4-0 Diesel	Beeston Creosote Works.
ZM32	M.		0-4-0 Petrol	Horwich Works.
DS49	S.		0-4-0 Petrol	Broad Clyst.
DS74	S.		Bo-Bo Electric	Durnsford Rd. Power Station.
DS75	S.		Bo Electric	Waterloo & City Line.
DS77	S.		C14	Redbridge Sleeper Depot.
DS600	S.		0-4-0 Diesel	Eastleigh Carriage Works.
DS680	S.		A1	Lancing Carriage Works.
DS681	S.		A1X	Lancing Carriage Works.
DS1169	S.		0-4-0 Diesel	Folkestone Warren.
DS1173	S.		0-6-0 Diesel	Engineer's Dept.
DS3152	S.	30272	G6	Meldon Quarry.
20	W.		0-4-0 Diesel	Reading Signal Works.
24	W.		0-4-0 Petrol	Taunton Engineer's Dept.
27	W.		0-4-0 Petrol	Reading Signal Works.
PWM650	W.		0-6-0 Diesel	

* Numbered in E. & N.E. Region Departmental stock.

This edition published 1995 by BCA
by arrangement with Ian Allan Publishing
an imprint of Ian Allan Ltd, Terminal House,
Station Approach, Shepperton, Surrey TW17 8AS.

All rights reserved. No part of this book may be
reproduced or transmitted in any form or by any
means, electronic or mechanical, including photo-
copying, recording or by any information storage
and retrieval system, without permission from the
Publisher in writing.

© Ian Allan Ltd 1976

CN 3117

Printed by Ian Allan Printing Ltd,
Coombelands House, Coombelands Lane,
Addlestone, Surrey KT15 1HY

Front cover: *Class A4 4-6-2 No 60034* Lord
Farringdon *and A1 4-6-2 No 60153* Flamboyant
seen at Kings Cross. Colour-Rail

Back cover, top: *Fresh from overhaul, Class
Q1 0-6-0 No 33010 is depicted at Hither Green.*
Colour-Rail

Back cover, bottom: *'County' class 4-6-0
No 1026* County of Salop *seen at Shrewsbury shed.*
Colour Rail